# THE EVOLUTION OF LIFE

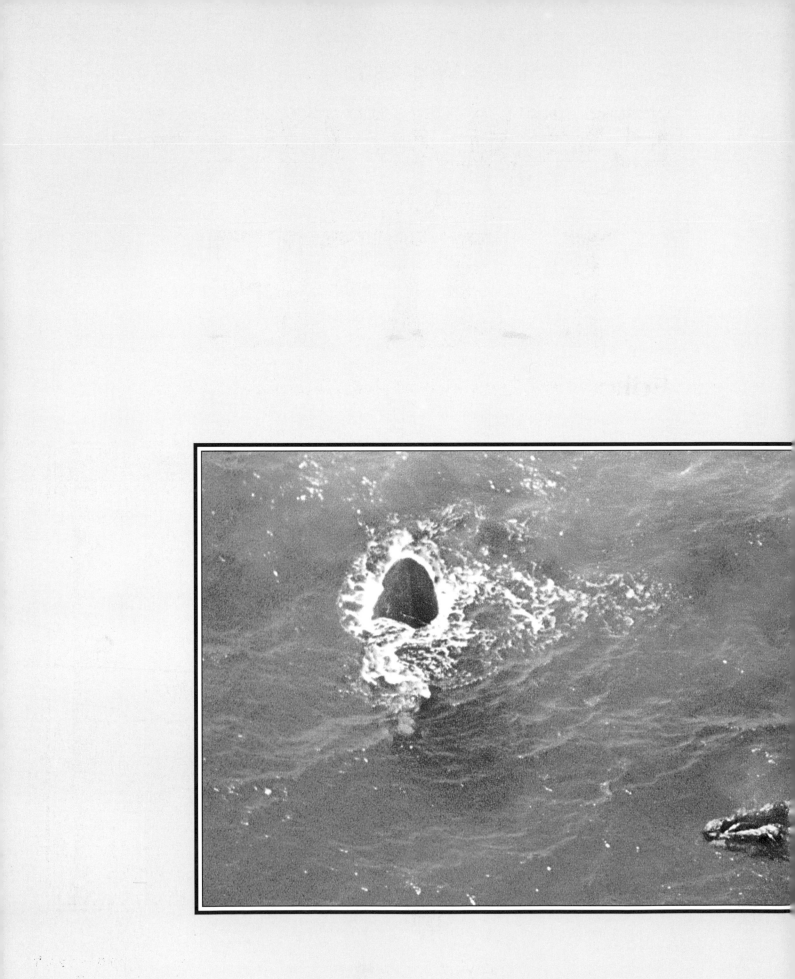

# THE
# EVOLUTION
## OF
# LIFE

### Edited by Linda Gamlin and Gail Vines

Oxford University Press

New York 1987

**Senior Editor** Lawrence Clarke
**Art Editor** John Ridgeway
**Designers** Ayala Kingsley,
Niki Overy
**Picture Editor** Alison Renney

**Advisors**
Dr John Barrett, Department of
Genetics, University of Cambridge
Professor Noel Carr, Department
of Biological Sciences, University
of Warwick
Dr Bernard Dixon, Former Editor
of New Scientist
Professor Sir Hans Kornberg FRS,
Professor of Biochemistry,
University of Cambridge

**Contributors**
Dr Jonathan Adams (27)
Dr Michael Benton (11, 12, 13,
14, 16)
David Burnie (20)
Dr Euann Dunn (15)
Dr Peter Forey (3)
Linda Gamlin (5, 19)
Jerry Lockett (24)
Dr Peter Moore (6, 7)
Dr Howard Platt (8)
Dr Andrew Pomiankowski (1)
Dr Andrew Scott (21, 26)
Dr Brian Tomsett (2)
Dr Bryan Turner (9)
Dr Gail Vines (4, 10, 17, 18)
Dr Martin Wells (8)
Dr Stephen Young (22, 23, 25)

AN EQUINOX BOOK

Planned and produced by:
Equinox (Oxford) Ltd,
Littlegate House,
St Ebbe's Street
Oxford OX1 1SQ

Copyright © Equinox (Oxford) Ltd
1986

Published in the United States
of America by Oxford University
Press, Inc. 200 Madison Avenue,
New York, NY 10016

Oxford is a registered trademark
of Oxford University Press

LOCN 86-23617

**Library of Congress
Cataloging-in-Publication Data**
Gamlin, Linda.
    Evolution of life.

    Bibliography: P.
    Includes index.
    1. Biology   2. Evolution.
I. Vines, Gail.
II. Title.
QH308.2.G34 1987   574   86-23617
ISBN 0-19-520532-4

Printing (last digit):
9 8 7 6 5 4 3 2
Printed in Spain

**Introductory pictures** (pages 1-8)
1 Cnidaria (◊ page 72)
2-3 Southern Right Whales
4-5 Reticulated python (◊ page 188)
7 Bee with orchid (◊ page 63)
8 Jellyfish (◊ page 70)

# Contents

# Introduction

We will never understand all of life – there are too many kinds of living organisms, living in too many different and subtle ways. But today we do have some idea of the range and variety of living things, and of the processes of life – and even of why it is that each creature has come to be the way it is.

The first stage in understanding is simply to *describe* – we should at least be able to say what kinds of organisms there are on Earth, what they look like, where and how they live. Systematic attempts to list all the animals and plants in the world began in the 17th century, and so far biologists have named about a million species. This may seem a phenomenal number, but modern estimates suggest that it is very much the tip of the iceberg – there could be 10 million species, and perhaps as many as 40 million. Many as yet unknown species are thought to live in the tropical forests, the details of which have hardly begun to be described. At first sight then, it seems that the endeavors of the last three centuries have scarcely given us the barest outline of life's diversity.

We need not be too disheartened, however. As has been clear since the 18th century – following in particular the work of the great Swedish taxonomist Linnaeus – the vast majority of living things are variations on a relatively few basic themes. These basic themes or "ground plans", number no more than a hundred, at a conservative estimate, and we can be reasonably sure that we know most of them – even though the deep oceans and the tropical forests may still spring surprises. It seems likely, too, that most of the millions of species that have not yet been described belong to just a few prodigiously successful groups, such as the insects or the nematodes. In short, although we do not yet know all the varieties of life, we do probably know the main forms of life. These forms, and the ways in which they are classified, are described in the first half of this book.

More difficult than mere description is explanation. Why are there so many different kinds of organism? Why does each one take the form it does, and live as it does? And how does each one perform the necessary tasks of life – feeding, growing, developing, reproducing?

Before the 18th century, most people simply accepted that God had made living things they way they are, and that was the end of the matter. But in the 18th century a few naturalists began to frame the idea of what we now call evolution: the idea that living things do not stay the same from generation to generation, for ever and ever, but change as the generations pass. In this way – so some 18th century biologists began to suggest – modern animals and plants developed from more primitive ancestors, which in turn had evolved from yet more primitive types, and so on, back to the first appearance of an incredibly simple microscopic ancestor, at some time in the distant past.

However, no-one in the 18th century could come up with convincing reasons as to why such evolution should occur, or how it could come about, and there was a strong religious opposition to the idea. So the theory of evolution was not widely accepted until the middle of the 19th century, when Charles Darwin suggested a plausible mechanism, natural selection, and collected a huge amount of evidence to support the idea that evolution had occurred.

Darwin managed to convince most biologists that evolution had occurred, and that natural selection was the main driving force, but there was an important gap in his theory as he himself was well aware. Evolutionary processes cannot work unless the offspring are, in general, similar to their parents. But they must also be somewhat different from their parents – because if they were always exactly the same then there would be no change from generation to generation. How can offspring be the same as their parents – and yet be different as well?

The basic explanation of heredity did not come from Darwin but from his near contemporary, Gregor Mendel. He it was who first suggested that the various characteristics of animals and plants were passed from generation to generation in the form of coded "factors" – which later became known as "genes". These could change by processes which we now call mutation and recombination (◗ page 24). Twentieth century biologists refined Darwin's ideas of evolution and combined them with Mendel's theories of heredity to produce the general theory of "neo-Darwinism". Neo-Darwinism may not provide a complete explanation of the forces and mechanisms that have made living things they way they are, and, as will be seen, it still gives rise to controversy. But the theory can properly be said to provide the core of modern biology.

In the last half-century, the story has been taken a step further, as the molecular basis for Mendel's observations has been revealed. Since the 1940s, biologists have known that genes are made of the material deoxyribonucleic acid, or DNA. In the 1950s, Francis Crick and James Watson described the structure of DNA and showed how DNA could reproduce itself. They also revealed how it could make proteins, which, as enzymes, fashion all the other materials of which cells are made and determine their function. In the 1960s, Crick and his colleagues showed how the code in the DNA was translated into protein. Thus it is that the once so mysterious processes of heredity can now be explained in chemical terms.

## Explaining life

The breakthroughs made in molecular genetics are characteristic of a thread that has run through biology for much of the 20th century. On the one hand, we can observe that animals and plants obtain nourishment, grow, breathe, seek mates, reproduce and die. On the other hand, biochemists have shown that every living thing is made up of a miscellany of organic molecules, mainly proteins, fats, sugars and nucleic acids. Increasingly, biologists have sought to relate the living processes they observe to underlying chemical changes, and some of their achievements in this endeavor are described in the second half of this book. Thus it is now possible to say exactly how muscles contract, by the remarkable interaction of the two types of protein they contain, or to describe the process whereby our eyes respond to light and send a nerve impulse to the brain. The complex mechanisms called photosynthesis that enable plants to capture the energy of sunlight are understood, and so are the chemical pathways by which we break down food and make use of it in our bodies.

Yet, despite these and many other successes, it would be a mistake to think that biologists have all, or even most, of the answers. To a very great extent, biology is still in its infancy, and this is what makes it such an exciting subject. Progress has been much faster in some fields than in others – molecular genetics is way out ahead, whereas subjects such as embryology and ethology (behavior) trail behind. In both these subjects there are some researchers studying molecular mechanisms (starting from the bottom and working up so to speak) and others studying whole organisms (working from the top down). No doubt they will eventually meet, as the classical and molecular geneticists have met, but it is difficult at present to see how, or where, or even when. Indeed, in the case of behavior, there is still fundamental disagreement about how to approach the subject. In this research, as in much of biology, there is the basic problem of pinning down something quantifiable, measurable or verifiable, from the complex organic whole. The lament of the population geneticist, Richard Lewontin, is applicable to a great deal of biological research: "What we can measure is by definition uninteresting and what we are interested in is by definition immeasurable."

Despite these difficulties, biology today is inspired by the hope that all the functions of life can ultimately be explained in chemical terms. This knowledge is valuable partly for its own sake: it is satisfying to know how we and other living things function. But it is also of practical value, because the more we understand the more we can seek to influence, both for our own good, and for the good of the millions of fascinating creatures with which we share this planet.

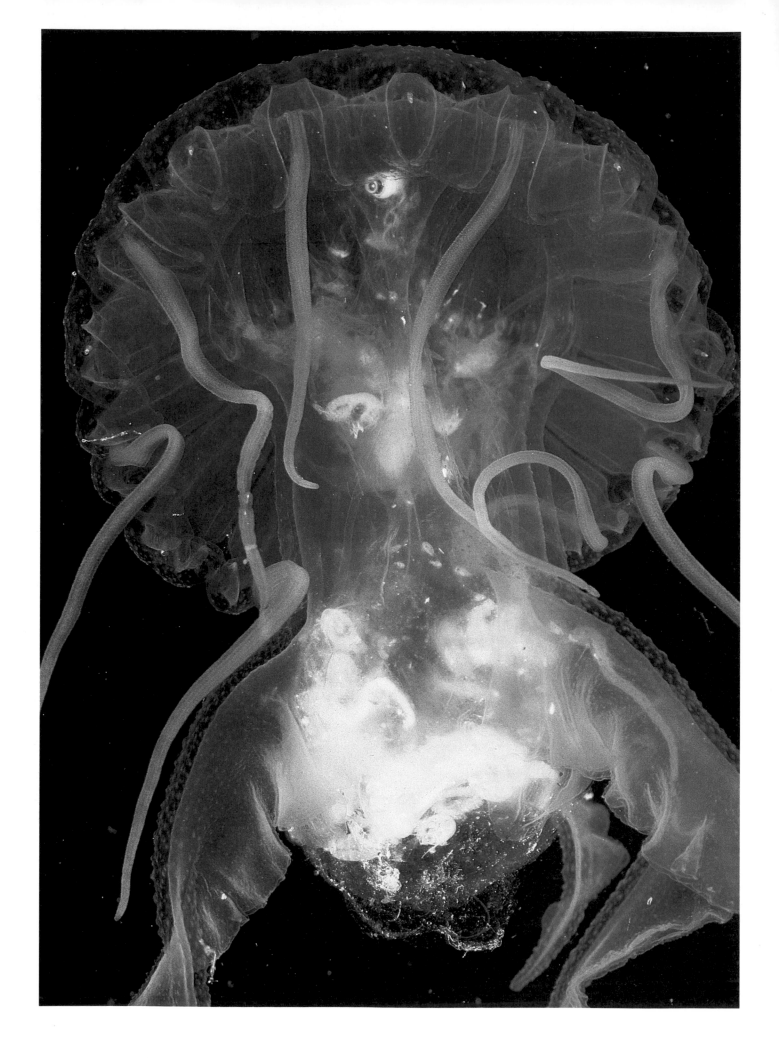

> *The basis of natural selection...Adaptation, genetic variation, coevolution...Forms of sexual selection...How species arise...Macro- and microevolution...Molecular evolution...PERSPECTIVE...Ideas of evolution...Observing evolution...Breeding...Selection not the only force in evolution...What is a species?... Hopeful monsters... Human/ape evolution*

In recent years there has been much criticism of the Darwinian theory of evolution. Banner headlines in the popular press have announced that "Darwin got it wrong" or "Darwinism is dead", but these pronouncements arise from a fundamental misunderstanding. The question of whether evolution has occurred is not in doubt. Charles Darwin (1809–1882) established that all modern species have descended from one or a few simple ancestral forms, and a century of research has amply confirmed his conclusions. What biologists have been arguing about in recent years is Darwin's claim that *natural selection* was the principal cause of change, and that the same types of selective forces have operated at all stages of the evolutionary process.

## Natural selection

The theory of natural selection is based on the combination of three simple ideas. The first is that organisms vary – two individuals of the same species are rarely exactly alike. The second is that these variations can affect their ability to survive and produce offspring. The ones that leave more descendants are, in general, likely to be the ones that live longest (although ability to secure a mate can be a factor in some species), and those that live longest are the ones that gather food more efficiently, survive the rigors of the environment, and avoid or deter predators. The ones to succumb will, by and large, be those that are less able to cope with these challenges. In other words, the organisms that are better adapted will tend to produce more offspring. Combine these with the third idea – inheritance – and you have natural selection. Those that are better equipped leave more offspring, and, if the features that promoted their survival are heritable, these features will become more common in future generations.

No one doubts that natural selection can and does occur. It has been simulated countless times in the laboratory, and observed in action in the wild (◆ page 11). What is now being questioned is the idea that natural selection is the major force behind *all* evolutionary change. Much of this questioning is a reaction to the orthodoxy of neo-Darwinism – the synthesis of Darwin's theories and Mendelian genetics which has dominated evolutionary thinking for most of this century. Ideas about evolution are difficult to test because the events being studied are over, and there is no chance of an action replay. Evolutionary processes are also very slow, so despite the fact that evolution is still going on, it is generally difficult to observe and measure. This means that theoretical arguments are very important in studying evolution, and, because the theories are hard to test, the danger of slipping into an unquestioned orthodoxy is very real. The current spate of alternative ideas represents an attempt to refine and improve the theoretical framework of neo-Darwinism. Even if many turn out in the end to be wrong, it is still a valuable exercise.

### Darwin and Wallace

The idea of evolution was not an original one, even in Darwin's time. But each time it had been proposed, the proponent was reviled, ridiculed or ignored. Darwin was well aware of this, so when he became convinced that evolution had occurred, he kept it to himself. The essential idea came to him during his time as ship's doctor and naturalist on board HMS Beagle, but, following his return to England, over 20 years passed before he published "The Origin of Species". During this time he gathered together a vast amount of evidence in favor of his theory. As well as carrying out meticulous observations and experiments, he read widely and asked endless questions of other scientists.

The amassing of evidence became an end in itself, and Darwin kept on delaying the publication of his ideas. Eventually he was stung into action by a letter in 1858 from Alfred Russel Wallace. Wallace lived in the Malay Archipelago and the idea of natural selection came to him, so he said later, during a bout of malarial fever. Natural selection was also the cornerstone of Darwin's theory – because it provided a plausible driving force for evolution. Wallace, however, did not know of Darwin's theories, and was unaware that he had stumbled on the same idea. So when he sent Darwin an outline, asking his opinion of it, he had no idea what a terrible blow it would be to the man who had spent 20 years substantiating the same theory. Both scientists acted in a thoroughly gentlemanly fashion. They agreed to simultaneously publish short accounts of their ideas, and thereafter Wallace took a back seat, leaving Darwin to hastily prepare an abstract of his proposed "big book". That "abstract" was "The Origin of Species" and it ran to over 400 pages. This book succeeded, where all its predecessors had failed, in making the case for evolution. Darwin had collected so much evidence, and so carefully prepared responses to possible criticisms, that from then on the fact of evolution was established.

▲ *Charles Darwin is often called the "father of modern biology". He would have been remembered as a great scientist even without "The Origin of Species", for his detailed studies of barnacles, orchids, plant movements and a variety of other subjects.*

▲ *The English naturalist, Alfred Russel Wallace spent much of his life in Malaysia, financing his private research by sending exotic butterflies back to England for collectors. He made a study of animal distribution and founded the science of biogeography.*

# Natural Selection

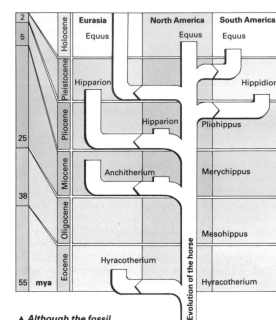

| | | Eurasia | North America | South America |
|---|---|---|---|---|
| 2 | Holocene | Equus | Equus | Equus |
| 5 | Pleistocene | Hipparion | | Hippidion |
| | Pliocene | Hipparion | | Pliohippus |
| 25 | Miocene | Anchitherium | | Merychippus |
| 38 | Oligocene | | | Mesohippus |
| | Eocene | Hyracotherium | | Hyracotherium |
| 55 mya | | | | |

*Evolution of the horse*

Equus

Pliohippus

▲ Although the fossil record for the horse shows a clear progression of form, this should not be seen as a steady "march of progress". As the tree above shows, other horse species appeared along the way, only to die out. And some of the species shown on the right, while successful in one continent, became extinct in other regions.

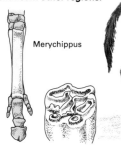

Merychippus

Mesohippus

## The gradual approach

While on HMS Beagle, Darwin read a controversial new book – Charles Lyell's "Principles of Geology". Lyell (1797-1875) was opposed to catastrophe theories and interpreted geological history as a steady uninterrupted process, a view that is considered largely correct today. He showed how the forces now at work could account for all features of the Earth if there had been sufficient time for them to achieve their effects. This uniformitarianism clearly influenced Darwin, and he applied it to his own theory, proposing that the same observable processes which molded a population could also, given time, turn that population into a new species, and eventually found a whole new order, class or phylum. Darwin's uniformitarianism is one aspect of his theory now criticized by some scientists. They suggest that "microevolution", or small adaptive changes within a species, is distinct from "macroevolution", which governs the appearance of new species and larger groups (♦ page 19).

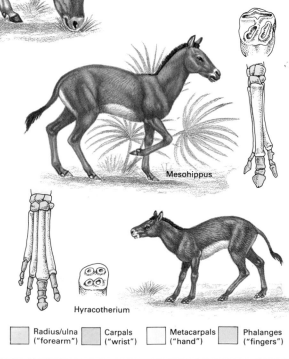

Hyracotherium

| | Radius/ulna ("forearm") | | Carpals ("wrist") | | Metacarpals ("hand") | | Phalanges ("fingers") |
|---|---|---|---|---|---|---|---|

▲ ◄ An example of slow, progressive change is seen in the evolution of the horse. Starting with the dog-like Hyracotherium, equine fossils display a gradual lengthening of the limbs, plus a reduction of the digits from five to three, and finally to one. The teeth (shown in cross-section) enlarge, with infolding of the enamel, to give a tougher grinding surface for eating grass (♦ page 123). At the same time, the jaw muscles enlarge and the jaw lengthens, to provide more room for attachment of the jaw muscles.

► Some biologists think that stabilizing selection alone keeps creatures like Nautilus unchanged. Others believe that the way in which a creature develops restricts the possibilities for change. Thus the way in which its shell grows could confine an animal to certain shapes. The idea of developmental constraints is controversial, linked to the punctuated equilibrium theory (♦ page 19). Even if such constraints exist, they cannot explain the total absence of change, because they can only limit variation in some directions, not all.

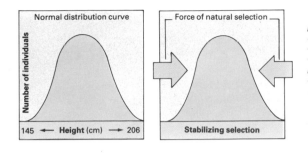

Normal distribution curve

**Number of individuals**

145 ← **Height (cm)** → 206

Force of natural selection

**Stabilizing selection**

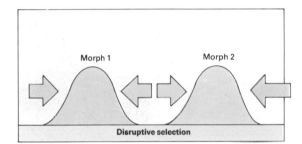

Original population    New population

**Directional selection**

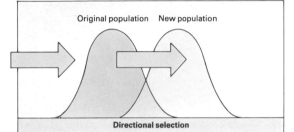

Morph 1    Morph 2

**Disruptive selection**

◄ *The variation found in a population can be represented as a frequency distribution. For example, consider height in a human population: a few people are small or tall, and a very few are very small or very tall. But most fall in the middle range. This gives a bell-shaped curve, which is the typical frequency distribution found in nature. Evolution can be thought of as changes in the frequency distribution. Stabilizing selection penalizes extremes and tends to keep a character at an intermediate value. It may explain why species like Nautilus, which inhabit very stable environments with few competitors, have apparently been unchanged for millions of years. Under directional selection (as for increased tooth height and leg length in horses), the distribution is shifted in one direction. Disruptive selection creates a curve with more than one peak and leads to polymorphism, where two or more distinct forms exist. This may occur in a diverse habitat where it pays, for example, to have different forms adapted to different parts of their environment.*

## Natural selection in action

*The best chance of observing natural selection in action occurs when there is a fairly sudden and drastic change in the environment. Such a change occurred on the Galapagos island of Daphne in 1977, when a severe drought greatly reduced the abundance of seeds, particularly small seeds. The ground finch, Geospiza fortis, whose staple diet is seeds, was subject to severe selection. Many birds died, but those with bigger beaks survived best, being able to cope with the bigger, harder seeds. Because larger beaks are found on larger birds, substantial changes in body size also resulted. So due to selection G. fortis has evolved, at least temporarily, into a larger bird with a larger beak.*

*Another superb example of natural selection in action took place in England during the 19th century, caused by pollution from smoky factories. This blackened tree trunks and killed off lichens that normally grew on the bark. Peppered moths, which rested on these trees during the day, and were delicately camouflaged to match the lichens, lost their protection and became vulnerable to birds. A mutation, which changed their coloration to a uniform black, spread through the population in areas of heavy industrialization. Such mutations, (known as melanism, after the brown-black pigment melanin) are quite common in many species, but are not usually favored by natural selection. In industrial areas, there are now several species of melanic moths, as well as melanic spiders and ladybirds, but with pollution control, the incidence of melanic forms is declining.*

▲ *The peppered moth, in its original and melanic forms.*

## Breeding: selection speeded up

*To substantiate his idea of natural selection, Darwin drew a parallel with the artificial selection practiced by plant and animal breeders. The most extreme result of this can be seen in dog breeds, all of which are derived from the same genetic stock – the wolf. In a few thousand years artificial selection has produced such opposites as the chihuahua and the Great Dane, the greyhound and the Saint Bernard. The response to natural selection is rarely so rapid, since it is not as ruthless as human selection; favored individuals have only a slightly increased probability of survival, and unfavored forms are only eliminated slowly. Natural selection may vary from year to year, and it rarely acts consistently across the species' whole range.*

## Adaptation

The most striking product of evolution by natural selection is adaptation – the way in which organisms seem to fit exactly with the external world in which they live. Many appear to be so perfectly attuned to their environment that it is easy to think of them as being "designed" to fill a particular role. But it is important to remember that natural selection is a blind force, and there is no design involved. Genetic variation (◆ page 24) produces random, undirected changes which are then rejected or accepted by natural selection. This rather haphazard process slowly builds up the adaptations which we observe. They are not perfect adaptations, precisely because they are arrived at by this blind process. Usually the imperfections are not obvious – thousands of years of selection having minimized their flaws. But some species do show obvious defects, such as the giant panda, a herbivore descended from carnivorous ancestors. Its digestive system makes a poor job of breaking down the bamboo shoots which it eats, and the panda must consume huge quantities of food to survive. Other features confirm that the panda has come to bamboo rather late in its evolutionary career. Its ancestors clearly had rounded paws with very short toes – not the thing for plucking and holding bamboo shoots. The panda has acquired a sixth digit, fashioned from a small piece of bone in the wrist. What looks like our thumb is in fact an evolutionary afterthought, added to the bear's paw to give it some sort of manual dexterity. Evolution has to make do with what is available – it can never go back to the drawing board and produce an ideal design.

Adaptations relate not only to the physical environment but also to other organisms. Between predators and prey, for example, there is an "arms race", where each improvement in a prey's defenses is matched by improvement in the predator's skill in attack (◆ page 234). This sort of coordinated adaptation, involving two or more species together, is known as "coevolution".

▲ *A superb example of adaptation is seen in the flower mantids, which capture insects by mimicking the flowers which they visit for nectar. The mantid keeps perfectly still, then grasps the insect as it flies within reach.*

◄ *The panda is a member of the Carnivora, a relative of the dogs, cats and bears. It has six digits on its forepaws. The sixth is produced by the elongation of a wrist bone, an adaptation for feeding on bamboo.*

### Storytelling
*Some adaptations are so obvious as to be beyond dispute, but sometimes the description of something as an adaptation is mere "storytelling". A few biologists have been guilty of wild speculation – one even explained the pink color of flamingoes as a camouflage against the setting sun. This sort of approach has recently been criticized and more scientific ways of studying adaptation advocated. Before describing something as an adaptation, there is a need for detailed observation, and experiments to reveal the nature of current selection pressures. For example, gulls remove eggshells from their nests shortly after the chicks hatch. By putting the eggshells back it was found that many more predators were attracted to the nest, suggesting that eggshell removal behavior is a defensive adaptation.*

*Another approach is the comparative method, which looks for a statistical correlation between features that appear to be adaptations and particular environmental conditions or ways of life. This involves considering a great many different species within the same taxonomic group.*

## Convergent evolution

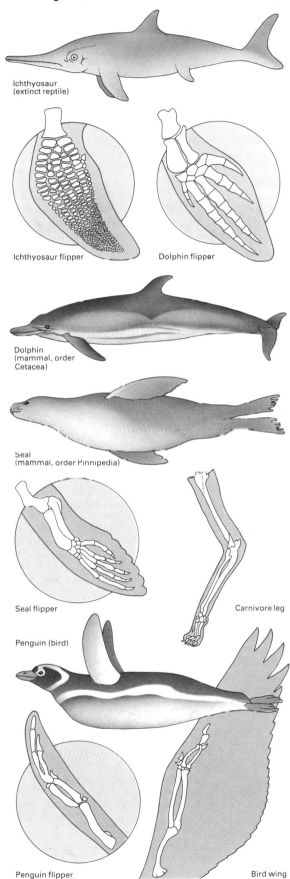

Ichthyosaur
(extinct reptile)

Ichthyosaur flipper

Dolphin flipper

Dolphin
(mammal, order
Cetacea)

Seal
(mammal, order Pinnipedia)

Seal flipper

Carnivore leg

Penguin (bird)

Penguin flipper

Bird wing

## Sexual selection

Something similar to an "arms race" can also occur between members of the same species in the process called sexual selection. This was first described by Darwin, who believed it to be the only significant evolutionary force other than natural selection.

The fundamental reason for sexual selection is that a female's reproductive success is limited by the number of eggs she can produce, whereas a male's reproductive success is limited by the number of females he can inseminate. So males often compete with each other for the most matings. This leads to selection, either through male competition or female choice. In the former case, males may compete directly, often by fighting, or they may try to monopolize the resources that females require. The result is that males can develop characters solely to fight or intimidate other males, like the antlers of red deer or the huge size seen in male elephant seals. The elephant seals often get badly injured, but the prize is high – the dominant four percent of males achieve an astonishing 85 percent of all the matings.

In the other type of sexual selection, females choose a mate, often using quite arbitrary characteristics. These may originally have developed as species recognition signals, but exactly how a female preference first develops is not fully understood. However, once it is established, it pays males to exaggerate the character that the females prefer, because then they will get more matings. But this process can get out of hand. Males become more and more extravagant in trying to stay ahead of each other, and become burdened with costly appendages used in display. The result is the elaborate plumage of the peacock and male birds of paradise. These birds illustrate the point that, in natural selection, passing on your genes is what matters. A mutant peacock without the extravagant tail feathers would probably live much longer than a normal male, but as he would never get a chance to mate, his mutant gene would die with him.

◀ To any environmental problem there are a limited number of solutions, and this results in "convergent evolution". These four marine animals, all descended from terrestrial ancestors, share some adaptations such as streamlining and paddle-like forelimbs. But seals and penguins still come out on land to breed, which restricts their body design. They show one solution to the environmental challenge, while the dolphin and ichthyosaur represent another. In cases of convergence, apparent similarities often conceal basic differences – as shown by the anatomy of the forelimbs. Comparing the penguin and the seal, the flipper has been derived from quite different structures – the wing of a bird, and the leg of a carnivorous mammal. A bird's wing has a reduced number of digits, so these could not spread out to form a flipper. Instead the penguin's limb bones are flattened and broadened.

▼ The single grotesquely enlarged claw of the male fiddler crab is a product of sexual selection. The male uses the claw to signal his ownership of territory to other males, and to attract females for mating.

*The idea that acquired characteristics can be inherited has had many supporters*

▼ The plant breeder, Trofim Lysenko (right) espoused Lamarckian ideas and rose to prominence in Stalinist Russia. Lamarck's ideas were officially favored for ideological reasons: they offered a way by which the improving efforts of one generation could be passed on genetically, as well as socially, to the next. Years of Russian plant improvement programs were based on erroneous Lamarckian ideas.

► Jean Baptiste de Lamarck (1744–1829), envisaged an evolutionary process driven by a "besoin" or need for improvement. The idea of inheritance of acquired characters, with which he is usually associated today, was a secondary part of his theory. The playwright, George Bernard Shaw, proclaimed Lamarck the saviour of evolution, rescuing it from the "senseless accident" of natural selection.

## Lamarckism

The best-known alternative to Darwinism is the theory of Jean Baptiste de Lamarck (1744–1829), proposed in 1809. This is often represented as the "inheritance of acquired characters" – the passing on to the offspring of features acquired by the parents. But that is only part of Lamarck's theory. More importantly, he believed that all organisms had a desire to improve themselves – a "besoin" or "need" as he called it. This striving translated itself into physical change, which was then inherited. The classic example was that of a giraffe, evolving a longer and longer neck by continually stretching toward higher branches for food.

One major objection to Lamarck's theory was that all this upward mobility would leave the world devoid of simple, primitive creatures. He attributed the continuing existence of the lower orders to spontaneous generation, that is, the power of non-living substances to spontaneously create living organisms. Spontaneous generation was finally disposed of by Louis Pasteur (1822–1895), who showed that, if the raw materials were adequately sterilized, living things did not emerge.

## Use and disuse

The idea of inheritance of acquired characters is not, in itself, incompatible with natural selection. If it did occur, it would just speed up the evolutionary process. Darwin himself believed that acquired features could be passed on, calling the process "use-and-disuse inheritance". For example, he thought that the drooping ears of many breeds of domestic animal were "due to the disuse of the muscles of the ear, from the animals being seldom much alarmed."

## Forces other than selection

Not all evolutionary change is attributable to selection – chance can play a part in several ways. When mating occurs a great many gametes are wasted. Only a few happen to combine in the new individuals, and these represent a random sample of the parents' genes. This sampling causes "genetic drift" – random changes in a gene's frequency. Purely by chance, a mutant gene can get into many offspring and so increase in frequency, even replacing the original gene completely. This is much more likely to happen in small populations than large ones, where selective forces tend to overwhelm the effects of drift.

Chance irregularities can also be important on a larger scale, and may determine which evolutionary path is followed. For example the Indian rhinoceros has one horn yet its close relative, the African rhinoceros, has two. The number of horns appears to make no specific adaptive difference. What matters is having a horn, or horns, for defense against predators. Probably slight differences in developmental pathways, rather than selective differences, caused the two rhinoceroses to evolve differently.

Another major nonselective force is linkage (♦ page 23). A gene which happens to be right next to one which is being positively selected will spread by "hitchhiking" – benefiting from the success of its neighbor.

▲ The Austrian biologist, Paul Kammerer (1880–1926) believed in the inheritance of acquired characters. He claimed to have demonstrated this in several species, including the midwife toad. But when his toads were exhibited, it was found that the crucial characteristic – a pigmented nuptial pad on the forelimb – had been faked. Doubts remain whether Kammerer himself committed the forgery.

## Weismann, Crick and the central dogma

In 1890 the German biologist August Weismann (1834–1914) proposed that acquired characters could not be inherited, since the germ line, the cell lineage leading to eggs and sperm, was separate from the soma, the cells of the body. Weismann's observation is not universally valid – in plants, for example, the germ and soma are not distinct – but the essence of his idea survived, and still seems largely correct: genetic changes occur haphazardly, and are not influenced by changes in the organism.

This idea was substantiated by the discovery, over 60 years later, that DNA could be translated into protein, but that the reverse process did not occur. This led to Francis Crick's "central dogma": that information flowed out of DNA, never into it.

However, there is an intermediate between DNA and protein, "messenger RNA", and it was later found that RNA could sometimes be translated back into DNA, through the action of enzymes produced by retroviruses (♦ page 28). Recently this has led an Australian biologist, Ted Steele, to suggest that the central dogma might not always hold true. If a gene in a somatic cell underwent a mutation, which proved favorable, that cell could multiply, and some of the mRNA molecules from the mutant gene might be carried to the germ cells by a virus and translated into DNA, which would then be inherited. Attempts to demonstrate that this can occur have so far failed.

### The selfish gene

The phenomenon of altruism, in which an animal puts itself in danger, or gives up the opportunity of mating, in order to benefit another animal, is difficult to explain in evolutionary terms. Worker bees, for example, do not reproduce, and will even give up their lives for the hive: they sting intruders and the act of stinging kills them. How could a trait which causes premature death evolve?

In 1962 Wynne-Edwards proposed that altruism evolves for the "good of the group" or for the "good of the species" – groups with altruists do better than groups of selfish individuals, so only altruistic groups persist. But there is a fatal flaw in this argument. In a group of altruists, a "selfish" mutant individual, which avoided the costs of altruism while still reaping the benefits, could arise. The whole system would then break down, as the gene for "selfishness" spread through the group.

Looking at evolution from the point of view of the gene provides a much better explanation for altruism, at least between related individuals. A "selfish gene" is only concerned with its own survival, not that of the individual in which it is carried. If it can get the individual to perform an act of altruism which benefits other individuals carrying the same gene, so much the better. Obviously the offspring of that individual are likely to carry the gene, but so are its brothers, sisters, parents, and even cousins. Calculations show that an individual will share, on average, about as many genes with a brother or sister as with its child. This makes sense of the behavior of Florida scrub jays, and other birds, which help their parents raise younger siblings rather than breeding themselves.

Most altruism is in fact directed at close kin, and can be explained in this way. But many cases are known of animals acting altruistically toward non-relatives, and even to members of another species. For example a baboon may help another in a fight, only to receive help itself later. Dolphins and whales often support distressed animals at the surface allowing them to breathe. This behavior has been observed across species, and there are cases where dolphins have saved humans from drowning. Such behavior probably evolves through reciprocation: an animal helped now will be able to return aid at a later date.

▼ Suricates keep watch for predators. These members of the mongoose family take turns in staying with the young, while the rest of the group go foraging. Some carers are related to the young – they may be elder siblings – and their "altruism" can be explained by kin selection. But this is not always so, because unrelated individuals can join a social group. Where the carer and the young are not related, reciprocation must be invoked to explain the "altruistic" act. The suricates' behavior is in contrast to that of lions, where an unrelated male joining the pride will kill the cubs that are present. This can be explained by kin selection, since the new male shares no genes with the cubs, and by killing them brings the lionesses into breeding condition more quickly.

## Adaptive radiation

◄ *Soon after being formed by volcanic eruption, the islands of Hawaii were colonized by a honey-creeper from mainland America. That was about 5 million years ago. In the absence of other birds, the ancestral honeycreeper adapted to fill the full range of avian ecological niches, and each species has developed a beak-shape to suit its particular diet.*

**Nectar and insects**

**1** Apapane
(*Himatione sanquinea*)
Beak unspecialized

**2** Iiwi
(*Vestiaria coccinea*)
Takes many
caterpillars

**Insects**

**1** Kauai akialoa (*Hemignathus procerus* –
possibly extinct)| Probes for insects in dead wood

**2** Maui parrotbill (*Pseudonestor xanthophrys* –
possibly extinct) Rips off bark and crushes twigs
to remove insects, mainly beetle grubs

**3** Akiapolauu (*Hemignathus wilsoni*)
Chips at dead wood with straight lower bill,
then probes for insects with upper bill

**Fruit**

Ou (*Psittirostra psittacea* –
possibly extinct)
Feeds largely on fruit

**Seeds**

Grosbeak finch
(*Psittirostra kona* –
extinct) Crushed hard,
dry seeds of trees

Ancestral honeycreeper

---

### The species concept

*The species concept is based on the common-sense observation that members of a species look alike. Either they all look the same, or there are a few characteristic types – males and females, for example, or workers and queens in social insects. (Domesticated species, such as the dog, are an exception to this, because artificial selection has produced a great variety of disparate types.) The species, as defined in this way, usually turns out to be a discrete, isolated unit in a biological sense. Within the group all individuals can actually, or potentially, interbreed.*

*Not every species is this clear-cut. Some have "fuzzy edges" and can interbreed to a certain extent with neighboring species. On the other hand, many species are divided into distinctive-looking subspecies or varieties that rarely interbreed, though they could theoretically do so.*

*Despite these exceptions, the species concept is biologically valid. Organisms that are adapted to one way of life will not benefit by mingling their genes with others whose adaptations lie in different directions. So isolating mechanisms have evolved, to keep different species from interbreeding.*

### Speciation

So far we have considered natural selection as a process which creates and maintains adaptation. But Darwin in *The Origin of Species* extrapolated from this to the formation of new species. He maintained that the same gradual process of natural selection produced both results. Such a continuum between adaptation and speciation can clearly be seen in the "adaptive radiation" of the Hawaiian honeycreepers.

A similar radiation has occurred in the Galapagos Islands, where the original colonizer was a species of finch. The Galapagos finch species differ little, except in their diets and their beaks. Recently, it has been found that they use the beak shape to recognize members of the same species during courtship. The fact that birds reject suitors with the wrong type of beak is an effective *isolating mechanism* (◆ page 17).

For over a century biologists have been arguing about the importance of *geographical* isolation for speciation. Darwin, after much equivocation, decided that it was largely unimportant, and that speciation could occur simply by divergence and the development of a suitable isolating mechanism. This view was later rejected by many for Ernst Mayr's allopatric speciation model.

Mayr argues that within large populations, individuals have an integrated set of adaptations, or a "coadapted gene complex". New

## Isolating mechanisms

Isolating mechanisms often involve species recognition signals – such as the crests, or long tail plumes of birds. A change in the plumage can set one group apart from another – females will only respond to the male if he looks right. The songs, calls and movements of courtship can also change, as can specific odors. The timing of breeding is another important component of isolation. A new species that switches its breeding season is instantly cut off genetically from the parent species. In species with internal fertilization, incompatibility can also act as an isolating mechanism.

In some closely related species there are no obvious differences, except in courtship behavior. In these cases, changes in mating preferences alone may have caused speciation.

## Ring species

Discrete reproductive groups generally come into existence very slowly. During speciation there can be considerable similarity and interbreeding between the diverging groups (which are described as varieties or subspecies). This is seen in "ring species", such as the one involving herring gulls and lesser black-backed gulls. These two species trace their ancestry to a Siberian species which spread to the west and the east, slowly diverging and forming a chain of subspecies. Each one can and does breed with the subspecies adjacent to it, but where the two extreme populations overlap, in northern Europe, the gulls do not interbrood. They are rightly considered to be distinct species, but the dividing line between them is clearly arbitrary.

◄ A mixed herd of horses and horse-zebra hybrids (known as zebroids). Like asses or mules, zebroids are generally infertile, due to differences in the chromosomes of their parents. In the wild, selection favors the evolution of isolating mechanisms that stop individuals of two related species such as this from mating and thus wasting their reproductive effort.

genes are unlikely to fit in with the existing gene complex, and any tendency of peripheral populations to adapt to novel conditions in their area is canceled out, because of gene flow from the parent population. Change and speciation are only possible when peripheral populations become isolated genetically. A new, isolated population will be founded by a small number of individuals from the main population, who quickly multiply, so that their genes become much more common than they were in the parent population. Gene frequencies are changed and the individuals in the new population will be homozygous at many more loci. This changes the nature of the genetic background, so the conservative influence of the "coadapted gene complex" breaks down. New genes can then become established more easily, promoting rapid change and speciation. When the peripheral population mixes again with the parental population, either they coexist or they compete, in which case one drives the other extinct.

Mayr's theory has been very influential and is part of the punctuated equilibrium model (page 19), but it has recently been heavily criticized. There is little evidence that large populations are actually so resistant to change as Mayr claims. Nor is there evidence that major genetic upheavals are associated with speciation. The matter is not yet resolved, but Darwin's view is once again gaining popularity.

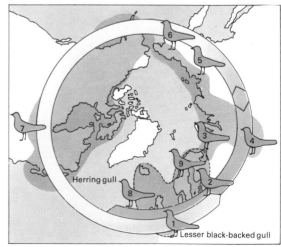

▲ In northern Europe, the herring gull and lesser black-backed gull are clearly distinct species, but they are linked by a series of interbreeding forms, in a classic "ring species".

1 Larus fuscus graellsi
2 L. fuscus fuscus
3 L. fuscus antellus
4 L. fuscus heuglini
5 L. argentatus birulaii
6 L. argentatus vegae
7 L. argentatus smithsonianus
8 L. argentatus argentatus
9 L. argentatus omissus

*The fossil record is so patchy that it has been likened to a dozen pages torn at random from a long novel*

### The Red Queen Model
*Another approach to understanding macro-evolution is to ask how communities of plants and animals have evolved. Two modes are likely. If the species in the community are closely coadapted then change in one species is likely to promote change in others. This mode of evolution is known as the Red Queen Model after Lewis Carroll's "Through the Looking-Glass", where the Red Queen says "it takes all the running you can do, to keep in the same place". Species have to evolve just to keep up with the rest of the community. In the contrasting Stationary Model, evolution is driven principally by environmental changes.*

*These two models make different predictions about patterns of change. The Stationary Model predicts that there will be no extinction in a constant environment, but that in a periodically changing environment, rapid bursts of extinction will occur. The Red Queen Model predicts that, regardless of the environment, species will go extinct at the same constant rate. Such predictions can be tested against the pattern of change seen in fossils of oceanic plankton, obtained from deepsea cores; these also record changes in the environment. So far only two tests have been completed – the results of one supported one model and one the other.*

*An exception to either model is when species evolve a new grade of organization, for example flight. It will take many millions of years before this character can be perfected, and during that time there would be continual selective pressure to do so, irrespective of any environmental change or species interactions.*

## Fossils

The process of adaptation can be observed in progress, and so can speciation, to a lesser extent. But the evolution of larger groups, like birds or insects, occurs so slowly that we cannot hope to see it in action, and it can only be studied by looking at fossils.

Darwin was well aware that his view of evolution as a gradual and continuous process was not borne out by the fossil record, which was full of gaps, and offered few intermediates between major groups. But paleontology was still in its infancy, so it was reasonable to dismiss the absence of intermediates as due to poor fossilization. Becoming a fossil is a chancy business and only a minute fraction of living forms are preserved. The chances of a fossil later coming to the surface and being found are also slight. All this makes the fossil record a very patchy and selective record of the Earth's history. The finding of a living coelacanth, presumed extinct since the Jurassic (◗ page 98), is evidence of this.

Some fossil lineages, such as that leading to modern horses, do show a gradual succession of intermediate forms. But more often in the fossil record there are long periods of no change ("stasis"), interspersed with short periods of more rapid change. In 1971 Stephen Jay Gould and Niles Eldredge argued that this "punctuated equilibrium" pattern was not due to poor fossilization – it was real. Drawing on Mayr's allopatric speciation model (◗ page 16) they developed a new theory to explain it. They argued that stasis was due to coadapted gene complexes and developmental constraints (◗ page 10) which both act to prevent change. These conservative forces could only be overcome

▲▼ *Well-preserved fossils, such as this saber-tooth tiger skull, lizard and holostean fish, tell us much about evolution, but the number of species represented by the fossil record is only a tiny fraction of all past life forms.*

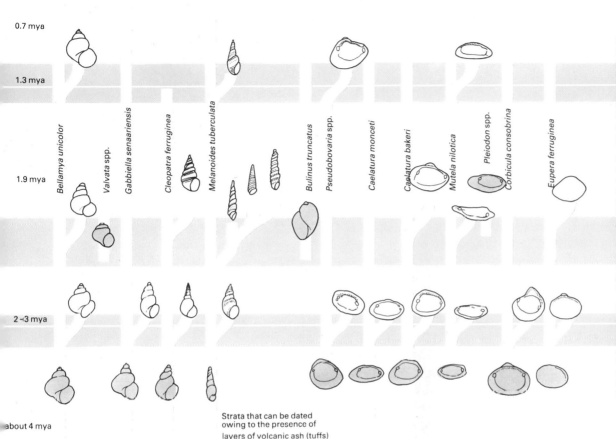

0.7 mya

1.3 mya

1.9 mya

2–3 mya

about 4 mya

*Bellamya unicolor*

*Valvata spp.*

*Gabbiella senaariensis*

*Cleopatra ferruginea*

*Melanoides tuberculata*

*Bulinus truncatus*

*Pseudobovaria spp.*

*Caelatura monceti*

*Caelatura bakeri*

*Mutela nilotica*

*Pleiodon spp.*

*Corbicula consobrina*

*Eupera ferruginea*

A

B

C

◄ *The fossil mollusks of Lake Turkana in northern Kenya, form a remarkably complete sequence. They seem to show a pattern of stasis broken by short bursts of change, when new species evolved only to become extinct later. These appear to be linked with a fall in the level of the lake. Two such eras of rapid change are noted here, (A and C) and a third may have occurred between them (B). But difficulties in dating make it impossible to tell if B represents a long or short period of time. Although these fossils seem to show a pattern of stasis and rapid change, they do not necessarily substantiate the punctuated equilibrium theory. The periods of "rapid" change are 5,000– 50,000 years long, quite sufficient for large changes to have occurred according to Darwinian theory. Alternatively, changes in the pH of the water could have directly affected shell shape, without any genetic change.*

Strata that can be dated owing to the presence of layers of volcanic ash (tuffs)

## Hopeful monsters

*The debate between gradualists and those who see evolution as a sporadic, jumpy process has been going on for a long time. Before Darwin, there were evolutionary theories proposed by the French biologist Étienne Geoffroy Saint-Hilaire (1772–1844) and by the Scottish writer Robert Chambers (1802–1871), both involving abrupt changes. These "saltations" were supposed to happen during growth of the embryo and result in a completely new type of creature appearing instantaneously. Only in this way, they thought, could fundamentally novel groups have originated. Darwin's uniformitarianism (* page 10) was, to some extent, a reaction to these theories. Like many scientists, he felt that they simply substituted one sort of miracle (saltation) for another (divine creation). His belief that major groups evolved by the accumulation of minute adaptive changes later became part of the dogma of neo-Darwinism. It was challenged in the 1940s by the geneticist Richard Goldschmidt (1878-1958), who revived the idea of saltations and described the mutant forms that founded new lineages as "hopeful monsters". Goldschmidt's theory found few supporters, but since the 1970s biologists such as Stephen Jay Gould have re-examined these ideas in a more favorable light. Although they would not advocate sudden and miraculous changes, they do believe that the . founding of new groups involves a different type of change from that which produces adaptation.*

in isolated peripheral populations. The new species that arose from the populations would then reinvade the parent population and drive it extinct. The lack of intermediates was thus due to them existing only for short periods in small numbers.

The punctuated equilibrium model involves two separate ideas. The first is that evolution proceeds in fits and starts, not at a constant, gradual speed. This is not really a very contentious claim, especially when one realizes that paleontologists have a rather odd attitude to time – for them, a "short period of rapid change" would occupy tens of thousands of years, and the changes taking place would be imperceptible in a human lifetime. The second, and more significant claim, is that macroevolution is decoupled from microevolution – it proceeds by different mechanisms and, perhaps, in different directions.

But what exactly are those different mechanisms? One that has been proposed is species selection – not to be confused with the old idea of "for the good of the species" (* page 15). It postulates some form of linkage between certain apparently unconnected features of species. For example, there is a trend in the fossil record toward larger size, so that related species in succeeding fossil strata often become bigger and bigger. This could just be due to the pressure of natural selection continually favoring individuals of increased size. Alternatively the trend could be explained if species with larger size speciated more quickly, or had greater species longevity. This independent mechanism of macroevolution could conceivably work in the opposite direction from natural selection, but there is no real evidence to suggest that it occurs.

## Molecular evolution

Thanks to advances in molecular biology over the last 20 years, it is now possible to study directly the rates at which genes evolve. One unexpected finding was that a great many proteins exist in two or more forms within a species. This is known as protein polymorphism, and it is far more prevalent than was expected.

To understand why this high level of protein variation exists, biologists had to think again about mutation. According to the traditional view most mutations are harmful, since they cause aberrant proteins to be produced. They are eliminated by natural selection because they cause death or a severe loss of fitness to their owners. Only a small percentage of mutations turn out to be useful and these are selected. If the very high observed level of protein polymorphism was maintained by selection in the same way as other polymorphisms (◀ page 11), the number of individuals that would have to die, or fail to breed, in each generation would outstrip the reproductive capacity of most species. So to account for the enormous variation observed, a new class of mutations had to be proposed. These are known as neutral mutations, because they cause little or no alteration of a protein's function and so remain unaffected by selection.

The "neutral theory" of molecular evolution was put forward in 1968, by the Japanese geneticist Motoo Kimura. He proposed that neutral mutations spread by the random process of genetic drift (◀ page 14), a mechanism first proposed in the 1930s.

Kimura also proposed that because neutral replacements occur at random, they accumulate at a regular rate. This explained the observations that had already been made using universal proteins such as hemoglobin or cytochrome c, and comparing their amino acid sequence in different groups of animals. If the number of amino acid differences between two groups was counted, and compared with approximate dates for the separation of their lineages, calculated from the fossil record, it was found that the number of amino acid differences was proportional to the time since separation. For example, human alpha-globin differs at 4 amino acid sites from a rhesus monkey, 17 sites from a calf and 71 sites from a carp. According to fossil evidence, our ancestors separated from those of the rhesus monkey 25 million years ago, from those of the cow 90 million years ago, and from those of the carp 400 million years ago. This gives a consistent rate of change of about one amino acid substitution every 5-6 million years (per pair of proteins).

Such observations form the basis of what is known as the "molecular clock". The rate of the molecular clock for an average protein is about one amino acid substitution every million years, but each protein has its own particular rate of change. Proteins with very specific functions change very little. For example, histone H4 binds over its whole surface to DNA and is vital for maintaining DNA stability. Calf H4 differs at only 2 out of 102 amino acid sites when compared to pea plant H4: a rate of change of only one amino acid site every 500 million years.

In contrast, the globin molecules, which also have a long ancestry, show a restricted rate only at the active heme site. The heme site is where globin binds to a heme group, giving hemoglobin, the bloodstream's oxygen-carrying molecule. The rest of the globin molecule forms a loose supporting skeleton, and here the detailed structure is not particularly important. It is in this part that variation abounds, and the evolutionary rate is about 500 times that of the heme site.

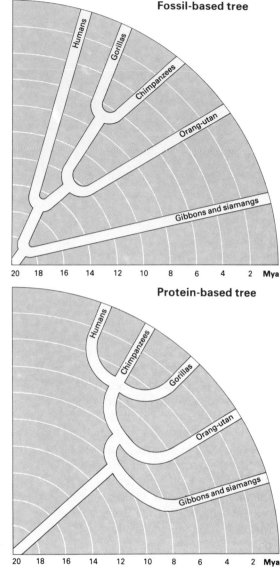

**Fossil-based tree**

**Protein-based tree**

▲ *The fossil-based evolutionary tree of the apes has had to be rejected in favor of one based on molecular evidence. DNA and protein studies show that the human line split off from the gorillas and chimpanzees only 5 million years ago.*

### The human puzzle

*Confidence in genealogies derived from molecular data now often exceeds that from fossils. Until the 1970s the main theory of human evolution – based on the scanty evidence of the fossil record and some guesswork – proposed that the split between the human and ape lines occurred about 15 million years ago. Molecular comparisons indicate a much closer relationship between Man and the African apes, and put the time at which they split at just 5 million years ago. Yet upright-walking, human-like fossils, over 3·5 million years old, found in Ethiopia, and fossilized footprints found in Tanzania show that hominids walked upright at this time. If the split with apes occured at 5 million years, this leaves only 1·5 million years for some dramatic evolutionary advances. But many proteins have now been examined and each gives the same date, so 5 million years is now accepted as correct.*

## 2

# Genetics

*Pioneers of genetic study...The discovery of chromosomes...Classical and molecular genetics... The genetic revolution...Introns, junk DNA and pseudogenes...PERSPECTIVE...Why individuals differ... Fruit flies...Sex linkage...Jumping genes*

When Charles Darwin wrote *The Origin of Species* he admitted to just one serious objection to his theory. How could descent with modification take place, when any favorable change that occurred spontaneously in an animal or plant, was bound to be diluted in subsequent generations? Darwin's problem was that he saw the process of inheritance as a blending of the father's and mother's features, a view that probably had its origins in the ancient idea of blood as the hereditary material (a notion that lingers on in such terms as "blood line", "blood relation" and "royal blood"). Darwin never resolved this particular difficulty, though he often seemed to get close to the answer. "No one can say...why the child often reverts in certain characters to its grandfather or grandmother...", he wrote. Unknown to him, the same sort of observations were being made, and the answer worked out, by an Austrian monk called Gregor Mendel (1822–1884).

The explanation for Darwin's observation is simple enough: the character which is observed in both grandparent and child is produced by a unit of hereditary material – now called a gene – that is passed on, largely unchanged, from one generation to another. It is not blended, so there is no dilution. But its effects can be masked – hence its disappearance in the intervening generation. The effects of genes like this are described as "recessive" – others genes have effects that are not masked, and these are described as "dominant". The essence of Mendel's idea is that inheritance is mediated by discrete units or particles – hence it is known as "particulate inheritance", as against the earlier ideas of "blending inheritance".

What set Mendel on the right track were breeding experiments with pea plants, which revealed several pairs of alternative features, one of which was dominant and the other recessive. If a tall variety of pea was crossed with a short variety, for example, all the offspring were tall. But short plants reappeared in the next generation: when two of the tall plants obtained from the first cross were interbred, about a quarter of their offspring were short.

Most monastic gardeners with a harmless interest in natural history would have stopped there, but Mendel had a mathematical turn of mind. Why a quarter, he asked? He made hundreds of crosses and, with his helpers, counted thousands of plants until he came up with the answer. When he looked at more than one pair of characters at a time he found yet more amazing ratios – 9:3:3:1 and even 27:9:9:9: 3:3:3:1. Mendel saw that there was a mathematical logic to these complex figures, and this led him to the explanation. In any one animal or plant each gene had an opposite number. It could be exactly the same gene, or a different version of that gene. When the animal or plant mated, its offspring got only one of the pair: the other came from the other parent. The illustration overleaf shows how this produces the characteristic "Mendelian ratios".

▲ *Gregor Mendel, the Austrian monk whose careful plant-breeding studies founded the science of genetics. His experiments included crossing a short variety of garden pea, such as the one shown below, with a tall variety.*

**Why is particulate inheritance not obvious?** *The results Mendel obtained from crossing tall and short pea plants were unexpected. After all, when a tall man marries a short woman their children are likely to show a range of heights, and most will be about average – as one would expect if inheritance was "blending". Inheritance of discrete units of information – "particulate inheritance" – was difficult to accept because it is far from obvious. The reason for this is that it only becomes apparent when a trait is determined by a single gene. Most characters are "polygenic traits" determined by many separate genes, so that each individual gene makes only a small difference to the end result.*

### Mendel's pea experiments

*When Mendel crossed a tall pea variety with a short one, all the progeny grown from the seeds (the F1) were tall. But when two of these F1 plants were crossed, about one quarter of their progeny (the F2) were small. Mendel explained this by assuming that each plant had a "double dose" of each hereditary factor (now called "genes"). The offspring received one from each parent. And the effects of one masked the effect of the other – tall (T) was dominant while small (t) was recessive.*

*Dominance is not always as complete as this. In the cross shown in the center, between red and white species of campion, there is incomplete dominance, and the F1 progeny appear pink. This looks like "blending inheritance" but in the next generation (F2), white and red flowers reappear in a 1:2:1 ratio. This ratio is also seen in the genotype of the F2 pea plants when tall and short plants are crossed, but, because T is dominant in its effects, it appears as a 3:1 ratio there.*

*When Mendel crossed a pea variety having round yellow seeds with one having green wrinkled seeds, all the progeny produced round yellow seeds. When two of these were crossed, their progeny (the F2) showed four different possibilities in a 9:3:3:1 ratio, as shown on the far right. Mendel realized that two pairs of characters (green-yellow, round-wrinkled) segregating independently of each other could produce this effect: yellow and round were dominant.*

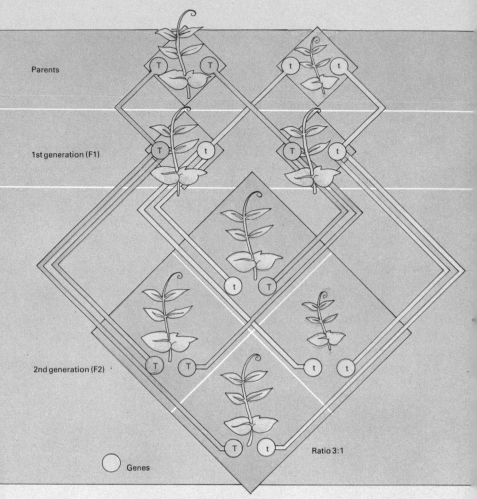

Parents

1st generation (F1)

2nd generation (F2)

○ Genes

Ratio 3:1

◄ *The common European hawthorn, growing in three different habitats, and producing dramatically different shapes as a result. All are situated at about the same latitude and within a few miles of the sea, but differ in their exposure to wind and grazing animals. The one on the far left has the most protection from both and has developed into a large handsome tree, over 12m tall. The one nearest the coast (top) suffers constant saltspray and buffeting winds which have stunted it and molded its shape by killing all buds and small branches on the seaward side. The third is in pasture land and was probably nibbled by grazing animals when small, producing a spreading bush, scarcely 1m high. These trees probably have much the same genotype, but their phenotype has been strongly molded by the environment. Their offspring, however, will not be affected by this, because characteristics produced by the environment are not inherited (◊ page 14).*

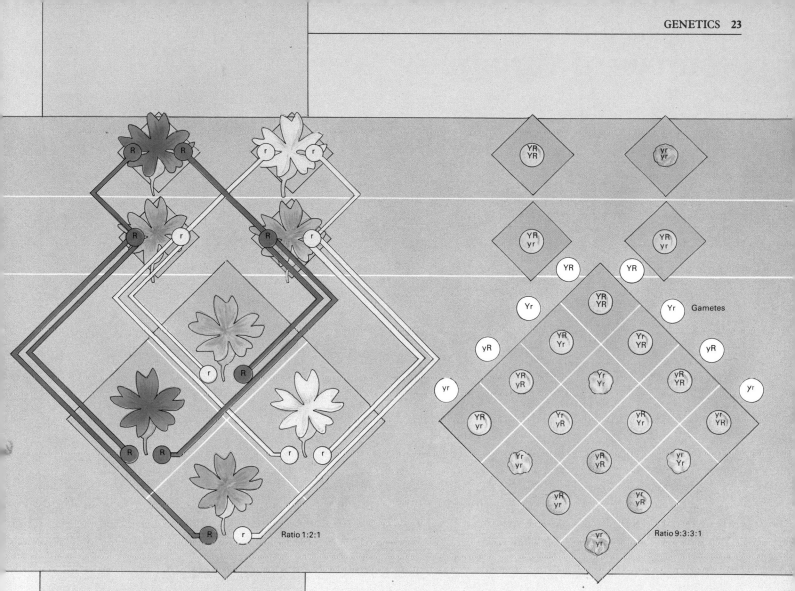

Ratio 1:2:1

Gametes

Ratio 9:3:3:1

### Keywords in genetics
*Pairs of alternative characters, like tall or short, and red or white flowers, are coded for by genes that occupy the same place or locus (plural loci) on a chromosome. The various genes found at a single locus are called alleles. Although only two alleles per locus are shown here, many loci have several alleles.*

*When an organism carries two identical alleles (eg TT or tt) it is said to be homozygous at that locus. When it has different alleles at a locus (Tt, Rr) it is heterozygous. Recessive characters (shown by a small letter) are only expressed in the homozygous state. Inbred lines, as in self-fertilizing plants like the pea, tend to be homozygous at many loci. The progeny of a cross between two inbred lines are called hybrids and these are heterozygous at many loci. The first generation of hybrids from a cross are known as the F1, the second generation as the F2.*

*Because of dominance, two organisms may show the same feature (such as being tall), although they have a different genetic makeup (TT or Tt). The organism's appearance is known as its phenotype, and its genetic makeup as its genotype. Environmental factors also influence the phenotype – a poor diet will stunt growth, for example.*

Mendel's work went sadly unnoticed in his lifetime, but at the beginning of the 20th century it was rediscovered, and soon afterward another piece of the puzzle was fitted into place. Microscope observations of cell nuclei showed them to contain elongated particles that took up certain dyes very strongly, and were therefore called "chromosomes", from the Greek for "colored bodies". Cells producing eggs and sperm showed an interesting sequence of events, known as meiosis (♦ page 24), in which the chromosomes paired up and then separated, so that each gamete got only one of the pair. The link with Mendel's work was quickly realized – all could be explained if his hereditary particles were carried on the chromosomes.

The discovery of the chromosomes also explained certain exceptions to Mendel's laws. Although some characters segregated independently of each other (producing 9:3:3:1 ratios), other characters tended to be inherited together. This phenomenon, known as linkage, was explained by the genes being near each other on the same chromosome. That they could occasionally become separated was attributed to crossing over between chromatids (♦ page 25).

Geneticists subsequently used linkage to "map" the chromosomes. This is done by measuring the frequency with which linked genes can be separated (the recombination rate). Genes that are right next to each other on the chromosome are unlikely to be split apart by crossing over, so they are always inherited together – they are said to be "tightly linked". The further apart the two genes are, then the greater the chance of a crossing-over event occurring between them, and on this basis linear "gene maps" of the chromosomes can be constructed.

# Sources of Variability

1 **Interphase I/early prophase I:** Chromosomes are just distinguishable. DNA replication is taking place, so most base sequence mutations will occur here, although they can happen at other times too, when DNA is being repaired.

2 **Mid prophase I:** Chromosomes shorten and thicken. They have already duplicated into two chromatids, but these remain together. They have paired up with their homologous chromosomes to form bivalents.

3 **Metaphase I:** Bivalents line up along the equator of the spindle.

4 **Anaphase I:** Chromosomes separate, one of each pair to either end of the spindle.

5 **Telophase I/Interphase II:** The cell has divided and each part now has only half the parent's chromosomes

(although they are still split into chromatids).

6 **Prophase II:** Chromosomes shorten and thicken as at Prophase I, but with no chromosome duplication.

7 **Metaphase II:** Chromosomes line up as before.

8 **Anaphase II:** Chromatids separate to form chromosomes.

9 **Telophase II:** Each cell divides to give four gametes and chromosomes disperse.

▶ *When meiosis was observed, in the 1900s, the link with Mendel's hereditary factors (genes) was clear. If the genes for pairs of characters (tall-short, red flowers-white flowers) were located opposite each other on homologous chromosomes, that would explain why the offspring always received one gene from the mother and one from the father, and always possessed only two versions of the gene.*

Gametes

Zygotes produced by self-fertilization

▲ *Reassortment of the chromosomes occurs during meiosis, because the set that each gamete receives is a random one. With 4 chromosomes, as in this example, 16 different combinations are possible in the gametes, and this would give 256 (16×16) possible combinations in the offspring of two parents. When the effects of crossing-over are added to this, the number of different recombinants is almost infinite. Recombination may make sex worthwhile even for self-fertilizing plants like the pea.*

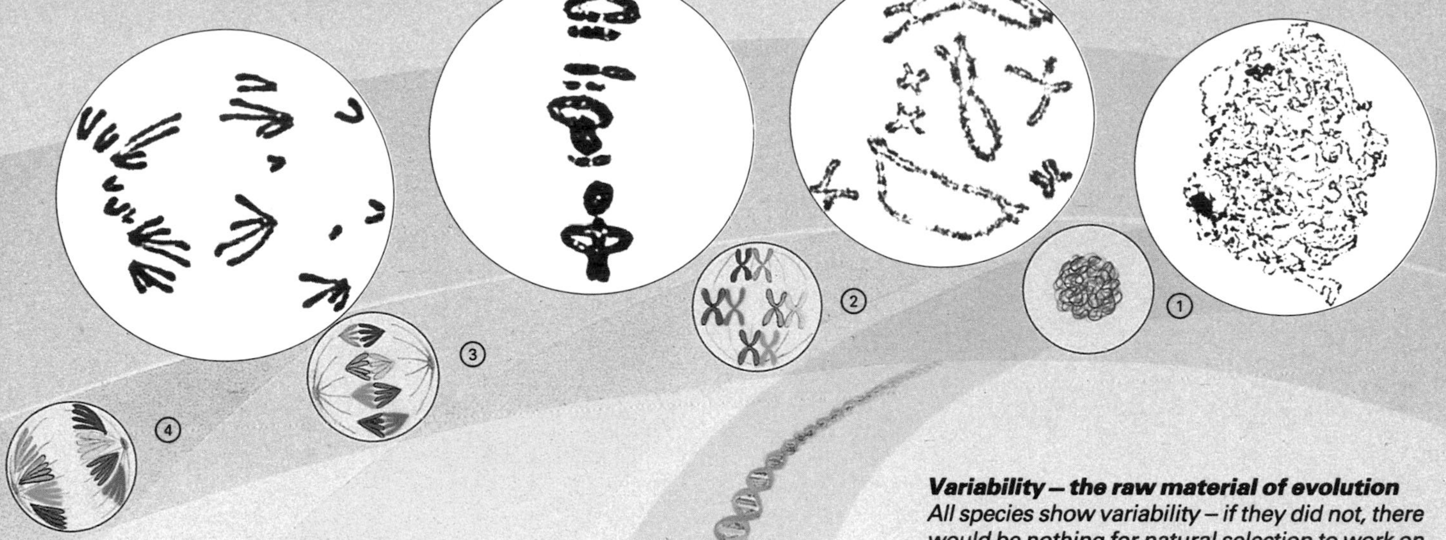

## Variability – the raw material of evolution

All species show variability – if they did not, there would be nothing for natural selection to work on and evolution would not occur. The original source of all variation is mutation – changes in the genetic material at the DNA level (see below). Mutations are essentially random in nature and most are either neutral (◊ page 20) or harmful in their effects: the chance of a random change improving a highly specialized molecule like an enzyme is very small indeed. Harmful changes tend to be weeded out by natural selection, but many such mutants are recessive, and can persist because the normal dominant gene masks their effect.

The second factor in maintaining variability is recombination either between chromosomes, through mechanisms such as crossing over (center), or the reassortment of chromosomes that occurs during meiosis (left). These processes reshuffle the changes produced by mutation, and may come up with winning combinations.

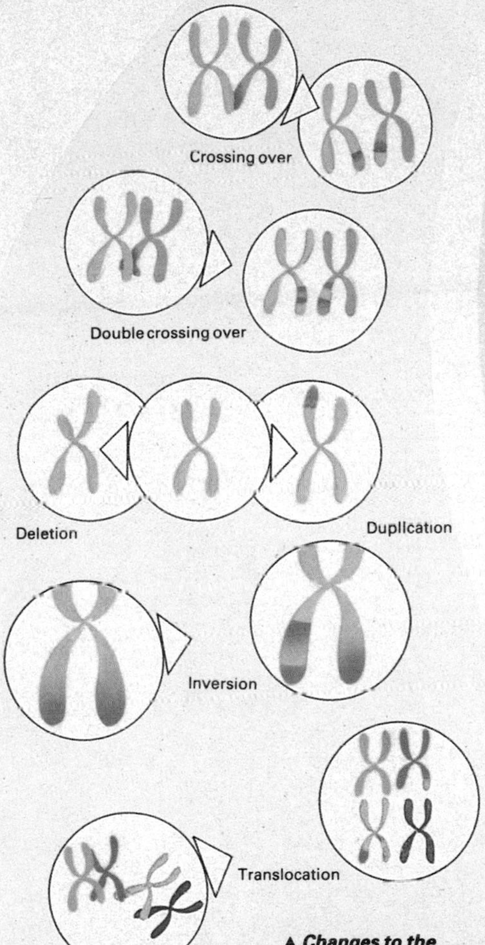

Crossing over

Double crossing over

Deletion

Duplication

Inversion

Translocation

DNA

Point mutation

Insertion

Deletion

● Site of mutation
Adenine
Thymine
Guanine
Cytosine

Sugar-phosphate chain

▲ Changes to the chromosome generally occur when the homologous pairs lie close together during prophase I. The most important and frequent change is crossing-over, in which the chromatids break and then exchange segments when they rejoin. Less common changes include deletion and duplication, in which a segment of DNA is lost, or duplicated, and inversion, which turns a segment of DNA back to front. In translocation, non-homologous chromosomes exchange pieces.

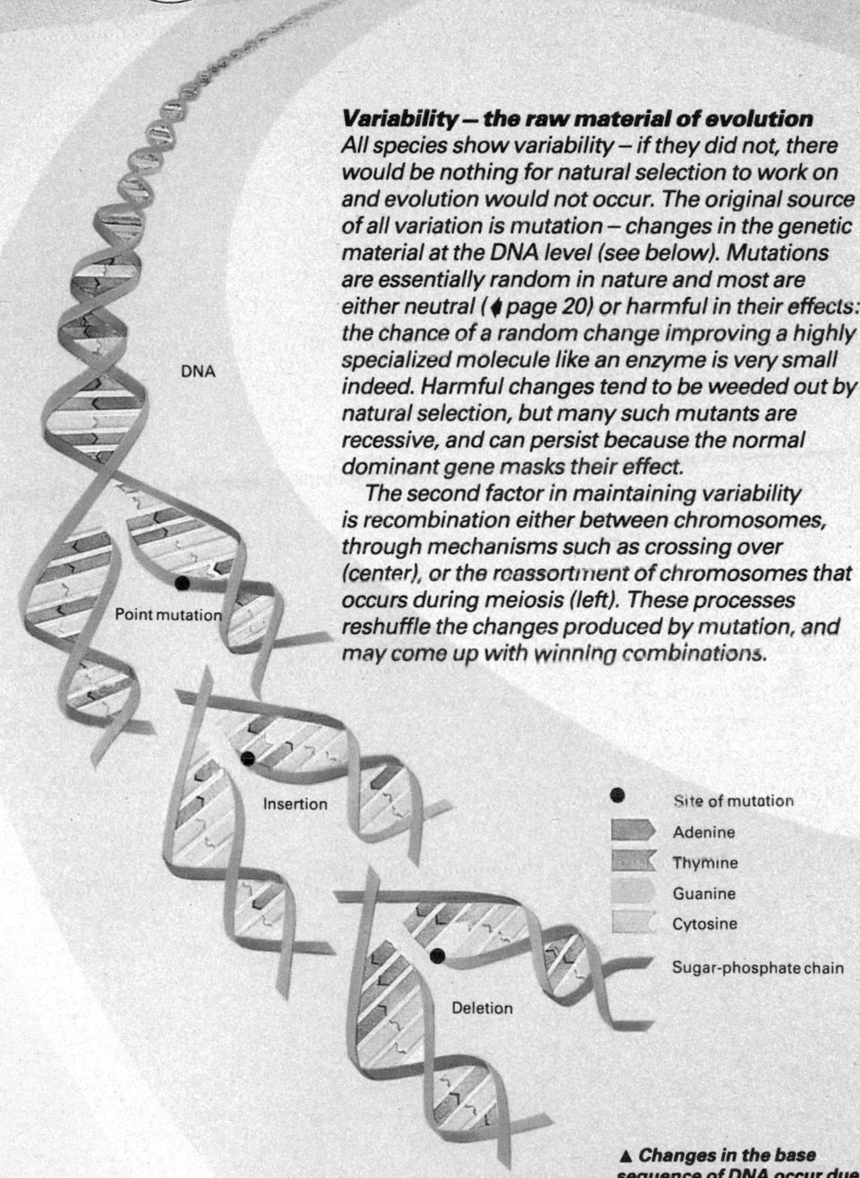

▲ Changes in the base sequence of DNA occur due to inaccurate copying during DNA replication or repair (but not as frequently as this diagram implies). Some such changes produce no change in the amino acid sequence of the gene's product, because of redundancy in the genetic code: most amino acids have several codons (◊ page 140). Even if the mutation does produce a change in the gene product, a physiological effect may not result. Such neutral mutations tend to build up in the genome (◊ page 20).

This type of study that Mendel pioneered – in which the genes are looked at via their effects, using breeding experiments – forms the basis of what is known as "classical genetics". Although the early geneticists would have liked to tackle the questions of "molecular genetics" – what genes were, and how they produced their effects – they could not begin to do so. The techniques of biochemistry, which were needed to unravel these questions, were still relatively crude. Nevertheless, by the late 1930s, important advances were being made, by using microorganisms – mostly bacteria and fungi. These were chosen because they can be grown on an artificial medium, made up in the laboratory from a gel containing simple, defined nutrients. Changes in growth can be observed with one nutrient missing, or a new one added. Forms that had undergone mutation were often unable to grow unless some extra nutrient was supplied. It became clear that this was because these mutants lacked a particular enzyme which, in normal cells, allowed that nutrient to be synthesized from simpler molecules. Studies of such mutants led to the conclusion that the genes' products were largely proteins of some kind: either enzymes or structural proteins. Since other cell constituents, such as fats, carbohydrates or, pigments, are synthesized by enzyme-controlled pathways, coding for proteins allows the genes to produce and control the entire cell contents.

On the basis of such experiments, two American scientists, Beadle and Tatum, proposed in 1941 that each gene – as identified by techniques of classical genetics – produced a single enzyme. This became known as the "one-gene-one-enzyme hypothesis" (although later it had to be modified to one-gene-one-polypeptide-chain). A few years later, in 1944, it was demonstrated that the nucleic acid DNA was the genetic material, rather than protein, the other constituent of the chromosomes. This was done by introducing purified DNA into one bacterial strain from another, and showing that genetic information had thereby been transferred.

As a result of these extensive genetic studies of microorganisms, a great deal of knowledge about them was accumulated. Popular laboratory organisms, such as the bacterium *Escherichia coli*, became so fully understood, and their chromosomes so thoroughly mapped, that they were the obvious choice for all further investigations. Thus two French scientists, Jacob and Monod, working in the 1940s, '50s and '60s, chose *E. coli* for their studies of how genes are switched on and off. They elucidated a system that was beautifully neat and logical. It depended on some molecule – a product, intermediate or raw material of the process being controlled – combining with a protein known as a "repressor", which in turn could control expression of the gene. For example, *E. coli* bacteria only produce lactose-degrading enzymes when lactose (a sugar) is added to their growth medium. Normally a protein repressor prevents the lactose-degrading enzymes from being produced by binding to a special "operator site", located beside the genes for these enzymes. When lactose is present, it combines with the repressor which then cannot bind to the operator site. This allows the genes to be expressed. Turning genes off is achieved by some molecule – usually the product of the reaction in question – combining with a normally inactive protein repressor. This activates the repressor and allows it to bind to the operator site. Jacob and Monod found that the enzymes of a particular metabolic pathway were often coded for by a string of neighboring genes, so that all were switched on or off together. Such sets of genes became known as "operons".

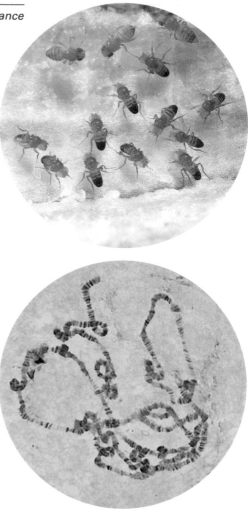

▲ *Fruit flies are useful in genetics because large numbers can be kept in a small space (usually milk bottles), and they have giant chromosomes in their salivary glands (below).*

**The man who put fruit flies on the map**
*Early on, geneticists realized that to study inheritance, experimental organisms with short breeding cycles and many offspring would be advantageous. Fruit flies* Drosophila *were ideal because their generation time is about two weeks. They also have the advantage of only possessing four pairs of chromosomes (the fewer the better for genetics) and in having unusual "giant" chromosomes in their salivary glands. These giant chromosomes greatly aid genetic mapping because the irregular bands all along them make different sections distinctive. Furthermore, when a gene is being expressed the chromosome expands into a "puff" around that point, and this can be used to corroborate mapping results.*

*The first person to use* Drosophila *for genetic experiments was T. H. Morgan (1865–1945), an American who began, at the turn of the century, by thinking Mendel's newly-rediscovered ideas rather dubious, but went on to lay the foundations of classical genetics. Morgan and his co-workers established incontrovertibly that the genes were on the chromosomes, discovered crossing over, identified sex chromosomes and sex linkage, invented the technique of genetic mapping based on linkage and extensively mapped* Drosophila's *chromosomes. Morgan was awarded the Nobel Prize in 1933, but his most lasting legacy is the tiny fruit fly, still an essential experimental tool in genetics.*

◄▲ *A European cuckoo laying her egg. (The egg in her beak is one of the host's which she removes.) These birds parasitize a number of species, and some produce brown eggs while others lay blue eggs, to match different hosts' egg color. The female cuckoo chooses a host of the same species as raised her, so that her eggs will match theirs. But cuckoos with differently colored eggs are not separate subspecies – they mate freely with any male cuckoo – so how is the blue and brown distinction maintained? Sex-linkage is thought to be the answer. In birds, females are XY and males XX. So the egg color gene could be on the Y chromosome, and thus be donated by the female alone.*

◄▼ *The gene for ginger-colored fur in cats is carried on the X chromosome only, and is codominant with the allele for brown fur. Pure ginger color can only occur in a female if both her X chromosomes carry the gene, but any male with the gene on his X chromosome will be pure ginger, there being no equivalent locus on the Y chromosome. Tortoiseshell coloring, a mixture of ginger and brown, can only be produced by two X chromosomes, so it is only seen in females. This picture shows a tortoise-shell female with kittens fathered by a ginger male. (There are other genes at work here, producing tabby striping and white patches, but these are not sex-linked.) The expected result (right) is equal numbers of ginger males, brown males, tortoiseshell females and ginger females. In fact this cat produced no ginger females but 5 ginger males – there is always an element of chance, which is why breeding experiments have to be replicated hundreds of times.*

## Sex determination and sex linkage

In most higher organisms, the sex of an individual is determined by a pair of sex chromosomes. In one sex these will be identical (denoted as XX) while the other sex will have two dissimilar chromosomes (XY). In most vertebrates, many invertebrates and some plants, females are XX, and males XY. But birds, moths, butterflies and some fish have XY females and XX males.

If sex chromosomes only determined sex, the story would be a simple one, but other genes are carried on these chromosomes. Some are present on both, but others are confined to the X or the Y – for example, the mutant genes giving rise to color-blindness in humans. Consequently, these defects are much more common in men than women: a phenomenon known as sex linkage.

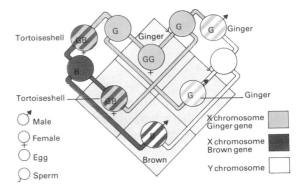

Tortoiseshell

Tortoiseshell

Ginger

GB

G

Ginger

G

Ginger

GG

B

GB

G

Ginger

Brown

♂ Male
♀ Female
○ Egg
♀ Sperm

X chromosome Ginger gene
X chromosome Brown gene
Y chromosome

**Mimicry and polymorphism**

*Papilio dardanus* female, morph B (mimics *Amaurus niavius*)

▼ *The mudpuppy, a type of salamander, has an extraordinary amount of DNA in its genome – 20 times more than some other amphibians of the same size.*

► *The advantages of polymorphism are not always clear, but in some butterflies it is related to mimicry (♦ page 230). Within a single African species, Papilio dardanus, some females mimic one type of noxious butterfly, other females mimic another type, while the males are nonmimetic. Mimicking more than one type of toxic butterfly allows the mimic to be less numerous than the model.*

*Amaurus niavius* (toxic model)

## The genetic revolution

At the same time as Jacob and Monod were working with *E. coli*, other geneticists were looking closely at the genetic material itself – DNA. Watson and Crick's discovery of its structure, in 1953 (♦ page 142), had opened the way, and by the 1970s it became possible not only to work out the base sequence of a given gene, but also to synthesize short pieces of DNA of known base sequence. Such techniques have given the geneticist much more powerful means of investigation.

Equipped with these new techniques, geneticists have begun to study the genome of higher plants and animals, and to look at micro-organisms in much more detail. A series of astonishing discoveries have resulted from these studies, which have revolutionized genetics. The picture that is now emerging shows the genome of higher organisms (those with eukaryotic cells) to be organized in a far less simple and logical way than those of bacteria – and even they have features that were previously unsuspected. The neat, economical systems that earlier geneticists found are far from universal.

One discovery is that, in higher organisms, genes involved in a common function are not organized in operons, as found by Jacob and Monod. They can be scattered about on different chromosomes or clustered in groups, but each is controlled and expressed individually. Another unexpected feature of the genes of higher organisms are "introns" – one or more short sequences of DNA that interrupt the coding sequence of a gene. Before being translated into protein, the sections of messenger RNA coded for by these introns are cut out, to create a continuous genetic message. This process is called RNA

### The genetics of polymorphism

*Some species show two or more different forms – a condition known as polymorphism. To avoid the mixing of genes for the different forms, some special genetic arrangement is clearly required. In butterflies such as Papilio dardanus, the genes for each different morph are grouped together in a tightly linked complex on one chromosome, rather than being distributed around the chromosomes, as they are in most butterflies. Once the mimetic morphs had become established, there must have been a strong selective pressure favoring closer linkage between the genes producing the pattern.*

### Retroviruses: reading the message back

*Until recently, it was thought that all genetic information was stored as DNA, but then viruses with RNA as their genetic material were discovered. Some RNA viruses have a specialized process to allow their RNA to be used to make more RNA, while others, known as retroviruses, convert their genetic material into DNA upon infection of the host. The ability to produce DNA from RNA depends on an enzyme called reverse transcriptase, and is the basis of many of the more bizarre events now known to occur in genes, including gene duplications from RNA, and the generation of some types of "jumping gene". Whether retroviruses are always involved in these events is not certain – ordinary cells may produce reverse transcriptase without retroviruses, but this has yet to be proved.*

*Papilio dardanus* male
(non-mimetic)

*Danaus chrysippus*
(toxic model)

▶ **Prion particles of the type
that cause scrapie in sheep,
magnified 100,000 times.
These particles apparently
contain nothing but protein,
and are 100 times smaller
than the smallest viruses.**

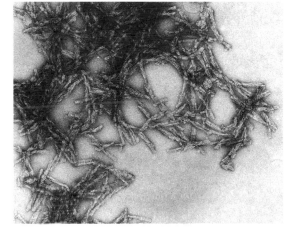

*Papilio dardanus* female,
morph A (mimics
*Danaus chrysippus*)

## Life without nucleotides

*The discovery that RNA could act as the genetic
material was not all that surprising as RNA is very
similar to DNA. But some recently discovered
organisms apparently reproduce themselves
without any form of polynucleotide. At least two
disorders, scrapie in sheep and goats, and
Creutzfeldt-Jakob disease in humans, appear to be
caused by infectious particles called prions. Both
cause a slow degeneration of the nervous system,
but they seem to consist of little more than a single
type of protein. At present it is not certain whether
they contain any nucleic acid – if they do, it is in
minute quantities – but they are capable of initiating
synthesis of new prion particles. A surprising
discovery is that host DNA in healthy tissues
contains sequences producing the prion protein. If
the prion protein is a constituent of normal cells,
how does it change to cause an infection? One
possibility is that the prion protein is modified in
some way during infection, the invading particles
altering the preexisting molecules, perhaps by the
action of a coenzyme. Or there may be a very small
polynucleotide in the prion particle which has not
yet been detected.*

splicing. How the introns got there in the first place is an intriguing
question. It may be that short genes sometimes join up into a single
larger gene, and that the introns are bits of intervening DNA that got
left behind. Evidence for this is seen in the hen lysosyme gene, which
has three introns. These divide the gene into four pieces (exons)
which are found to correspond to the functional units of the enzyme.
Exons 2 and 3 contain the active site of the enzyme, exon 2 being able
to act as an enzyme by itself. Exons 1 and 4 code for structural sections of the protein which are not enzymatically active.

It has also been discovered that higher plants and animals have
much more DNA in each cell than do bacteria. Some, but not all, of
this can be explained by their greater size and complexity. However,
some species have a lot more DNA than other closely-related groups,
for example, the mud puppy, which has 20 times more DNA than
some other amphibians of comparable size – and 20 times more than a
human being. Because this DNA does not seem to be essential it has
been called "junk" DNA. In fact, most higher organisms have redun-
dant DNA: short sequences repeated thousands of times. Some of
these are located near the center or ends of the chromosome and
appear to control its activities. Other repeated sequences are probably
useless, and may be generated by gene duplication, or perhaps by
retroviruses (◀ page 28). The abundance of RNA in the cell gives
retroviruses plenty to work on, and could account for the high number of repeated genes – as many as 300,000 copies per genome in some
cases. The new DNA can be inserted anywhere on any chromosome,
not just at the site of the original gene.

Not all repeated genes are junk. For example, the genes that produce ribosomal RNA in animals and plants are present in very large numbers, presumably because cells need many ribosomes to synthesize their proteins (♦ page 140). In other cases, copies of a gene may code for slightly different products which are used at different stages in the development of the organism. In mammals, for example, there are several copies of the hemoglobin gene. Some of these produce a hemoglobin adapted to the needs of the adult, while others code for a slightly different molecule, more suited to the developing fetus, which must obtain its oxygen from its mother's blood, rather than from the air.

Sets of related genes such as this are called gene families. A surprising finding was that some genes associated with gene families are not true genes, because they have mutations which prevent them from being expressed. These have been called pseudogenes, and they are a type of junk DNA. But while they have no immediate function, they may provide the molecular "raw material" on which natural selection can operate. The evolution of a new kind of gene is probably more straightforward, using a duplicated copy of an existing gene than starting from scratch because many of the essential features of the new gene are already there. The pseudogene has built-in control mechanisms, including segments that signal transcription of the gene (copying into messenger RNA) to begin and end.

Perhaps the most surprising of all the discoveries of the past decade has been that of transposons or "jumping genes", first postulated in the 1940s, but only accepted in the 1970s. These elements do not really "jump", but they do throw off copies that can insert themselves elsewhere in the genome, on any chromosome. From an evolutionary viewpoint, the ability of some genes to occasionally move around the genome is thought to enable more rapid change, and could be particularly important in forming new species.

### Life in the fast lane

*No one knows why the genome of eukaryotes (higher plants and animals) is organized so differently from that of prokaryotes (bacteria), but it could be related to fundamental differences in the way they live.*

*Bacteria are generally fast-growing organisms whose evolutionary success and survival relies on rapid growth, short generation time and many progeny. To achieve this, all processes must be streamlined, so their genomes tend to be small to allow rapid replication. Responses to environmental change must also be prompt, and having genes grouped in operons probably allows efficient and rapid changes in gene expression with minimal energy loss.*

*Most eukaryotes, by contrast, are complex organisms with long life cycles. Because their environment and food source do not vary greatly, they do not need such rapid and great changes in gene expression. Fewer progeny are produced, so a complex genome, taking a lot of time and energy to replicate, is acceptable. In fact, genetic complexity is probably an ingredient in the success of the eukaryotes.*

*The exceptions in eukaryotes are those that compete directly with the fast-living prokaryotes – soil fungi, for example. They too must grow and reproduce quickly so they have smallish genomes (about 10 times the size of E. coli), few repeated sequences, and reasonably fast responses to changes in the environment.*

*Ironically enough, it was features such as short generation time that endeared these fungi and bacteria to geneticists in the first place – and thus allowed a somewhat misleading picture of gene expression to become established.*

### Barbara McClintock and the jumping gene

*In the 1940s, the American geneticist Barbara McClintock first published her odd results from breeding experiments with maize. To explain them, she suggested there were genetic elements which changed the expression of seed-color genes, making the seeds dotted rather than a solid color. The strangest thing about these genetic elements was that they seemed to move from chromosome to chromosome, but not by crossing over.*

*At that time the idea of genes jumping about at random was alien to genetic thinking, and many scientists found it difficult to accept this explanation. It was only in the 1970s that jumping genes were discovered in other organisms, including bacteria where they are responsible for transferring antibiotic resistance from one plasmid (a small genetic unit, not part of the main loop of bacterial DNA) to another. The final proof for jumping genes, more properly called transposons, needed advanced DNA technology. Sections of DNA of known sequence were analyzed and a new segment of DNA – the transposon – was later shown to be present in the original sequence. In 1983, Barbara McClintock was awarded the Nobel Prize for discoveries made 40 years previously.*

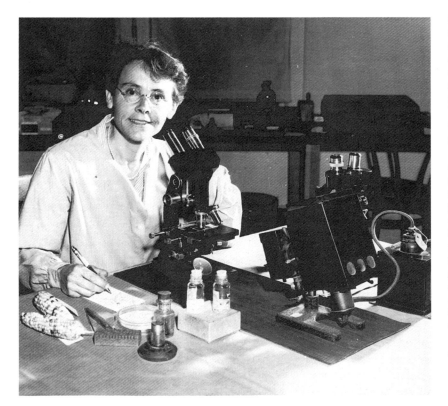

◄ *Barbara McClintock at work in 1947.*

# Classification

Controversies in classification...The early taxonomists
...Linnaeus...Evolutionary classification...Hennig and
cladistics...PERSPECTIVE...The urge to classify...
Molecular comparisons and the "molecular clock"...
Legacy of Linnaeus, the binomial system...Phenetics

### Classification – practice and theory

*Classification is really two subjects in one. The first, taxonomy, is simply an exercise in ordering living things, and summarizing our knowledge about them. The second deals with the philosophical framework – it tries to explain why some organisms are more closely related and others less so. Modern explanations are evolutionary ones, whereas earlier ones relied on a Creator, or even mathematical patterns. Systematics is a term which embraces this theoretical background and includes taxonomy, the more practical side.*

### Classification – old and new

*The urge to classify things – assign them to groups and give them labels – is a universal human trait. The natural world was first subjected to such a process millions of years ago, when our earliest ancestors coined words like "bird", "fish", or "snake". Such a crude classification was modified with increasing awareness of the natural world, so that, for example, flying animals with fur were distinguished from birds and given their own name – bats. Many naturalists subsequently tried to elaborate on these basic systems, including Aristotle who resolved the living world into 14 groups – mammals, birds, fish and so on. This was reasonable enough, but he then went on to subdivide the groups, by arranging creatures in them according to size. This results in an artificial classification, because it is based on one characteristic only and the groupings it produces are generally not confirmed by looking at other sorts of similarities. Modern taxonomists try to achieve "natural" classifications that reflect the true relationships of the organisms involved. This is done by examining a range of characteristics.*

One of the most heated debates to emerge in biology during the past decade has concerned the seemingly uncontroversial – and some might say, unexciting – subject of classification. On one side of the debate are the traditionalists, who favor a method known as evolutionary taxonomy, and on the other are the cladists, who follow a system that was originally inspired by a German biologist, William Hennig, in the 1960s. Broadly speaking, Hennig's aim was to introduce a more methodical and scientific approach to classification, which had previously been rather subjective and idiosyncratic – more an art than a science. But the change in method also involved a change in attitude. Some of the preconceptions that had dominated taxonomy for almost a century were challenged, and this is where the controversy originated – during which cladists were accused of many things, even of being creationist.

## Librarians of the living world

"When men do not know the names and properties of natural objects ...they cannot see and record accurately" lamented the English naturalist John Ray (1627?–1705). The problem was that most animals and plants had a confusing abundance of local names, and there was no convenient way of describing them intelligibly to another naturalist. Ray set out to catalogue the living world and to introduce some order by grouping animals and plants that were clearly related. In the 18th century the same objective inspired Carl von Linné (1707-1778), a Swedish botanist whose ambitious *Systema Naturae* founded the modern science of taxonomy. He is usually known by the Latinized version of his surname, Linnaeus.

Both Ray and Linnaeus believed that their classifications revealed the work of the Creator. Linnaeus noted the hierarchical pattern of nature, whereby smaller groups could be assembled into larger groups, and he devised names for these that are still used today: species, genus, order and class. He saw this hierarchy as part of a divine plan of creation, as did the taxonomists who followed him and elaborated his system. But in the 19th century a different interpretation was put on these natural hierarchies by Charles Darwin (1809–1882). Darwin used the evident success of the Linnaean system as one line of argument for his theory of "descent with modification", neatly turning the classificatory schemes into evolutionary trees. He also urged that classifications should try, in future, to represent genealogy. As the cladists see it, that was where the trouble began.

In the century that followed, taxonomists tried to fulfil Darwin's objective and they employed all the available evidence in determining genealogy, including fossils. One popular method for compiling evolutionary trees (on which the classification was then based) was to try to follow lines of descent back, through the available fossil forms. The pitfalls of such a process only became evident later (page 33).

▲ The English naturalist John Ray was the first to attempt a classification of living things based on anatomical similarities. He anticipated the work of Linnaeus, in trying to devise a natural classification rather than an artificial one.

Snake  Lizard  Newt  Eel

## Cladistic method

► 1 The first step in the cladistic method is to draw up a table summarizing the features of the animals or plants being compared: these are referred to as the "taxa". The table of characteristics shown here (right) is very much simplified – in a real analysis far more characters would be considered. Note that two types of character are excluded: those confined to one of the taxa, and those present in all four taxa. These are not considered because they do not allow any comparisons to be made. The four taxa to be classified are a snake (A), a lizard (B), a newt (C) and an eel (D). At first sight, it looks as if the eel and the snake might belong together in one group, and the lizard and newt in another, but this proves to be incorrect...

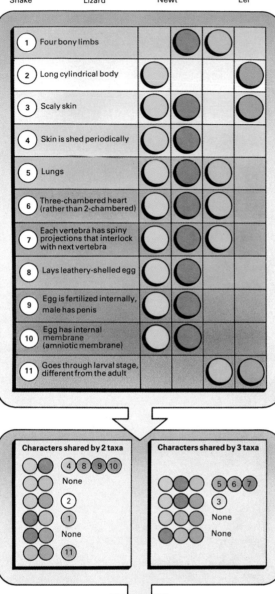

1. Four bony limbs
2. Long cylindrical body
3. Scaly skin
4. Skin is shed periodically
5. Lungs
6. Three-chambered heart (rather than 2-chambered)
7. Each vertebra has spiny projections that interlock with next vertebra
8. Lays leathery-shelled egg
9. Egg is fertilized internally, male has penis
10. Egg has internal membrane (amniotic membrane)
11. Goes through larval stage, different from the adult

► 2 The next step is to summarize the shared characters. This is done by considering each pair of taxa – A and B, A and C, A and D, B and C etc. The points they have in common (but which no other taxa have) are noted. The process is repeated considering each trio of taxa, A, B and C, A, B and D.

**Characters shared by 2 taxa**

4 8 9 10
None
2
1
None
11

**Characters shared by 3 taxa**

5 6 7
3
None
None

► 3 This data is then applied to the 15 possible branching diagrams that are possible for four taxa. If a character is shared by B and C only, it is noted at the point where B and C (but no other taxa) diverge. There are no numbers at the bottom branching points as features common to all four were excluded initially.

## Fossils: the taxonomist's problem

The approach to fossils is one of the key differences between cladism and evolutionary taxonomy. Hennig believed that classifications should be based solely on the observable characters of living animals, with no preconceptions about how they had evolved. He suggested that fossils should be dealt with separately, and an independent cladogram established for them. This could then be compared with the cladogram of living forms.

Cladists now include fossils and living forms in their studies, but they still look at living forms first, establish a cladogram, and then attempt to fit the fossils into this scheme. They also avoid designating any fossil as an ancestor, on the grounds that there is no objective way of knowing what features an ancestral form would have had.

## The molecular evidence

A powerful new tool that has become available to taxonomists in the past 25 years is that of molecular comparisons. The simplest technique, conceptually, is DNA hybridization, in which single DNA strands of two species are combined and the extent to which they stick together assessed. The more closely the two species are related the more pairing there will be between their DNA strands.

Another simple method is to immunize an animal, such as a rabbit, with cells from one species – a kangaroo, say – and see how the rabbit's antibodies react to another species, such as a wallaby. A strong reaction indicates that the kangaroo and wallaby are closely related. Both these techniques give crude measurements of relatedness. More sophisticated methods involve determining and comparing the base sequences of DNA or RNA, or the amino acid sequences of proteins that are common to many species. As well as providing data on relatedness, this method can illuminate another dimension – that of time. Many changes in the amino acids of proteins are neutral and accumulate at a fairly constant rate. This forms the basis of the "molecular clock" (◆ page 20).

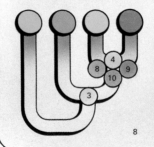

▼ **5 The cladist attempts to exclude primitive characters at the outset, but relies on other false guides being outnumbered by true guides. For this reason it is important to consider as many characteristics as possible.**

| ① | ② |
|---|---|
| A close look at the developing snake embryo shows that it has signs of a pelvic girdle – the bony frame to which the hindlimbs are attached. And some snakes show tiny vestigial hindlimbs, an indication that the characteristic has been secondarily lost – in other words, the ancestors of snakes had limbs. | In the absence of limbs, a long cylindrical body gives a powerful means of movement, whether on land, in water, or through silt on the sea bottom. The snake and the eel have both arrived at this shape independently of each other – an example of convergent evolution (◆ page 13). The phenomenon of parallel evolution also produces false guides. |
| ③ | ⑪ |
| The fossil record suggests that the ancestors of the newts had a scaly skin, but that this has been secondarily lost in modern amphibians. | Study of the embryos of snakes and lizards shows that they go through stages similar to the larval stage of the newt, but they are completed inside the egg. In the vertebrates as a whole, a larval stage is a primitive characteristic, completed inside the egg in more advanced taxa. Cladists try to exclude such characters from their initial table of characteristics. |

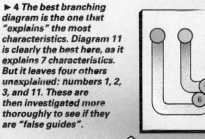

► **4 The best branching diagram is the one that "explains" the most characteristics. Diagram 11 is clearly the best here, as it explains 7 characteristics. But it leaves four others unexplained: numbers 1, 2, 3, and 11. These are then investigated more thoroughly to see if they are "false guides".**

The problem with fossils is that they only record the harder parts of the body, and generally only the bones and teeth. The soft parts, which are crucial in discerning most relationships, are missing. Secondly, the fossil record is very patchy, so the chances of a vital link in the chain being absent are high. Thirdly, the designation of a fossil as being "ancestral" to living species is fraught with dangers, for there is no foolproof way of distinguishing a genuine ancestor from a now-extinct relative or descendant of that ancestor.

Beyond these practical difficulties, lay a much more serious conceptual problem. Evolutionary classifications were always based on certain assumptions about the course of evolution. If the classifications that emerged were then used to draw conclusions about the evolutionary process, those original assumptions were inevitably confirmed as fact, and given more plausibility than they might in fact have deserved.

Cladists addressed these problems and attempted to construct a method that would be more objective and scientific than the intuitive approaches of the past. The least controversial aspect of the new approach was the system for discerning relationships and this is now widely used in taxonomy. In principle, it involves drawing out all the possible cladograms – branching diagrams – for the number of organisms to be classified. With four organisms there are 15 possible dichotomous cladograms, for five organisms 105 cladograms, for six organisms 945 and so on. Computers have now taken the drudgery out of this process.

The next step is to make a table showing all the salient features of the creatures to be compared. Features belonging to all of them are considered irrelevant, as are features possessed by only one – *comparisons* are the essence of the cladistic method. The similarities are then compared with all the possible branching diagrams, and the "best" one selected. This is the one that leaves the fewest similarities unexplained – a principle known as parsimony. One important rule underlying this method is that the organisms can only be placed at the tips of the cladogram, and not at the branch points. This keeps the number of alternative diagrams to a manageable number, and facilitates comparisons between them.

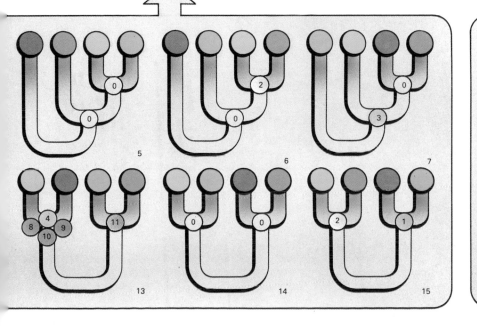

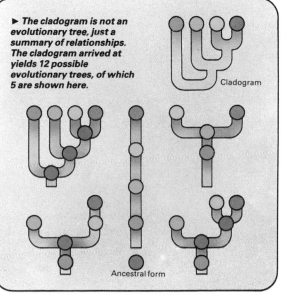

► **The cladogram is not an evolutionary tree, just a summary of relationships. The cladogram arrived at yields 12 possible evolutionary trees, of which 5 are shown here.**

Cladogram

Ancestral form

**See also**
Evolution 9-20
Non-flowering Plants 45-58
Development 161-168

The second, and more controversial, aspect of cladistics is the designation and naming of groups. Hennig proposed that only monophyletic groups should be named, because only they could be defined by the possession of certain common characteristics. A monophyletic group contains all the descendants of a hypothetical ancestor – the class Mammalia is a good example.

Evolutionary taxonomists, however, think that paraphyletic groups are acceptable. "Reptiles" and "fish" are examples: both are incomplete monophyletic groups because some of their descendants have been taken out and classed separately. In the case of reptiles, it is the birds that have been given this special status, and evolutionary biologists justify this on the grounds that birds are *very* different from reptiles, having diverged a great deal from them.

The differences between evolutionary taxonomists and cladists run much deeper than this, however. The latter have sometimes been accused of having a narrow, unrealistic view of evolution, always portraying speciation as a dichotomous branching. Such criticisms stem from a misunderstanding of the cladogram which is not intended as an evolutionary tree, only as a summary of relatedness. More seriously, cladistics has in the past been identified with "creationism" because of the claim, by some cladists, that classification can be practiced without reference to any particular evolutionary theory. Such statements were seized on by creationists as a rejection of the whole idea of evolution, but this is a misrepresentation. Cladists simply stress the need not to approach classification with preconceptions about evolutionary events.

▲ **Linnaeus, in the traditional costume of the Lapps. His earliest attempts at classification involved long cumbersome descriptive names. The binomial system provided an elegant solution to these problems.**

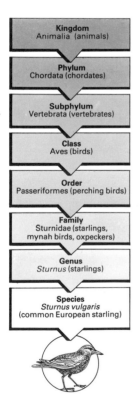

| Kingdom |
| --- |
| Animalia (animals) |

| Phylum |
| --- |
| Chordata (chordates) |

| Subphylum |
| --- |
| Vertebrata (vertebrates) |

| Class |
| --- |
| Aves (birds) |

| Order |
| --- |
| Passeriformes (perching birds) |

| Family |
| --- |
| Sturnidae (starlings, mynah birds, oxpeckers) |

| Genus |
| --- |
| *Sturnus* (starlings) |

| Species |
| --- |
| *Sturnus vulgaris* (common European starling) |

▲ **Taxonomy firstly recognizes and names species. These have a biological identity (◆ page 16), whereas the higher taxonomic groups are more abstract concepts.**

### Carl von Linné
*Classification was controversial, even in Linnaeus's time. An English clergyman wrote that "...nothing could equal the gross prurience of Linnaeus's mind...". The source of offense was his scheme for classifying plants, which rested solely on their reproductive organs. (Although concentrating on one feature could have led, as Linnaeus acknowledged, to an artificial classification, it turned out that this particular feature was fundamental, and gave a largely natural scheme.) Linnaeus, far from playing down this aspect of his scheme, fanned the flames with yet more erotic descriptions: "The actual petals of a flower contribute nothing to generation, serving only as the bridal bed, which the great Creator has so gloriously prepared, adorned with such precious bed curtains, and perfumed with so many sweet scents in order that the bridegroom and bride may therein celebrate their nuptials...."*

### Taxonomy by numbers
*Phenetics is a method of objective classification that relies on comparing vast numbers of characteristics in an effort to assess overall similarity. Its underlying aim is to be methodical and objective, like cladistics, but it differs in its approach, and in allowing absence of a characteristic to count as a similarity. The total number of similarities between organisms is calculated and used to pair the organisms off, and arrange the pairs into a hierarchy. Computers are essential for resolving the vast amounts of data. Phenetics is useful with large numbers of similar organisms that are difficult to classify otherwise.*

### The binomial system
*A legacy of the Linnaean classification is the binomial system. This gives each organism a generic name (eg Sturnus) and a specific name (vulgaris). The two together denote the species – Sturnus vulgaris, the common starling. As a young man Linnaeus had tried to follow the earlier system of creating a name that incorporated all the distinctive features, but this led to impossibly complicated names of up to ten Latinized words.*

### A rose by any other name...
*Although the binomial system has been very successful in many ways, it has not fully achieved one of Linnaeus's original objectives – that of improved communication through standardization of nomenclature. Classifications are regularly revised and updated in the light of new information, and when this happens the scientific name has to be changed. For example, the bluebell was originally designated Hyacinthus non-scriptus by Linnaeus, but this was later changed to Agraphis festalis, then to Scilla festalis, Scilla non-scripta, Scilla nutans and Endymion non-scriptus. The latter name stuck for many years but has recently been changed, first to Hyacinthoides non-scripta and then back to Scilla non-scripta again. By contrast, the common name "bluebell" has remained the same throughout and this makes it a more useful label, at least among English-speakers. On the other hand the scientific name has the advantage of meaning the same thing in different countries. Some common names, such as "chickweed" and "groundsel", are used on both sides of the Atlantic, but they refer to completely different plants.*

# Bacteria, Viruses and Protozoa    4

*By weight, more than half of all living creatures...
The principal groups within the protozoa...Success
of the bacteria...Viruses – life at its very simplest...
PERSPECTIVE...Leeuwenhoek, founder of microbiology...
Pasteur – microbiology begins in earnest...Bacteria and
disease...Discovery of viruses*

**Mastigophora**

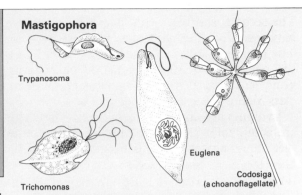

▲ *The commonest mastigophorans, the euglenids, are
mostly photosynthetic, but are not true autotrophs because
they need to absorb some amino acids, and can live in
darkness if given nutrients. There are also more animal-like
forms in this group, such as the colonial choanoflagellates
and the parasitic trypanosomes. Some have a mouth and
gullet, others engulf their food, as amebae do (♦ page 170).*

Single-celled organisms are estimated to account for over half the total
weight of living creatures in the world. Yet they are invisible – at least
to human eyes. It was only in the 17th century that they were first
observed, by Leeuwenhoek, and not until the 19th century were they
extensively studied.

The wealth of living things visible through the microscope were
originally called "animalcules" by Leeuwenhoek, but later came to be
called "microorganisms" or "microbes". These terms are really rather
meaningless, because they cover a host of unrelated creatures, which
have little in common except that they are mostly too small to be seen
without a microscope (the largest are just visible as tiny specks) and
generally consist of only a single cell (though some form loose colonies). A few groups are clearly related to multicellular organisms,
notably the yeasts, which are fungi (♦ page 39) and the single-celled
algae (♦ page 47), but even with these groups taken out, a very diverse
collection of organisms remains. Nevertheless, it can be split into
three general categories: viruses (which lack cells altogether), bacteria
and cyanobacteria (which have prokaryotic cells) and protozoa (which,
along with all other higher organisms, have eukaryotic cells).

Each of these groups includes a great many different types of
organism, but the protozoa is probably the least satisfactory group of
the three. Even its name is an anachronism, dating back to misguided
19th-century attempts to force microorganisms into a rigid two-king-
dom view of the natural world. Some – including the bacteria, yeasts
and algae – were designated as plants because they had rigid cell walls,
and the rest were classed as animals. The names protophyta, "first
plants", and protozoa, "first animals", were given to them. The latter
name has stuck, despite the fact that some protozoans, such as *Euglena*, produce their food by photosynthesis – a distinctly plant-like
ability. The less contentious name "protists" (or more correctly "eukaryotic protists") is sometimes used instead, but this is sometimes
credited with a much broader meaning (♦ page 159) and its use can
lead to confusion.

## The protozoa

The protozoa are enormously varied, but they can be split into three
fairly distinct groups on the basis of how they move about. The Mastigophora have one or more whip-like flagella for locomotion, while
the Ciliata have shorter and more numerous cilia (♦ page 211). Among
the Sarcodina, the amebae have given their name to a particular style
of movement (♦ page 212) but not all sarcodinians move in this way.
Those with shells, such as the foraminiferans, show a modified type
of ameboid movement, but radiolarians and heliozoans with spiky
internal skeletons either float in the plankton or, in one exceptional
species, row themselves along.

**Sarcodina**

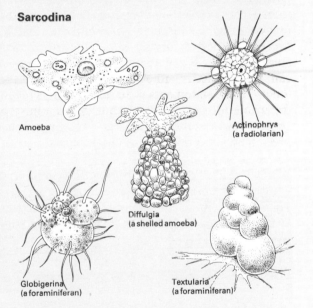

▲ *The Sarcodina include the amebae, many of which build
protective shells around themselves using grains of sand,
and the foraminiferans, which are enclosed in a chalky cell.
This has many small holes through which the pseudopodia
can extend. The radiolarians and heliozoans also have a
skeleton, in some species an internal one of fine, spiky
processes, radiating from the core of the cell.*

**Ciliata**

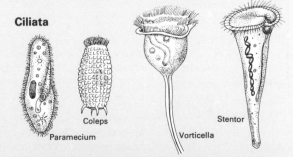

▲ *The Ciliata include some of the most complex single cells
in existence. Their cilia, of which there may be thousands on
each cell, are used for movement and to convey food to the
specialized "mouth" which leads to a gullet. In sessile forms,
such as Stentor and Vorticella, feeding is the only function of
the cilia. Cilia are fundamentally much the same as flagella
(♦ page 211) but they are shorter and more numerous.*

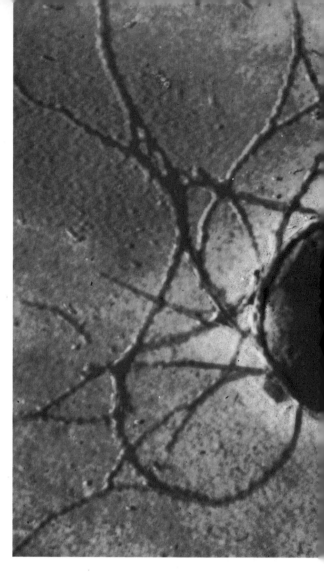

Other features distinguish the three protozoan groups, apart from their form of movement. For example, the ciliates are characterized by having at least two nuclei per cell – usually a larger one that governs growth and metabolism but disintegrates during sexual reproduction, and a smaller one that survives sexual reproduction. It appears that the smaller nucleus contains the "master set" of genetic information from which the large nucleus is generated. This contains multiple copies of the genes, which are needed to control the activities of the cell.

## Bacteria and cyanobacteria

The word bacterium is inevitably associated, in most people's minds, with disease, but in fact most bacteria do not cause disease, and many diseases are caused by other microorganisms. The majority of bacteria are saprotrophs feeding on dead or waste matter, while some bacteria and all cyanobacteria are autotrophs (◗ page 148). A few of the myxobacteria are even predators, killing other bacteria, algae and yeasts by secretion of toxins, and then digesting them externally.

The first living things were probably bacteria-like, and the group is still abundantly successful. Nowhere on earth is bacteria-free, and extreme environments are generally their exclusive domain. Some can live embedded in the Arctic ice, while others thrive in deep-sea hydrothermal vents where temperatures can be well above boiling.

The success of the bacteria is due to their high rate of reproduction and mutation – which enables populations to adapt quickly to changing circumstances – and to their enormous chemical versatility. Almost nothing is inedible to the bacterial saprotrophs – some species can even break down oil, and while most plastics are as yet immune, it is possible that bacteria capable of decomposing them will eventually evolve – or be artificially bred in the laboratory. Other unique biochemical functions include nitrogen fixation (◗ page 153).

Despite their chemical diversity, bacteria have many basic features in common. The internal structure of their cells is fairly simple and they lack many of the features seen in higher organisms. These traits characterize them as prokaryotes (◗ page 156). Furthermore, the bacterial cell wall is distinctive, being constructed of a unique polysaccharide called peptidoglycan. It is extensively cross-linked to provide a very strong protective covering for the cell. Penicillin and related antibiotics act by interfering with the synthesis of peptidoglycan, so producing a weak cell wall, which cannot resist osmotic pressure and bursts as water floods into the bacterial cell.

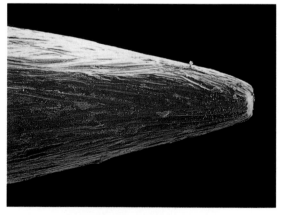

## Viruses – minimal life

Viruses pose particular problems for definitions of life, because they cannot replicate except within the cells of bacteria, animals or plants, and because they form crystals. Most viruses consist of little more than a protective coat, usually made of protein, and, inside it, one long molecule of nucleic acid (RNA or DNA). This virus particle begins to multiply once it has penetrated a host cell. Typically, the nucleic acids are produced first, and then the proteins. Each nucleic acid is packaged into a protein coat within the host cell, and the new virus particles then break out to infect other cells.

In the mid 1950s researchers had come to think of viruses as packets of nucleic acid in a protein box. But some viral coats, it transpired, contain fats and carbohydrates as well. By the 1970s researchers had also discovered enzymes in some viruses – most strikingly the enzyme reverse transcriptase in retroviruses (◗ page 28).

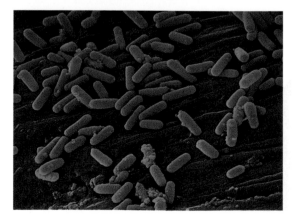

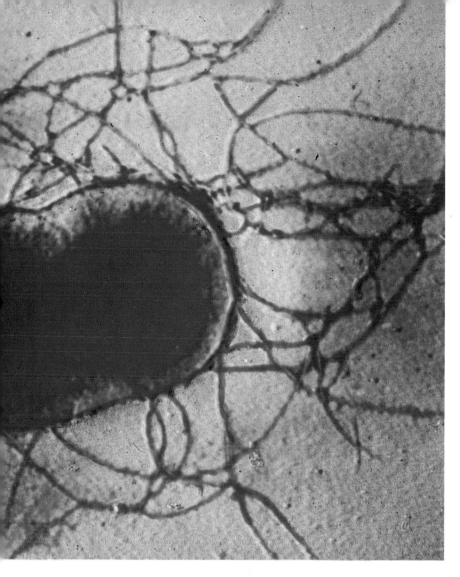

### Archebacteria

Some of the bacteria that inhabit odd ecological niches – living at physical extremes or having peculiar nutritional requirements – appear, on the basis of their RNA sequences, to be as different from other bacteria as they are from the eukaryotes. Carl Woese of the University of Illinois has pioneered the study of these so-called archebacteria, which he distinguishes from the eubacteria.

The archebacteria contain three main groups – the extreme halophytes, that can tolerate very salty conditions, the methanogens, that metabolize carbon dioxide to produce methane (♦ page 148), and the thermophiles that inhabit hot springs and depend on sulfur as an energy source. By comparing the nucleotide sequences of their RNA molecules (♦ page 32), Woese has mapped the relatedness of these organisms, as well as other prokaryotes and representatives of the eukaryotes. Most revealing is the 16S-RNA molecule from the ribosome. This molecule is present in every living organism and always has the same role in the synthesis of proteins. Looking at the changes in the sequence of this RNA molecule, Woese notes a striking divide within the prokaryotes, a division that is backed up by other biochemical studies. The lipids in the membranes of archebacteria, for instance, are strikingly different from those in eubacterial membranes.

### Leeuwenhoek – founder of microbiology

Antonie van Leeuwenhoek (1632–1723), a Dutch draper who made glass lenses as a hobby, opened up a new world for scientific study. He constructed microscopes made out of a single lens that were nonetheless capable of magnifying some 280 times. His exquisitely crafted devices revealed a seething world of minute and diverse organisms invisible to the naked eye. He called these creatures "animalcules" and, in a series of letters to the Royal Society in London during the mid-1670s, described his observations in admirable detail. His curiosity drove him to examine a great variety of environments. He looked, for instance, at the intestines of animals and found what we now call protozoans. Among the moss and debris of gutters he saw a variety of life, and he discovered in his own mouth, snake-like bacteria known as spirochetes, of which he wrote: "I have had several gentlewomen in my house, who were keen on seeing the little eels in vinegar: but some of them were so disgusted at the spectacle, that they vowed they'd never use vinegar again. But what if one should tell such people in future that there are more animals in the scum of a man's mouth, than there are men in a whole kingdom?"

In the century after Leeuwenhoek, little progress was made in microbiology, because few could equal his skill in grinding lenses to the accuracy required for simple microscopes. Compound microscopes, using two or more lenses, were available, but at that time suffered from serious optical defects which produced a distorted image. Not until the mid-19th century were technological advances made in optics that paved the way for good compound microscopes.

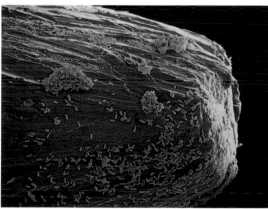

▲ Micrograph of the flagellate bacterium, Proteus mirabilis. The hair-like protein filament in many bacteria is called a flagellum, but it is quite different from the flagella of protozoa and other eukaryotic cells. It has been suggested that the latter be called an undulipodium. Apart from structural differences, the bacterial flagellum moves by rotation at the base (♦ page 212), whereas in eukaryotes movement is generated all along the length of the flagellum (♦ page 211).

◄ A sequence of photographs taken with a scanning electron microscope to illustrate the size of bacteria in relation to the point of a pin. The magnifications are 35 times, 175 times, 890 times and 4,375 times respectively. Because of their rigid or semi-rigid cell walls, all bacteria have fixed shapes, and these are used to classify them. The bacteria shown here are rod-like, the other two main types being spherical (known as "cocci") and corkscrew-like (known as "spirochetes").

### Louis Pasteur

*Microbiology begins in earnest with Louis Pasteur (1822–1895), who did much to establish the role of microorganisms in both fermentation and disease. Pasteur began his microbiological research by solving a practical problem. In Lille, a manufacturer of alcohol from sugar beet was having difficulties with some batches. Pasteur noticed that healthy wort contained microscopic globular structures, while unhealthy batches contained long threads – a sign, it transpired, of contamination by nonfermenting bacteria. Pasteur established that particular microorganisms were responsible for fermentation, and went on to show that microorganisms also caused decay. In the process he settled the long-running dispute over "spontaneous generation" – the notion that life could arise today out of nonliving matter. He showed that life comes only from life, at least under the conditions prevailing on Earth today.*

### Linking bacteria with disease

*Robert Koch (1843–1910), along with Pasteur, did much to confirm the nature of bacteria and their role in disease. Koch, a young German medical officer, was the first to show that a disease, anthrax, was caused by bacteria. He devised simple ways of growing bacteria in the laboratory and he improved techniques of fixing and staining microorganisms so they could be more readily identified under the microscope. His research did much to reveal that each infectious disease is caused by a specific microorganism. In later years, Koch discovered the bacteria responsible for TB and cholera, and inspired a flurry of investigations into bacteria at the root of other diseases.*

Viruses are usually considered to be disease-causing parasites, external invaders of cells. But recent findings in molecular biology suggest that viruses are better thought of as anarchic fragments of nucleic acid, that have escaped from the genomes of other organisms. They are only partially free, because they must return to the host genome to reproduce, essentially using the cell as a factory to produce more viruses. Occasionally they may also pick up genes from their host and deposit them in the genome of another host, perhaps one of a different species. Evidence that viruses have carried genes across otherwise inviolable species' boundaries is growing.

An even smaller and simpler class of disease-causing agents was discovered only in 1971. Called viroids, these pathogens are simply molecules of RNA, just 250–400 base pairs long, with no protective coat. So far these naked RNAs have been shown to cause about a dozen diseases, but only in higher plants.

How viroids damage the cells they infect is still mysterious. Their RNA does not seem to code for any viroid proteins, and they may exert their pathogenic activity by directly interfering with RNA synthesis or processing in the host cell. They may represent life at its very simplest: doing nothing but being replicated out of control by enzymes within the infected cells.

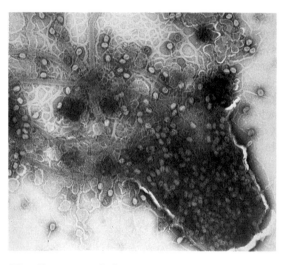

▶ *Destruction of a bacterial cell by a bacteriophage (virus). The cell is packed with virus particles (light ovals with stalks); this has burst the cell membrane.*

▼ *Dr Robert Koch achieved great public acclaim for his pioneering work on a number of diseases, especially anthrax.*

### The discovery of viruses

*The discovery that something much smaller than bacteria could cause disease came in 1892, when a Russian scientist, Dimitri Ivanovski, showed that healthy tobacco plants could be infected with juice from plants suffering from mosaic disease. The sap had been filtered to remove bacteria, yet the plants were still infected by some "filterable" agent, invisible under the microscopes of the day, and small enough to pass through the submicroscopic pores of clay filters. Ivanovski was unsure whether a toxin, rather than an organism capable of replicating, was responsible for the disease. M.W. Beijerinck of Delft University called the infectious liquid a "virus" – which originally meant simply "poison". Researchers went on to find the exact size of the filterable agents, by using a series of graded filters, and to identify viral diseases in animals. The first of these was foot-and-mouth disease in cattle, whose virus was identified in 1902, to be followed by a host of human diseases such as yellow fever, measles and smallpox.*

## 5

# Fungi

*Fungal characteristics...The sex life of the higher and lower fungi...Adaptability of fungi...PERSPECTIVE...The several origins of fungi...Life histories of the slime molds...How fungi attack plants...Lichens – a case of mutualism or parasitism?*

Fungi are everywhere. An average cubic meter of air contains millions of fungal spores, and whenever one such spore lands on a suitable food-source, it begins to grow, breaking down the food-source and absorbing nutrients from it. Hence bread goes moldy, fallen fruit rots and timbers slowly decay. The fungi that produce these changes are all saprotrophs – organisms that live on the dead bodies or waste materials of other organisms. Some of these saprotrophic fungi can switch to being parasitic if the opportunity arises, while other fungi are obligate parasites – that is, they cannot live in any other way. Whether saprotrophs or parasites, the fungi are all confirmed heterotrophs (◗ page 169) – none can synthesize complex carbon compounds from carbon dioxide gas, as plants can. Despite this, fungi were traditionally regarded as plants, mainly because of their immobility. But their resemblance to plants is entirely superficial. Apart from lacking the ability to photosynthesize, almost all fungi lack cellulose, the universal cell-wall polymer of plants. Most have cell walls made of chitin (also a strengthening component of arthropod exoskeletons) while yeasts have two unusual polysaccharides, mannan and glucan. Of the true fungi, only a group of lower fungi, called the oomycetes, have any cellulose, and they have several other odd features that set them apart from the fungi as a whole.

Fungi show another difference from plants in their storage compounds, which never include starch – the insoluble polysaccharide favored by plants. Oil may be used instead, or a polysaccharide known as trehalose, or even glycogen, the glucose polymer that animals employ as a short-term energy store.

Fungi are also distinct from plants in their basic structure. Apart from some lower fungi and the single-celled yeasts, most fungi consist of branching filaments, known as hyphae, which can grow only at the tips. The hyphae collectively make up the "mycelium" of the fungus. Unlike typical plant and animal tissues, fungal mycelium is not compartmentalized into cells. In the lower fungi there are generally no divisions or "septa", except where reproductive bodies develop, or where injury occurs, and the part needs to be sealed off. The cytoplasm within the hyphae contains many minute nuclei, and moves about freely by cytoplasmic streaming – a directed movement of the cytoplasm (◗ page 157) which serves to transport nutrients around the mycelium. Among the higher fungi, septa *are* present, but they have a pore in the middle that allows the cytoplasm through. In the Basidiomycotina, there is an interesting elaboration of this, with small pieces of membrane on either side of the pore, that can act as instant "plugs" if the hypha is cut. Even in these septate fungi, the organization of the cell (strictly called a "division") is unusual, in that there can be two nuclei in each cell, and these nuclei generally have different sets of genes in them.

## Evolution of fungi

*Almost nothing is known about how fungi evolved, but it is widely accepted that they are polyphyletic – that is, they include several separate lineages which evolved independently. The most clearly distinguished of these is the Myxomycota, or slime mold lineage (◗ page 43), which has little in common with the "true fungi".*

*It was once believed that algae were the ancestors of the true fungi, but this is now a discredited idea, except in the case of the oomycetes. This small group of lower fungi includes the parasitic molds that afflict fish, as well as plant diseases such as the downy mildews and the potato-blight fungus, Phytophthora, which caused the 19th-century potato famine in Ireland. These oomycetes have several odd features, including cellulose in their cell walls and a method of synthesizing lysine (an amino acid) that is uncharacteristic of fungi, but is found in all plants. This has led to the suggestion that the oomycetes are descended from the brown algae.*

*The rest of the fungi are derived from neither plants nor animals, but represent a separate and independent line of multicellular evolution.*

▲ *Cup fungi produce their spores on the inner surface, and rely on an explosive discharge for dispersal.*

▼ *A bracket fungus growing on a dead branch. Its spores are produced on the underside.*

*The sexual processes of fungi are immmensely varied and complex*

## Fungal sex

The presence of nuclei of different genetic constitution in higher fungi – a state known as heterokaryosis – is a by-product of their rather odd sexual processes. This does not involve the release of gametes, but comes about (as in some lower fungi) through the fusion of hyphae. In some species, there are different mating types and fusion can only take place with one of the opposite type – an approximate parallel to male and female sexes, although the different mating types are identical in appearance. In other species, there are no such restrictions. The oddest feature of sex in higher fungi – and the one that produces heterokaryosis – is that the nuclei do not join up when the hyphae fuse. They remain distinct until just before spore formation. This is a fairly short interval in the Ascomycotina, where hyphal fusion leads directly to the formation of a fruiting body and thus to spore production, but in the Basidiomycotina, most of the life cyle is taken up by a heterokaryotic mycelium.

In lower fungi the sexual processes are rather different, and fusion of the nuclei usually *does* follow directly on from fusion of the hyphae, where this occurs. However, several of the Mastigomycotina release gametes, instead of having hyphal fusion. The elaborate fruiting bodies, such as toadstools, that are a conspicuous feature of sexual reproduction in the higher fungi are absent in the lower fungi.

The lower and higher fungi also differ in their methods of asexual reproduction. In lower fungi, the typical asexual spores are formed by division of the cytoplasm inside a distinct structure known as a sporangium. This is lacking in the higher fungi, whose asexual spores are produced individually, at the tips of the hyphae.

Another important difference is that all members of the Mastigomycotina have motile spores which swim by means of a flagellum – something not seen in the higher fungi, nor, indeed, in the Zygomycotina. In some taxonomic schemes, these are not regarded as fungi at all, because they have flagella at some stage in their life cycle and fungi are defined as being nonflagellate (♦ page 159).

Beyond these broad generalizations, it is difficult to characterize the sexual processes of fungi for they are immensely varied and complex. Many species, as well as reproducing sexually, can generate asexual spores in two or even three different ways.

▶ *The bread molds,* Mucor, *belong to the Zygomycotina and are well-known examples of lower fungi. Their life cycle (above) includes producing spores asexually in a distinctive sporangium, a characteristic of the lower fungi. Their sexual process involves hyphal fusion, although this is not true of all lower fungi. The mushrooms* Agaricus *are good examples of higher fungi, whose life cycles are typified by complex sexual processes, heterokaryosis, and elaborate fruiting bodies. Asexual reproduction is rare among the Basidiomycotina, but less so among the Ascomycotina, which produce spores at the tips of the hyphae.*

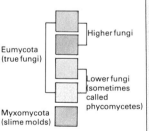

Eumycota (true fungi)
Higher fungi
Lower fungi (sometimes called phycomycetes)

Myxomycota (slime molds)

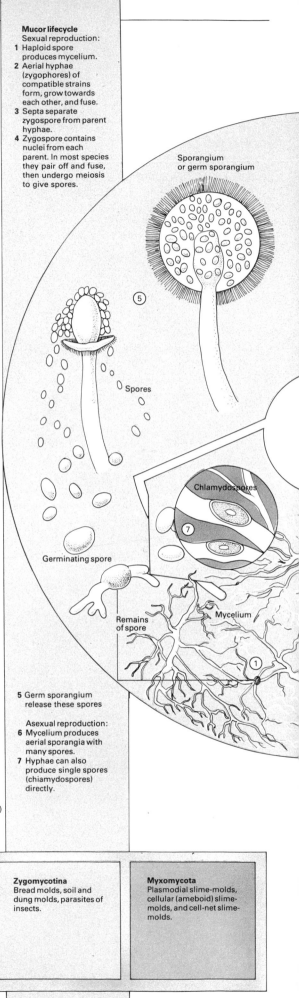

**Mucor lifecycle**
Sexual reproduction:
1 Haploid spore produces mycelium.
2 Aerial hyphae (zygophores) of compatible strains form, grow towards each other, and fuse.
3 Septa separate zygospore from parent hyphae.
4 Zygospore contains nuclei from each parent. In most species they pair off and fuse, then undergo meiosis to give spores.

Sporangium or germ sporangium

Spores

Chlamydospores

Germinating spore

Remains of spore

Mycelium

5 Germ sporangium release these spores

Asexual reproduction:
6 Mycelium produces aerial sporangia with many spores.
7 Hyphae can also produce single spores (chiamydospores) directly.

**Basidiomycotina** (or basidiomycetes)
Mushrooms, toadstools, puffballs, stinkhorns, earthstars, coral fungi, jelly fungi, and brackets; plant parasites: smuts and rusts.

**Ascomycotina** (or ascomycetes)
Many small wood-decaying fungi, truffles, most lichens; plant parasites: powdery mildews and ergots; penicillin mold; yeasts, including commercially used strains.

**Mastigomycotina**
Aquatic fungi, on dead or living water plants; soil fungi; plant parasites: potato blight and downy mildews; fish parasites. This group includes the chytrids, hypochytrids and oomycetes, and is probably polyphyletic.

**Zygomycotina**
Bread molds, soil and dung molds, parasites of insects.

**Myxomycota**
Plasmodial slime-molds, cellular (ameboid) slime-molds, and cell-net slime-molds.

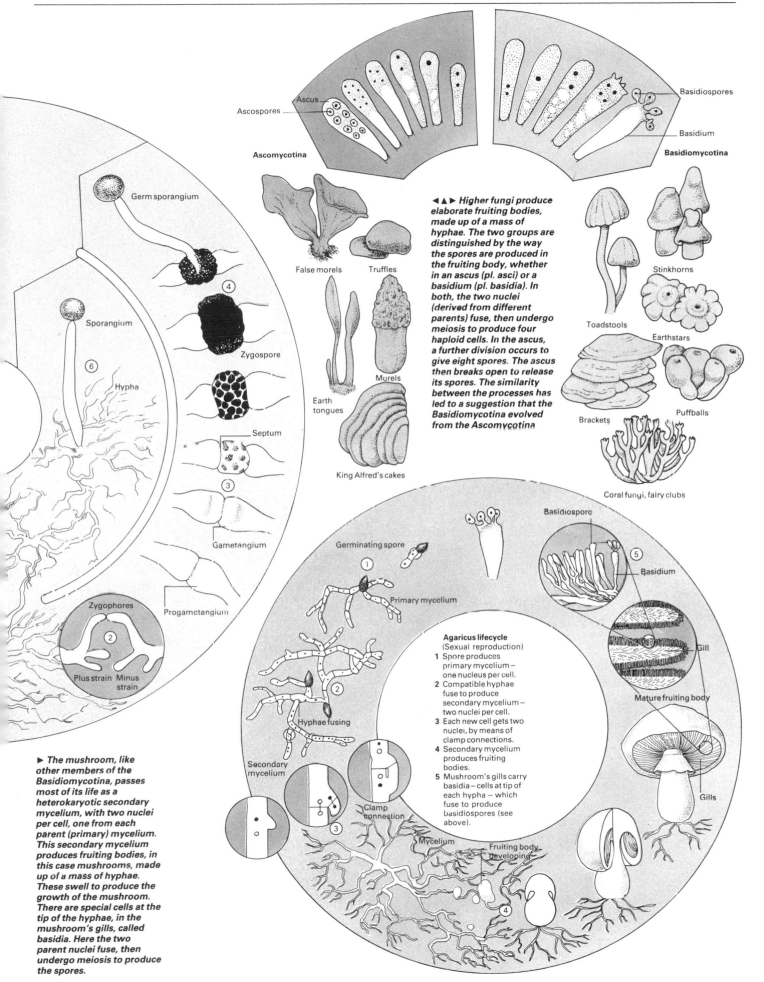

Ascospores

Ascus

**Ascomycotina**

Basidiospores

Basidium

**Basidiomycotina**

Germ sporangium

Sporangium

④

⑥

Hypha

Zygospore

Septum

③

Gametangium

Zygophores

②

Plus strain   Minus strain

Progametangium

False morels

Truffles

Earth tongues

Morels

King Alfred's cakes

◄▲► *Higher fungi produce elaborate fruiting bodies, made up of a mass of hyphae. The two groups are distinguished by the way the spores are produced in the fruiting body, whether in an ascus (pl. asci) or a basidium (pl. basidia). In both, the two nuclei (derived from different parents) fuse, then undergo meiosis to produce four haploid cells. In the ascus, a further division occurs to give eight spores. The ascus then breaks open to release its spores. The similarity between the processes has led to a suggestion that the Basidiomycotina evolved from the Ascomycotina*

Stinkhorns

Toadstools

Earthstars

Brackets

Puffballs

Coral fungi, fairy clubs

Basidiospore

Germinating spore

①

Primary mycelium

⑤

Basidium

Gill

Mature fruiting body

Secondary mycelium

②

Hyphae fusing

**Agaricus lifecycle**
(Sexual reproduction)
1 Spore produces primary mycelium – one nucleus per cell.
2 Compatible hyphae fuse to produce secondary mycelium – two nuclei per cell.
3 Each new cell gets two nuclei, by means of clamp connections.
4 Secondary mycelium produces fruiting bodies.
5 Mushroom's gills carry basidia – cells at tip of each hypha – which fuse to produce basidiospores (see above).

Clamp connection

③

Mycelium

Fruiting body developing

④

Gills

► *The mushroom, like other members of the Basidiomycotina, passes most of its life as a heterokaryotic secondary mycelium, with two nuclei per cell, one from each parent (primary) mycelium. This secondary mycelium produces fruiting bodies, in this case mushrooms, made up of a mass of hyphae. These swell to produce the growth of the mushroom. There are special cells at the tip of the hyphae, in the mushroom's gills, called basidia. Here the two parent nuclei fuse, then undergo meiosis to produce the spores.*

*The way in which some slime molds produce their spores is one of the most remarkable phenomena of the natural world*

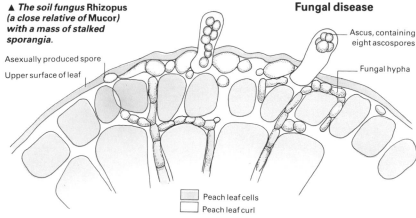

▲ *The soil fungus Rhizopus (a close relative of* Mucor*) with a mass of stalked sporangia.*

Asexually produced spore

Upper surface of leaf

**Fungal disease**

Ascus, containing eight ascospores

Fungal hypha

Peach leaf cells

Peach leaf curl

### Attacking plants

Plant parasites are found among both lower and higher fungi. Generally they attack plants by gaining entry through the stomata on the leaves, or through a wound. Once a spore has germinated, it sends out hyphae that insinuate themselves between the cells of the host plant. Specialized hyphae, known as haustoria, may also penetrate the cells to suck out nutrients. Once established, the fungal mycelium throws up fruiting bodies, and often these produce the characteristic symptoms (and names) of the different diseases: powdery mildews, downy mildews, rusts and smuts.

▲ ▶ *Fungal diseases of plants cause huge agricultural losses each year. The plant rusts (right) belong to the Basidiomycotina, whereas peach leaf curl (above) is caused by a member of the Ascomycotina. Auxin, a plant hormone which promotes growth, is secreted by the hyphae of the leaf-curl fungus. This produces uneven growth within the leaf, and causes typical symptoms.*

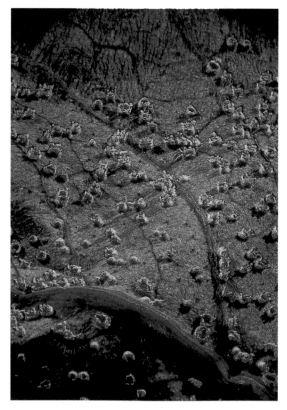

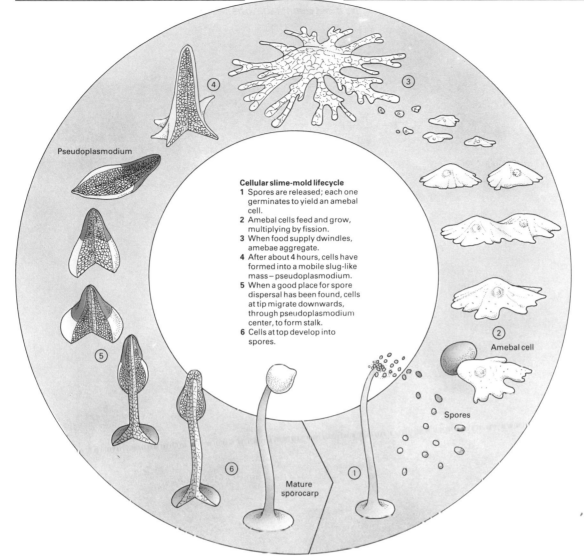

Pseudoplasmodium

**Cellular slime-mold lifecycle**
1 Spores are released; each one germinates to yield an amebal cell.
2 Amebal cells feed and grow, multiplying by fission.
3 When food supply dwindles, amebae aggregate.
4 After about 4 hours, cells have formed into a mobile slug-like mass – pseudoplasmodium.
5 When a good place for spore dispersal has been found, cells at tip migrate downwards, through pseudoplasmodium center, to form stalk.
6 Cells at top develop into spores.

Amebal cell

Spores

Mature sporocarp

◄ The life cycle of one of the cellular slime molds, Dictyostelium. The individual cells live in soil and feed on bacteria which they engulf in the same way as protozoan amebae (♦ page 170). They continue to grow and divide until food supplies dwindle, then some amebae begin to secrete a hormone-like chemical which attracts others. They, in turn, secrete more of the attractant, so new waves of amebae move toward the accumulating pile of cells. In Dictyostelium, the cells eventually form a pseudoplasmodium, which can move about and responds to stimuli such as light and heat, just as any multicellular animal would. This extraordinary mass of cells seeks out a suitable place for release of the spores, and once this has been found, the cells that formed the "head" of the pseudoplasmodium migrate to become a stalk, which develops a cellulose sheath for rigidity. These stalk cells do not contribute their genes to the spores – an intriguing example of altruism (♦ page 15).

▼ The fruiting bodies of a plasmodial slime mold. In this group, the spores germinate to produce gametes, which then fuse

## Slime molds

Slime molds (Myxomycota) fall into two main types, of which only one bears even a superficial resemblance to fungi. This group normally exists as a plasmodium – a multinucleate mass of protoplasm, that flows over the surface of rotting logs, engulfing microorganisms and decaying plant matter. The plasmodium has a net-like structure which, except for its lack of cell walls, is similar to fungal mycelium. When it reaches a dry area, the plasmodium produces a stalked, feathery or coral-like fruiting body. Meiosis occurs here and haploid spores are produced, which later germinate to produce gametes. These fuse to form a zygote, from which a new plasmodium grows.

Cellular slime molds, the second group, have no plasmodium and spend much of their time as single cells, indistinguishable from protozoan amebae (♦ page 35). The way in which these cells can come together and cooperate to produce their spores, is one of the most remarkable phenomena of the natural world. This is not a sexual process (none is known in these slime molds), but simply a matter of individual cells cooperating to lift their asexually produced spores up into the air.

It is interesting that a very similar type of life cycle occurs in the Myxobacteria, which come together to produce fruiting bodies. These bacteria are clearly unrelated to the slime molds, so the similarity must be due to convergent evolution.

*See also*
*The Origin of Life 143-154*
*Cell Structure and Evolution 155-160*
*Movement 205-212*
*Reproduction 235-248*

## The success of the fungi

Prodigious spore production is one reason for the success of the fungi. Another is their immense capacity for variation, which allows them to adapt rapidly and opportunistically to changes in the environment. When fungi are cultured in the laboratory, sections of the mycelium frequently develop visibly different characteristics. These may be a result of the normal proces of mutation (◀ page 25) but they can also be due to other genetic changes, related to the unusual way in which fungal genes are organized. Where the mycelium contains nuclei of genetically distinct types, for example, partial or total loss of one type of nucleus can occur, changing the characteristics of the fungus. Furthermore, some important metabolic pathways are coded for, not by the nuclear genes, but by genetic particles in the cytoplasm. Uneven distribution of such particles, for example during budding in yeasts, can lead to some daughter cells showing marked differences in their metabolism.

Nongenetic changes are possible too. Many fungi respond to environmental fluctuations by altering their own characteristics. Of particular interest are the mycelial fungi that disintegrate to form single yeast-like cells in certain conditions. This is a particular feature of some parasitic fungi that attack animals and plants, such as the one that causes Dutch elm disease. The yeast-like form is more easily transported in plant sap and the fungus switches to this state in response to a flow of water around its cell walls. The fungus that causes "thrush" infections in humans shows a similar switch, but the trigger in this case is the normal human body temperature, 37°C.

▲ *In puffballs, the spore-producing gills are inside a pear-shaped or globular fruiting body. This may release its spores through a pore, as above, or by rupture of the fruiting body, which becomes thin and papery when mature.*

### Lichens

*A lichen is not one organism but two: an intimate partnership between a single-celled alga or a cyanobacterium, and a higher fungus – usually one of the Ascomycotina. The alga or cyanobacterium is enmeshed in the fungal mycelium, but obtains enough light to photosynthesize. Some of its food is passed on to the fungus, which cannot survive alone – even if nurtured in a laboratory, it will fail to reproduce without the alga. Oddly enough, the algae do quite well alone, and actually grow faster when freed from the fungus. This raises the interesting possibility that what looks like a case of mutualism may actually be one of parasitism.*

*When they reproduce sexually, lichens release ascospores (or basidiospores), which contain no algal cells. They rely on encountering the right type of alga when they germinate. Most lichens also have a form of asexual reproduction, in which chunks of the mycelium, complete with algal cells, break away from the parent mycelium and regenerate a new lichen. In addition to this, some produce small spherical packages of hyphae, known as soredia. These are specialized for dispersal, and contain one or more algal cells.*

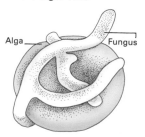

◀▶ *In lichens, each algal cell is enclosed by fungal hyphae. The soldier lichen (left) has column-like outgrowths of the thallus, which bear red apothecia, containing the spore-sacs (asci). The dusty appearance of the lichen is due to the many soredia thrown off from the surface.*

Alga

Fungus

# Non-flowering Plants

## 6

*The immense variety of form...The bewildering collection of algae and their reproductive strategies... Mosses and liverworts...Clubmosses, horsetails and ferns...The pollen grain and seed – doing without a watery environment...Conifers and other gymnosperms...PERSPECTIVE...Colorful ecology of algae...Plants with shells...Relics of the coal forests... Ginkgos, "living fossils"*

Plants with flowers belong to a distinctive group, known as the angiosperms. They probably had a single evolutionary origin, or comprise, at most, two different lineages. Not so the non-flowering plants. Everything from a microscopic one-celled alga up to a giant redwood tree may be covered by this term: seaweeds, mosses, ferns, horsetails, cycads and conifers, as well as many minor orders, are lumped together solely on the basis of not having flowers.

Yet the lack of flowers *is* significant. These specialized reproductive structures appeared at a late stage in plant evolution, and the groups without them are relics of earlier times. Several had periods of huge success in distant geological eras, when there was no competition from flowering plants. As well as being more numerous then than now, some were also much larger. Giant relatives of today's clubmosses made up the Carboniferous swamp forests and contributed their remains to the coal seams. The non-flowering plants are, in a sense, a catalogue of plant evolution, marking the steps it has taken since the simplest one-celled plants first appeared on Earth.

▲ *The largest seaweeds, the kelps, can achieve lengths of 30m or more, and form "kelp forests".*

▼ *Strands of Spirogyra, one of a hugely successful group, the filamentous green algae.*

## The algae

Taxonomy – the business of classifying living things – is essential to the study of biology. To make sense of something as complex as the living world one needs meaningful names for things, and names cannot be applied until the great diversity of organisms has been categorized. But taxonomy only works because there is extinction. If some animals and plants did not die out, everything would grade imperceptibly into everything else, and the pigeon-holing of life into neat categories would be impossible.

In groups like the algae, taxonomists could be forgiven for wishing that a little *more* extinction had occurred. The variety of forms, ranging from single-celled organisms with animal-like features, up to large and distinctly plant-like seaweeds, is bewildering. Many are obviously dead-ends in evolutionary terms, while others look tantalizingly (but perhaps misleadingly) like higher plants. The impossibility of drawing any sharp dividing lines between multicellular algae, single-celled algae and photosynthetic protozoa such as *Euglena* (◀ page 35) is reflected in the many different taxonomic schemes, some more satisfactory than others, but none of them perfect. A few of the organisms considered here as algae – the dinoflagellates, for example – would be classed as protists in other taxonomic systems, and the relationships between other groups would be represented differently. Indeed, some taxonomists do not include any of the algae in the plant kingdom (◆ page 159). This sidesteps the problem of dividing unicellular algae and other microorganisms from multicellular algae, but it ignores the obvious relationship between the green algae and the higher plants.

Algae include single-celled organisms, as well as a huge variety of multicellular forms

It is quite clear that the algae include several different lineages that have evolved independently. Four would be a conservative estimate, but there might be six or more. The engulfing of photosynthetic bacteria by a larger host organism (◆ page 159) could account for the origin of them all, with a different bacterium and host being involved in each lineage. The algae are usually classified by their color, that is, by the pigments involved, directly or indirectly, in photosynthesis. These pigments are thought to be relics of those that the original bacteria contained. For example, the pigments of red algae could well be derived from those of cyanobacteria. The red algae owe their distinctive coloration to phycoerithrin, one of a group of pigments termed phycobilins. It is similar to the blue phycobilin of cyanobacteria (this pigment is the origin of their old name, "blue-green algae"), with just a slight chemical difference making the pigment red rather than blue. Indeed, the red algae contain small amounts of the same blue-colored phycobilin as found in the cyanobacteria.

## Range of form
Each of the algal groups probably began as a single-celled organism. (A possible exception here is the brown algae, which could be an offshoot of the green algae.) Some groups, such as the dinoflagellates, stayed unicellular, apart from forming loose colonies. Others went on to produce multicellular forms, although many unicellular species survived and flourished as well. What is so interesting about the algae is the huge variety of multicellular forms, particularly in the green algae. This group seems to have undergone a phase of evolutionary experimentation, during which it has tried out every conceivable way of building cells up into larger and more complex bodies.

The most successful of the green algae are undoubtedly the filamentous forms and many of these are now pests of our lakes and reservoirs. The filamentous system is of special interest because it has developed a stage further in a group called the Chaetophoraceae. Here the filaments grow in two directions, horizontally to form a flat plate, and vertically to form an erect system. This bears many resemblances to the primitive land plants and may well indicate how a structure suitable for growth out of water could have developed.

In both green and brown algae, the filamentous system has been further developed, to create a complex, intermeshed mass of filaments, known as pseudoparenchyma. This type of solid tissue is of considerable importance in the evolution of the brown algae because it has permitted the development of large body size, particularly in the kelps, where seaweeds up to 35m in length are found.

## Reproduction in the algae
Asexual reproduction is found throughout the algae, but even in the simple, unicellular forms there is some sort of sexual process. In *Chlamydomonas*, for example, a deterioration in their environment causes the cells to divide, forming 8 to 32 flagellated gametes, which look just like miniature versions of the normal cells. When two join up, the resulting cell, the zygote, has a double set of chromosomes (diploid). It therefore undergoes reduction division, or meiosis (◆ page 24), and produces four daughter cells with just one set of chromosomes (haploid). This is a form of sexual reproduction, even though the sexes look exactly the same: there are two physiologically different strains, and they must find a gamete of the other type to mate with (◆ page 238).

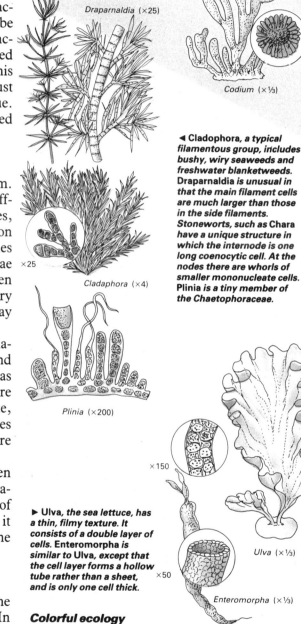

► **Codium is a seaweed whose tissues are a mass of interwoven filaments. This type of tissue, known as pseudoparenchyma, is also found in the larger species of brown algae.**

*Chara* (×⅛)

*Draparnaldia* (×25)

×12

*Codium* (×⅓)

◄ **Cladophora, a typical filamentous group, includes bushy, wiry seaweeds and freshwater blanketweeds. Draparnaldia is unusual in that the main filament cells are much larger than those in the side filaments. Stoneworts, such as Chara have a unique structure in which the internode is one long coenocytic cell. At the nodes there are whorls of smaller mononucleate cells. Plinia is a tiny member of the Chaetophoraceae.**

×25

*Cladaphora* (×4)

*Plinia* (×200)

×150

► **Ulva, the sea lettuce, has a thin, filmy texture. It consists of a double layer of cells. Enteromorpha is similar to Ulva, except that the cell layer forms a hollow tube rather than a sheet, and is only one cell thick.**

×50

*Ulva* (×⅓)

*Enteromorpha* (×⅓)

### Colorful ecology
*The different pigments which the various groups of algae possess allow them to exploit a range of ecological opportunities. The green algae, like the higher plants, contain chlorophylls a and b, which absorb light most efficiently in the red and the blue ends of the spectrum. The light energy in between these wavebands is reflected, which is why the pigments look green. In well-illuminated regions – on land and in the upper layers of water – this pigment system has clearly proved to be very efficient. Green algae are not confined to aquatic habits, but are found on the trunks of trees, in the*

| Green algae | Red algae | Brown algae | Diatoms, golden-brown algae and yellow-green algae | Dinoflagellates | Euglenoid protozoa | |
|---|---|---|---|---|---|---|
| Inner layer of cellulose; outer layer of pectin; rigid | Inner layer of cellulose; outer layer of pectin and mucilaginous polysaccharides; rigid | Inner layer of cellulose; outer layer of pectin plus gelatinous material, notably alginic acid or "algin"; rigid | Pectin impregnated with silica; rigid | Cellulose; generally rigid, but with gaps where pseudopodia can extend | No cell wall, so cell is flexible | **Cell wall** |
| Chlorophyll a, chlorophyll b, α-carotene, β-carotene, some xanthophylls | Chlorophyll a, chlorophyll d, η-carotene, some xanthophylls, phycobilins | Chlorophyll a, chlorophyll c, β-carotene, fucoxanthin and other xanthophylls | Chlorophyll a, chlorophyll c (diatoms only), β-carotene, various xanthophylls including fucoxanthin | Chlorophyll a, β-carotene, η-carotene, various xanthophylls | Chlorophyll a, chlorophyll b, α-carotene, β-carotene, η-carotene, other carotenids, various xanthophylls | **Pigments** |
| Mostly starch (an insoluble polysaccharide) but oil in a few | Starch, but of a chemically unique type | Short-chain polysaccharides (soluble), such as laminarin, plus an alcohol, mannitol | Oil | Starch | Paramylum, an insoluble polysaccharide | **Energy storage compound** |
| No | No | No | No | Yes | Yes | **Capable of heterotrophic nutrition?** |
| Plant-like seaweeds; filamentous forms; thin sheets of cells; single giant cells; colonial forms; single cells | Plant-like seaweeds, but none very large; filamentous forms; thin sheets of cells; single cells | Plant-like seaweeds, including the largest-known algae, kelps; filamentous forms | Single cells; loose colonies; small filamentous forms (golden-brown algae only) | Single cells; loose colonies | Single cells only | **Structural types** |

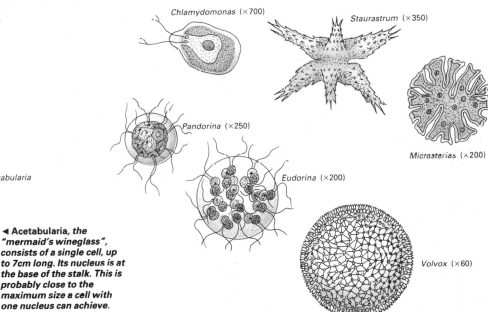

Chlamydomonas (×700)

Staurastrum (×350)

Pandorina (×250)

Micrasterias (×200)

Eudorina (×200)

Volvox (×60)

Acetabularia

◄ **Chlamydomonas, with its two flagella, is typical of the motile unicellular algae. The individual cells of colonial forms, and the gametes of multicellular algae, often resemble Chlamydomonas, suggesting a close relationship. Desmids, such as Staurastrum and Micrasterias, are classed as green algae, but resemble diatoms in some ways, notably their symmetrical forms and sculpted cell walls.**

◄ **Acetabularia, the "mermaid's wineglass", consists of a single cell, up to 7cm long. Its nucleus is at the base of the stalk. This is probably close to the maximum size a cell with one nucleus can achieve.**

◄ **Pandorina consists of 16 cells, packed together leaving just a small hollow at the center and enclosed by a layer of mucus. Eudorina comprises 32 cells, embedded in a jelly-like sphere. The cells seem fairly independent but there are fine threads of cytoplasm connecting them. Volvox colonies contain up to 50,000 cells, on the surface of a mucus sphere. Its cells show more interdependence than those in smaller colonies, with some being specialized for reproduction. At 0·5mm, Volvox is probably as large as this type of colony can be.**

surface layers of soil, in ice and snow, and even within crystalline rocks.

The greens have difficulties, however, when faced with the problem of living under any great depth of water. As light passes through water it is gradually absorbed, scattered and reflected. Often 80 percent is lost in the top 10m, although some light penetrates to about 200m and even as far as 1,000m in very clear water. But light is also changed in its spectral composition as it passes downward, with a strong selective absorption in the red region. Chlorophyll becomes rather inefficient under these conditions and accessory pigments are needed to collect the scarce light and pass the energy on to chlorophyll. Pigments that absorb light in the blue-green wavebands, which penetrate water best, are particularly useful. The brown algae have fucoxanthin, a pigment which absorbs well in the intermediate wavebands, and as a result they are able to perform more efficiently than the greens in deeper water. The reds have phycoerythrin which is also a valuable receptor of green light, and it is these algae which have proved most successful in living at great depth – one was recently discovered at a depth of 286m in the clear seas off the West Indies.

Sexual reproduction in multicellular algae often involves specialized cells which produce the gametes. For example, the brown alga *Ectocarpus* produces its gametes in special sex organs. The gametes, like the plants, are haploid, but the zygote resulting from fusion is, of course, diploid, and it grows into a diploid *Ectocarpus* plant. Despite the chromosomal difference, this looks identical to the haploid plant in every respect. This plant reproduces asexually, by means of spores, and since the formation of spores is preceded by meiosis, the next generation is once again haploid. Two types of haploid spore are formed which grow into new male and female haploid plants.

This type of life cycle, involving a haploid gametophyte (gamete-producer, with one set of chromosomes), and a diploid sporophyte (spore-producer, with two sets of chromosomes), is common in algae, and is known as an "alternation of generations". It also occurs in terrestrial plants, but here the haploid and diploid stages look quite different ( page 50).

The two generations also look different in more specialized groups of brown algae. In the kelps for example, the characteristically massive thallus – the familiar seaweed – is the diploid sporophyte generation. By meiosis, it produces two types of haploid spore. These are released and germinate respectively into male and female gametophytes: microscopic, branched filaments that float on the surface of the sea. On each of these the sexual organs develop. The egg cell never leaves the female gametophyte, but is sought out by the swimming male cells. After fertilization, the zygote develops into the the embryo of a new sporophyte generation, which relies on being washed inshore and finding a good anchor-point for its survival. This life cycle – with the sporophyte long-lived and conspicuous, and the gametophyte small and transitory – parallels that of land plants such as ferns, but it is a completely independent line of evolution.

Among red algae, the alternation of generations is even more complex and some species have a three-generation life cycle, with an additional sporophyte stage which is retained on the gametophyte. In all groups, the number of exceptions to, and variations on, the "normal" life cycle is staggering. The enormous diversity of form seen in the algae is paralleled by their reproductive strategies.

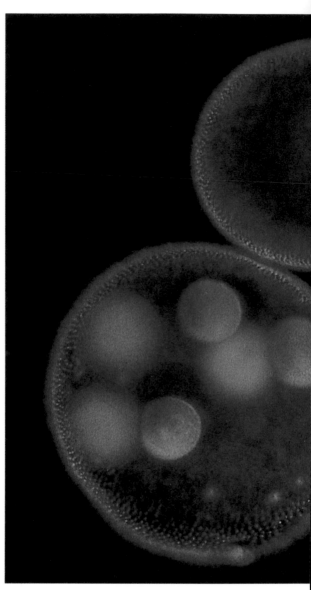

◄ The red seaweed, Corallina, has a chalky shell which gives it support, conserves moisture, and probably also affords some protection from animals.

▲ ► Volvox produces daughter colonies asexually, as shown on the right. These stay within the parent colony, until large enough to be released.

### Plants with shells

*In both the red and green algae, some species use calcium carbonate to form a kind of skeleton, encasing their softer tissues with layers of lime, thus giving them support and protecting them from desiccation in times of drought. This type of skeleton is found in branched reds, like* Corallina, *and in encrusting forms like* Lithophyllum. *In the greens, a group of freshwater filamentous forms, the stoneworts, have exploited the system. These lime casings have aided their preservation as fossils, and stoneworts are known from 420 million years ago. It is even possible that some of these calcareous algae may have conducted the first tentative experiments in the conquest of the land. But this line of development proved of little long-term value for terrestrial living.*

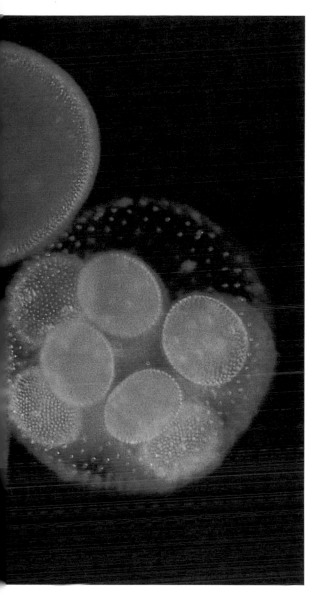

## Mosses and liverworts

Five hundred million years ago, all the continents of the Earth were, quite literally, a desert – not because it was particularly hot or arid, but simply because very few living things had established themselves on land. Although the waters teemed with life, around them there was nothing but a silent, inanimate landscape of rock, with perhaps a powder-like layer of unicellular algae in places. But by 400 million years ago the pioneers of terrestrial life were to be found. One such pioneer was a seemingly insignificant little plant, no more than a tiny plate of alga-like cells, colonizing the edges of lakes and ponds. Here it was bathed in moisture which enabled its delicate cells to survive. The fossils of this plant, known as *Sporogonites*, show that it had tiny projections below it that were probably used for absorbing water and nutrients – some of the first roots the world had seen.

Apart from its primitive roots (strictly called rhizoids), one of the most distinctive features of *Sporognites* was the presence of upright, spore-bearing structures on the upper surface of the plant. The correlation between this and the living mosses and liverworts – presumed descendants of *Sporogonites* – is striking. In these plants, the spore-bearing structures, called sporogonia, consist of cells that are fundamentally different from those of the main plant body (the thallus) because they contain two sets of chromosomes rather than one. As in the algae, meiosis precedes spore-production, so the spores are haploid, and they germinate to produce a new haploid gametophyte thallus. This type of alternation of generations is assumed to have been a feature of *Sporogonites*, as it is in the living bryophytes (mosses and liverworts). It has continued to this day in all terrestrial plants, even the flowering plants, although in them it is very highly modified so that the gametophyte cannot be seen, but completes its brief existence inside the tissues of the sporophyte.

The sexual phase of the life cycle occurs on the gametophyte, and the fertilized egg then develops into the sporophyte. At its most basic, in the bryophytes, this part of the life cycle depends upon the ability of a sperm to reach an egg cell by swimming, and for this to happen the gametophyte must be covered by a film of moisture – which means staying close to the ground in damp habitats.

**Daughter colony formation in *Volvox***

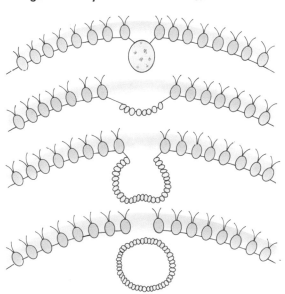

◄▼ *A modern liverwort and a reconstruction of the fossil bryophyte* Sporogonites. *Bryophyte spores are formed on a stalk to aid dispersal by the wind.*

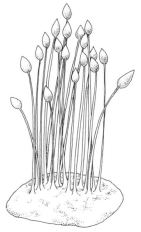

*The life cycles of non-flowering plants show increasing adaptation to life on land*

Two other factors have also limited the growth potential of bryophytes and restricted them to humid environments. Firstly, the thallus has no protective covering so it could easily be dried out, and secondly, it lacks a well-developed system of structural support – in most species there are no woody tissues to strengthen stems and permit extensive upward growth. As a consequence, most bryophytes are no more than a few centimeters tall.

Despite these restrictions, the bryophytes are widespread and numerous, and within the two basic types – mosses and liverworts – there is a diversity of forms. Some of the liverworts have retained the primitive gametophyte thallus, a flat mass of cells on which male and female sex organs are formed. Others, the leafy liverworts, have a more complex thallus, and the sexual organs are often enclosed in specialized, enlarged leaves called perianths. These leafy liverworts seem to be more recent in their evolutionary origin, for their fossils can only be traced back about 64 million years.

The mosses, on the other hand, can be traced back in the fossil record for well over 300 million years, to the swamp forests of the Carboniferous (◆ page 54). Their gametophyte – the familiar moss plant – is a more complex organism than a liverwort, differentiated into stems and leaves. There are two main groups: pleurocarpus mosses which grow in creeping mats or form trailing wefts over tree trunks, and acrocarpus mosses, which have upright shoots and so form dense cushions. The moss plant begins its life as a protonema – a chain of cells resembling a filamentous green alga. This gives rise to buds, each of which develops into a genetically identical moss plant. In liverworts, there is no protonema, and the spore develops directly into a thallus. Some botanists think that this different start in life indicates an independent evolutionary origin.

The mosses' sporophyte generation is also more complex than that of the liverworts. It is at least partly self-supporting, and even has specialized openings, called stomata, which take in carbon dioxide to fuel photosynthesis – these are not present in the moss leaf, but *are* seen in the sporophytes of ferns and higher plants. The extreme top of the capsule forms a distinct lid and, as the mature capsule dries, this breaks away to reveal a set of protective teeth over the entrance to the spore sac. These teeth respond to changes in the humidity of the atmosphere, opening when it is warm and dry to release the spores into the air.

As in liverworts, the long stalk of the sporophyte has an important role in dispersal. Because the spores are released from some height above the thallus, they are therefore kept away from the dampness on the ground and are likely to be carried further in the wind. This is perhaps the clearest way in which the bryophyte has left its aquatic history behind it and is taking advantage of the new opportunities offered by life on land.

- Gametophyte
- Egg
- Sperm
- Sporophyte
- Sporangium
- Spore
- Pollen grain

*Bryophytes (eg mosses), pteridophytes (eg ferns) and gymnosperms (eg pines) all show alternation of generations, in which a sporophyte (spore-producing) generation alternates with a gametophyte (gamete-producing) generation. The sporophyte results from the fusion of gametes, so it has a double dose of chromosomes (diploid) whereas the gametophyte has a single dose (haploid). To produce haploid spores, sporophyte cells undergo meiosis (◆ page 24) just before spore formation.*

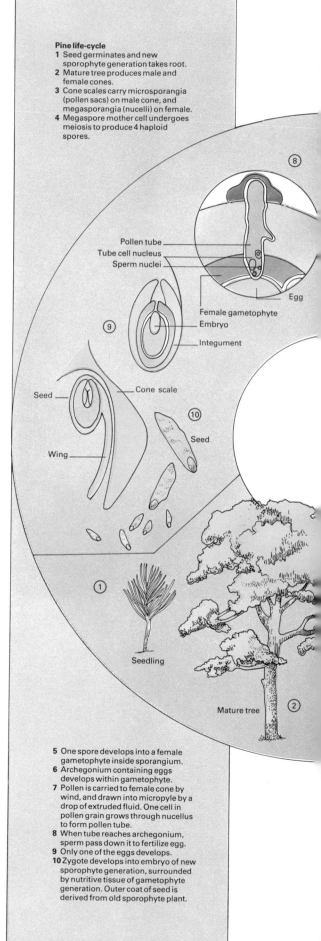

**Pine life-cycle**
1 Seed germinates and new sporophyte generation takes root.
2 Mature tree produces male and female cones.
3 Cone scales carry microsporangia (pollen sacs) on male cone, and megasporangia (nucelli) on female.
4 Megaspore mother cell undergoes meiosis to produce 4 haploid spores.

Pollen tube
Tube cell nucleus
Sperm nuclei
Egg
Female gametophyte
Embryo
Integument
Cone scale
Seed
Seed
Wing
Seedling
Mature tree

5 One spore develops into a female gametophyte inside sporangium.
6 Archegonium containing eggs develops within gametophyte.
7 Pollen is carried to female cone by wind, and drawn into micropyle by a drop of extruded fluid. One cell in pollen grain grows through nucellus to form pollen tube.
8 When tube reaches archegonium, sperm pass down it to fertilize egg.
9 Only one of the eggs develops.
10 Zygote develops into embryo of new sporophyte generation, surrounded by nutritive tissue of gametophyte generation. Outer coat of seed is derived from old sporophyte plant.

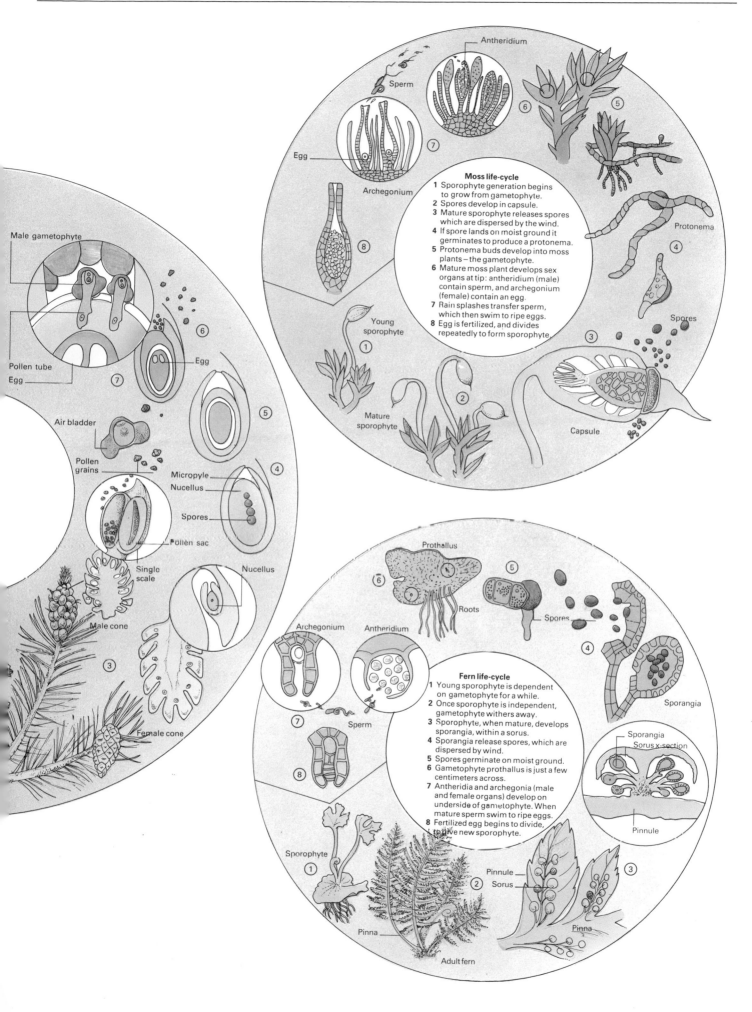

**Moss life-cycle**
1 Sporophyte generation begins to grow from gametophyte.
2 Spores develop in capsule.
3 Mature sporophyte releases spores which are dispersed by the wind.
4 If spore lands on moist ground it germinates to produce a protonema.
5 Protonema buds develop into moss plants – the gametophyte.
6 Mature moss plant develops sex organs at tip: antheridium (male) contain sperm, and archegonium (female) contain an egg.
7 Rain splashes transfer sperm, which then swim to ripe eggs.
8 Egg is fertilized, and divides repeatedly to form sporophyte.

Antheridium
Sperm
Egg
Archegonium
Young sporophyte
Mature sporophyte
Capsule
Spores
Protonema

Male gametophyte
Pollen tube
Egg
Egg
Air bladder
Pollen grains
Micropyle
Nucellus
Spores
Pollen sac
Single scale
Nucellus
Male cone
Female cone

**Fern life-cycle**
1 Young sporophyte is dependent on gametophyte for a while.
2 Once sporophyte is independent, gametophyte withers away.
3 Sporophyte, when mature, develops sporangia, within a sorus.
4 Sporangia release spores, which are dispersed by wind.
5 Spores germinate on moist ground.
6 Gametophyte prothallus is just a few centimeters across.
7 Antheridia and archegonia (male and female organs) develop on underside of gametophyte. When mature sperm swim to ripe eggs.
8 Fertilized egg begins to divide, to give new sporophyte.

Prothallus
Roots
Spores
Archegonium
Antheridium
Sperm
Sporangia
Sporangia
Sorus x-section
Pinnule
Sporophyte
Pinnule
Sorus
Pinna
Pinna
Adult fern

▲ *In a damp southern beech forest in New Zealand, mosses, ferns and lichens flourish, many growing on the trees as epiphytes.*

▶ *The spore capsules of mosses respond to changes in humidity, opening up when the air is dry, to ensure good dispersal.*

▼ *Many liverworts reproduce asexually by releasing "gemmae" from special cups on the thallus, to be dispersed by rain.*

### Standing tall

*The tallest mosses, like* Polytrichum, *grow to about 30cm. They are able to do this because specialized central cells in their stems assist in support – and perhaps in water movement, as the vascular systems of higher plants do.* Polytrichum *also shows other advanced features, which make it better adapted to terrestrial life than most mosses. Its leaves have many ridges, or lamellae, through which gas exchange takes place. When conditions are dry, and there is the risk of too much water loss through the lamellae, the sides of the leaves roll over and cover these more delicate parts. Despite these features, it is very unlikely that* Polytrichum *and its relatives are on the main line of evolution leading to the higher plants. They are not found until relatively late in the geological sequence, about 50 million years ago, long after the ferns and their allies had appeared.*

### Simple survivor

*Apart from the two major groups of bryophytes – the mosses and the liverworts – there are some oddities which do not fit comfortably into either group. One such is* Anthoceros *and its relations, which may resemble the ancestral bryophytes. They have a flat thallus with simple, root-like rhizoids, and vertical sporophytes rising from it. Moreover, the cells of the gametophyte are very like those of an alga, containing one large chloroplast, rather than several chloroplasts per cell. Unlike most bryophytes, the sporophyte lacks a globular spore-producing structure at the tip. Instead, it is a column-shaped mass containing spores, which grows from the base and splits at the top to release the spores.*

## Changing tactics

*Although the clubmosses, horsetails and ferns evolved alongside the mosses and liverworts, they differ from them in one important respect. Their sporophyte is no longer a "parasite" on the gametophyte – it leads an independent existence and is the most conspicuous and persistent part of the plant's life cycle. The diploid generation dominates rather than the haploid.*

*The mosses and liverworts had taken what turned out to be a "dead end", because the need for the sperm to swim to the eggs restricted the gametophyte to damp habitats and small size for ever. By transferring the emphasis to the sporophyte generation, the ferns and their allies opened up all sorts of new possibilities. But the ferns are not as free from the need for water as higher plants, because they still require a damp spot for the short-lived gametophyte to inhabit. Its small, inconspicuous, plate-like thallus can only develop when the fern's spore lands in a moist environment. The sperm cells swim across the thallus to the eggs and fertilize them (♦ page 51). Once fertilized, the egg begins to develop into a new sporophyte which soon becomes self-supporting, for it has its own green, photosynthetic tissues. Small fronds grow upward and the main stem, or rhizome, begins to differentiate. At this stage the gametophyte is surplus to the new embryo's needs and it soon degenerates.*

▲ *Horsetails produce their spores in fleshy, cone-like structures at the tips of special white or brown shoots. The green shoots usually appear later and consist of a central stem with regular whorls of spiky branches.*

## Clubmosses, horsetails and ferns

One of the problems to confront the early plant colonists of the land was that of support. Without water to buoy up the plants, and allow them to extend their light-absorbing leaves, they were forced to remain small and spreading, as most mosses and liverworts have done. Yet great advantages could be gained by plants with more elaborate structures: an erect, branching canopy of shoots could compete far more effectively for the available light and also distribute itself more widely by airborne spores. It is just such a plant, called *Cooksonia*, which is recorded in the fossils of sediments 410 million years old as one of the first colonists of the land. *Cooksonia* grew alongside *Sporogonites*, the ancestral bryophyte, but it held far more promise for the future: this was the forerunner of the ferns, clubmosses, horsetails, conifers, and, possibly, of the flowering plants – in other words, most of the modern vegetation of the world.

Upright stems, like most evolutionary advances, bring other problems in their wake. A tall plant immediately comes up against the problem of water loss in the air, so water has to be replaced from the damp soil, and water conduction is therefore essential. *Cooksonia* was admirably equipped to cope with these problems, for it had evolved specialized cells in its stems, called xylem elements, which were the forerunners of wood. They were constructed of a toughened material, lignin (♦ page 136), for support, and because they were dead and empty, they could also be of use in transporting water through the stems. As moisture evaporated from the plant's branching shoots it created the force to draw water up from the soil via the xylem elements. To minimize water loss from the plant, *Cooksonia* had a thickened outer layer of cells.

With the development of this internal conducting and support system, a great variety of opportunities became available to plants, for they could grow tall and form high canopies. The shade cast by the taller forms offered a new habitat suitable for types which could not cope with the high light intensities and drought of the upper canopy, but could grow in the dim, moist niches near the ground.

The force of natural selection resulted in some early plants becoming very large. Many of these, such as the giant clubmosses and horsetails, were forming extensive swamp forests by 345 million years ago, at the end of the Devonian period. These were the first of the great swamps that built up the coal measures with their black, waterlogged, undecayed remains. These massive plants – up to 40m or more – have living descendants, but these are very tiny in comparison: present-day horsetails only grow about 1m in height, while the clubmosses seldom exceed 30cm. More efficient plants, such as swamp-cypresses, have taken over the role of swamp-forest dominants.

The ferns also evolved during Devonian times, and lived alongside the giant clubmosses and horsetails (the three groups are collectively known as pteridophytes). The ferns were characterized by their compound fronds arising from a central trunk or stem. They did not grow as large as the giant clubmosses and horsetails but some, the tree ferns, were over 18m tall – and still are, for they have survived to the present day. Many of the early ferns, however, were smaller, and, like their modern relatives, probably lived on the forest floor, by streams and in other deeply shaded places. Forms such as bracken, which can survive in open grassland, are rare. Bracken owes its success to a very effective means of vegetative reproduction, by spreading rhizomes, so it can do without the gametophyte phase.

*The giant clubmosses and horsetails were up to 40 times taller than their modern counterparts*

### Relics of the coal forests

The pteridophytes are an ancient and diverse group of plants, but only the ferns have survived in any great numbers. The giant clubmosses and horsetails, which built up the coal seams of the world, have very few living relations, but those that have survived are of particular interest to botanists. The small clubmosses include the cone-bearing Lycopodium, whose "cones" are specialized parts of the fronds which carry the sporangia. As in ferns, the spores are all of one type and grow into a gametophyte which bears both male and female reproductive structures. However, another clubmoss, Selaginella, produces male and female spores from separate sporangia. Although they are shed, the female spores never germinate into an independent gametophyte plant. Instead the haploid tissues develop within the wall of the spore and bear their egg cells there. The smaller male spores release swimming sperm which seek out and fertilize these eggs. This separation of male and female gametophytes, and their reduction in size and duration, is of great evolutionary interest because it resembles the process that occurred in the progymnosperms (◊ page 57). Plants of this type – with separate male and female spores – are said to be heterosporous, in contrast to the more primitive homosporous type.

The horsetails Equisetum have an unusual growth form in that their leaves are reduced to small scales and occur in whorls around the stems and branches. Like the Lycopodium clubmosses they bear their sporangia in specialized cones and are homosporous.

One other unusual pteridophyte is Psilotum, the whisk fern, which is a splendid example of a living fossil, closely resembling some primitive Devonian pteridophytes of 350–400 million years ago. This tropical plant has no leaves at all, its stems doing the work of photosynthesis. The sporangia are produced on very short side branches.

### Primary colors

Like the green algae and the bryophytes, all pteridophytes contain chlorophyll a and chlorophyll b, which give them their green color. This is a good reason for regarding all three groups (together with the flowering plants and gymnosperms, which also share these pigments), as having a common origin. Paleobotanists currently believe that both the bryophytes and the pteridophytes evolved from members of the green algae as they colonized the land around 400 million years ago.

▲ The earliest clubmosses were small creeping forms like those alive today. But from them evolved giant species such as Sigillaria and Lepidodendron. These clubmosses colonized swamps and their remains probably built up into domed masses of peat. Over millions of years, the accumulated plant debris, prevented from decomposing by lack of oxygen, gradually turned into coal.

Sigillaria
Lepidodendron
Living clubmoss
Human

▲ In most species of ferns, all the leaves carry spores. These are produced by sporangia which develop on the underside of the leaf, usually covered by disks of protective tissue, or sori, which turn brown and papery as the spores ripen.

◄ The adder's tongue fern is unusual in several ways. It produces only one frond each year, and this divides to give a pointed, oval "leaf" and a more slender central stalk bearing up to 40 pairs of spore cases. This specialization of one part of the sporophyte for spore production is seen in a few other fern species as well, and parallels the evolutionary development that led to the seed ferns.

▼ Spike moss, a type of Selaginella clubmoss from the forests of Costa Rica.

◄ Found only in the tropics, tree ferns are remnants of a form of vegetation that once dominated the Earth. Their trunk is derived from the fern's stem, which is equivalent to the horizontal underground rhizome in bracken. This trunk rarely branches, has no bark on the outside, and cannot increase in girth as the tree grows. Tree ferns also lack the extensive root system of gymnosperm and angiosperm trees. Despite these disadvantages, tree ferns grow 18m tall, and up to 25m if supported by other trees.

▼ The kidney fern of New Zealand is a species of filmy fern, whose fronds are only one cell thick. Because of this they can only survive in 100 percent humidity: in rainforests, beside waterfalls or in wet streamside crevices.

*In the ice ages, conifers dominated the northern hemisphere*

▲ ◄ *Cycads from southern Africa, and their massive cones, which house the reproductive structures.*

► *Monterey pine, native only to the Monterey area of California, is a reminder that during the ice ages, conifers were much more widespread. These trees at Monterey are an isolated population, descended from pines left behind as the conifers' range shrank at the end of the ice ages.*

## Pollen power

The pollen grain represents a major advance in evolution and the gymnosperms are living descendants of the first pollen-producing plants. All gymnosperms seem to rely on wind for pollination.(Although some botanists have claimed that the cycads may be insect pollinated.) The trouble with using wind is that enormous quantities of pollen have to be released to allow for a very high failure rate. But it is probably economical in the long run because there is no need for showy flowers or attractive nectar.

Perhaps their independence from insects is one reason why conifers are so successful in the far north, where the winter is long and severe, and the summer very brief. They can complete the process of pollination quite early in the spring, before insects are abundant, thus giving the embryo a full growing season to begin its development.

## Triassic tree

The ginkgo is a "living fossil", descended from trees that date back to the Triassic, some 200 million years ago. Apart from its leaves, the ginkgo differs from the main group of living gymnosperms – the conifers and their allies – in several ways, particularly in the details of its reproductive process. Its female sporangia are not in protective cones, but lie naked on the tips of specialized shoots. The pollen is produced by catkin-like structures and carried on the wind. As in the cycads, the pollen grains release flagellated sperm which swim to the egg cells and fertilize them. This is a primitive characteristic that has been lost in the conifers. The seed of the gingko develops a fleshy orange-colored coat with a nauseating smell of rotting cheese. Within is an edible kernel, however, for which the ginkgo was cultivated: its name means "silver apricot" in Chinese.

► *The maidenhair tree or ginkgo was first described in 1690, from a cultivated tree in Japan. It was presumed to be extinct in the wild, but later a small relict population was found, confined to a remote part of China. Its remarkable leaves are superficially like those of angiosperms, but differ in that there is no central vein. Instead the veins radiate from the leaf stalk. The leaves of this, or a very closely related species, have been found fossilized as far back as the Triassic period. This is the sole living representative of an order of gymnosperms that were once widespread and diverse.*

## Seed ferns and cycads

The bryophytes and pteridophytes have one obvious weakness as land plants and that is their dependence on a watery environment for their gametophyte generation, and hence for sexual reproduction. The answer to this problem was provided by the development of two new structures, the pollen grain and the seed.

Heterospory – the development of separate male and female spores, producing separate male and female gametophytes – was the first step in this new development. The next was adequate protection from desiccation for the gametophyte. One simple way of protecting the female gametophyte was to retain it on the sporophyte, preferably wrapped up in sporophyte tissues. But this placed additional responsibility upon the male, for it had to travel further, and often horizontally rather than down toward the ground. The male gamete also had to penetrate the sporophyte tissue to achieve fertilization of an egg cell. The evolutionary answer to this problem was to make the male gametophyte as small as possible, encase it in a protective waterproof wrapping of resistant material, and release the entire package – a pollen grain. Some fern-like plants, the progymnosperms, were developing in this direction 370 million years ago and their descendants, the gymnosperms (ginkgos, conifers, cycads and their allies), proved a very successful group.

The progymnosperms were woody plants, growing up to 30m with robust branches and fern-like leaves, some of which bore sporangia, often of two kinds, male and female. These were probably the ancestors, not only of the gymnosperms, but also of the seed ferns. The seed ferns, or pteridosperms, were the first plants with true seeds. The seed was essentially a female gametophyte retained on the parent plant and wrapped in sporophyte tissue (the sporangium itself – now called the nucellus) plus an extra layer, the integument. The need for a seed arises from keeping the female gametophyte attached to the parent plant – the function of dispersal, previously fulfilled by the air-borne spores, is now lost. But the new plant must still be carried away from its parent in order to find a suitable place to live, and so the seed takes on the task of dispersal.

The seed ferns flourished for millions of years only to become extinct in the Cretaceous, but the cycads still survive in some tropical areas, and these living descendants of the early seed plants exhibit some primitive and some more advanced reproductive features. One notable primitive feature is that the pollen grains germinate to liberate swimming sperm – in other gymnosperms the sperm are non-mobile. The sperm travel over the moist surface of the female cycad cone to reach the egg cell.

## Ginkgos and conifers

Although the cycads are a very ancient group of gymnosperms, they are certainly not the most successful. Having reached their peak of development and distribution about 150 million years ago, they went into decline and are now rather scarce and scattered around the tropics. Other types of gymnosperm had evolved around 300 million years ago, including the ginkgos, the yews and their allies, and the conifers. The latter group produced a great variety of species with leaf types ranging from the tiny scale-like leaves of the cypresses to the long, sharp needles of the pines. The conifers were able to conquer a far greater range of environments than the cycads, and now predominate in the cold boreal zone.

The conifers' method of protecting the sensitive gametophyte is basically similar to that of the cycads. The female gametophytes are retained within sporophyte tissue, deep inside the female cone, while the pollen grains have a tough wall made of an extraordinarily resistant material, called sporopollenin. This keeps the delicate male gametophyte from becoming desiccated on its journey through the air to the female cone. Reaching its target is very much a matter of chance, but, once there, the pollen grain is drawn into the female sporangium by the contraction of a drop of exuded fluid.

Once inside, it germinates to produce a tube, but there is no release of motile sperm cells. The tube carries passive male cells which are released within the egg cell and fertilize it (◀ page 51). This process is a very slow one, as is the maturation of the new sporophyte embryo, and the period between the arrival of the pollen at the female cone and the eventual release of new seeds may be as long as two years.

Once released, the seeds must be dispersed from the parent tree. To aid dispersal, many conifer seeds have extensions to their coat which form a wing and catch the wind. Some are more elaborate still, as in junipers, where the cone scales become swollen and fleshy to form a berry-like covering. This is attractive to birds, which digest the "berry" and pass the seeds unharmed in their droppings.

One reason why the conifers have been so much more successful than the cycads is that their structure is much more elaborate. The cycads never got beyond producing whorls of fern-like leaves borne at the tops of short, woody trunks – far greater size and complexity of canopy structure had been seen in the primitive giant horsetails. The conifers, by contrast, produced branching crowns supported by robust boles which were capable of attaining very great heights. Even today the group can boast the tallest trees in the world, from the kauri pines of New Zealand which grow to 50m, to the immense redwoods of California, which grow to over 100m.

### Reasons for resin
*The stems and leaves of many of the conifers are permeated by a system of ducts which contain a sticky, aromatic, oily material called resin. It is this material which gives pines their characteristic smell. Its function is to inhibit the growth of microbes, and deter insects from feeding on the tree. But there are some insects, like the pine bark beetle, which, far from being discouraged by its presence, have actually developed ways of using it for their own ends. The female bark beetle takes up the resinous chemicals as she feeds and converts them into pheromones (message-bearing chemicals) which act as sex-attractants and draw the males to her.*

### Evergreen advantages
*The majority of conifers are evergreen and this particular feature has probably made them well adapted to both high latitudes and high altitudes. There are several possible explanations why the evergreen habit is so successful in these areas. The obvious one is that they may manage to keep up their photosynthetic activity during the winter – the summer is very short at high latitudes and this restricts plant growth. In fact, measurements show that conifers shut down activity for the winter just as deciduous trees do. What they can do, however, is pick up their photosynthesis very quickly as soon as spring occurs. They do not have to wait until their leaf canopy has expanded because it is already present. The evergreen leaf may also serve as a store for nutrients, which is quite an important feature for plants growing in the northern regions where the soils are often impoverished. The moisture-retentive needle leaf is also advantageous where shortages of water occur due to icing-up.*

▶ **Growing in the Namib Desert in southern Africa is the extraordinary gymnosperm Welwitschia mirabilis, *a lone species with no close living relatives. A massive woody stem-cum-rootstock, up to 1m in diameter, is largely buried in sand. From its apex grow long, strap-shaped leaves of indefinite length, often reaching 2m or more. Welwitschia *is capable of growing under extreme drought and survives because the leaves can absorb moisture from the fog that rolls in over the Namib from the Atlantic Ocean – the only available water. Welwitschia *is usually classified with the gymnosperms.**

## 7

# Flowering Plants

*Plant evolution...Descendants of the magnolia family?
...Pollination and fertilization...Wood and water...
PERSPECTIVE...Leaves – the source of all flower parts...
The endosperm that nourishes the young plant...Seed
dispersal...The dodo's role in one tree's germination*

**Parts of a flower**

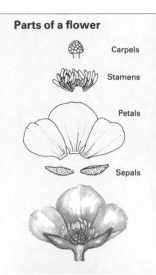

Carpels

Stamens

Petals

Sepals

◄▼ *Ornamental cherries
have been cultivated for
thousands of years in Japan
and subjected to intense
artificial breeding, to
produce the double flowers,
profuse long-lasting
blossom and wide variety of
colors available today. Such
intensive breeding can have
some odd effects, as here,
with the carpels of each
flower being replaced by
tiny leaves. This abnormal
flower is a reminder of the
fact that all the parts of the
angiosperm flower – the
sepals, petals, stamens and
carpels – originally evolved
from ordinary leaves that
became specialized for
reproduction.*

Over 80 percent of all living green plants are angiosperms, or flowering plants. In that sense, they are the present pinnacle of plant evolution. But really it is wrong to think of them as a cut above other groups such as the ferns or conifers. Way back in geological history they all had a common origin, but have developed along separate lines. The fact that the other groups still survive shows that in certain circumstances and environments they are superior to the angiosperms, although they are generally not as widespread.

It is therefore misleading, in some ways, to describe one group as primitive and another as advanced. By these descriptions biologists do not necessarily mean that the more primitive group is inadequate, nor that it is ancestral to the advanced group. The term simply means that the "primitive" form has retained more of the features which emerged early on during the process of evolution. In this sense, the flowering plants *are* the most advanced, for they have both emerged and diversified later in geological history, and have accumulated a greater range of new and innovative features.

Where the flowering plants came from is still something of a mystery, but their expansion, both geographically and in terms of taxonomic diversity, was little short of explosive. Some time in the Cretaceous – the geological age of chalk-forming seas and a land dominated by dinosaurs – the flowering plants began to make their presence felt. About 110 million years ago they were a negligible element in the vegetation of the world, which was then dominated by gymnosperms. But by 100 million years ago many of the flowering plant families had appeared and the group was well on the way to global domination.

Some botanists believe that angiosperms evolved from a gymnosperm ancestor, while others prefer the idea of a seed-bearing fern (◀ page 57) as the immediate progenitor. It is probable that the earliest angiosperms were woody shrubs or trees, and something is known of their leaves and pollen grains, because these features have been preserved in the fossil record. Unfortunately, the most important bits, the flowers themselves, are very scarce in fossil remains, at least until the late Cretaceous, so one can do little more than guess at their form.

The dearth of plant fossils means that ancestral types must be reconstructed, as far as possible, from living forms. One important method is to establish which modern families have retained most of the primitive features in their leaves and stems, by comparing them with fossils, and then to assume that their flowers resemble those of the early angiosperms. This method points to the magnolia family, Magnoliaceae, and the water-lilies, Nymphaceae, as being among the most primitive. Certainly, magnolia-like flowers were present on earth about 100 million years ago, and magnolia-like pollen is present in much older rocks.

## The first flowers

*The earliest angiosperm flowers developed from ordinary leaf-bearing shoots and all the flower parts are derived from leaves. The uppermost leaves were fertile and female, bearing ovules. In the course of evolution, these leaves wrapped themselves around the ovule to form the carpel – an important angiosperm innovation which protects both ovule and seed. The next set of leaves were also fertile, but they were male, and these became modified into stamens. Lower down the leaves lost their chlorophyll and became colored – the petals. Some of these developed sugar-secreting nectaries which attracted insect pollinators. Finally, some leaves retained their original appearance and served to protect the reproductive parts – these are known as the sepals.*

## Packaged seed

*The most notable feature of the angiosperm plant is its flower, though not all are scented, colorful affairs – some flowering plants, such as the grasses, have inconspicuous green flowers, which are pollinated by wind. However, the flower is not the only distinctive feature of the angiosperms. The name "angiosperm" means "covered seed", and refers to the layer of tissue known as a carpel, which encloses first the ovule and later the seed. In gymnosperms ("naked seed") this is lacking. The carpel later develops into a fruit, which aids the seed's dispersal (◆ page 66).*

*Magnolias rely on beetles for pollination – and may have done so for some 100 million years*

If we accept the primitive nature of the magnolia flower, then the early angiosperms probably had upright, cone-like floral structures in which the flower parts – still betraying their leafy origins – were borne in a spiral sequence. The lowest of these were sepals which merged into the white or colored petal-like leaves above them. Then came stamens, and the spirally arranged carpels – the fleshy part containing the female reproductive cells.

The question of whether primitive flowering plants were pollinated by wind or by insects cannot be answered by the fossil record, so again, the pollination of the magnolia family and other "primitive" plants is the only available evidence. In the Magnoliaceae the pollen grains are transported by beetles which feed upon parts of the flower and carry pollen by chance when moving from one meal to another. This apparently clumsy method has clearly proved a satisfactory means of pollen transfer, from the plant's point of view. On the evidence of the Magnoliaceae, it seems likely that the most primitive angiosperms had already adopted insect pollination.

It is only fair to add that not all botanists agree that the magnolias are the most primitive of living flowering plants. Some prefer the idea of the earliest flowers being catkins, which would make families such as the hazels, birches and willows most primitive. All of these have wind-borne pollen, though in the case of the willows there is a strong development towards increasing reliance on insects.

### Breaching the defenses

Once the pollen grain has arrived at the female organ, it will clearly experience a more difficult task than that of the gymnosperm pollen (◀ page 51) in effecting fertilization, since all those layers of protective tissue have to be penetrated. The carpel is vase-shaped and it is on the narrow top (the stigma) that the pollen grain germinates, extruding a tube of gametophyte tissue which grows down into the stigma and the neck (the style) of the carpel, eventually arriving in the swollen base (the ovary) where the female gametophyte is housed. The pollen tube locates the egg cell and a nonmotile male gamete flows down the tube and fuses with the egg. The rate at which such pollen tubes can grow is quite surprising – as much as 35mm per hour.

▲ *The male catkins of a silver birch tree release their copious pollen, which is blown by the wind to the female flowers. In birches, these too are arranged in catkins, but in some other groups, such as the hazels, the female flowers are not in catkins and look quite different from the male flowers.*

### Two to one

*There is one major division within the flowering plants based on an apparently insignificant character, the number of cotyledons (leaf-like organs) produced by the germinating seed. Although the division seems a somewhat arbitrary one, it does in fact represent a fundamental split, and the separation may well date back to the origin of the flowering plants. Most of our familiar flowering plants, from dandelions to oak trees, belong to the larger of the two groups, the dicotyledons or dicots. They have two cotyledons, whereas the monocotyledons (monocots) have only one. This smaller group includes grasses, lilies, orchids and palm trees.*

*There are other differences, besides the number of cotyledons. The monocots mainly have simple leaves with parallel veins, in contrast to the variety of leaf-shapes and the complex network of veins found in dicots. The monocots also tend to have their floral parts in multiples of three, whereas in dicots this is an unusual number, five being much more common.*

◀ *The magnolia flower is considered "primitive" because all its parts – sepals, petals, stamens and carpels – are present in large numbers, and the number varies from one flower to another. Also, the parts are arranged spirally and none are fused. In more highly evolved flowers the parts are fewer, and of a fixed number. They are arranged in whorls, rather than spirally, and the flower is sometimes asymmetrical. Some of the parts may be lost, while some are fused to create new and more complex structures, as in the orchids.*

▶ *The flowers of the claret-cup cactus, like other showy blooms, serve to advertise the presence of nectar, and thus attract pollinating animals.*

### Energy-packed endosperms

One characteristic feature of the angiosperm seed is the endosperm – a "packed lunch" that nourishes the plant embryo during germination, and helps the young plant to become established rapidly. This food store is formed by sexual fusion in a remarkable process that parallels the fertilization of the egg. When the pollen tube reaches the ovule, two male gametes enter, but only one of these gametes fuses with the egg. The other fuses with two other haploid nuclei, and then divides repeatedly to form the endosperm. Thus the endosperm has three sets of chromosomes.

### Carnivorous plants

In general, plants provide a source of food for animals. But there are some plants which have managed partially to reverse this process and consume animals to supplement their intake of elements, such as phosphorus and nitrogen. It was once thought that these insectivorous plants could not absorb larger molecules from insects, nor gain any energy from them, but the use of radioactively-labeled amino acids has proved this to be wrong – the amino acids are absorbed. However, photosynthesis is still the main basis of their existence. Gaining extra minerals from insects simply allows them to live in places with poor soil.

Most insectivorous plants have highly modified leaves for trapping insects. The sundew's leaves are covered in glandular hairs or tentacles, containing digestive enzymes, to which insects become stuck. In the pitcher plants, the leaf forms an urn-shaped structure which contains the digestive fluids. Insects are attracted to the slippery rim by nectar, and when they fall in, arrays of downward-pointing hairs prevent their escape.

▼ *A lesser bladderwort catches a mosquito larva in one of the tiny bladders that develop at the margins of its leaves. The capture of aquatic insects enables bladderworts to live in peaty pools that are too poor in nutrients to support most plant life. Closure of the bladders is controlled by an electrical message, similar to a nerve impulse (♦ page 202).*

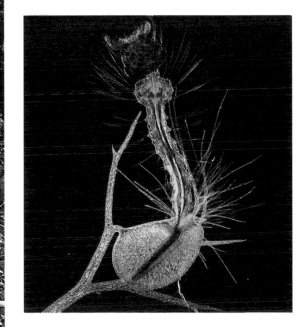

# Pollination

### Partners in pollen

A common evolutionary trend in the flowering
plants is for the number of floral parts to be
reduced and for some components to become
fused. Generally, this has resulted from closer
associations with specific animals as pollen
carriers. These are mostly insects, but in tropical
areas, where a year-round supply of nectar is
available, bird- and bat-pollination are relatively
common. Other small mammals, besides bats, may
also act as pollinators, but only one specializes in
eating nectar – the Australian honey possum.

   Whatever the animal involved, once a stable
pollination relationship has been achieved, there is
less wastage of pollen, and more "direct hits" on
the stigma, so the number of stamens and carpels
can be reduced. Fusion of parts may also occur,
often linked with a greater complexity of floral
structure. For example, the fusion of petals to form
tubular sheaths around nectar-bearing organs is
geared to the specialist pollinators. It makes the
nectaries of the flower inaccessible to those
without the appropriate mouthparts. Thus some
South American flowers have very long, curved
corollas and can only be pollinated by a few species
of hummingbirds with long, curved beaks. Flowers
such as honeysuckle and nicotiana (sweet tobacco)
likewise have a long tubular corolla that is
accessible to the long probiscis of a pollinating
moth, but excludes bees and flies.

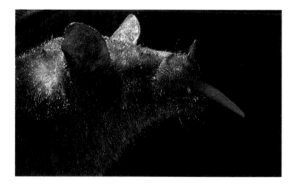

◄▲ *While feeding on the
nectar of a century plant,
a bat's head becomes
covered with pollen.*

▼ *The red velvety flower
of this orchid mimics the
abdomen of a certain
female wasp. Here a male
has just tried to mate
with the flower, causing it
spur to break open and
glue its pollen sacs to his
abdomen. Attempted
mating with another flower
will remove them.*

### The costs of pollination – and those that cheat

The use of insects for pollination has several
advantages, such as reduced wastage of pollen,
and increased chance of success. But these are
only achieved by the expenditure of considerable
energy on the part of the plant. The plant generally
offers food, in the form of nectar and/or pollen, and
it must advertise itself by means of large, colorful
and, in some cases, scented flowers.

   Some plants are apparently very generous in
their provision, such as the fig, which has an
exclusive pollination arrangement with a certain
species of wasp. The fig plant is completely
dependent on this insect and in winter it bears
sterile fruit, whose only purpose is to ensure the
survival of its pollen vector by providing it with
shelter – an extreme example of coevolution.

   Other plants are anything but generous. There
are some orchids whose flowers mimic the shape
and coloring of female insects. Each such orchid
specializes in a single insect species, and mimics
its female so realistically that the males attempt to
copulate with the flowers, thereby pollinating them.
A simpler deception is practiced by the early purple
orchid which has a well developed, curved spur to
its flower. In nectar-secreting orchids, this provides
the reward to the insect pollinators, but the early
purple orchid cheats, because its spurs are empty.

   Insects can also cheat, by removing the nectar
without effecting pollination. Some flowers of
leguminous plants (peas and beans) are regularly
robbed of nectar by bees that cut a hole near the
base of the flower. The leguminous flower is so
constructed that the insect has to crawl right inside
to reach the nectar – by cutting a hole in the petals,
they can get at their food supply more quickly.

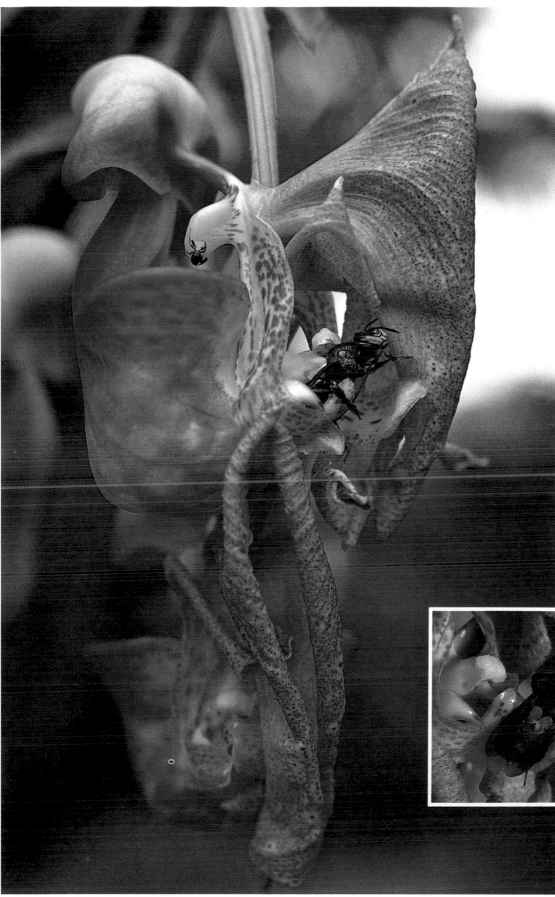

◄ Coryanthes orchids achieve pollination with a complex trap that ensnares bees. The flowers carry a reservoir of fluid in a vertical-sided chamber. The liquid contains drugs that attract the insects and make them drowsy, so bees clambering about the edge inevitably fall in. They swim around there until they find the only possible exit, which is a narrow ridge of tissue, level with the surface of the fluid. Crawling along this, the bee passes beneath the stigma and stamens. The latter glue two pollen sacs (pollinia) to the insect's back. A passageway then leads the insect out of the flower much higher up, away from the liquid reservoir – it is shown here leaving. The bee flies off, but is usually tempted to repeat the experience at another flower. This time, the flower's stigma picks up the pollinia from the male's back, and fertilization takes place.

▼ Pollen on the stigma of a cotton plant flower.

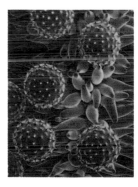

▲ A bee carrying a pair of Coryanthes pollinia. Even if it returns to the same flower, self-pollination will not occur, as the stigma is unreceptive just after the pollinia are removed.

*An extraordinary flexibility of form may account for the immense success of flowering plants*

### The wandering plant

*The fact that plants cannot move about as easily as animals makes the study of their geographical distribution particularly interesting and relevant to their evolutionary origins. Plant distribution was an important part of Darwin's evidence in "The Origin of Species". He remarked on the resemblance of plants on oceanic islands to those of the nearest mainland, and demonstrated that seeds could be carried by ocean currents or birds. The similarities of plants from widely separated mountain ranges he correctly attributed to glacial periods which encouraged the spread of plants from the higher latitudes. When the ice sheets retreated, these cold-loving plants would die out, except on mountain peaks. Much of the basic evidence for these speculations came from Darwin's close friend, Joseph Hooker. One of Hooker's observations – that the plants of South America, South Africa and Australia showed certain affinities – could not be explained at the time and remained a puzzle until the 1950s. Only then, with the acceptance of continental drift, did the explanation become established: these three continents had once been part of a single landmass (* page 124).*

## Wood and water

It is not only the flower which differentiates the angiosperm from the more primitive plants. The angiosperm also has more highly differentiated wood tissues than is seen in conifers. In particular it has tubular wood elements, called vessels, which are involved in the process of conducting water up the stems. These vessels are dead cells which are connected end-to-end by perforated plates, so permitting the water contained in them to form a long, uninterrupted column up the entire height of the plant. Comparable vessels are generally not found in the gymnosperms; they possess only tracheids which are narrower, and do not show perforations at the end wall: water passes from one tracheid to another laterally, through pits in the sides of the cell.

It is interesting to note that the wood of *Welwitschia*, an aberrant gymnosperm, *does* contain vessels, whereas many members of a primitive angiosperm family, the Winteraceae (winter's bark), lack vessels altogether. Recent discoveries of Winteraceae pollen grains in rocks aged about 110 million years, add to the case for regarding this group as close to the ancestral angiosperms. But the argument concerning the origin of vessels is complicated by the possibility that they may have evolved independently on several occasions.

◄ *Joseph Hooker collecting plants in the Himalayas, for the Royal Botanic Gardens at Kew, in London. Plant collectors and botanists such as Hooker discovered a great deal about plant distribution, and contributed valuable evidence for Darwin's evolutionary theories.*

► *The prisoner boab tree of Australia, a close relative of the African baobab, and similarly adapted to arid conditions. The swollen trunk stores water for the dry season. These trees do not keep growing throughout their lives, and large trees may even shrink in times of severe drought.*

### Flexibility of form

*One of the most remarkable features of the flowering plants is the variety of form, both vegetative and floral, which is found among them. Stems, leaves, roots, flowers and fruits all demonstrate an extraordinary flexibility of form, and it may be this fact rather than any specific feature (such as the water-conducting vessels, the flower, or the carpel) which accounts for the immense success of the flowering plants.*

*For example, many angiosperm leaves have elaborate protective measures against herbivorous animals, such as the prickly leaves of the thistles, or the irritant chemicals stored in brittle, hollow hairs, as in nettles. Other plants may be so rich in volatile, irritant oils that even the slightest skin contact can cause a severe reaction, as in poison ivy.*

*Storage is another role for the leaves. Some plants have thick, succulent leaves in which they store water, while others, such as the onion, use modified leaves (in the bulb) for food storage.*

*The leaves of sensitive plants are able to close up when touched, probably to make themselves seem less appetizing, while those of carnivorous plants can trap and digest insects.*

*The angiosperm also comes in a whole range of sizes. The great eucalyptus trees of Australia rival the redwoods in height, and the baobabs achieve gigantic girths, while at the other end of the scale are the tiny floating duckweeds, some of which are less than 1mm in diameter.*

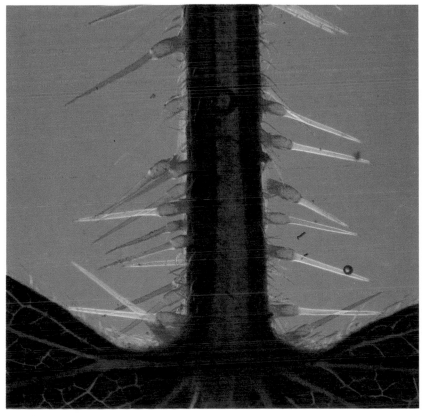

◀ The stinging hairs of a nettle contain acetyl-choline, histamine and other substances which together produce an irritant effect. The hairs have a small knob at the apex, which easily breaks off to reveal an ultra-sharp silica point. This penetrates the skin and injects the toxin.

▼ Duckweeds have no leaves or stems as such, and reproduce mainly by budding, only rarely producing tiny flowers in pockets at the edge of the plant. Their resemblance to seedlings of the water plants Pistia suggests that they could have evolved by pedomorphosis.

▲ The fact that worker
ants regularly take food
back to the nest, for other
ants to feed on, makes
them useful for seed
dispersal.

◄ Rosehips attacked by
greenfinches which "cheat"
by eating the seeds and not
the fruit. Plants must
produce excess seeds to
compensate for such losses.

▼ Without the dodo,
Calvaria major *could not
reproduce. Its seeds are
now coaxed into life by
feeding them to turkeys, or
turning in a gem polisher.*

## Spreading the seed

As the seed of a flowering plant matures, the carpel
that surrounds it develops to produce a fruit. The
sweet, juicy items we eat are just one type of fruit,
botanically speaking. The term also encompasses
such unappetizing products as burrs, acorns, pea
pods and thistledown. The structure of the fruit is
adapted for dispersal, either by animals or other
agents. Succulent fruits depend upon being eaten
by birds or mammals which benefit from the food
supplied by the carpel. The seeds are suitably
packaged to pass through the animal and be
deposited unharmed. (This is not always
successful, however, and the plants suffer many
lost seeds because the "wrong" animal eats the
fruit. Some animals even strip off the fruit and eat
the seeds, crushing the protective coat.) Just how
far the seeds travel depends upon the time spent in
the animal's gut and its pattern of movement. The
laxative effect of fruits may be of advantage to the
seed, speeding up its passage and thus minimizing
the damage done by the carrier's digestive system.

Other fruits, such as those of some violets, are
not ingested by the animals which disperse them.
In this case ants are the vectors, and they carry the
seeds off to their nest, where just a small and non-
essential part is consumed – a droplet of oil
produced especially for the purpose. The rest is left
to germinate. Fruits such as acorns and nuts offer
rich food that keeps well, and rely on mammals
burying them for winter stores. The forgotten ones
germinate next spring, having gained a double
advantage from their animal partners – planting as
well as dispersal.

Non-edible fruits can also be adapted to animal
dispersal, as in the case of burrs, which attach
themselves to fur or feathers, but many non-edible
fruits rely on inanimate forces, such as wind, or
water. Wind-dispersed seeds are equipped with
wings, parachutes, or fluffy plumes, to help them
float away from the plant.

## Doing without the dodo

A tree known as Calvaria major, *confined to the
island of Mauritius, was a puzzle to botanists for
centuries. Once quite common on the island, it had
gone into a decline until only 13 ancient trees were
left. These were all over 300 years old, and
although they produced healthy-looking seed each
year, none ever germinated. In the mid-1970s an
American ecologist, Stanley Temple, came up with
an explanation. He suggested that the tree's large
fruits had formerly been eaten by the dodo, a large
bird whose stone-filled gizzard exerted a powerful
crushing pressure. Adapted to withstand this
onslaught, the tree's seeds were protected by a
thick-walled seed coat. The dodo's gizzard pounded
away at the seed coat, made it much thinner, and
cracked it a bit, but not sufficiently to damage the
seed inside. When deposited by the bird, the seed
could germinate. But the protective wall was so
thick that without this rough treatment the seed
was trapped inside, unable to get out. So when the
dodo became extinct, 300 years ago, the tree's
seeds were unable to germinate. This is an extreme
example of the phenomenon of coevolution
between two species.*

## 8

# Lower Invertebrates

*A bewildering diversity of forms...Sponges – the simplest multicellular animals...Innovations of roundworms and wheel animals...A profusion of worms...Formidable predators...Segmentation and shells...PERSPECTIVE...Advantages of many cells...The difficulties of classification...Body cavities...Filter feeders...Intelligent invertebrates*

There is a bewildering diversity of lower invertebrates. They range from the beautiful conches and corals to the rather less attractive leeches, liver-flukes and slugs, from microscopic rotifers and thread-like nematode worms up to the massive giant clams. They include the seemingly inanimate sponges at one extreme and such cunning and speedy creatures as the octopus or squid at the other. Beneath these superficial differences, there lie even greater dissimilarities in internal organization and development.

Such diversity has led zoologists in the past to suggest that invertebrates arose more than once from protozoan stock: that there were several "experiments" in producing multicellular animals. But most zoologists now believe that all living multicellular animals (metazoans) are in some way related, having evolved from a single ancestor. This is not to say that multicellular animals necessarily evolved only once. Multicellularity may have arisen several times but only one type lasted the course, the others perishing long ago.

Beyond this simple fact, any measure of zoological consensus ends. The relationships between the more primitive invertebrate animals has traditionally been a rich field for taxonomic speculation. Attempts to make any sense of them receives no help from the fossil record as the small soft-bodied early metazoans left little or no trace, and by the time fossils with hard parts appear, most of the higher invertebrates are well represented. Nevertheless, there remains the evidence of the living animals to puzzle over: an immensely rich fauna of relatively simple forms.

## Why be many-celled?

With the benefit of hindsight, it is easy to see why having a body consisting of many cells is an advantage. It allows individual cells to specialize in what they do and this division of labor makes for greater efficiency and the possibility of a large body size. Single-celled organisms are limited in size by the need for gases and food molecules to diffuse between the cell surface and the center. Over a certain size, diffusion is too slow a process to sustain the central mass of protoplasm and a circulatory system is needed. Also, protoplasm has the consistency of raw egg white. So without the development of a skeleton to support a large body, life out of water would be impossible.

But advanced features like circulatory systems and skeletons – which allow rapid movement, colonization of the terrestrial environment, flight and so on – evolved after the appearance of multicellularity itself. So what was the primary advantage that the first metazoan had over its protozoan colleagues? Protozoans had existed for perhaps a billion years before the first metazoan and were by then exceedingly sophisticated organisms in their own right, much as they are today. So what happened to make being bigger better?

Nobody knows the answer for sure. But one possibility is that a change occurred in the feeding relationships of protozoans, resulting in the emergence of the first predators. Some protozoans began to eat other protozoans. So here was a new problem of survival – how to avoid being eaten?

Probably by chance, cell division may occasionally have been imperfect, and the daughter cells may have failed to separate completely. If this continued to happen, a large blob would be formed, and it is clearly much more difficult to eat a blob of cells than it is to consume a single cell. Therefore, there could have been an advantage in "sticking together". And a small advantage is all evolution needs to get started on.

Of itself, this would only explain why "colonies" of cells might persist. Colonial algae such as Pandorina or the even larger Volvox exist today (◊ page 47). But this is not the full multicellular condition, if by that we imply a complex division of labor. But there is an interesting property of spherical blobs of cells – those on the inside would be out of contact with the environment and therefore food. So there is a maximum size a blob can be before the internal cells begin to die. Volvox "solved" this problem by being hollow. Another solution would be for those on the outside to pass a proportion of their food to those on the inside. Why they should do this apparently altruistic act may be explainable by theories of kin selection (◊ page 15). However it happened, this would be the beginnings of a division of labor and the true metazoan condition. And so the juggernaut of metazoan evolution began to roll.

◄ *A community of hydroids, corals (notably the leaf-like sea fan, and the convoluted brain coral in the foreground), and sponges (including yellow tube sponges, and red encrusting sponges) from the Caribbean. Although sessile, they are all animals, not plants. They live on tiny food particles suspended in the water.*

*Despite their appearance flatworms share several characteristics with comb-jellies*

Many of the lower invertebrates are highly successful in terms of abundance and species diversity, and, in spite of their simple body plans, they are highly evolved organisms. Indeed, one of the pitfalls that systematists have to be wary of is equating simplicity of structure with primitiveness. Seemingly advanced, complex creatures with little genetic adaptability may become extinct when competition from newly evolving forms becomes severe. Simple organisms with the ability to diversify rapidly can thus be at an evolutionary advantage over more complex species.

### The simplest metazoans

Apart from puzzling creatures like *Trichoplax* and the mesozoans (◀ page 69), many zoologists believe the sponges to be the simplest multicellular animals (metazoans). At one time sponges were considered to have diverged a long way from the main line of metazoan evolution, for they seemed to be little more than two-layered bags of cells, without any true tissues or organs, and with relatively little cellular interdependence. This can be dramatically demonstrated by forcing a living sponge through a fine mesh. The individual cells are able to survive despite being separated from each other. In time they will even reorganize themselves into a new sponge body.

One characteristic of sponges is that the inner layer of cells each has a collar around a single flagellum, a feature once thought to be unique among metazoans. These unusual cells are known as "collar cells". Another peculiar feature is the embryological process called "reversal of layers". Larval sponges are ciliated on the outside and on changing into adults the ciliated and non-ciliated cells were thought to swap places. For these reasons, sponges were at one time put into a subkingdom of their own. More recently, however, collar-cells have been observed in several other metazoan groups, and it has been demonstrated that the "reversal of layers" does not actually happen. Larval ciliated cells are shed or resorbed, while the collar-cells are formed in the inner layer from previously undifferentiated cells. Sponges are also now known to have many of the "advanced" features of higher invertebrates, including contractile tissue, cellular recognition systems, immune systems and a matrix between the two cell layers (mesoglea) which seems to be made up of true connective tissue. So the modern view is that sponges really *are* metazoans.

The next three phyla to be considered present the zoologist with a greater problem than was first thought. The cnidarians (previously called coelenterates) are radially symmetrical animals such as sea anemones, jellyfish, corals and hydroids. The ctenophores are the less familiar comb-jellies or sea gooseberries, abundant open-water predators. The third group, the platyhelminths or flatworms, consist of three types of flat, bilaterally symmetrical worms: the flukes and tapeworms (both parasites), and the non-parasitic flatworms also called the turbellarians.

All three phyla have a similar bodyplan consisting of an outer and an inner layer of cells separated by a kind of matrix, the mesoglea. This matrix is the bit which puts the jelly in jellyfish: in the others it is thinner but has a similar gelatinous consistency. These animals have only very rudimentary organ systems, that is, discrete sets of cells with specialized functions. The major innovation over the sponge condition is the continuous inner layer – the gut – providing a cavity for the efficient digestion of food. In sponges each cell works alone, engulfing and digesting its own food particles.

▲ *The basic type of comb-jelly has a globular body and swims with rows of comb-like plates, made up of fused cilia. Some more highly evolved comb-jellies are elongated and have an undulating movement produced by muscle fibers in the mesoglea.*

▼ *The sea anemone is a single large polyp, whereas corals are colonies of many tiny polyps, encased in a skeleton. Hydroids may be colonial, like corals, or individualists, like sea anemones. The basic body plan of the polyp is very similar in all three.*

**Cnidarian life cycle**

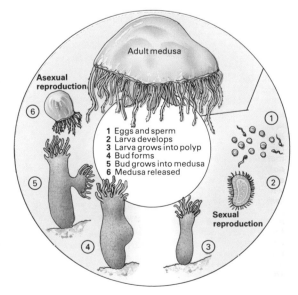

Adult medusa

Asexual reproduction

1 Eggs and sperm
2 Larva develops
3 Larva grows into polyp
4 Bud forms
5 Bud grows into medusa
6 Medusa released

Sexual reproduction

## Trichoplax *and the mesozoans*

*Just over 100 years ago, a minute blob of cells, no more than 0·5mm in diameter, was first found in a seawater aquarium and given the name of* Trichoplax adherens. *These very simple animals have flattened bodies composed of two layers of flagellated cells separated by a loose layer of contractile cells. They behave rather like amebae, creeping about and continuously changing shape. Some zoologists believe* Trichoplax *to be a direct descendant of the original metazoan ancestor, but others think it may be a degenerate form of some other group of invertebrates.*

*Unlike* Trichoplax, *the mesozoans are all parasites. Most have two layers of cells, but these differ fundamentally from the body layers of other multicellular animals: in one mesozoan, a long multinucleate "axial cell" lies at the center of the worm-like body, with the outer layer of cells arranged around it in a spiral. Mesozoans may be simple animals, related to early metazoans, or again they could be the degenerate descendants of some other group, such as the flatworms.*

## *Problematic phyla*

*In addition to the major groups of invertebrates, there are many minor groups that are often very difficult to classify, because they show no clear-cut relationship to any other phylum. The beardworms, or Pogonophora (♦ page 154) for example, lack a gut entirely, and while this may well be a secondary loss, it makes it difficult to compare them with other invertebrates. Consequently they are placed in a phylum of their own.*

*Beardworms were first discovered in 1900, but as recently as 1956 another completely new phylum of animals was discovered, the gnathostomulids. These worm-like animals live deep in marine sediments, where oxygen is virtually absent. There are now 54 known species and most are only 0·5 – 1·0 mm long. It has been suggested that they are related to the flatworms, but some features argue against this, and taxonomists are far from agreed as to what should be done with this strange group. It seems likely to lead a nomadic existence around the lower invertebrate phyla for some years to come, before finding a permanent resting place.*

▲ *A colorful flatworm swims through the warm waters of the Great Barrier Reef with graceful undulating movements of its body. Although a few inhabit tropical rainforests, most non-parasitic flatworms are aquatic, feeding on protozoa and small invertebrates.*

◄ *A generalized cnidarian life cycle, showing the two forms: free-swimming medusa and sedentary polyp. The medusa is, in effect, an inverted polyp with the mouth and the tentacles pointing downward. In jellyfish, the medusa predominates, and the polyp stage is small and transitory. In the hydroids, the polyp is the important form and in sea anemones and corals the medusa stage has been lost entirely.*

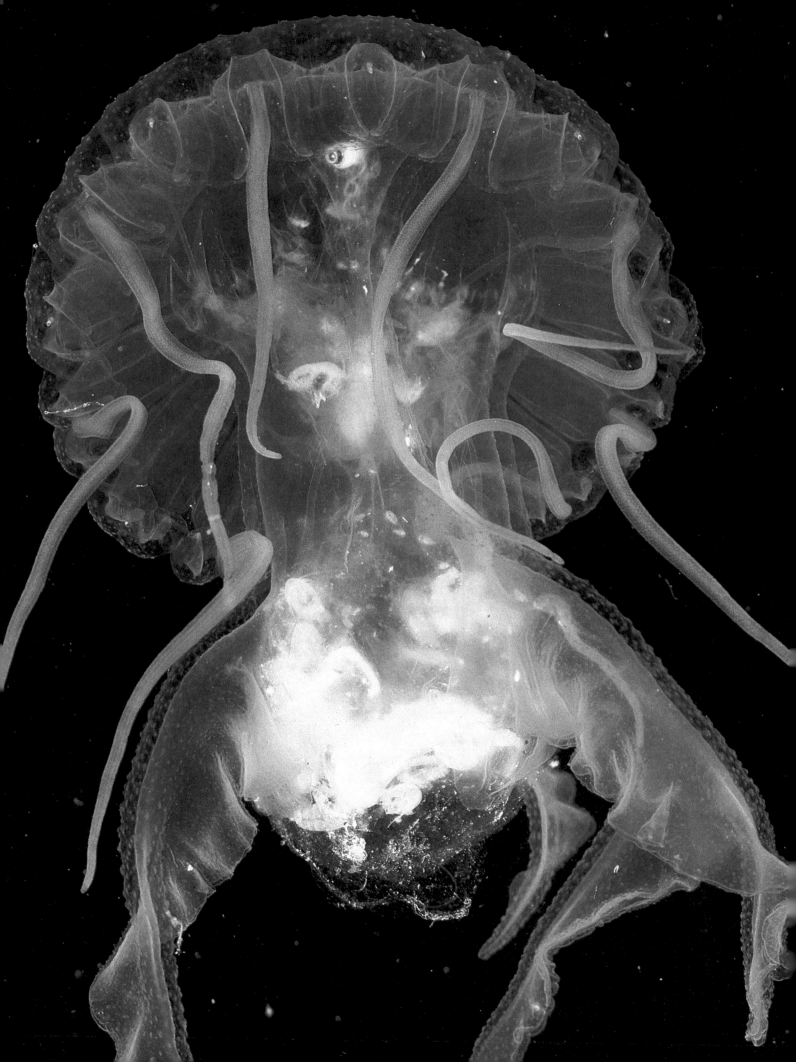

Traditionally, the cnidarians and ctenophores have been united as a single group because they share radial symmetry. The radial symmetry of ctenophores is, however, incomplete and there are many profound differences between the two groups. For example, ctenophores are hermaphrodites, do not form colonies and lack the typical stinging cells of the cnidarians, known as nematocysts. On the other hand, the flatworms share several characteristics with the comb-jellies. There is no overwhelming case for linking any two of the groups, and zoologists might in the end have to settle for saying that all three diverged before the fundamental characters of each developed.

## A profusion of worms

A group which *does* appear to be related to the flatworms and has evolved from them is the ribbon-worms or proboscis worms (Nemertea). Like the flatworms they have a ciliated epidermis, solid bodies and tubular excretory organs called protonephridia. But they have several advances over the flatworms, including their gut, which has an anus and is therefore "one-way". They also possess a primitive circulatory system and a special feeding structure, the proboscis.

The next stage in evolution is best represented by the nematodes (roundworms) and the rotifers (wheel animals). Typical features are the consistent presence of an anus, a well-developed muscle system, and fewer cilia on the body surface. These animals also retain the same cell number once adult, so that growth consists of increasing cell size rather that quantity, an interesting innovation that proved to be something of a dead-end in evolutionary terms.

Besides the nematodes there are six other phyla of worm-like creatures which achieve about the same level of sophistication, although they are distinctly different in some respects: the hair-worms, scale worms, spiny-skinned worms, priapulus worms and spiny-headed worms. These tiny worm-like creatures all tend to look very much alike without the aid of a microscope, but properly magnified, the structural variety they reveal is astonishing. Of all of them, however, by far the most successful are the nematodes. The unusual structure of their cuticle, which is keratinized to make it highly impermeable, and their efficient locomotion has resulted in their penetrating almost every conceivable habitat. They are found in all marine and freshwater sediments, and in terrestrial soils. As parasites they are in almost all animals and plants, and are responsible for many human diseases.

▲ A free-living freshwater nematode. There are over 12,000 named species of nematode, but many more undoubtedly remain to be discovered. They are almost ubiquitous and occur in staggering numbers. Non-parasitic forms include the "eelworms" found in soil.

▼ Rotifers grazing on the cells of a green alga. The pointed tail helps them keep their grip. A chewing structure, the mastax, made of tough cuticle, opens up a variety of dietary possibilities to rotifers. Some are predatory, while a few are parasitic.

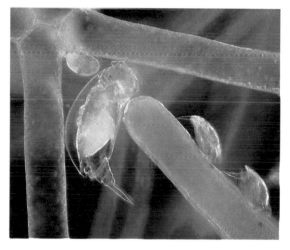

► Not a seaweed, but a colony of bryozoans, or moss animals. Each tiny "cell" contains an individual animal enclosed in a box-like shell with a lid. From this protective shell, each animal extrudes its lophophore to feed – they can be seen forming a fuzzy halo around the colony.

◄ The jellyfish Pelagia noctiluca has four membranous extensions of its mouth which hang down below the tentacles and assist in feeding. It produces a luminescent mucus if alarmed – this probably helps to deter predators by warning of the jellyfish's painful sting.

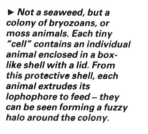

## Moss animals

Moss animals (ectoprocts or bryozoans) are small but abundant colonial filter-feeders, forming fronds, encrusting mats and even stem-like structures. Each colony consists of a number of individuals or zooids, each enclosed in a calcareous box or tube, feeding by means of a lophophore – a ring of ciliated tentacles. They might, at first glance, be mistaken for small corals or colonial hydroids, but structurally they are much more complex than the cnidarians. For one thing, they possess a body cavity known as a coelom (♦ page 74), a feature of more advanced invertebrates. Muscles attached to the animal's box-like body case can contract to increase the pressure of the body fluid in the coelom, and this inflates the lophophore. If the lophophore is threatened, retractor muscles pull it back into the body case and a hard operculum closes to protect it.

# Invertebrate Body Plans

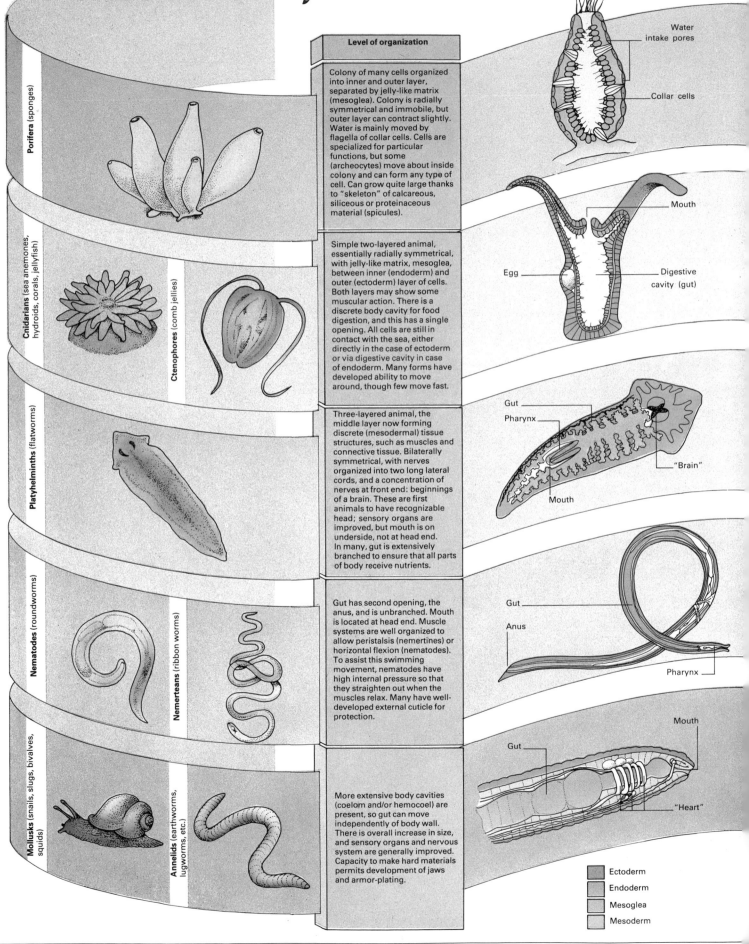

**Porifera** (sponges)

**Level of organization**

Colony of many cells organized into inner and outer layer, separated by jelly-like matrix (mesoglea). Colony is radially symmetrical and immobile, but outer layer can contract slightly. Water is mainly moved by flagella of collar cells. Cells are specialized for particular functions, but some (archeocytes) move about inside colony and can form any type of cell. Can grow quite large thanks to "skeleton" of calcareous, siliceous or proteinaceous material (spicules).

Water intake pores

Collar cells

**Cnidarians** (sea anemones, hydroids, corals, jellyfish)

**Ctenophores** (comb jellies)

Simple two-layered animal, essentially radially symmetrical, with jelly-like matrix, mesoglea, between inner (endoderm) and outer (ectoderm) layer of cells. Both layers may show some muscular action. There is a discrete body cavity for food digestion, and this has a single opening. All cells are still in contact with the sea, either directly in the case of ectoderm or via digestive cavity in case of endoderm. Many forms have developed ability to move around, though few move fast.

Mouth

Egg

Digestive cavity (gut)

**Platyhelminths** (flatworms)

Three-layered animal, the middle layer now forming discrete (mesodermal) tissue structures, such as muscles and connective tissue. Bilaterally symmetrical, with nerves organized into two long lateral cords, and a concentration of nerves at front end: beginnings of a brain. These are first animals to have recognizable head; sensory organs are improved, but mouth is on underside, not at head end. In many, gut is extensively branched to ensure that all parts of body receive nutrients.

Gut

Pharynx

"Brain"

Mouth

**Nematodes** (roundworms)

**Nemerteans** (ribbon worms)

Gut has second opening, the anus, and is unbranched. Mouth is located at head end. Muscle systems are well organized to allow peristalsis (nemertines) or horizontal flexion (nematodes). To assist this swimming movement, nematodes have high internal pressure so that they straighten out when the muscles relax. Many have well-developed external cuticle for protection.

Gut

Anus

Pharynx

**Mollusks** (snails, slugs, bivalves, squids)

**Annelids** (earthworms, lugworms, etc.)

More extensive body cavities (coelom and/or hemocoel) are present, so gut can move independently of body wall. There is overall increase in size, and sensory organs and nervous system are generally improved. Capacity to make hard materials permits development of jaws and armor-plating.

Mouth

Gut

"Heart"

| | Ectoderm |
| | Endoderm |
| | Mesoglea |
| | Mesoderm |

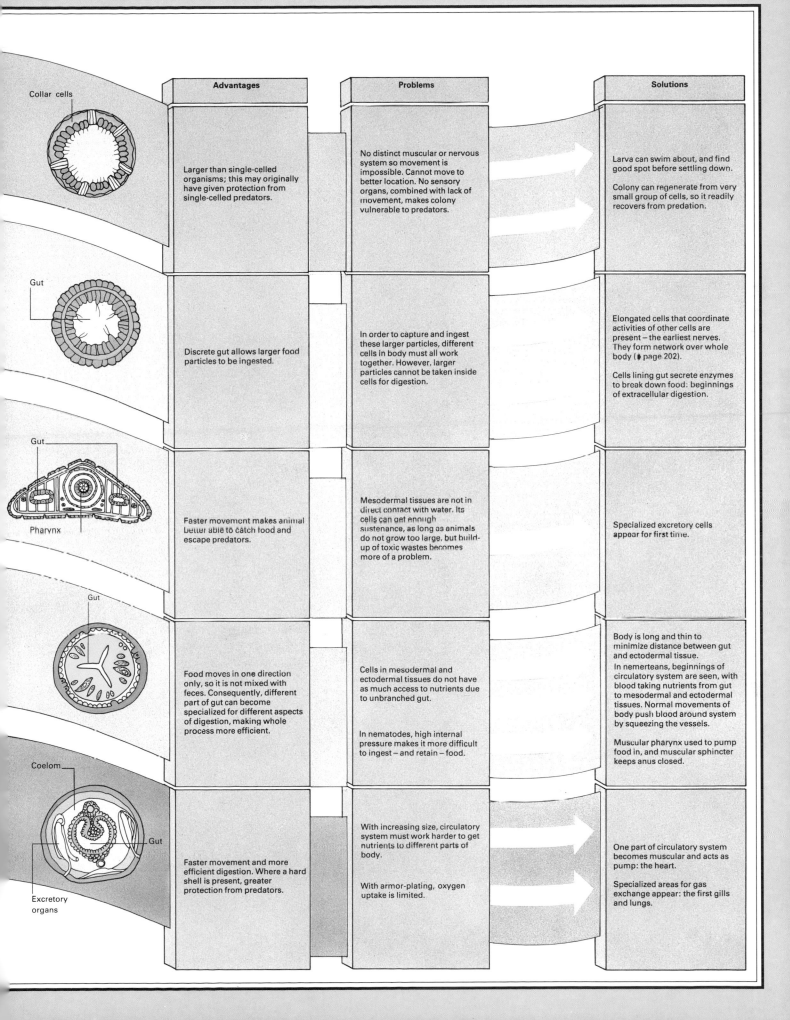

| | Advantages | Problems | Solutions |
|---|---|---|---|

**Collar cells**

Larger than single-celled organisms; this may originally have given protection from single-celled predators.

No distinct muscular or nervous system so movement is impossible. Cannot move to better location. No sensory organs, combined with lack of movement, makes colony vulnerable to predators.

Larva can swim about, and find good spot before settling down.

Colony can regenerate from very small group of cells, so it readily recovers from predation.

**Gut**

Discrete gut allows larger food particles to be ingested.

In order to capture and ingest these larger particles, different cells in body must all work together. However, larger particles cannot be taken inside cells for digestion.

Elongated cells that coordinate activities of other cells are present – the earliest nerves. They form network over whole body (♦ page 202).

Cells lining gut secrete enzymes to break down food: beginnings of extracellular digestion.

**Gut**

**Pharynx**

Faster movement makes animal better able to catch food and escape predators.

Mesodermal tissues are not in direct contact with water. Its cells can get enough sustenance, as long as animals do not grow too large, but build-up of toxic wastes becomes more of a problem.

Specialized excretory cells appear for first time.

**Gut**

Food moves in one direction only, so it is not mixed with feces. Consequently, different part of gut can become specialized for different aspects of digestion, making whole process more efficient.

Cells in mesodermal and ectodermal tissues do not have as much access to nutrients due to unbranched gut.

In nematodes, high internal pressure makes it more difficult to ingest – and retain – food.

Body is long and thin to minimize distance between gut and ectodermal tissue.

In nemerteans, beginnings of circulatory system are seen, with blood taking nutrients from gut to mesodermal and ectodermal tissues. Normal movements of body push blood around system by squeezing the vessels.

Muscular pharynx used to pump food in, and muscular sphincter keeps anus closed.

**Coelom**

**Gut**

**Excretory organs**

Faster movement and more efficient digestion. Where a hard shell is present, greater protection from predators.

With increasing size, circulatory system must work harder to get nutrients to different parts of body.

With armor-plating, oxygen uptake is limited.

One part of circulatory system becomes muscular and acts as pump: the heart.

Specialized areas for gas exchange appear: the first gills and lungs.

*Annelid worms achieved greater size by segmentation*

## Body cavities

Most animals measuring more than a few millimeters across have fluid-filled body cavities, which arise in the course of their development. These cavities are often classified into three types: pseudocoelom, hemocoel and coelom.

The first of these is thought to be derived from the blastocoel – the cavity that is formed when the multiplying cells of the fertilized egg first form a hollow ball (◆ page 162). In some groups, like the rotifers, the blastocoel cavity apparently persists and is called a pseudocoelom. The second type of cavity, the hemocoel, is found in arthropods and the majority of mollusks – animals that have an "open" circulatory system (◆ page 184). The name hemocoel is given to the cavities in the mesoderm within which the blood circulates. The third type of cavity, the coelom, is also located in the mesoderm, and is formed (◆ page 89) when the mesodermal tissue splits to create internal spaces or encloses a space as it develops from the ectoderm.

The formation of a coelomic space typically results in two layers of muscle, one lining the body wall and the other surrounding the gut. This is advantageous because it allows the gut to move independently of the rest of the body. (The hemocoel confers similar advantages on mollusks and arthropods.) The coelomic fluid can also supplement the circulatory system by transporting oxygen, and it can become the container in which eggs or sperm are stored before release. Ducts to the outside carry the eggs or sperm, and can also remove wastes. The presence of a large fluid-filled body cavity has also been exploited in locomotion. Contraction of the muscles surrounding a part of the body can squeeze out the fluid, leading to an extension elsewhere, the basis of many sorts of movement by soft-bodied animals.

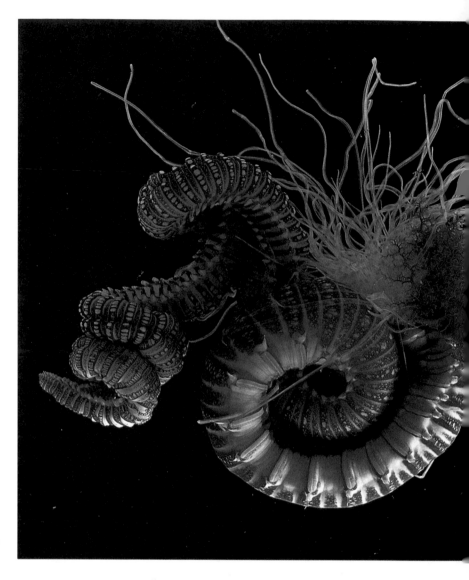

▶ **Two species of filter-feeding polychaete annelids, the one above having been removed from its protective tube.**

## Filter feeders

Many lower invertebrates specialize in the collection of minute particles (single-celled algae, animal larvae and organic debris) from the sea. Among polychaetes, these filter-feeders have multiplied the appendages of the head, to form a crown of tentacles through which a water current is drawn by cilia. The bivalve mollusks catch food in a different way, using their gills, which are greatly extended to form fine filters (◆ page 77). Water is drawn in through an inhalent siphon, filtered, and then spat out through an exhalent siphon.

In addition, there are many minor groups of filter-feeders, and several of them, including the phoronid worms, the moss animals (◆ page 71), and the lampshells (◆ page 78) have a specialized organ for feeding, known as a lophophore. This consists of a ring of ciliated tentacles surrounding the mouth. Because the tentacles are hollow, containing an extension of the coelom, they can be forced in and out by changes in body-fluid pressure. The similarities between the feeding apparatus suggest that, despite their superficial differences, these minor groups may be related to each other.

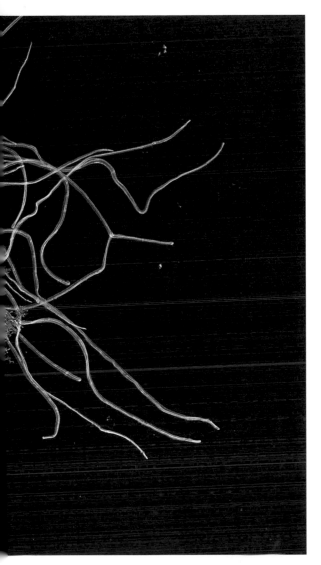

## More of the same: segmentation

Flatworms, nematodes, and the like are successful creatures. They manage to be very numerous and widespread in a variety of habitats, but they are necessarily small. A world populated by such creatures was waiting for exploitation by opportunists that were able in some manner to grow bigger.

The annelids were the first group to achieve this sort of breakthrough, and they did it in an interesting way: by replicating the same structures over and over again, thus getting a large animal "on the cheap", genetically speaking. This phenomenon is known as metameric segmentation. If considered a segment at a time, an annelid is a simple creature. Each segment includes a nervous ganglion capable of organizing basic sequences of movements via its muscles. It also includes a length of gut, blood vessels, excretory and reproductive apparatus: nothing very remarkable or sophisticated, for all these structures are already present in flatworms or proboscis worms. What the annelids hit upon was the advantage to be gained from stringing together a whole series of such units, with little or no increase in nervous complexity. Peristalsis, with each segment in turn becoming long and thin and then short and fat, introduces new possibilities for forcing a way through the substrate. With lateral extensions to each segment (parapodia) a form of walking became possible, and an increase in the size of the parapodia made for efficient swimming. Increased size, more powerful sensory equipment, and the development of hardened jaws, made annelid worms formidable predators.

We know little about the early history of the annelids. Fossils with a distinctly annelid look about them are found in Precambrian rocks, and it seems likely that these evolved into the range of creatures we find today: predators and detritus feeders, burrowers, parasites and a host of filter-feeding organisms. A regular feature of animal evolution is that each new "design" rapidly diversifies, devising a whole range of new ways of doing old jobs. As the first successful large animals, it is not surprising that the annelids gave rise to a wide variety of specialized forms.

▶ *A free-living polychaete worm. The parapodia of polychaetes are muscular, paddle-like extensions from each segment. They bear two bundles of bristle-like chaetae and a pair of sensory tentacles, the cirri. The polychaetes get their name from the fact that they have many chaetae per segment, whereas oligochaetes have just a few, and the leeches have none.*

▶▶ *Most leeches are blood-suckers, but some feed on small invertebrates. They are believed to have evolved from the oligochaete annelids – of which the earthworm is the most familiar example – by becoming specialized for a predatory or parasitic way of life. Unlike other annelids, they lack chaetae altogether, and instead have suckers at each end of the body to aid locomotion.*

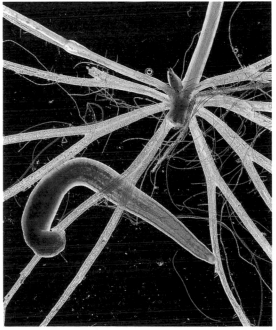

*Some desert snails can survive for years between infrequent rains*

## Mollusks: the unsegmented solution

Hard on the heels of the annelids, the members of a second group of animals were increasing in size in quite a different way. The mollusks are not segmented, and they represent a quite separate development from the root stock of platyhelminth-like creatures. Their most characteristic feature, the shell, probably evolved quite early, providing a protection for the exposed back of the animal as it crawled along the seabed. Covering any part of the body limits gas exchange, however, so a parallel development would have been the specialization of a part of the body surface for the collection of oxygen – gills – and the means to distribute it to the rest of the body – a more efficient, oxygen-carrying circulatory system. Mollusks have a very characteristic sort of gill, the ctenidium, which is one reason for believing that, despite their very diverse appearance, they all shared a common ancestor. Gills are necessarily delicate and were enclosed in a cavity below the shell – the mantle cavity, another persistent molluskan feature. Also typically molluskan, though best developed in the gastropods (slugs and snails), is the radula, a rasping tongue which equips them to eat plants, as gardeners know all too well.

The mollusks fall into five main groups, but two of these – the chitons and the tusk shells – are not very numerous. A third group, the cephalopods (squids, octopuses and cuttlefish) also have relatively few species, but their remarkable advances in intelligence and speed make them of particular interest (◗ page 78). The remaining two

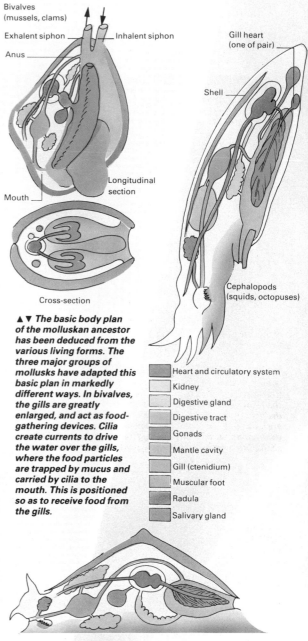

▲ ▼ *The basic body plan of the molluskan ancestor has been deduced from the various living forms. The three major groups of mollusks have adapted this basic plan in markedly different ways. In bivalves, the gills are greatly enlarged, and act as food-gathering devices. Cilia create currents to drive the water over the gills, where the food particles are trapped by mucus and carried by cilia to the mouth. This is positioned so as to receive food from the gills.*

Heart and circulatory system
Kidney
Digestive gland
Digestive tract
Gonads
Mantle cavity
Gill (ctenidium)
Muscular foot
Radula
Salivary gland

Hypothetical mollusk ancestor

► *Mussels – typical bivalve mollusks – in the process of filtering water for food. Both siphons are visible – the inhalent one is edged with sensory tentacles, which monitor the water as it is taken in, while the exhalent siphon has a smooth edge.*

▼ *The articulated shells of chitons earned them the name coat-of-mail shells. It was once believed that their shell was a primitive feature, a reminder of their segmented past, but the idea that mollusks evolved from segmented ancestors is now disputed.*

### Molluskan puzzles

*The chitons or coat-of-mail shells are, for the most part, inconspicuous creatures, living on the surface of rocks between the tidemarks, browsing on the film of algae. Their characteristic feature is the dorsal shield: eight overlapping strips of shell which allow the animal to curl up like a woodlouse. Their interest to zoologists is their relative simplicity: they have a small brain, rather unsophisticated sensory organs, and a ladder-like nervous system, not unlike that of a flatworm. The chitons are plainly primitive mollusks, and their eight shell plates used to be seen as a lingering indication of a segmented ancestry. In view of the current debate over whether ancestral mollusks really were segmented, the evolutionary status of the chitons is uncertain. Their articulated shells may be secondary features, acquired for defensive purposes, rather than the vestiges of segmentation.*

*◄ In modern cephalopods, the shell is greatly reduced, internalized or lost. The body has a streamlined shape, and the mantle cavity has become a muscular organ, used for jet propulsion. To sustain the more active way of life there are improvements in the sensory, nervous and circulatory systems. The main heart is larger, and a pair of extra hearts boost the supply of blood to the gills.*

Gastropods (snails, slugs)

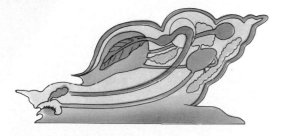

*▲▼ In gastropods, the body has been twisted through 180° (torsion), so that the mantle cavity is at the front. This allows the animal to withdraw its head into the mantle cavity when danger threatens. In many terrestrial gastropods, the gills are lost and the mantle cavity acts as a lung. Many gastropods, such as this sea slug (below), have lost their shells, but most still undergo torsion as a relic of their past.*

groups far outnumber the others, and have adapted to an enormous range of niches worldwide. In the case of gastropods (slugs and snails) this includes terrestrial habitats, with the coiled shell offering protection from drought, so that some desert snails can survive for years between infrequent rains. Those without shells – the slugs – are protected by a layer of mucus. Gastropods come in a wide range of sizes, from tiny millimeter-long sea slugs to some of the largest invertebrates. They include herbivores, browsing animals (which use the radula to rasp off thin layers of algae), scavengers and even outright predators. The commonest victims of predatory gastropods are bivalve mollusks (see below), which cannot easily escape. The radula is used to bore a hole in the shell of the bivalve. Some cone shells however, prey on fish, which they stab with a poisoned harpoon, an extreme modification of the radula.

The second highly successful class of mollusks, the bivalves or lamellibranchs (oysters, clams and mussels), have developed their gills as feeding devices (◀ page 74). Most bivalves move around rather little, preferring to stay hidden beneath the mud or sand, with only their siphons protruding. Despite their unobtrusive life-style, bivalves are important animals so far as we are concerned. As "shellfish" they are eaten in enormous quantities, they clog up our underwater machinery, and some of them, including the misnamed shipworm, devote their lives to the destruction of jetties and boats, using the sharp edges of their shells to bore into the wood.

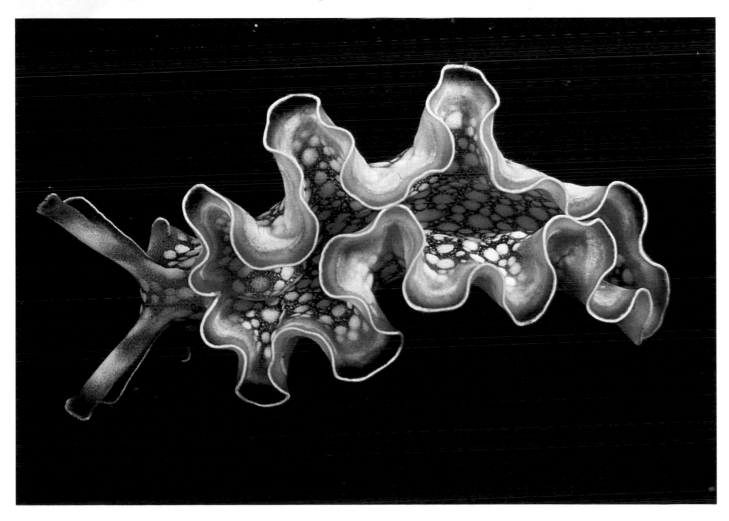

► *Fossil ammonites, one sectioned to display the inner chambers. By using these as gas-filled floats, the early cephalopods achieved great success. The ammonites underwent numerous radiations and extinctions during the Mesozoic, and are much loved by geologists, because each strata has its own distinctive species. They died out altogether at the same time as the dinosaurs.*

### The thinking invertebrates

The aristocracy of the phylum Molluska is a group called the cephalopods: the squids, cuttlefish and octopuses. The first cephalopods were hardly distinguishable from gastropods and had small coiled shells. There was, however, a critical difference. Cephalopod shells were chambered, with sections partitioned off as the animal grew and moved forward. Successive chambers were drained of water and became filled with gas, so that the animals were able to float in mid-water, out of reach of the bottom-crawling predators, but themselves able to drop on their prey from above. The success of this tactic was immediate. By the mid-Paleozoic, cephalopods, notably the nautiloids and ammonites, dominated the seas. Some species attained lengths of 4m – the first really large animals that the world had seen.

Catastrophe followed. The ancestors of the ray-finned fish evolved in freshwater and returned to the sea. They were faster and more maneuverable than earlier fish, and it nearly finished the cephalopods. Eventually, nearly all of the shelled forms were eliminated, so that today only Nautilus exists, a relic of times past (◆ page 11).

The cephalopods survived by becoming increasingly fish-like. The armored shell was progressively reduced, which besides lightening the animals, allowed the wall of the mantle cavity surrounding the gills to adopt a new and more active role as a muscular ventilating device: ciliary circulation of water across the gills would be inadequate for animals as large and active as cephalopods. From there, the wall of the mantle progressed to become a means of producing a powerful water jet, a novel and highly effective form of movement (◆ page 210). Jet propulsion gave cephalopods as much mobility as fish. They could escape suddenly, forward or backwards, and they could pounce on their unsuspecting prey. Alongside this increase in speed, cephalopods have developed brains that are larger than those of any other invertebrate, and eyes and organs of balance that show astonishing parallels with those of vertebrates (◆ page 218).

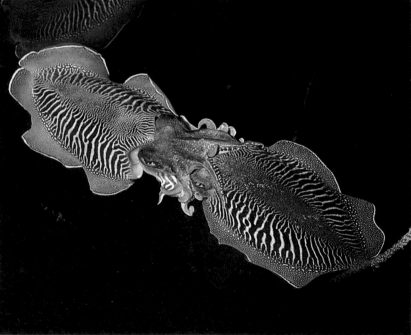

### Lampshell

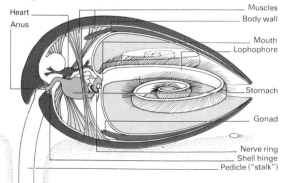

Heart
Anus
Muscles
Body wall
Mouth
Lophophore
Stomach
Gonad
Nerve ring
Shell hinge
Pedicle ("stalk")

▲ *Mating in cuttlefish, as in other cephalopods, involves transferring a packet of sperm, using a special tentacle, the hectocotylus. Here two male cuttlefish make a misguided effort to mate.*

◄ *In bivalve mollusks, the two halves of the shell are exactly equal, but in lamp shells the top and bottom halves of the shell are structurally distinct. The internal organs are also differently arranged.*

### Lampshells — not what they seem

The brachiopods or lampshells provide a good example of convergent evolution in invertebrates. They look very similar to bivalve mollusks, having two roughly equal halves to the shell, but this similarity is deceptive: within is an animal quite unlike a mollusk. Like bivalves, lampshells are filter-feeders, but they sift food particles from the water by means of a lophophore (◆ page 74). As in bivalves, the shell protects this delicate feeding apparatus. The brachiopods' modest place in the modern invertebrate world represents a substantial decline from their heyday. Fossil shells show nearly 30,000 species, now mostly extinct.

## 9

# Arthropods

*An all-over suit of armor...The key to success...The drawbacks of growth...Evolutionary history...Insects – 90 percent of all arthropods...Pioneers of land and air... PERSPECTIVE...The first arthropods...Water bears and sea spiders...Silk production...Undiscovered insects*

▲ *A Pacific lobster with its newly molted cuticle.*

Four out of every five animal species alive on earth today are arthropods, members of a prolific and diverse group which includes the insects, crabs, shrimps, spiders, scorpions, millipedes, centipedes and a host of lesser-known organisms. The phenomenal success of these invertebrates can be attributed, at least in part, to their external skeleton – an all-over suit of armor, which varies in form from the smooth shiny casing of a beetle, to the soft flexible bag covering a caterpillar, or the chalky "shell" of a crab. The exoskeleton is made of a specialized polysaccharide (◗ page 130) called chitin, although in crustaceans this is combined with calcium salts for extra hardness.

The main advantage of having the skeleton on the outside lies in the strength-to-weight ratio. For a given quantity of skeletal material, a thin, tubular structure is far stronger than a solid rod-like skeleton, such as our own. And besides providing something for the muscles to pull on (◗ page 207), an external skeleton offers support and protection to the internal organs. Paradoxically, the value of such a skeleton in protecting the body's organs is best shown by the vertebrates, for despite having an internal skeleton, their most vital organs are effectively surrounded by bone – the skull cradles the brain and the ribcage encases the heart and lungs. In addition to these structural roles, the exoskeleton gives arthropods some defense against predators, parasites and pathogens. It lines the fore and hind regions of the gut as well as part of the reproductive system. In terrestrial arthropods it also lines the respiratory structures: the tracheae of insects, millipedes and centipedes, and the lung-books of spiders and scorpions.

### Growing pains

*Although the exoskeleton is highly adaptable, it has one great drawback: it limits the size of the arthropod. To grow bigger the animal must discard its old exoskeleton and grow a new and bigger one to replace it. During this period of molting the animal lacks support and is very vulnerable to predators. In water, support is less of a problem because water is dense and buoys the flabby animal up. On land, arthropods have to inflate themselves with air to keep their body-shape while the new exoskeleton is hardening. The larger the animal, the more severe the problem becomes, which explains, perhaps, why terrestrial arthropods are relatively small. The largest land-dweller, a longhorn beetle, Titanus giganteus, from the Amazon basin, is just 20cm long, whereas the largest marine arthropod, the Japanese spider crab Macrocheira kaempferi, has a leg span of 3·5m.*

### The trilobites

*The trilobites were a group of primitive arthropods, now extinct, but once abundant in the warm seas of the Cambrian and Ordovician periods (between 400 and 600 million years ago). Most trilobites were bottom dwellers, moving over sand or scavenging in mud for food. They were ovoid in shape, strongly flattened and segmented, with a size range from a microscopic 0·5mm to a gigantic 70cm. Each body segment had a pair of jointed limbs. These were in two parts (biramous), with an outer gill-bearing branch and an inner branch. On the four pairs of limbs immediately behind the head this inner branch was developed for walking. Biramous limbs are also found in the crustaceans, suggesting a possible common ancestry, although not everyone is agreed on this.*

## Arthropod origins

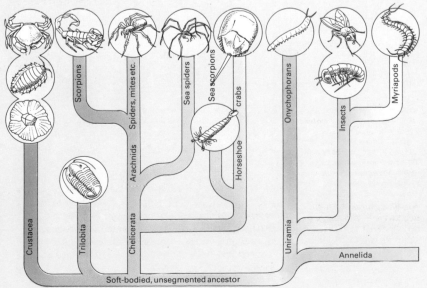

Scorpions • Spiders, mites etc. • Sea spiders • Sea scorpions • crabs • Onychophorans • Insects • Myriapods

Crustacea • Trilobita • Chelicerata • Arachnids • Horseshoe • Uniramia • Annelida

Soft-bodied, unsegmented ancestor

◀ *The arthropods are no longer considered to be a single phylum with a common segmented ancestor. Instead, they are thought to include at least three major lines that have evolved independently from unsegmented worm-like animals. The extinct trilobites may be a fourth independent line, or they could be related to the crustaceans.*

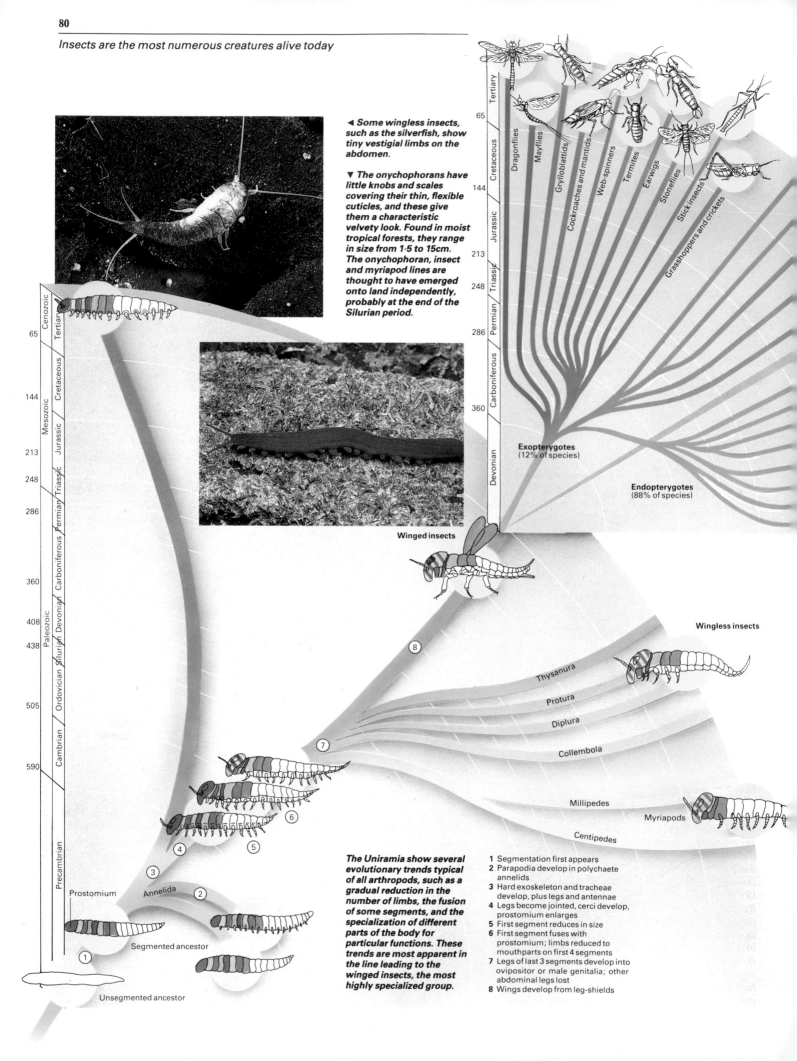

◄ Some wingless insects, such as the silverfish, show tiny vestigial limbs on the abdomen.

▼ The onychophorans have little knobs and scales covering their thin, flexible cuticles, and these give them a characteristic velvety look. Found in moist tropical forests, they range in size from 1·5 to 15cm. The onychophoran, insect and myriapod lines are thought to have emerged onto land independently, probably at the end of the Silurian period.

Tertiary
Cretaceous
144
Jurassic
213
Triassic
248
Permian
286
Carboniferous
360
Devonian

Dragonflies
Mayflies
Grylloblattids
Cockroaches and mantids
Web-spinners
Termites
Earwigs
Stoneflies
Stick insects
Grasshoppers and crickets

**Exopterygotes** (12% of species)

**Endopterygotes** (88% of species)

**Winged insects**

Cenozoic
65
Tertiary
Cretaceous
144
Mesozoic
Jurassic
213
Triassic
248
Permian
286
Carboniferous
360
408
Paleozoic
438
Devonian
Silurian
Ordovician
505
Cambrian
590
Precambrian

Prostomium
Annelida

**Winged insects**

8

**Wingless insects**

Thysanura
Protura
Diplura
Collembola

Millipedes
Myriapods
Centipedes

7

6

4
3
5
2

1

Segmented ancestor

Unsegmented ancestor

The Uniramia show several evolutionary trends typical of all arthropods, such as a gradual reduction in the number of limbs, the fusion of some segments, and the specialization of different parts of the body for particular functions. These trends are most apparent in the line leading to the winged insects, the most highly specialized group.

1 Segmentation first appears
2 Parapodia develop in polychaete annelids
3 Hard exoskeleton and tracheae develop, plus legs and antennae
4 Legs become jointed, cerci develop, prostomium enlarges
5 First segment reduces in size
6 First segment fuses with prostomium; limbs reduced to mouthparts on first 4 segments
7 Legs of last 3 segments develop into ovipositor or male genitalia; other abdominal legs lost
8 Wings develop from leg-shields

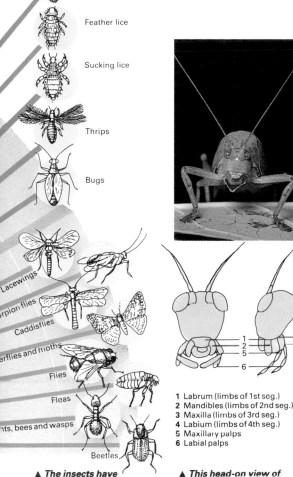

Book lice and bark lice

Feather lice

Sucking lice

Thrips

Bugs

Lacewings

Scorpion flies

Caddisflies

Butterflies and moths

Flies

Fleas

Ants, bees and wasps

Beetles

1 Labrum (limbs of 1st seg.)
2 Mandibles (limbs of 2nd seg.)
3 Maxilla (limbs of 3rd seg.)
4 Labium (limbs of 4th seg.)
5 Maxillary palps
6 Labial palps

▲ The insects have diverged enormously, largely as a result of their domination of terrestrial habitats. The most ancient of the insects are the dragonflies and mayflies, whose fossils are found in coal seams of the Carboniferous period.

▲ This head-on view of a katydid, or bush-cricket, shows the multiple mouthparts, which are all derived from the limbs of the first four segments. The insect's organs of hearing are also visible, as membrane-covered openings on its legs.

## Sugar armor

*Arthropod exoskeletons gain their strength from a mixture of proteins and a polysaccharide called chitin, which is made up of N-acetyl-glucosamine: glucose with an amino-acetyl group attached. The long chitin molecules form bonds between the amino groups, and the proteins are also cross-linked making the exoskeleton rigid. (Softer, more flexible cuticles, such as those of caterpillars, have undergone less cross-linkage than the hard exterior of a beetle or scorpion.)*

*The fact that all arthropods use chitin in their exoskeleton might seem an odd coincidence, since they are no longer thought to have descended from a common ancestor. But N-acetyl-glucosamine is one of the constituents of bacterial cell walls, chitin-like compounds are found in annelids, and chitin itself forms the cell wall of many fungi. So the fact that several arthropod groups have independently developed it, is not all that surprising. Its presence in all arthropods seems to be an example of convergent or parallel evolution (♦ page 13), and suggests that chitin has some special advantages for this type of exoskeleton which no other molecule can match.*

## Evolution of the arthropods

The arthropods have an evolutionary history of more than 600 million years, but, unfortunately, there are no fossils of their earliest ancestors. Because they share an exoskeleton and jointed limbs, biologists once assumed that all arthropods arose from the same stock. Yet recent studies of living arthropods suggest that there are three main lines which evolved independently: the Crustacea, the Uniramia and the Chelicerata. One major difference is that the limbs of crustaceans are branched (biramous) whereas those of insects and myriapods are always unbranched, even in their embryonic stages – hence their new name "Uniramia". Chelicerates also have unbranched limbs but they lack antennae and have a different set of mouthparts, in particular a pair of pincer-like structures called chelicerae. Finally there are fundamental differences between the groups in the way the legs and jaws move, which suggest that each developed limbs independently.

Of the ancestors themselves, little is known, and only the worm-like onychophorans provide any real evidence. The construction of their body wall and excretory system is distinctly annelid-like, but they also have appendages that could have been the forerunners of the insects' segmented limbs, as well as insect-like antennae, and tracheae for breathing. All this suggests that the Uniramia evolved from annelid stock, but the ancestors of the other groups – the crustaceans and chelicerates – remain a complete mystery.

Although separate, these three arthropod lines show signs of parallel evolution – that is, they have changed in similar ways during their evolutionary development. The ancestors of the arthropods had one pair of limbs per segment, but most modern species have fewer appendages, especially in the abdominal region, and their body segments have become fused to form larger structures with specialist functions, such as the head, with its complex mouthparts.

## The insects

About 90 percent of all arthropods are insects – more than a million species are known. Their most remarkable feature is, undoubtedly, the power of flight – something no other invertebrate group has achieved. Whereas in birds and bats the wings are modified legs, insects' wings developed from plates that once covered the tops of the limbs. Fossil insects have been found showing these plates, which probably started out as protective shields for vulnerable leg joints, but then became useful for gliding, and eventually developed into powerful flying organs.

Winged insects can be divided into two groups on the basis of how they develop. The majority (88 percent) of insect species have a larval stage – a caterpillar, maggot or grub – that is distinctly different from the adult. These insects, called "endopterygotes", undergo a complete change, or metamorphosis, to the adult form. This requires them to enter a dormant, pupal stage while the larval structures are transformed into adult characteristics. Typical endopterygotes include beetles (order Coleoptera), bees, wasps and ants (Hymenoptera), flies (Diptera) and butterflies and moths (Lepidoptera). The other group of insects, known as "exopterygotes", have no equivalent of the caterpillar stage: they hatch from the egg as miniature adults, but without wings or reproductive structures. This 12 percent of the class Insecta includes the grasshoppers, crickets and locusts (Orthoptera), termites (Isoptera), bugs (Hemiptera), dragonflies (Odonata), mayflies (Ephemeroptera) and cockroaches and mantids (Dictyoptera).

## Water bears

The tiny animals known as "water bears" are a puzzle to zoologists and are often placed in a phylum of their own – the Tardigrada. Their affinities are far from clear, but they are thought to be related to the Uniramia. The biggest is no more than 1mm in length, yet these tiny animals have a nervous system, specialized mouthparts for sucking plant juices, a digestive tract, legs with hooked claws and a chitinous exoskeleton. They also show signs of segmentation.

Tardigrades are remarkably abundant, particularly in rainwater gutters. A few species are found in freshwater or marine habitats, but most live in the thin water film that covers the leaves of mosses. Well adapted to this unpredictable habitat, they have an extraordinary capacity to tolerate desiccation (◊ page 192). If water becomes available again the tardigrades swell up and begin to function normally. This can occur many years later – some dried moss kept in a museum for over a century yielded living tardigrades.

▲ A dragonfly's wings are operated directly by the flight muscles, whereas in some advanced insects, a different mechanism has evolved (◊ page 205).

▼ The very small size of water bears makes classification difficult. But their intricate structure suggests descent from much larger animals.

▶ A ladybird emerges from its pupa. The insertion of a pupal stage into the life cycle allows the larva and adult to specialize in different directions.

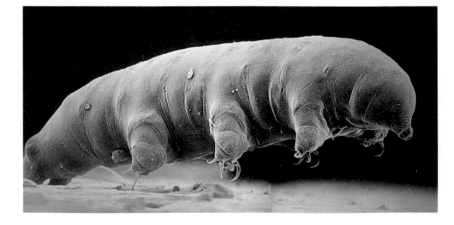

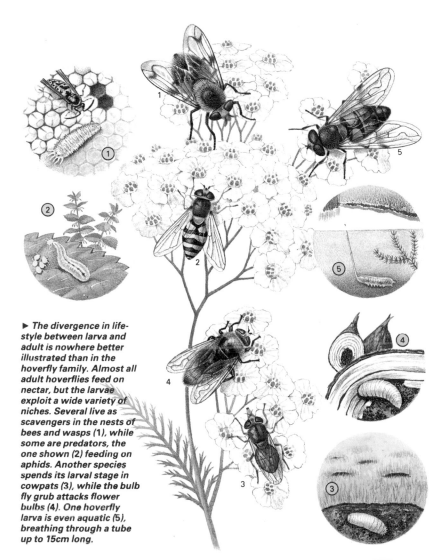

▶ The divergence in life-style between larva and adult is nowhere better illustrated than in the hoverfly family. Almost all adult hoverflies feed on nectar, but the larvae exploit a wide variety of niches. Several live as scavengers in the nests of bees and wasps (1), while some are predators, the one shown (2) feeding on aphids. Another species spends its larval stage in cowpats (3), while the bulb fly grub attacks flower bulbs (4). One hoverfly larva is even aquatic (5), breathing through a tube up to 15cm long.

### A different way of life

The first winged insects were probably exopterygotes, so-called because their wings develop externally, whereas in endopterygotes, such as butterflies, beetles and flies, the wings develop inside the pupa.

Endopterygotes developed from their exopterygote ancestors when the latter were already well established, in the late Carboniferous, but they have gone on to become enormously successful. Today there are seven times as many endopterygote species as exopterygote, and the beetles alone boast at least 350,000 species, accounting for a third of the world's animal species. One reason for this enormous expansion is the flexibility their three-stage life cycle offers. Interposing a pupal stage, in which the body tissues are completely reorganized, allows the larva and adult to pursue fundamentally different ways of life. The adult, for example, can specialize in feeding on nectar and pollen — substances that would be highly unsuitable for a non-flying larva. And the larva too can develop a specialized way of life, such as parasitism, relying on the winged adult stage for dispersal. Winter survival is another benefit. The larvae can develop burrowing forms that overwinter in the soil or in wood, surviving periods of cold that prove fatal for the adults.

### Inside the pupa

The larva of an endopterygote looks completely different from the adult, but its internal organs are often much the same. The typical adult features, such as wings, mouthparts, segmented legs and reproductive organs, are all of ectodermal origin – that is, they develop from the outermost layer of body cells. In fact, the beginnings of all these structures are there in the larva as "imaginal buds", little clusters of cells, waiting for the right conditions to trigger them into action. What happens inside the pupa is that the larva's fat reserves (which account for much of its body weight) are broken down, and used to fuel the growth of the adult structures.

Hormones control the transformation. In the larva there are large amounts of the juvenile hormone which suppresses the development of the imaginal buds. The juvenile hormone level later decreases, either in response to the larva's growth, or at an external signal such as temperature or daylength. When it drops below a certain level, pupation occurs.

### History repeated

Exactly how endopterygotes developed from exopterygotes is not known. However, the process seems to have been partially repeated, in more recent times, by one family of exopterygotes. The family involved is the Aleyrodidae, tiny whiteflies, which often infest cabbages. They are members of the Hemiptera (bug) order, but whereas most Hemiptera are typical exopterygotes, the whiteflies have a sedentary larva which goes through a stage known as a pseudo-pupa before reaching maturity. The larva stops feeding, thickens and develops a pill-shaped outer covering within which it develops into an adult.

Horseshoe crabs are not crabs at all, but marine relatives of the spiders

**Sea spiders**
*Pycnogonids (above) are a curious group of marine chelicerates. Despite their common name, sea spiders are only distantly related to the true spiders. Pycnogonids feed on sessile animals such as sea anemones, corals and bryozoans, pulling them off with their chelicerae. Because the animal has no real body, many of the internal organs extend into the legs. Sideways extensions of the gut pass almost to the tips of the legs. The reproductive organs also extend into the limbs and females can be recognized by the bulges in their legs as the eggs develop within them.*

## Pioneers of land and air

The very first animals to move out onto dry land were the forerunners of insects, centipedes and arachnids. To colonize the land, arthropods had to overcome certain problems, principally that of desiccation. All land animals must reduce their loss of water, and the smaller they are the more critical this becomes, because small animals have a large surface area in relation to their body mass. Insects and arachnids (the terrestrial chelicerates – spiders, scorpions, ticks and mites) have a waterproof layer of wax that protects them from drying up, but myriapods do not, forcing them to keep to moist places in the soil and under leaf litter. For insects, the colonization of the land soon led to the conquest of the air: flight evolved early and is found in almost all insect groups. It enabled them to spread rapidly to new habitats and to exploit temporary or patchily distributed resources.

Thanks to this ease of distribution and to their great adaptability, insects (and to a lesser extent arachnids) have established themselves in virtually every available habitat on land. Yet they have failed to invade the sea. This absence might suggest that insects cannot adapt to marine conditions, but if the fly *Psilopa petrolei* can live and breed in something as inhospitable as pools of crude oil around the oil wells of southern California, then seawater is unlikely to pose an insurmount-

◄ *Pseudoscorpions are one of the six main orders of arachnids, or terrestrial chelicerates. Pseudoscorpions are generally quite small and have massive pincers but, unlike the scorpions, no tail. Here they are using their pincers to attach themselves to a beetle which will unwittingly transport them to a new, and perhaps more promising, habitat.*

▲ *A large, almost circular, carapace covers most of the horseshoe crab, Limulus. Underneath, there are four pairs of walking legs, plus abdominal appendages that are flattened to form gills. Despite the name, these are not crabs at all, but chelicerates, the sole survivors of a largely extinct marine group, which goes back 400 million years and included the extinct sea scorpions, or eurypterids.*

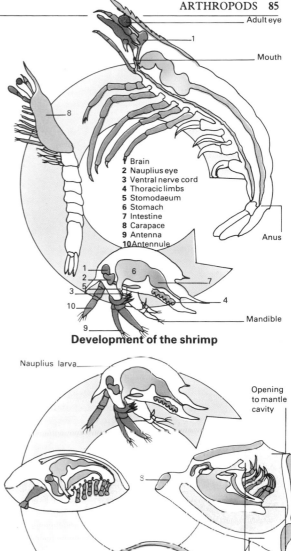

Development of the shrimp

1 Brain
2 Nauplius eye
3 Ventral nerve cord
4 Thoracic limbs
5 Stomodaeum
6 Stomach
7 Intestine
8 Carapace
9 Antenna
10 Antennule

Adult eye
Mouth
Anus
Mandible

able problem. Marine insects, however, would have to compete with the crustaceans, already well established in the sea: it seems as though the crustaceans have the ocean environment "sewn up". There is only one truly sea-dwelling insect, the ocean skater *Halobates*, which is a maritime version of the common pond skater, living at the interface of sea and air.

The other side of the coin is that crustaceans have largely failed to conquer dry land. A few, such as the fiddler crabs, come out briefly, and one, the robber crab, even climbs trees to feed on coconuts. But the only permanently terrestrial crustaceans are woodlice, and even they are not fully adapted to life on land, being largely confined, like the myriapods, to dark and humid crevices.

Despite having carved out their separate domains of land and sea, the insects and crustaceans do compete for the resources of freshwater habitats. But because aquatic insects have re-invaded freshwater from the land, most still breathe air, rather than using true gills to extract oxygen from water, as do the crustaceans. However, some have secondarily developed gill-like organs. A few spiders have also colonized freshwater, and, like most insects, they need to return to the air to breathe. Water spiders actually create a small aerial habitat underwater, by trapping a bubble of air in a silken bag.

Nauplius larva

Opening to mantle cavity

Anus
Hemocoel
Mouth

Development of the barnacle

◀▼ The water fleas (left), and copepods (below) are freshwater crustaceans, just visible to the naked eye as frenetically moving specks. Rather like the nauplius larva, they have large antennae which are used for movement, even in adults. The body is encased in a transparent shell. Both are seen here carrying their eggs, the water flea internally, the copepod in two external sacs.

▲ The basic crustacean body-plan, such as that of a shrimp, has been remodeled in barnacles to produce a sessile filter-feeder with a strong shell. The shell plates open at the top and the limbs move in and out: effectively the barnacle stands on its head and kicks food into its mouth. The pattern of development from the nauplius larva shows how this is arrived at.

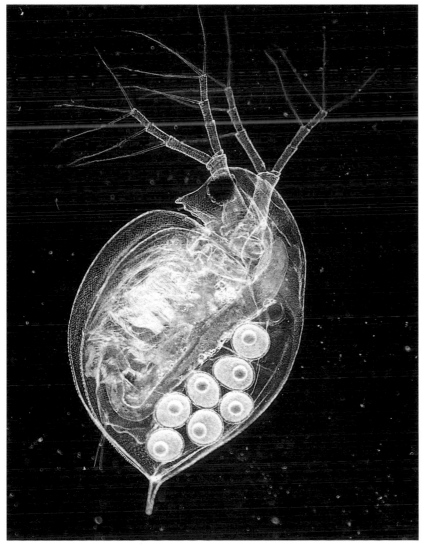

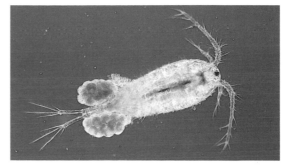

## The secrets of success

Why are the arthropods, in general, and the insects, in particular, so successful? There are many factors involved, but the absence of any other truly terrestrial invertebrates is probably important. Only the insects and arachnids have completely overcome the need for a watery or humid environment. On land, invertebrates have an advantage over vertebrates in being smaller and highly mobile. They are only 3–4mm long, on average, and this means that their habitats are also small. To large grazing animals like cows, grass is a more or less uniform carpet of food, but to small insects it is a highly varied habitat. The grass has roots, stems, leaves (with upper and lower surfaces), flowers, pollen and seeds. Given this huge range of microhabitats on one simple plant, it is clear that the terrestrial world as a whole contains a vast array of niches for tiny creatures. The sea also offers many microhabitats, although there are other invertebrates to compete with, and the overall variety of opportunities is far smaller than on land. Plants are limited to coastal waters and the ocean's upper layers, where sunlight can penetrate – this leaves the bulk of the sea as a very uniform, plantless habitat, and probably explains why there are fewer crustacean species than either insects or arachnids.

Arthropods are also notable for the adaptabililty of their body organs and structures – those originally used for one purpose can be readily modified by natural selection to take on others. The respiratory system of insects, for example, consists of branching tubes (tracheae) which ramify through the body, delivering oxygen to the cells. This system has also taken on a range of non-respiratory functions. The tracheae have been turned into air sacs which can cushion beating wings, or insulate flight muscles from the cold, or even act as resonators to amplify the singing of cicadas. Tracheae in the eyes of moths reflect light, to improve vision at dusk. Such flexibility gives the arthropods the potential to continually adapt to new conditions.

### Silk: the arthropods' synthetic fiber

*An interesting parallel development in three arthropod groups is the production of a liquid protein which hardens in air to form a strong elastic thread – silk. The most noted silk-producers are the spiders and mites, but some insects also produce silk, and so do a group of tiny myriapods known as symphylans. Most spiders produce several types which are used in different ways – as a lifeline, to construct webs, tunnels, funnels or other snares, or as a protective covering for eggs. Young spiderlings also use long strands of silk to disperse to new habitats, the silk strand being caught up by air currents and carrying the spiderling with it. Insects use silk mainly for protection. Many moths and butterflies produce it to support or encase the pupal stage. Silkworms, caterpillars of the moth Bombyx mori, are farmed for the dense silken cocoon they spin.*

▲ *Arachnids parasitizing another arachnid – red mites attached to the body of a harvestman.*

▼ *Fibers spun from liquid protein make up this garden spider's magnificent silken web.*

◄ *The order Solifugae go under a variety of common names, including sun-spiders, wind-scorpions and camel-spiders. Found only in warmer regions of the world, they are notable for their enormous chelicerae, which can represent a third of the body length in some species. Their bite is not venomous but depends on sheer muscle-power for its devastating effect. Here a sun-spider munches away on a locust.*

### Insects incognito

*Less than 80 years ago researchers discovered a new order of insects, the Grylloblattodea, living among the snowfields of the Canadian Rockies. They feed on lowland insects that are carried up on air currents and deposited on the snow. Grylloblattids share some of the characteristics of two insect orders, the cockroaches and the crickets, and they may be relics of an ancestral group. More recently, in 1982, a biologist studying tropical rainforest beetles found 600 new species living in just one type of tree. If other rainforest trees harbor similar numbers, there may be as many as 30 million insect species on Earth, rather than the 2–3 million of earlier estimates.*

*The effectiveness of five-fold symmetry...A unique way of moving and feeding...Variations on a theme... Evolutionary origin...PERSPECTIVE...Why five?... A common ancestor with the chordates?...The chewing apparatus of sea urchins*

**How tube-feet work**

1 The tube foot at rest.
2 Ampulla muscles contract, forcing fluid down into tube foot, which elongates. A stiff sheath of collagen around the foot prevents it from ballooning outwards.
3 Tube foot extends until it reaches a rock. Circular muscles at tip contract to raise centre, creating suction. Mucus strengthens its grip.
4 Ampulla muscles relax, allowing fluid back in, and longitudinal muscles contract, shortening tube foot and pulling starfish towards rock.

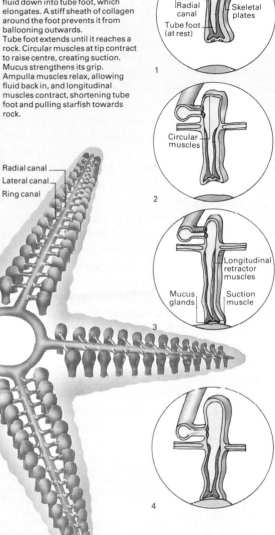

The headquarters of the US Department of Defense and a collection of spiny-skinned marine creatures have one striking feature in common: they both exhibit a five-fold radial symmetry. Like the Pentagon building with its five sides, a starfish has five symmetrically radiating "arms". Headless, brainless and unsegmented, these distinctive marine animals are the echinoderms – some 6,000 living species which include the starfish, sea urchins, brittle stars and sea lilies. Their pentamerism is virtually unique in the animal world.

Just beneath the surface of a typical echinoderm is a rigid skeleton – a series of fixed or movable plates (ossicles), each a single crystal of calcite (calcium carbonate). Often these plates bear spines, which can be quite painful for the unwary human.

Echinoderms have also invented a unique way of collecting food and getting about. Hundreds of hydraulically-powered "tube-feet" project through perforations in the skeletal plates. They are extended by pressurized body fluids contained in a network of vessels known as the water-vascular system. In most echinoderms the tube-feet bear suckers which can grip surfaces.

Starfishes can use their tube-feet to move around and to pull against objects in their environment. Many are active carnivores and prey upon shellfish, such as scallops, by prising the animals open. The scallop has powerful muscles holding the shell together but it is the first to become exhausted, because the starfish can bring fresh tube-feet into the struggle as the working ones tire. The adaptable tube-feet also help the animals to take up oxygen, which diffuses across the thin outer membranes. And at the tips of the arms, a few tube-feet are modified into eyespots.

◄▲► *The tube-feet of starfish are equipped with suckers, which enable them to grip surfaces – such as a scallop's shell (left). Each tube-foot and its associated ampulla has a central cavity, which is part of the coelom (◊ page 74). This cavity is linked via lateral canals to a radial canal running along the arm, and then to the central ring canal. However, a valve in the lateral canal prevents any movement of fluid out of the tube-foot. Fluid can only move into the foot, which it does if the pressure in the foot falls, thus maintaining the status quo. The role of the ring and radial canals is simply to compensate for any leakage and keep the tube-feet full.*

*The embryos of echinoderms show them to be related to the vertebrates*

The starfish's fellow echinoderms are variations on a common theme. The brittle stars move about using the whole of their long, slender arms as oars, hence their tube-feet are less well-developed and lack suckers. Surprisingly common on the bottom of the world's seas, they can form dense mats containing 1,000–2,000 animals per square meter. They flourish by catching small creatures and picking up organic debris from the ocean floor. When threatened by a predator, a brittle star may break off one of its own arms by simultaneously contracting the muscles between two "vertebrae" (modified ossicles) in the arm. The predator is often content to eat the arm and let its owner escape. In time, the brittle star can grow a new limb.

The sea urchins have dispensed with arms altogether and their ossicles are fused to form an external shell or "test", made up of closely fitted plates surrounding a spherical or flattened body. They move about and manipulate their food via rows of tube-feet and elaborate movable spines connected to muscles in the skin. Many sea urchins feed on algae and other large marine plants, or on barnacles and sponges. Some sea urchins, such as the heart-urchin and the sand dollars have bilateral symmetry superimposed on the basic pentamerous plan, so they have a definable "head" and "tail" which presumably helps them to burrow in sand.

The five-fold symmetry of the echinoderms is least obvious among the sea cucumbers, which creep over the sea floor, often at great depths in the ocean. Their sausage-shaped, muscular bodies have no arms or spines, although their skeleton persists as microscopic ossicles in the flexible body wall. Some live by catching plankton on their mucous-covered tentacles, which are modified tube-feet. Others eat the sediment and extract organic material from it.

A strikingly different group of echinoderms are the crinoids – the feather stars and sea lilies. Some 5,000 species of crinoids flourished in the Carboniferous era, but today only about 600 species remain. They are stalked and live permanently attached to the seabed. Their ten arms sport tube-feet that are modified into feeding tentacles, collecting detritus, plankton and microorganisms from the sea.

## A question of strength

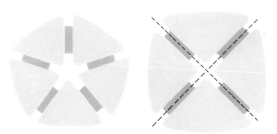

▲ *Five skeletal plates give an almost circular outline with no planes of weakness because none of the sutures lie opposite each other. A skeleton of four plates would have two planes of weakness, and six plates gives three such planes.*

### Why five?

*Fives are rare in the animal world. Why, then, have echinoderms chosen to develop a body that is divided into five parts arranged around a central axis – that is, a pentamerous radial symmetry? An appealing explanation is suggested by Professor David Nicols who argues that a five-fold symmetry gives the animal the strongest arrangement of its skeletal plates.*

*The plates of the adult echinoderm are knitted together by connective tissue, and these suture lines are the weakest point in the skeleton, especially as it develops. Hence it would be best for the animal to avoid having two suture lines directly opposite one another. Such a state of affairs can be achieved only by having an odd number of plates, and five is the smallest odd number that can give a basically circular cross section.*

▶ *In feather stars, or crinoids, the suckerless tube-feet collect minute food particles on their mucus-coated surfaces. They push the food particles towards a groove that runs down each arm to the mouth.*

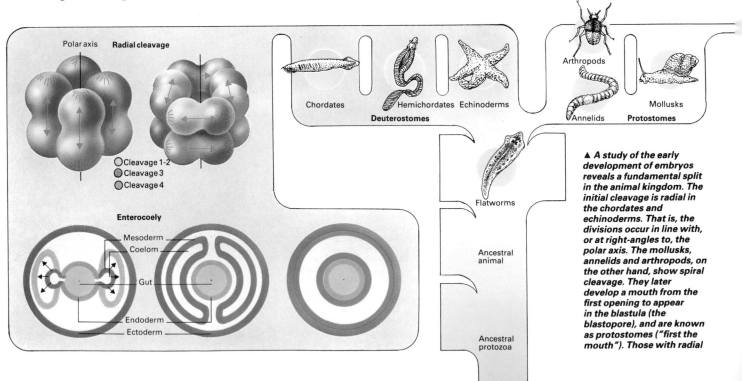

▲ *A study of the early development of embryos reveals a fundamental split in the animal kingdom. The initial cleavage is radial in the chordates and echinoderms. That is, the divisions occur in line with, or at right-angles to, the polar axis. The mollusks, annelids and arthropods, on the other hand, show spiral cleavage. They later develop a mouth from the first opening to appear in the blastula (the blastopore), and are known as protostomes ("first the mouth"). Those with radial*

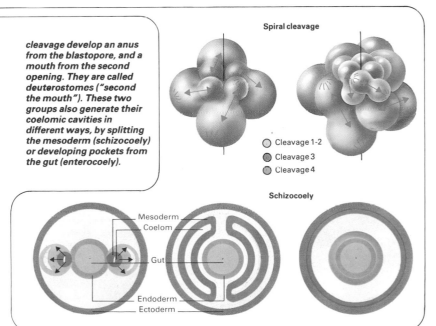

cleavage develop an anus from the blastopore, and a mouth from the second opening. They are called deuterostomes ("second the mouth"). These two groups also generate their coelomic cavities in different ways, by splitting the mesoderm (schizocoely) or developing pockets from the gut (enterocoely).

**Spiral cleavage**

○ Cleavage 1-2
● Cleavage 3
● Cleavage 4

**Schizocoely**

Mesoderm
Coelom
Gut
Endoderm
Ectoderm

### On the road to vertebrates

The embryonic stages of echinoderms mark them out from most other invertebrates. At a very early stage of development, an echinoderm is a simple hollow ball of cells, known as the blastula. In echinoderms, the first opening in this ball of cells develops into the anus, rather than the mouth as in other invertebrates. Such embryos are said to be deuterostomes. Apart from the echinoderms, the only major group to show this characteristic is the chordates, the group that includes vertebrates. The embryos of these two groups both show radial cleavage (see left) and form a coelom, or cavity, in a similar fashion. All this suggests that long ago the echinoderms shared a common ancestor with the chordates (◆ see page 93).

Another line of evidence comes from the larvae of the hemichordates, a minor group of animals closely related to the chordates. Their larvae are so similar to those of starfish that at first researchers mistook the hemichordate larva for that of an echinoderm. Despite this close resemblance, the creatures that led to the modern echinoderms must have split off from the chordate line very early on, probably in the Precambrian.

**See also**
Lower Invertebrates 67-78
Lower Chordates 91-94
Development 161-168

The evolutionary origin of the echinoderms is still controversial. They first appeared in the Cambrian (or perhaps even earlier) and became extremely abundant towards the end of the Paleozoic era. The radial symmetry that is so characteristic of the group probably arose in ancestors that were sessile, as the crinoids are today. Most fossil echinoderms were filter-feeders attached to the ocean floor and it makes sense to be radially symmetrical if one is a stalked creature surrounded on all sides by shallow seas, rich in planktonic food. Yet the fossil evidence does not provide a clear answer, in part because the oldest echinoderms, from the early Cambrian, were very diverse: as well as the eocrinoids and edrioasteroids which were sessile radially symmetrical creatures, they also include the carpoids, which were bilaterally symmetrical.

◄ **Fossil crinoids flourished in shallow, well-lit waters. These sessile forms were later replaced in coastal waters by free-swimming echinoderms, and the remaining sessile crinoids are mostly found in deep ocean water.**

▲ **A pearlfish leaves the safety of its sea cucumber host. It rests inside its body during the day, but, as far as is known, does not rely on the echinoderm for food. This is an example of a special type of symbiosis, known as inquilinism.**

### Living together

Echinoderms are striking individualists, on the whole. No echinoderm is a parasite – an unusual state of affairs, as most major groups of invertebrate animals contain at least a few parasitic members. Moreover, echinoderms rarely live commensally – in harmless association with other creatures. Yet there are a few interesting exceptions. In the Indo-Pacific, tiny brittle stars live on the undersurfaces of sand dollars. Other species of these commensal brittle stars inhabit the surface of feather stars, hanging onto their tentacles with their long arms. An outsider has also colonized one sort of echinoderm. The tropical pearlfish, which grows to about 12cm long, makes its home in sea cucumbers. This fish lives in the respiratory tree of the echinoderm, which is an outgrowth of the cloaca, the common exit of the reproductive and excretory systems. The pearlfish comes and goes through the anus of the sea cucumber, spending the day inside, and emerging to feed only at night.

### Aristotle's lantern

Sea urchins, in common with other echinoderms, lack jaws, but they compensate for this with a unique and complex chewing apparatus, known as Aristotle's lantern because it was first described by Aristotle. Five calcified plates, shaped rather like barbed arrowheads, are bound together by muscles and equipped with teeth. An urchin can protrude the lantern partially through its mouth to chew on algae and marine animals attached to rocks. Aristotle's lantern is a slow but efficient device, which enables urchins to feed on tough materials, including shell and cellulose, without having true jaws.

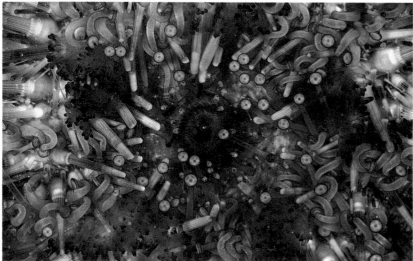

◄ **A mass of tube-feet and calcareous spines surround a sea urchin's mouth and help to manipulate its food. The five bony plates of the chewing apparatus – which were described as "lantern teeth" by Aristotle – break the food down into digestible pieces. This chewing apparatus allows sea urchins to feed on seaweeds and other tough foods.**

# Lower Chordates

*The phylum Chordata...Sea squirts and amphioxus...
The ancestor of vertebrates?...PERSPECTIVE...
Biochemical innovation in early free-swimming
chordates...Discovery of a conodont fossil...Fossil
calcichordates...Evolution of the bony skeleton...
Pedomorphosis – larvae that never grew up*

The phylum Chordata, which includes the lower chordates, fish, amphibians, reptiles, birds and mammals, is characterized by three main features. All chordates, at some stage in their lives, have a notochord – a strengthening spine made from cartilage that runs down the back. They also share a tubular dorsal nerve cord, just above the notochord, and at some stage, gill slits just behind the mouth. Most chordates belong to the subphylum Vertebrata. Their notochord is replaced, in the adult, by a bony backbone composed of separate elements, the vertebrae. The group of lower chordates – those that are not vertebrates – are less familiar, but they give us important clues about the origins of the group and of our own distant ancestors.

Among living chordates, only two groups lack a bony backbone: the tunicates, or sea squirts, and the cephalochordates, typified by the lancelet or amphioxus. Amphioxus exhibits, in rather diagrammatic form, the fundamental plan of vertebrates. Some 7cm long and roughly cigar-shaped, amphioxus has a tough notochord, a nerve cord running along the back, and gill slits along the sides of the chamber behind the mouth. It can swim through the waters by means of sideways contractions, much like a fish, using the blocks of muscles positioned along its body. Its elastic but incompressible notochord prevents the whole body from shortening when these muscles contract and allows the muscles to bend the body instead. As an adult it leads a sedentary life, half-buried in mud and sand on the seafloor, where it feeds by filtering organic particles from seawater. It draws the water in through its mouth and ejects it through the gill slits.

## A new way of life

The first free-swimming fish-like chordates probably appeared in the Ordovician, some 500 million years ago. These creatures, of which amphioxus is a living example, can be regarded as a major "advance" for the chordates, because, unlike the sessile, bag-like sea squirts (♦ page 92), individuals could exploit a variety of habitats, including the rich sea surface.

An advance in biochemistry probably played a part in their success. To fuel the muscles at the core of this more active life, the early free-swimming chordates exploited a new way of regenerating adenosine triphosphate, or ATP – the molecule that acts as a short-term energy store in the cell (♦ page 139). Cells release energy when they need it, by breaking off a phosphate from ATP, to form the energy-depleted form, adenosine diphosphate (ADP). When it comes to regenerating ATP, a ready source of phosphate is required, and the majority of invertebrates employ phosphoarginine for this purpose. All arthropods and mollusks, plus many bacteria, protozoans, cnidarians and flatworms, regenerate ATP in this way, but it seems to be a rather primitive process. In amphioxus and all vertebrates, another molecule, phosphocreatine, supplies the phosphate to rebuild ATP from ADP. Annelids, echinoderms and tunicates have both systems, so it seems as though, early in their evolution, the free-swimming chordates opted for the phosphocreatine system alone.

Phosphocreatine has a distinct advantage for a creature that needs a ready supply of energy to support an active life. Like phosphoarginine, it is formed from an amino acid (♦ page 134), in this case glycine, the simplest and most abundant of all amino acids. Because glycine is more readily available, the phosphocreatine system is more efficient, and it frees the much scarcer amino acid arginine for use in the synthesis of proteins. Thus the first fish-like animals ensured that they had a rich supply of energy for their active swimming in the sea, as well as plenty of protein to build muscle.

**Anatomy of amphioxus**

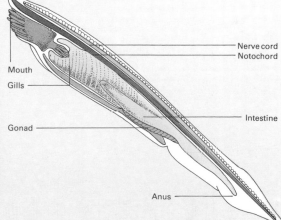

Nerve cord
Notochord
Mouth
Gills
Intestine
Gonad
Anus

◀ ▲ *The lancelet, or amphioxus, has a definite front end, but lacks well-developed sense organs and has little in the way of a brain. Moreover, the notochord runs right up to the "head", whereas in tunicate larvae – which are more plausible ancestors for the fish – it only strengthens the tail.*

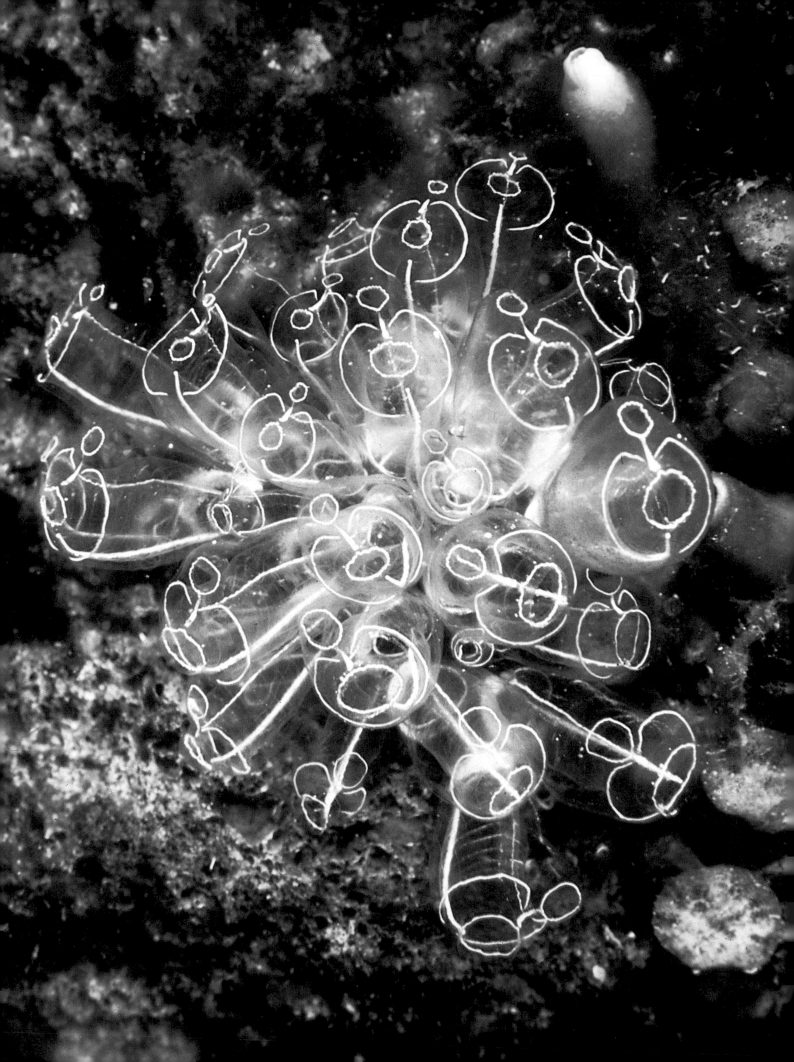

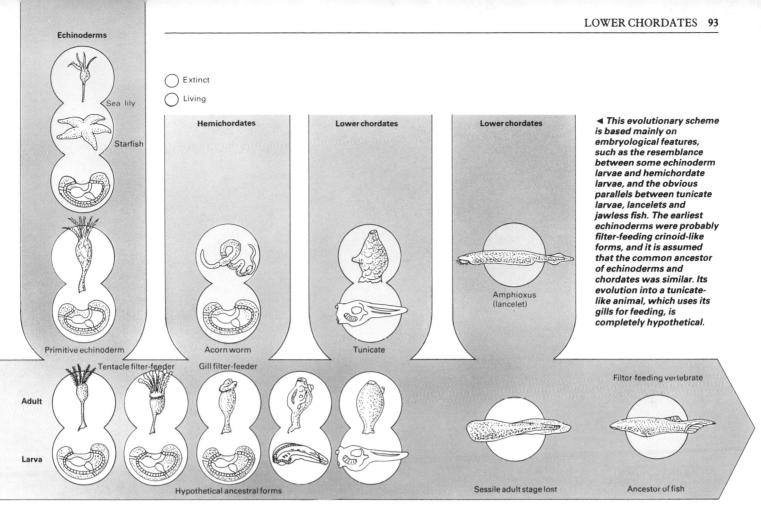

Echinoderms

○ Extinct
○ Living

Sea lily

Starfish

Hemichordates

Lower chordates

Lower chordates

Amphioxus
(lancelet)

◀ *This evolutionary scheme is based mainly on embryological features, such as the resemblance between some echinoderm larvae and hemichordate larvae, and the obvious parallels between tunicate larvae, lancelets and jawless fish. The earliest echinoderms were probably filter-feeding crinoid-like forms, and it is assumed that the common ancestor of echinoderms and chordates was similar. Its evolution into a tunicate-like animal, which uses its gills for feeding, is completely hypothetical.*

Primitive echinoderm

Acorn worm

Tunicate

Tentacle filter-feeder    Gill filter-feeder

Filter feeding vertebrate

**Adult**

**Larva**

Hypothetical ancestral forms

Sessile adult stage lost

Ancestor of fish

## Precocious and successful

*Slight changes in the relative rates of development of the body of an animal and of its reproductive ability may have major effects in evolution. Pedomorphosis, in which the sexual organs develop much more rapidly than the rest of the body, can be observed in some living amphibians (♦ page 101), and may have been a factor in the evolution of several species and groups. Indeed, it has been suggested that this process played a role in human evolution.*

*The change that occurred in the ancestors of the fish, and those of amphibians, seems to have been repeated in a group of living sea squirts, the larvaceans, which probably evolved from a tunicate ancestor. These do not have a fixed bag-like adult stage. Instead, the free-swimming larva becomes sexually mature without changing into the typical adult form.*

*◀▶ A group of sea squirts or tunicates. These bag-like animals take in water through an inhalent siphon, at the top, filter it through their gills, then eject it through the exhalent siphon at the side. As befits a sessile animal, the adult tunicate has a rather rudimentary nervous system, and the notochord that is a characteristic feature of the cephalo-chordates, such as amphioxus, is absent. Though well-developed in its tadpole-like larva (right), the notochord is lost during metamorphosis.*

Despite its resemblance to primitive jawless fish, several features of amphioxus indicate that it could not have been a direct ancestor to the vertebrates. Its excretory system is very different from the vertebrate kidney, in function and developmental origins. Furthermore, the creature has virtually no brain, and its notochord extends from the tip of the snout to the end of the tail – something not seen in any other chordate. Hence amphioxus and its fellow cephalochordates seem to have diverged from the line that led to vertebrates at an early stage.

The other group of lower chordates, the sea squirts, or tunicates, do not look at all like vertebrates, and are not really the sort of animal you would be proud to call your ancestor. Nevertheless, the sea squirts may give us a better idea of the vertebrate ancestor than amphioxus does. The adult sea squirt is a sessile bag-like organism with an outer coat made from protein and sugars. It lives attached to the seabed. Though itself an unlikely candidate for the progenitor of the fish, it has a free-swimming, tadpole-like larva about 1mm long, that looks much more promising. It has a definite head, a tough but flexible notochord that runs the length of the tail, and a hollow nerve cord above that. The sea squirt larva swims by swiftly moving its muscular tail in a fish-like manner. All these features suggest that it could be similar to the ancient chordate that evolved into the first vertebrate. But after a brief free-swimming existence, the larva settles on the seafloor and changes into the fixed adult condition. How then could the sea squirt larva have contributed to the adult form of succeeding generations?

Many biologists believe that both amphioxus and the ancestor of the fishes evolved from a chordate larva that simply never grew up. If it had precociously developed functional sex organs, so that it was able to breed, the adult fixed stage could quite easily have been dispensed with. This biological phenomenon, the development of adult sex organs in an otherwise juvenile body, is called pedomorphosis.

### From chalk to bone

The echinoderms' outer shell is made of crystals of calcite (calcium carbonate), familiar to us as chalk. But the bones of higher animals are strengthened by the mineral apatite (calcium phosphate). Exactly when the switch occurred in unknown, but the teeth of the conodonts (see below) contain apatite, and this is one reason for placing them with the chordates. The reason for the change from carbonate to phosphate is also far from certain. The fact that calcium carbonate is soluble in acids may be relevant. Perhaps a bone made of calcite would be eroded by acids in the body's tissues.

### Fossils that refuse to fit

The most widely accepted evolutionary scheme for the chordates and echinoderms is based on the embryology of living forms. Several common features of development link the two groups and point to the acorn worms as near relatives. Moreover, pedomorphosis provides a simple and plausible evolutionary origin for creatures like amphioxus and for the ancestral vertebrates.

Unfortunately, there are no fossils to support this evolutionary scheme, and certain fossils that might be ancestral obstinately refuse to fit in with it. Known as calcichordates, these occur in the Cambrian and Ordovician. Exactly how they lived is anybody's guess and it is even hard to say which end of the animal is which. But they would appear, in some respects, to be intermediate between echinoderms and chordates. Like echinoderms, they have plates of calcite (calcium carbonate) covering their bodies, and the calcified rings on their tail (or is it a stalk?) resemble the column of a crinoid. Yet these fossil animals are also bilaterally symmetrical (like chordates) and they might have had chordate-like gill slits – there is a series of marks on their flank that can be interpreted in this way.

A few paleontologists favor these anomalous creatures as descendants of some missing link between echinoderms and chordates, but most are more convinced by the embryological evidence. They prefer to classify calcichordates with a group of extinct echinoderms, known as carpoids, that were bilaterally symmetrical.

### A controversial fossil

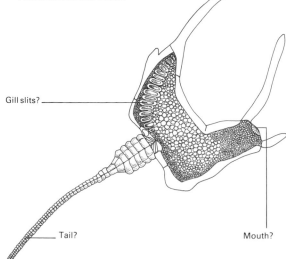

Gill slits?

Tail?

Mouth?

▲ The animals whose teeth are so abundant in the fossil record – the conodonts – remained elusive until recently. This fossil of a soft-bodied animal less than 4cm long was found in 1983, near Edinburgh, in Scotland. Typical conodont teeth were present in its head region.

◄ The calcichordates are among the most enigmatic and controversial of fossils. Some paleontologists see the parallel marks along the side of the body as gill slits, but others disagree. The opening labeled as a mouth here is regarded as the anus by some paleontologists.

### Dating with teeth

An intriguing feature of the fossil record, from the early Cambrian through to the Triassic (a period of about 400 million years), is the presence of conodont teeth. These teeth are so common and widespread that they can be used for dating rocks – distinctive forms occur at particular times. Until recently the owners of these teeth were a complete mystery – presumably the teeth were the only hard part in a soft-bodied animal. Soft bodies do fossilize occasionally, however, if the sediments in which they are buried are fine enough, and in 1983 a convincing conodont animal was found. The body is long with traces of segmented muscles and what may be a notochord. Broadly speaking it resembles a very thin and elongated amphioxus, and was probably related to it, if only distantly. How these incredibly successful animals lived, or why they eventually became extinct, is unknown.

*The diversity of fish...Jawless fish...The evolution of jaws...Fish without bones...Success of the ray-finned fish...Lobe-finned fish, ancestors of the amphibians... PERSPECTIVE...Reconciling Genesis and fossils...An aid to swimming...Last of the lungfish...Finding an "extinct" fish*

▲ *Hugh Miller, stonemason turned paleontologist.*

Most aquatic vertebrates are fish but, paradoxically, there is no single group called "fish" in the classification of the vertebrates. Whereas the terms "bird", "reptile" and "amphibian" each represent a single class of animal in taxonomy, "fish" corresponds to several separate classes – between six and nine, depending on which taxonomic scheme is followed. Three or more have living representatives. The two major classes alive today are the cartilaginous fish (sharks, dogfish and rays), and the ray-finned fish (salmon, herring and all the other familiar fishy species). Add to this the lobe-finned fish (lungfish and coelacanth), and the primitive jawless species, and it is clear that "fish" denotes a very diverse group. But, as the catch-all term might suggest, there is often a superficial similarity, and this is due to their shared way of life. Swimming demands particular adaptations, and the resemblance between a shark and a marlin, for example, or that between an eel and a lamprey, or a plaice and a ray, are all products of convergent evolution (◀ page 13).

### The first fish

The hagfish and lampreys are the last survivors of the earliest vertebrates: the jawless fish, or agnathans. These primitive fish were widespread in the seas of the Early Paleozoic, but most were quite different from the modern agnathans. Known as ostracoderms ("armor-skinned"), they all had thick bony plates covering the body. This heavy armor probably evolved as a defense against giant sea-scorpions, or eurypterids, which grew over 2m long and had pincers that could crush any unprotected animal.

During the age of the ostracoderms, some early fish evolved jaws, which was an important evolutionary advance. Jaws gave a better grip on food, helped to fend off predators, and enabled their owners to manipulate objects. Nutritional possibilities that were closed to the jawless fish began to be exploited by these novel animals, known as acanthodians and placoderms. In addition to jaws, they shared a second advance: strong, mobile fins which could be used in steering.

Cartilaginous fish – the sharks and rays – first appeared during the Devonian. The skeleton of these fish is made from cartilage, a tough flexible material similar to bone, but lacking its hard mineralization. The skeleton of all other vertebrates is initially made of cartilage, but as the embryo develops the mineral apatite is incorporated into the cartilaginous matrix to make bones. Hence biologists once thought that cartilaginous fish were very primitive, and had never evolved bone. But it is now known that all the earliest vertebrates had bone, so the cartilaginous fish must have evolved from fish with bones, and subsequently lost this characteristic. The only mineralized elements in a shark are its teeth and scales, and these are often the only parts to be fossilized.

### Miller's fish

*Many different groups of fish – the extinct ostracoderms, placoderms and acanthodians, as well as the earliest ray-finned fish and cartilaginous fish – are recorded in Devonian freshwater sediments. These remarkable fossils were found in the 1820s in the Old Red Sandstone of Scotland, by a stonemason, Hugh Miller (1802-56). He taught himself paleontology by studying these fossils, but being a deeply religious man, regarded them as relics of some ancient Creation. He believed that the heavily armored ostracoderms and placoderms were more advanced than living fish, and used them as an argument against the idea – put forward by Lamarck and others – that life had progressed from simple forms to complex forms. His books, which reconciled Genesis with geology, were immensely popular, and his suicide, in 1856, came as a terrible shock to Victorian society.*

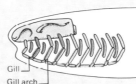

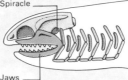

Gill
Gill arch

Spiracle

Jaws

◀ *Jaws are thought to have evolved from the gill arches of jawless fish. The exact details are uncertain, but it seems likely that the third gill arch developed into the jaw bones themselves, while the second gill arch became fused to the skull. The first gill arch was probably lost. The jaw hinge needed some extra support, and the fourth arch moved closer to the jaw to provide this. As a result the gill slit between the third and fourth arch was reduced to a small, round opening – the spiracle, still seen in some sharks.*

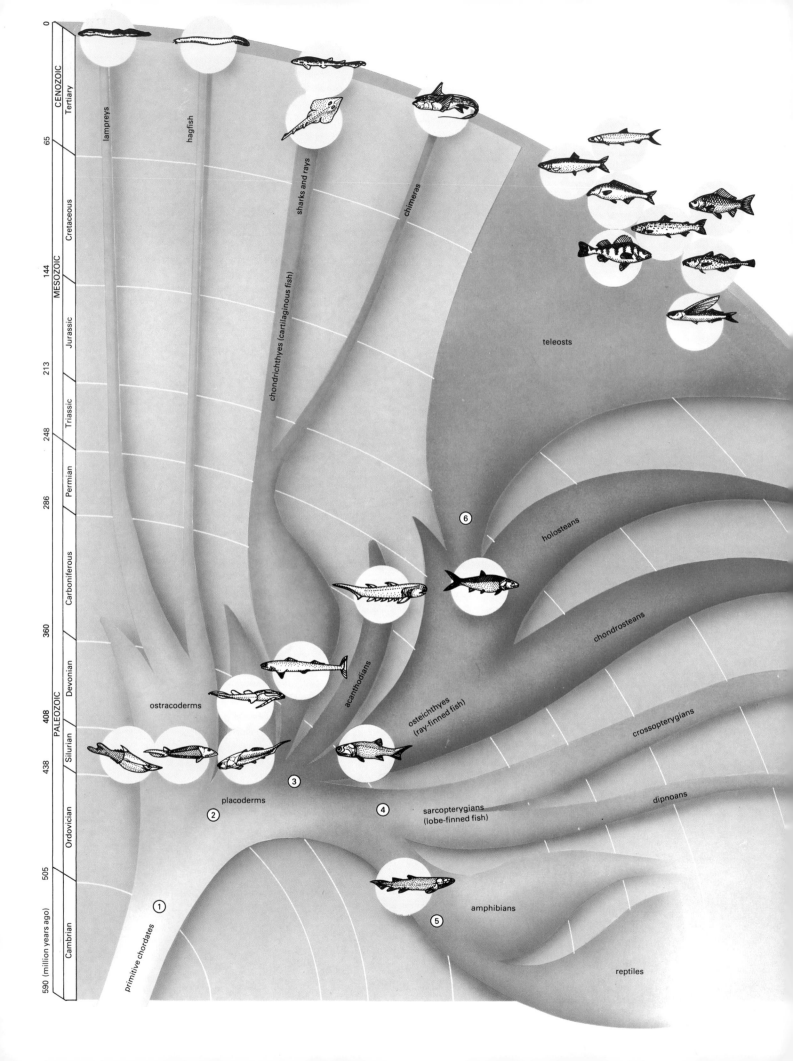

| 590 (million years ago) | 505 | | 438 | 408 | 360 | 286 | 248 | 213 | 144 | 65 | 0 |
|---|---|---|---|---|---|---|---|---|---|---|---|

PALEOZOIC

Cambrian | Ordovician | Silurian | Devonian | Carboniferous | Permian | Triassic | Jurassic | Cretaceous | Tertiary

MESOZOIC

CENOZOIC

primitive chordates

lampreys

hagfish

sharks and rays

chimeras

chondrichthyes (cartilaginous fish)

ostracoderms

placoderms

acanthodians

osteichthyes (ray-finned fish)

sarcopterygians (lobe-finned fish)

amphibians

reptiles

teleosts

holosteans

chondrosteans

crossopterygians

dipnoans

① ② ③ ④ ⑤ ⑥

1 First animals with a backbone appear
2 Hinged jaws and paired fins develop
3 Lungs develop, probably among freshwater fish in times of drought
4 Fleshy lobed fins develop, the forerunner of the tetrapod limb
5 Tetrapod limbs develop as the amphibian ancestors become more fully terrestrial
6 Swimbladder develops, probably from the lungs as the teleosts return to the sea

Invertebrates

Agnathans or jawless fish

"Fish"

Gnathostomes (jawed vetebrates)

Tetrapods (amphibians, reptiles, mammals and birds)

◀ *In this evolutionary tree, the width of each branch is roughly equivalent to the importance and abundance of the group, in terms of number of species. Except for living groups, these numbers are obviously estimates. They do not correspond to the actual number of species known from the fossil record, which is often very patchy and incomplete.*

▶ *A shoal of tarpon, typical teleost fish.*

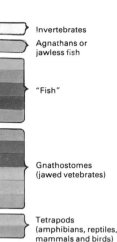

gars, bowfin

sturgeons, paddlefish

coelacanth

lungfish

## The ray-finned fish

The largest fish group, with more than 20,000 living species, is the ray-finned fish, also known, rather confusingly, as the "bony fish", despite the fact that agnathans and lobe-finned fish also have bones. The name was given to them because the other major fish group, in terms of numbers, is the cartilaginous fish, and the presence of mineralized bone was the simplest distinguishing feature between the two.

Ray-finned fish evolved at about the same time as the cartilaginous fish, and there are three major living groups. The first group, known as chondrosteans, appeared during the Devonian period, and were probably more agile than the early fish. They also displayed a greater range of adaptations: most of them were slender in shape, but some had very deep bodies, and others were protected by remarkably long spines. Only two groups of chondrosteans survive – the sturgeons and the paddlefish. The sturgeons have a few plates of bone set in the skin, as a vestige of their armor-plated ancestry.

The second step in the evolution of the ray-finned fish was taken by the holosteans; they had more flexible jaws, less armor and better developed fins. Such features made them more agile than their predecessors, and more adaptable in their feeding habits. Again only two groups survive: the gars and the bowfin.

The most advanced ray-finned fish, the teleosts, dominate the seas and rivers of today. The teleosts have specialized jaws in which the whole mouth can be pushed forwards in a sort of "pouting" expression, familiar to anyone who has kept goldfish. This allows teleosts to suck in small prey, and to feed with great precision. They are also lighter and more agile than the holosteans, and their tail fin is symmetrical. Most teleosts also have a specialized structure called the swimbladder, which allows them to control their buoyancy.

Another major group of fish, often known as the lobe-finned fish, arose in the Devonian, and became very diverse and numerous. There were two types of lobe-fins, lungfish and crossopterygians, and both types have living representatives, although these are rare remnants of their former importance. They are characterized by their elongated fins with a fleshy area in the middle, and by their lungs. The single living crossopterygian no longer uses its lungs for breathing, but the surviving lungfish have retained this ability. Like their ancestors they can either extract oxygen from the water with their gills, or breathe air by gulping it down into their lungs. The freshwater fish of the early Devonian needed this sort of versatility because the climate was very dry and warm, and many lakes and rivers became shallow and stagnant. Such water is low in oxygen, so the ability to breathe air was the key to survival for freshwater fish. It was from these slimy, stagnant waters, about 375 million years ago, that the earliest land-dwelling vertebrates – the first amphibians – emerged (◆ page 99).

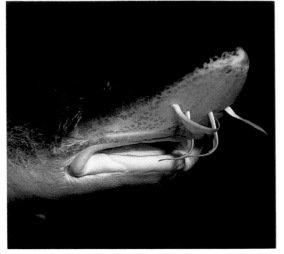

▲ Sturgeons are relics of some of the earliest ray-finned fish.

### Floating on air

*Sharks and their relatives, like human swimmers, rely largely on movement to keep them afloat. One of the great advantages that ray-finned fish have over their cartilaginous cousins is the swimbladder, a silvery sac just above the gut which is filled with gas. It is richly supplied with blood, so gas can be added or removed by the bloodstream to adjust the fish's buoyancy as it changes depth. In "The Origin of Species" Darwin suggested that the lungs of land animals had evolved from the swimbladder of fish, but it is now believed that the reverse is true. Lungs were probably present in all Devonian freshwater fish, as they needed to breathe air from time to time. These lungs later evolved into swimbladders in the modern teleosts, but retained their original function in lobe-finned fish. A few species of teleost living in poorly aerated water have gone back to using their swimbladder as a lung.*

### A living fossil: the coelacanth

*The coelacanths – a group of crossopterygians – were once assumed to have become extinct in the Jurassic period, about 200 million years ago. But in 1938, a fishing boat in the Indian Ocean caught a 2m-long fish of a kind never seen before. It was shown to Dr J.L.B. Smith of Rhodes University, South Africa, who recognized it as a living coelacanth – the only surviving crossopterygian. Despite intensive searching it was not until 1952 that another specimen was obtained, but now more than 80 coelacanths have been caught. They are known to live in deep water feeding on fish and squid. Their eggs are retained in the body and they give birth to live young.*

*The discovery of the coelacanth has interesting implications. It demonstrates that huge gaps in the fossil record do occur, for although the coelacanth has survived to the present day, there are no known fossils over a 200-million-year period. And it raises hopes for more such discoveries. If the coelacanth had remained undetected for so long, what other "living fossils" might be lurking in the ocean's unexplored depths?*

▲ The discovery of a coelacanth, in 1938, was as astonishing as finding a living dinosaur. It had been thought extinct for 200 million years.

▼ In the African lungfish the typical lobe-fins are reduced to long thread-like structures. It breathes by gulping air and survives dry periods in a burrow.

### Fish out of water

*Lungfish today live in hot areas of South America, Africa and Australia. Several species breathe air much of the time because the pools and swamps they live in become very stagnant and low in oxygen. Some that inhabit seasonal swamps can survive long periods with no water at all. At the beginning of the dry season they dig a burrow and curl up inside. Before the swamp dries out completely, the fish seals itself in with mud and secretes a coat of mucus to retain moisture. It then enters a state of "suspended animation" in which it can survive for a year or more.*

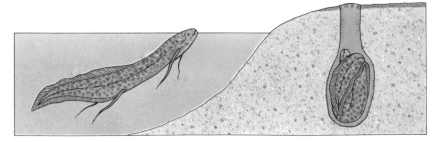

# Amphibians

## 13

*Emergence from the water...The first land vertebrate...
The Age of Amphibians...Living amphibians, last of
their line...PERSPECTIVE...Evidence about the amphibian
ancestor...A misunderstood fossil...Salamanders
that never grow up...The remarkable caecilians...
Breeding without water*

The majority of living amphibians start life as a tadpole, an aquatic larva that swims by thrashing its tail from side to side. Its tail has diagonal blocks of muscle, like those in fish, and at first the tadpole breathes by means of gills, but as its limbs grow the gills are resorbed and lungs develop instead. Like fish, it has a lateral line system for detecting vibrations in the water, and this too is lost as it matures. The old idea that "ontogeny recapitulates phylogeny" – in other words that embryology precisely re-enacts the evolutionary process – has long been discredited ( ◆ page 168), but the development of the tadpole, while not a true-to-life replay, is certainly an interesting parody of what happened 375 million years ago, when fish emerged from the water to conquer the land.

The oldest fossils that are clearly amphibian date from the late Devonian, and the best belong to a 1 meter-long animal named *Ichthyostega* ( ◆ page 100). It was obviously a land animal: it had four strong legs and it could have moved around quite efficiently. Its shoulder girdle was separate from the skull, so *Ichthyostega* could have swung its head from side to side, something that its aquatic forebears were probably unable to do. Such mobility of the head is unnecessary in water, because the whole body can be maneuvered much more easily.

## Amphibian ancestor

There are currently two theories about which group of fish – the lungfish or the crossopterygians – are most closely related to the amphibians. Both types of fish have lungs and "lobe fins" – fleshy fins with various bones and muscles inside. At present, the evidence seems to favor a group of fossil crossopterygians called rhipidistians. Their skulls are similar to those of an amphibian and the bones in the fleshy front fin can be matched with the bones in a newt or frog forearm. Most striking of all are the teeth: those of rhipidistians and early amphibians both have complex infoldings of enamel and are virtually indistinguishable.

Why these fishy ancestors of the amphibians ever made the step onto land is also a matter of some debate. Life in shallow, oxygen-depleted water was probably responsible for the evolution of features such as air-breathing lungs ( ◆ page 98), but what finally forced the rhipidistians out of water? Until recently it was believed that the eventual evaporation of their lakes or rivers was responsible: the image of a forlorn fish, lolloping slowly over the parched Devonian earth, peering about for another pond, is an enduring one. This now seems an unlikely scenario, however. The current view is that the amphibian ancestor left the water in response to the opening up of new terrestrial habitats. There were many small plants on the land already, and they seethed with insects, spiders and millipedes – their numbers as yet unchecked by any large predator. The young rhipidistians may have regularly come ashore to snap up prey in the damp undergrowth. They could already breathe air, and as they had muscular fins, they could probably have moved about on land, as living catfish sometimes do.

◄ Some species of catfish can move overland by pulling with their fins and making snake-like movements of the body. This is probably how the rhipidistian ancestors of the amphibians moved on land.

► The earliest amphibians are called labyrinthodonts – "labyrinth-tooths" – because of their elaborately infolded tooth enamel, as shown in this cross-section. Rhipidistian teeth are remarkably similar.

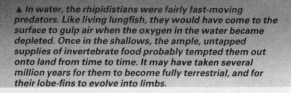

▲ In water, the rhipidistians were fairly fast-moving predators. Like living lungfish, they would have come to the surface to gulp air when the oxygen in the water became depleted. Once in the shallows, the ample, untapped supplies of invertebrate food probably tempted them out onto land from time to time. It may have taken several million years for them to become fully terrestrial, and for their lobe-fins to evolve into limbs.

*The early amphibians were generally larger than those alive today, and they had more waterproof skin*

Another difference between aquatic and terrestrial life is that, without the buoyancy of water, gravity exerts a greater pressure on the internal organs and limbs. *Ichthyostega* showed adaptations to counteract this. It had a strong rib cage with overlapping flanges to keep the internal organs uncrushed, and the legs were strong enough for it to hold its belly off the ground.

## The Age of Amphibians

The amphibians radiated and became very important land animals in the Carboniferous swamp-forests, 360-286 million years ago. The major group consists of the labyrinthodonts, fat, bulky animals, 50cm to 4m long – much larger than living amphibians. They were all carnivores, and they probably fed on invertebrates, such as giant dragonflies and cockroaches, as well as freshwater fish. Most had very flat skulls and small spiky teeth. Some forms evolved crocodile-like skulls, and these must have been specialist fish-eaters. They bore little resemblance to the amphibians we know today, and probably had a thick, scaly layer of keratin on the surface of the skin, making them more waterproof than modern amphibians. One group, the anthracosaurs, became increasingly terrestrial during the Carboniferous, and it seems likely that the reptiles evolved from them.

**A characteristic pattern of bones**

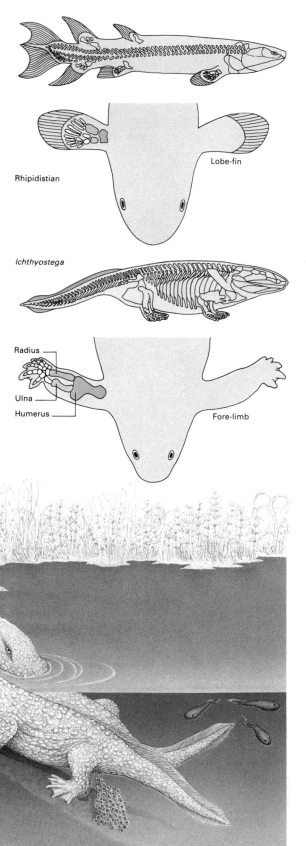

Rhipidistian

Lobe-fin

*Ichthyostega*

Radius

Ulna

Humerus

Fore-limb

► *The bones in the lobed fins of rhipidistian fish match up with those in amphibian limbs. Indeed all vertebrates, including ourselves, have this characteristic pattern of bones. Only the small bones at the tip of the fin became reduced, to give just five digits.*

▲ *Ichthyostega, the first amphibian, could have moved about on land quite efficiently, but like most modern amphibians, it must have returned to water to breed, and fertilized the eggs externally. There are no fossils of its larval form, but later, during the Carboniferous, fossilized tadpoles (known as "branchiosaurs") are quite common.*

**The witness of the flood**
*In 1731, the Swiss geologist Johann Scheuchzer (1672-1733) discovered a fossil which he believed was the skeleton of a sinner, drowned in the Biblical flood. He named the specimen* Homo diluvii testis: *"Man, a witness of the flood". Paleontologists now know that the skeleton is that of an extinct giant salamander,* Andrias, *dating back to the Miocene, 20 million years ago. It was about a meter long, comparable with the living giant salamanders of Asia which grow up to 1·5m.*

*In the 18th century geologists knew very little about fossils, and few people believed that any animal could have become extinct. This was tantamount to suggesting that God had made a mistake in one of his creations. Only in the 19th century did geologists become aware of the great variety of animals that had completely died out.*

▼ *The fire salamander's bright colors warn of its noxious skin secretions, which deter predators by inflaming the eyes and mouth. Unusually for amphibians, fire salamanders mate on land. The female is carried round on the male's back for a while, then gently lowered over the sperm package that he has deposited on the ground. She later gives birth to live young.*

## The living amphibians

The living amphibians are something of an enigma. They are classified as the Lissamphibia, a group quite separate from the labyrinthodonts and other extinct forms. How they are related to those archaic amphibians is not known, because the earliest fossil Lissamphibia are already fully fledged members of their respective groups: a distinctly frog-like frog first appears in the fossil record 240 million years ago. It is even possible that the two major groups of living amphibians – the newts and salamanders, and the frogs and toads – have evolved independently from the ancestral amphibian stock. Their relationship with the third group – the legless caecilians – is equally obscure.

What unites the living amphibians is the way water dominates their lives. As adults, most must live in damp habitats, although a few frogs and toads can survive arid conditions, often by sealing themselves in a burrow. But for the majority of amphibians, the thin skin must be kept permanently damp, because it acts as a "third lung", supplementing the animal's intake of oxygen. Amphibians must also lay their eggs in water, with the exception of the burrowing caecilians, the terrestrial salamanders and a few specialized frogs and toads, which either carry their eggs around, brood them in body cavities, or create a special moist environment for them (◗ page 102).

**The Peter Pan syndrome**
*Like other amphibians, many salamanders have an aquatic larval stage. In some groups, however, development stops there and the adult stage fails to materialize. Instead the larva develops sexual organs and is able to breed. This phenomenon, known as pedomorphosis, is seen in the Mexican axolotl, which is sometimes kept as a pet. It grows up to 30cm long, and has small, weak limbs, but retains the larva's tail-fin and external gills.*

*Many other species of salamander share this trait, but to different degrees, and a small environmental change may determine whether the salamander develops into the adult form or not. Some that never become adults can be induced to do so by feeding them thyroid gland from a calf, which contains the hormone thyroxine. The fact that a mammalian hormone has such a specific effect on an amphibian points to the common evolutionary origin of all land vertebrates.*

**Underground enigmas**
*The caecilians are a curious group of amphibians that have lost all trace of their limbs. Most of the 150 or so species are burrowers, but a few live in freshwater. Uniquely among the amphibians, some male caecilians have a penis for internal fertilization. The females of such species give birth to live young and in one species, the unborn young have rasping mouthparts for feeding on the lining of the mother's oviduct. In contrast to these advanced reproductive features, caecilians have tiny scales embedded in the skin – a primitive feature as far as amphibians are concerned.*

◀ *Burrowing caecilians are found in the soft, moist soils of tropical rainforest, or the warmer temperate forests. Most feed on insects or earthworms, and are preyed upon in turn by snakes. They are blind, but have a pair of tiny sensory tentacles beneath the vestigial eyes. Some give birth to live young, while others guard their eggs until they hatch.*

▲ A marsupial frog's young leaving the pouch.

◄ A tree frog's eggs, with young frogs inside.

▼ During courtship, the male Surinam toad grasps his mate, stimulating the skin on her back to swell. As the 100 or so eggs are laid, the male pushes them onto the female's back and each becomes enclosed by puffy skin. About 3 months later tiny adult toads emerge.

## Getting away from water

Amphibians generally need water in which to lay their eggs, but certain frogs and toads have escaped this requirement. In many cases, the avoidance of predators that consume eggs and tadpoles seems to be the reason for these adaptations, rather than a lack of water. Some tree frogs create a watery nest by producing a viscous secretion and beating it into a foam with their hind legs. The foam nest usually overhangs water and by the time it disintegrates and the tadpoles drop into the water below, they are swift enough to avoid predators. Another strategy is to lay the eggs on a leaf, protected by mucus, and for the tadpole stage to be completed inside the egg. The young then emerge as very tiny adults. Most foolproof of all, however, is parental care, as seen in the remarkable marsupial frog. The female lays her eggs with her rump above her head so that the eggs roll down her back and lodge in a special skin pouch. The male sits on her back, fertilizing the eggs, and later helps to seal the pouch over them. The pouch remains closed for several weeks until the young are ready to emerge.

Parental care is also a feature of some species that breed in water, such as the Surinam toad, where the eggs develop embedded in the female's back. In Darwin's frog, a group of males guard the female's eggs until the tadpoles begin to move about, then each male swallows 10-15 eggs, which develop inside his vocal sacs. More remarkable still is the Australian gastric-brooding frog in which the female broods the eggs in her stomach.

# Reptiles

## 14

*The Age of Reptiles...Better jaws and a watertight egg...Between reptiles and mammals...Crocodiles and alligators...Reign of the dinosaurs...PERSPECTIVE... How the amniotic egg works...Most ancient of the reptiles...Studying dinosaurs, believing in Creation... The extinction of the giants...Reptiles without legs... The living reptiles*

The era of amphibian dominance lasted for about 80 million years, and the present Age of Mammals has run for less than 65 million years. Both are overshadowed by the intervening Age of Reptiles, which endured for over 225 million years and produced some of the most astonishing creatures the world has ever seen. Although the dinosaurs were clearly the pinnacle of reptilian achievement, they were just one group among many. Besides the dinosaurs there were the therapsids, plesiosaurs, ichthyosaurs, rhynchosaurs, pterosaurs and several other reptilian success stories.

Reptiles first evolved from amphibians in response, it seems, to major changes in terrestrial habitats during the Carboniferous. The first forests appeared, with tall trees that offered a new range of habitats. Insects also flourished, and many new groups evolved. The evolution of these plants and insects created novel sources of food and shelter that were ripe for exploitation by fully terrestrial predators and herbivores.

During the late Carboniferous, several groups of amphibians began to diverge from their fellows and became more specialized for terrestrial life. Typically small animals, 10-20cm long, they evolved strong and efficient jaws adapted for feeding on insects. In place of the very low skulls typical of amphibians, these early reptiles had higher skulls, which allowed more room for the jaw muscles. The high skull enabled these muscles to run vertically from the back of the skull to the lower jaw and exert a strong crushing force on prey. In the early amphibians, the muscles fanned out inside the skull and could produce only a quick snap of the jaws.

Yet reptiles needed more than efficient jaws to exploit the new terrestrial habitat. More than anything, they had to escape the need to lay their eggs in water. The key to success was a watertight egg, and developing such an egg was the definitive step that separated reptiles from their amphibian ancestors. Once the reptiles had mastered land-living they began to diversify. In the Carboniferous and Permian the reptiles radiated into four or five major lines, distinguished primarily by the arrangement of openings in the side of the skull. In a primitive reptile skull there was an opening for the nostril and one for the eye. Among living reptiles, only the turtles and tortoises have a skull like this, termed the anapsid ("no opening") condition. Although strong and rigid, the skull is also heavy and provides relatively little space for jaw muscles. In the three or four other lines, extra openings developed, reducing the weight of the skull and providing attachment sites for the jaw muscles that ran up inside the skull at the back. The line that led to the dinosaurs, birds, crocodiles and lizards had two openings on each side, and is therefore called the diapsid line. The two other lineages both had one opening on either side (♦ page 105) but it was differently placed in relation to the skull bones.

## The innovative egg

The amniotic egg made its debut with the reptiles, and it was the innovation that allowed vertebrates to become fully terrestrial. It differs from the eggs of fish and amphibians in two crucial ways. First, it has a leathery shell (or, in birds, a hard shell) which protects the developing embryo and yet allows oxygen, carbon dioxide and water vapor to pass through. It effectively encloses the embryo in its own little pool of water and nutrients. Second, it contains three extra membranes. The amnion encloses the embryo itself, and has a protective function, while the allantois is a collecting bag for waste materials as well as a respiratory organ. A third membrane, the chorion, encloses the embryo, the yolk sac and the allantois. It is separated from the egg shell by the albumen or "egg white", which acts as a reservoir of water and protein.

Reptiles, birds and mammals are collectively called "amniotes" because they all possess an amnion, although most mammals no longer lay eggs. The allantois is also present in mammals, and forms part of the placenta.

The first known fossil of an amniotic egg is about 260 million years old. The problem with such fossils is that their parentage is a matter of guesswork, but it seems reasonable to suppose that this was the egg of a reptile, and it was probably laid by an early archosaur or therapsid. In later geological strata, dinosaur eggs are a common find.

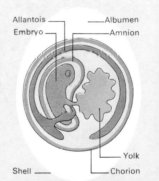

Allantois — Albumen
Embryo — Amnion

Shell — 
Yolk
Chorion

◄▼ *The membranes of the amniotic egg all develop as outgrowths from the embryo. The allantois carries out gas exchange, a task performed by the embryo's external gills or membranous tail in fish and amphibian eggs. The allantois is much more efficient, allowing amniotic eggs to be larger. The allantois also collects waste products, so these are left behind at hatching, relieving the young of toxic wastes.*

CENOZOIC

65

MESOZOIC

Cretaceous

144

Jurassic

213

Triassic

248

Permian

286

PALEOZOIC

Carboniferous

(million years ago)

0

monotremes

marsupials

placentals

multituberculates

ankylosaurs

ceratopsians

ornithopods

stegosaurs

sauropods

carnosaurs

birds

deinonychosaurs

ornithomimosaurs

coelurosaurs

pterosaurs

mammals

prosauropods

theropods

crocodilians

dicynodonts

cynodonts

rhynchosaurs

archosaurs

pseudosuchians

lepidosaurs

pelycosaurs

therapsids

gorgonopsids

SYNAPSID

DIAPSID

EURYAPSID

ANAPSID

AMPHIBIANS

REPTILES

plesiosaurs

ichthyosaurs

turtles and tortoises

In this evolutionary tree, the width of each branch is roughly equivalent to the importance and abundance of the group, in terms of number of species. Except for living groups, these numbers are estimates since the fossil record is incomplete. For example, there are only about 300 recognizable species of dinosaur known in total from fossils, although they dominated the Earth for 200 million years. By comparison, there are 2,800 living species of lizard.

The prosauropods were bipedal and quadrupedal animals 2–5m long.

The sauropods were quadrupeds ranging from 5 to 30m long. They included the massive *Brontosaurus* and *Diplodocus*.

The sauropodomorphs were all herbivores.

The theropods were all carnivorous bipedal animals ranging in size from chicken-like creatures to the huge *Tyrannosaurus*.

The ornithopods, such as *Iguanodon*, were mostly bipedal and lacked the bony armor of the other ornithischians.

The ceratopsians, stegosaurs and ankylosaurs all had armor made of bone. Its weight forced them to be quadrupedal.

The saurischians ("lizard-hips") are distinguished from the ornithischians ("bird-hips") by the arrangement of the hip-bones. However, the birds evolved from the saurischians, not the ornithischians. A bird's hipbone is only superficially similar to that of the ornithischian dinosaurs.

The ornithischians were all herbivores and showed novel features of the skeleton, compared with saurischians. Apart from the different hip-bone, they also had an extra bone at the front of the lower jaw. In some ornithopods, known as duck-billed dinosaurs, this extended chin was used in feeding.

The dinosaurs are distinguished from other diapsid reptiles by one major feature: erect gait. This was also seen in the pterosaurs and in the later pseudosuchians, but it was the dinosaurs which exploited the full potential of erect gait by becoming bipedal at quite an early stage. Some later reverted to quadrupedalism, but retained a distinctive dinosaur feature, linked to bipedalism: their hindlegs were twice the length of their forelegs. Dinosaurs also had the fifth toe much reduced in size, possibly as an adaptation to running. Bipedalism made carnivorous dinosaurs highly effective predators, able to seize prey with their forelimbs as they ran.

The pterosaurs were flying or gliding reptiles, and detailed fossils obtained from fine lake sediments show them to have had hair. They were probably warm-blooded.

The pseudosuchians ranged in size from 0.5m to 5m. Some of the smaller ones were bipedal, showing certain improvements in the ankle joint, though not as fundamental as those of the dinosaur line.

The turtles and tortoises are carnivores, herbivores or omnivores; teeth have been replaced by a horny beak. They show the sprawling gait of the early reptiles; in turtles the limbs have developed into paddles.

The plesiosaurs and ichthyosaurs were unique marine reptiles that fed on fish and squid. The plesiosaurs probably came ashore, but ichthyosaurs never left the water, even giving birth to live young.

All crocodilians are carnivorous and have a secondary palate, like that of mammals, as an adaptation to feeding in water. They have many distinctive anatomical features.

The mammal-like reptiles are distinguished from other reptiles by their synapsid skulls and differentiated teeth. Later therapsids acquired various mammalian characteristics.

The rhynchosaurs were heavily-built, herbivorous quadrupeds that flourished before the Age of Dinosaurs. The disappearance of their food-plant – a seed fern – was probably responsible for their demise.

Lepidosaurs, lizards and snakes differ from crocodilians and dinosaurs in their skulls (below). Most are carnivores. All lizards have a sprawling gait, although a few can stand bipedally for a short while.

Mammals are difficult to define, because the fossil record shows a full range of reptile-mammal intermediates. The character chosen to define mammals is the single-boned lower jaw (♦ page 107).

tuatara

amphisbaenians

lizards

snakes

The synapsids include the mammal-like reptiles (pelycosaurs and therapsids) and the mammals. The extra opening on each side of the synapsid skull made it lighter, and provided attachment sites for the jaw muscles that run up inside the skull.

The diapsids are a large group, comprising lizards, snakes, crocodiles, rhynchosaurs, pterosaurs, dinosaurs and birds. In these animals the skull has two openings on each side, which achieve much the same ends as the single opening of the synapsid and euryapsid skulls.

The archosaurs and their descendants (dinosaurs, birds, pterosaurs and crocodiles) are diapsids, but they all have an extra opening behind the nostril and in the lower jaw. Again, the additional openings are thought to be advantageous because they lighten the skull.

The euryapsids (plesiosaurs and icthyosaurs) are all extinct. Their skulls had a single opening on each side, as in the synapsid skull, but it was developed in a different place, higher up on the skull.

The anapsids include the earliest reptiles. Their skulls had no opening apart from the eye and nostril; though strong and rigid, they were also very heavy. Such skulls have persisted only in a group which has made a virtue of strength and heaviness – the turtles and tortoises.

*Many different groups of reptiles appeared and flourished before the dinosaurs, including the mammal-like reptiles and the crocodilians*

## The mammal-like reptiles

The first group of reptiles to become important, both in terms of numbers of species and in variety of adaptations, were some mammal-like reptiles known as pelycosaurs. This group included both carnivores and herbivores, and the latter were probably the first large plant-eaters to live on land.

The pelycosaurs were replaced in the mid Permian (260 million years ago) by more advanced mammal-like reptiles, the therapsids. Some species, the dicynodonts, lost most of their teeth and developed beaks. They were the dominant herbivores worldwide, and some were up to 5m long and must have weighed as much as a hippopotamus. Among the early carnivorous therapsids, known as gorgonopsids, some were like saber-toothed cats with great canine teeth, others very like dogs, and yet others like small shrews. During the late Permian and most of the Triassic, the therapsids were very diverse, and dominated the earth. The more advanced carnivores, known as cynodonts are believed to have had hair, for their skulls show small pits on the snout, which in modern mammals accommodate nerves and blood vessels for the touch-sensitive whiskers. If there were whiskers there was probably fur, and this points to the therapsids being endothermic or "warm-blooded". All in all, we would probably have unhesitatingly called these creatures mammals if we came across one, though, like the duck-billed platypus, they probably still laid eggs.

## Forerunners of the mammals

A progression of mammal-like reptiles can be followed through time as they acquired one "mammalian character" after another. The primitive pelycosaurs were not very mammal-like but they did show some differentiation of their teeth, instead of a row of similar teeth throughout the jaw, as in typical reptiles.

The principal carnivorous therapsids (the cynodonts) take the story further. Their limbs were longer and, in later forms, they moved underneath the body. Living lizards are sprawlers – their legs stick out sideways, with the elbows and knees permanently bent. The earliest pelycosaurs had the same ungainly pose, but the cynodonts had begun to tuck their legs underneath their bellies. This semi-erect posture is seen in crocodiles when they run. Finally, the legs moved right under the body to give the erect posture of later cynodonts and their descendants, the mammals. Dinosaurs and birds also evolved erect posture independently of the mammalian line. This rearrangement of the body allows the animals to take longer strides, and eliminates the typical reptilian waddle, so it can run much faster. Erect posture also allows an animal to become bipedal, as in human beings, dinosaurs and birds. Finally, an erect animal can support a heavier body weight, which is why elephants and dinosaurs could get so much bigger than earlier land animals. A sprawling elephant would be impossible, since it could not heave its belly off the ground.

The later cynodonts showed a number of important trends towards mammalian characters in the skull as well. The teeth became fully differentiated, and a secondary hard palate developed, separating the flow of air through the nose from the food in the mouth. Most reptiles do not have a secondary palate, and they have to eat or breathe: they cannot do both at once.

The number of bones in the jaw, and the way in which it hinged with the skull also changed. In typical reptiles, the lower jaw hinges on

▲ *The green turtle is an ocean-going species.*

### Packaged for survival

*The turtles and tortoises found a successful approach to life 215 million years ago and have scarcely changed since. They all have horny beak-like jaws instead of teeth, and a protective outer shell, made up of keratin-and-bone plates, which are firmly linked to the skeleton at various points of attachment. Most can pull their head and legs back into the shell for protection, and this enables them to resist predators. The cumbersome shell does put some limits on their diversity, but nevertheless there are land-dwellers, aquatic and burrowing forms – and even a few that take to trees.*

◀ *There are only 21 species of crocodiles and alligators left today. All are aquatic, and rather similar in appearance. In their heyday the crocodilians were much more diverse.*

▶ *The change in dinosaur gait involved the legs moving underneath the body. The ancestors of the dinosaurs may have had a semi-erect gait, like modern crocodiles.*

**The upright stance of dinosaurs**

Ichthyostega

Crocodile

Dinosaur

▲ *Crocodiles sometimes tuck their legs underneath their bodies and run for short distances. The dinosaurs developed upright gait more fully and later became bipedal.*

**The reptile-mammal transition**

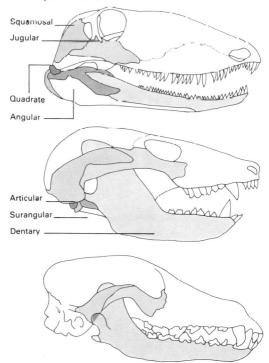

Squamosal
Jugular
Quadrate
Angular

Articular
Surangular
Dentary

▲ *Primitive mammal-like reptiles had five bones in each half of the lower jaw, but mammals only have one main bone, the dentary. The three missing bones from the reptile jaw have become part of our middle ear – the hammer, anvil and stirrup bones that improve our hearing. Most stages in this remarkable transition can be followed through the Triassic, in the fossils of the therapsids.*

the skull at the very back: it forms a simple flap which can only go up and down. In mammals, the hinge is placed forward, and it allows other more complex movements of the jaw. We can chew our food, whereas reptiles can only bite and swallow.

The first mammal arose from this stock, in the late Triassic, more than 210 million years ago. By this time most of the mammal-like reptiles had died out. A few continued into the middle Jurassic, but the last therapsid disappeared more than 160 million years ago.

**The diapsids**

The diapsids arose in the late Carboniferous and the first really important sub-group, the archosaurs, came on the scene in the late Permian. They started as medium-sized carnivores, and initially fed on fish, labyrinthodont amphibians and small mammal-like reptiles. They diversified during the Triassic, and split into two lines that led eventually to the crocodiles and the dinosaurs. Toward the end of the Triassic, there was a mass extinction event and most of the mammal-like reptiles and labyrinthodont amphibians disappeared, together with several reptile lines. With many niches vacant, the two archosaur lines took their chance to diversify.

During the Jurassic and Cretaceous periods, crocodiles were important aquatic predators, feeding on fish and vertebrates that ventured near the water. Indeed, some early crocodiles were fully terrestrial, and they probably lived much as wild cats and dogs did later. In the late Cretaceous, one giant 16m crocodile fed on dinosaurs.

The dinosaurs were the second archosaur line to emerge during the Triassic. The first dinosaurs were small and medium-sized bipedal carnivores – the theropods – and it was from them that the birds probably evolved. Within a few million years, the first large dinosaurs had come on the scene, and thereafter the dinosaurs evolved along five or six main lines, which dominated terrestrial faunas for almost 150 million years (◀ page 104). They showed this great potential because they evolved after a mass extinction had cleared the board for them. Dinosaurs ranged from chicken-sized creatures up to giants 30m long, the largest terrestrial animals of all time.

*Abundant fossils in limestone cliffs show how different groups of extinct reptiles inhabited the coastal waters and the shoreline*

## Dinosaurs and the Victorians

As the 19th century progressed, more and more fossils were found and the dinosaurs, in particular, seized the popular imagination. Life-size models of several species were exhibited at the Crystal Palace gardens in London, and the public flocked to see them. The models were made under the supervision of the great paleontologist Richard Owen who managed to combine his enthusiasm for fossils with a continuing belief in the Creation story. (Nonetheless, when the New York City authorities asked for a similar set of models for Central Park, they were attacked as "anti-religious" and the idea was dropped.) Owen managed never to be very explicit about his own views, but most people reconciled fossils and Creation by regarding Genesis as an account of the last in a long series of creations. This theory was severely shaken by finds of human remains in association with extinct animals like mammoths and woolly rhinoceroses.

## The great extinction

The dinosaurs became extinct 65 million years ago, and their disappearance opened the way for the expansion of the mammals (♦ page 117).

In considering why the dinosaurs died out it is important not to forget all the other animals that died out at the same time – the pterosaurs, ichthyosaurs and plesiosaurs, as well as many planktonic organisms and larger invertebrates, notably the ammonites (♦ page 78). There are also the survivors to consider: the crocodiles, mammals, birds, lizards, fish and most plants. The current theories about dinosaur extinction (of which there are literally hundreds) fall into two categories: change of climate or extraterrestrial catastrophe. The main climatic-change theory says that, as temperatures fell all round the world in the late Cretaceous, the warm lush dinosaur habitats began to disappear and cooler coniferous forests took their place. The dinosaurs were unsuited to this new environment and slowly declined.

The extraterrestrial theories suggest that a large asteroid hit the earth, either sending up a huge cloud of dust, which blocked out the Sun, or giving off poisonous arsenic or osmium. The evidence for this is that the uppermost Cretaceous rocks include unusually high concentrations of iridium, an element normally found only in meteorites and asteroids. The weakness of these theories is that such a catastrophe would have wiped out most other living things, particulary plants.

Extraterrestrial theories clearly involve a more rapid extinction than climatic theories, but methods of dating ancient rocks are too imprecise to be of help here. Geologists cannot tell if the dinosaurs all died out in a week or over 10,000 years.

▶ **The reptiles reached the peak of their diversity and success during the Mesozoic Era. During this time, they not only dominated the land, but also evolved swimming and gliding types. The fauna of southern England in the early Jurassic Period shows this diversity very well.**

A Jurassic landscape
1 *Megalosaurus* (carnosaur – carnivorous dinosaur)
2 *Scelidosaurus* (stegosaur – armored herbivorous dinosaur)
3 *Dimorphodon* (pterosaur – gliding reptile)
4 *Plesiosaurus* (plesiosaur – long-necked swimming reptile)
5 *Ichthyosaurus* (ichthyosaur – fish-shaped swimming reptile)

## Losing legs

A thin cylindrical fish such as an eel can move about quite efficiently on land, but the earliest terrestrial vertebrates had short, fat, fishy bodies and needed to evolve limbs to get about. Having become well adapted to life on land, however, several different groups of reptiles have rediscovered the legless state.

Snakes are the main group of legless reptiles. The more primitive ones – the boa constrictors and pythons, which squeeze their prey to death – show vestiges of their hind limbs, in tiny claws. These the male uses to caress the female during courtship. Boas and pythons also have two lungs, whereas the more advanced poisonous snakes have only one. In all snakes a transparent scale covers the eye instead of an eyelid, and the ear has no opening. These look like adaptions to burrowing and suggest that snakes evolved from a burrowing lizard.

Legless lizards, such as the slow worm, have followed a parallel evolutionary path, but in more recent times, and are not as fully adapted to burrowing: an external ear opening is present, as is the normal reptilian eyelid. Limbless species occur in several lizard families, so the loss of limbs must have occurred independently several times.

Strangest of all are the amphisbaenians, sometimes called worm-lizards, although they are not really lizards. Most are entirely legless, but some have miniature front legs which they use for digging. Others dig by means of hard, sharp ridges on the head, which bore into the soil as the reptile twists and turns in its burrow.

▲ In attaining their thin, elongated body-shape, poisonous snakes, such as this green palm viper, have dispensed with one of their lungs. Other paired organs, such as ovaries and kidneys, are arranged in tandem, rather than side-by-side.

◄ One group of lizards, the skinks, has many legless species and several others that have tiny almost-useless limbs. In a few skinks, the hindlegs are an optional extra: they can lie flattened against the body when not in use.

► The tuatara is a solid, heavily-built reptile, up to 65cm long. Last of the archaic lepidosaurs, it can operate at unusually low temperatures for a reptile, remaining active at only 12°C, whereas other reptiles require temperatures of at least 25°C. The tuatara can live to be over a hundred years old.

◄ The bony helmet of the green basilisk lizard is best developed in the male. These lizards are unusual in that they can run on their hindlegs at speeds of up to 11km per hour.

## Last of the reptiles

The most numerous living reptiles, the snakes and lizards, are, like the living amphibians, something of an afterthought. They belong to a group called the lepidosaurs, which arose during the Age of Dinosaurs. The archaic lepidosaurs, known as sphenodontids, have left a single survivor, the tuatara, which inhabits small islands and rock-stacks off New Zealand. It lives in woodland and is largely nocturnal.

Lizards developed as an offshoot of the sphenodontids in the Jurassic, and the snakes appeared in the mid Cretaceous. Although they originally evolved from a burrowing lizard, the snakes later radiated to produce terrestrial, tree-dwelling and even sea-going species.

# Birds

## 15

*Controversy continues over the origins of birds...Fossil birds and their niches...Adaptations for flight...Feathers – structure, types and colors...PERSPECTIVE...The discovery of the reptile-bird Archaeopteryx...Influence of the ice ages on bird evolution...The roc, moas and other extinct giants...Home-builders without rival*

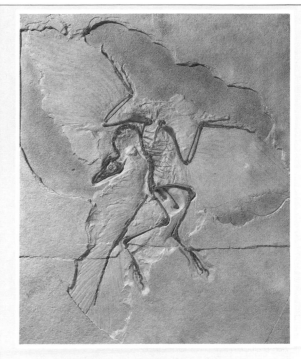

▲ ▼ *Archaeopteryx as a fossil and in a reconstruction.*

The fossil *Archaeopteryx* discovered in the mid-19th century showed a tantalizing blend of reptile and bird characters. About the size of a crow, it bore a long bony tail and sharp-toothed, unquestionably reptilian jaws. And yet its remarkable covering of feathers scarcely differed in patterning and structure from those of modern flying birds.

Despite being hailed as a "missing link" between reptiles and birds, *Archaeopteryx* has raised almost as many questions as it has answered. The lack of a deep sternum, or breastbone (to which the flight muscles are attached in living birds), points against *Archaeopteryx* having been a true flying bird. The presence of clawed digits on the wings have suggested to some a semi-arboreal existence in which *Archaeopteryx* clambered up trees, using both wings and feet, before gliding down in pursuit of insect prey. In the mid-1970s this scenario was challenged by some paleontologists, notably John Ostrom, who cast *Archaeopteryx* as a ground-dweller, running on strong hind legs and using its forelimbs for seizing prey. He interpreted its plumage as serving a primarily insulative role, an idea that has important implications for the origins of birds, even though the ground-dwelling hypothesis has since been largely discarded. The most recent appraisal strongly supports the belief that *Archaeopteryx* was indeed capable of rudimentary flight, and supposes that in lieu of a sternum, the sturdy collarbone – the "wishbone" – served as anchorage for the necessary muscles. *Archaeopteryx* is dated to the mid-Jurassic, some 150 million years ago.

The question of why feathers evolved – whether for flight or insulation – is linked to ideas about how and when birds originated. Until the mid-1970s the traditional view was that, during the Triassic period, a group called the thecodonts or "stem archosaurs" gave rise to two separate lines, both originally cold-blooded. The first was the dinosaurs, while the second went on to become the birds. In this scheme, warm-bloodedness was thought to have evolved late in the development of birds, as it did in mammals.

Following a reexamination of bioenergetics and anatomy, John Ostrom and his colleagues proposed a new phylogeny in which birds were directly descended from dinosaurs (◗ page 112). The most revolutionary aspect of Ostrom's proposal was that birds had inherited their high metabolic rates, endothermy, and, most probably, their feathers, from dinosaurs rather than developing them as original features. The idea that birds had evolved from small bipedal dinosaurs like *Microvenator* had been proposed 100 years earlier on purely anatomical grounds by Thomas Huxley, but had then fallen into disrepute. This new line of reasoning resurrected the idea, and it is now much in favor, although the question of whether the dinosaurs were truly warm-blooded is still being debated (◗ page 189).

### Discovering Archaeopteryx

*In the 19th century the printing process known as lithography relied on blocks of exceptionally fine-grained limestone to transfer images drawn on the stone on to paper. One of the few quarries to supply "lithographic limestone" was at Solnhofen in Bavaria, West Germany. The stone was split like slate, and each surface then had to be carefully inspected for flaws. During this process many curious fossils were discovered. The quarrymen took them to a local doctor, Friederich Haberlein, who exchanged them for medical treatment. Haberlein's steadily growing collection of fossil plants, invertebrates, fish and reptiles showed that the quarry had been formed by a vast inland sea, where chalky silt had settled out of the water.*

*It was in this quarry, early in 1861, that a fossil was found which the workmen immediately knew to be different from any of their previous finds. The skeleton was clearly that of a reptile, but fanning out from the delicate bones were unmistakable impressions of feathers. In most rocks, only bones are preserved as fossils, but here the feathers were clearly recorded due to the fineness of the deposits. Archaeopteryx had been discovered.*

# Flight and Feathers

### The flexible feather

Feathers are formed entirely from the protein keratin that also makes up our fingernails and skin. As the basal cells of vertebrate skin multiply outward, they are gradually deprived of oxygen and nourishment, and then become filled with keratin. In birds this dead tissue has become elaborated into feather structures. These almost certainly evolved from reptilian scales, but exactly how is not known: only fully evolved feathers are found in the fossil record.

Most modern birds are covered in a variety of feather types. Over the soft, downy, heat-conserving layers are vaned or "contour" feathers, which streamline the body, those on the wings and tail also helping to create the lift and propulsion needed for flight. A third type of feather, the filoplume, is thin and hair-like and tells the bird if its feathers are disarrayed; it may also be sensitive to air currents during flight.

Filoplume feathers are found in all birds, but some special types of feather are restricted to particular species or groups of birds. One desert bird, the sand grouse, has tightly coiled breast feathers that are highly absorbent, and can be used to carry water from drinking holes back to the nestlings. Another specialized type of feather is the powder down of the heron family. These curious patches of feathers fray continuously, producing a powder that the bird uses to cleanse its feathers of the oil and slime picked up from eating fish. It applies the powder, leaves it to soak up the dirt for a while, then preens it out.

Finally, feathers give birds their distinctive appearance and communicate messages of sex and status to other individuals. The striking colors of plumage are achieved in a variety of ways. The blacks, grays, browns and buffs result from natural pigments widespread in the animal kingdom, while yellows, oranges and reds originate from carotenoid pigments obtained through the bird's diet. Greens, blues and violets are produced, like the colors on the surface of soap bubbles, by the refraction of light on feather structure.

Primaries

Digits

Alula

Carpals (wrist bones)

Radius

Ulna

Humerus (upper arm)

Secondaries

Scapula (shoulder blade)

Backbone

Rib

Clavicles or furcula ("wishbone")

Sternum (breastbone)

Pelvis

Femur (thigh)

Pygostyle (tailbone)

Keel (carina)

Digits

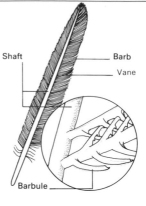

Shaft

Barb

Vane

Barbule

▲ From the feather's strong shaft branch out hundreds of barbs, each a miniature feather bearing hundreds of barbules. Each barbule is tipped with hooks that mesh into barbules on the next parallel barb.

Trachea
Air sacs

Syrinx

Lung

Air sacs

▲ Light weight and an efficient metabolism to maintain a high body temperature (41-43.5°C according to species) are the keys to success for birds. The chief limb bones, and some skull bones and the pelvis are hollow. A system of air sacs provides for a one-way flow of air through the lungs, greatly assisting uptake of oxygen and disposal of carbon dioxide.

◄ Flying underwater, these Magellanic penguins get their main propulsion from their wings, which have lost all power of flight. Auks also swim mainly with their wings (as did the now-extinct flightless great auk). But most diving birds swim with webbed feet.

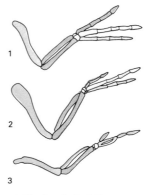

▲ The forelimb of the dinosaur Microvenator (1), a possible ancestor of Archaeopteryx (2) and living birds (3). Already in Microvenator five digits are reduced to three. In Archaeopteryx the digits were probably used for capturing prey.

▲ Triple exposure of a blue tit in flight. The downstroke provides the power, the feathers closed flat against one another. The primary feathers open up for the "recovery" stroke.

▼ The wings of birds are shaped for their particular way of life. Shown here are those of an albatross (1) – long, straight and tapering for sustained gliding in winds and air currents over the sea; a common swift (2) – long, swept-back, narrow and tapering for high-speed flapping flight; and a hummingbird (3) – short and tapering and capable of turning over completely so that both up- and downstrokes provide lift for hovering.

## Built for flight

All birds' wings share the same basic "teardrop" shape in cross-section, but the overall design and motion of wings differ markedly. The largest flying birds, like eagles, vultures and storks, are best adapted to a gliding style of flight, maximizing lift by having an extensive wing area. Such birds utilize updraughts over cliffs and mountainsides, or the columns of warm rising air called thermals.

The albatrosses, likewise, seldom resort to flapping flight, but use a different gliding principle. To extract lift from stormy ocean winds in high latitudes they have evolved long rigid tapering wings capable of cleaving air at speed while maintaining deft control. The wandering and royal albatrosses claim the largest wingspan of modern birds, up to 3·4 meters from wingtip to wingtip.

Most small birds can neither soar efficiently nor turn strong winds to their advantage. Instead they must generate their own motive power, and they achieve this by flapping flight, the powerful downstroke producing lift, and the twisting of the wing (especially the wingtip) producing forward propulsion. Flapping flight achieves the highest air speeds found in birds. Although estimates of maximum speeds – around 320km per hour by

diving falcons and swifts – are possibly exaggerated, half this speed is not unlikely over short distances. Even small birds such as sparrows can muster 50 or 60km per hour when pressed.

Such performances are achieved only by marked physiological adaptations. Birds have the highest body temperatures of all warm-blooded animals, some 41–43·5℃, compared with 37℃ in humans. This temperature is maintained by an energy-rich diet and extremely rapid digestion. The large heart pumps sugar-rich blood to the flight muscles at a prodigious rate: 300 beats per minute in the turkey vulture (a leisurely flier) and 615 per minute in the ruby-throated hummingbird. Our own pulse rate of 80 to 120 per minute is sluggish by comparison.

Uniquely, birds also possess several (usually five) pairs of air sacs which route air from the lungs to all parts of the body, even to hollows in the bones. The air sacs also create a one-way system which pushes air through the lungs more efficiently than the in-and-out system of mammals. This unique feature minimizes the stale air in the lungs, thus maintaining an oxygen-rich supply to the blood. Air sacs also provide an extensive cooling surface to dissipate the intense heat generated by flight – birds have no sweat glands.

*Flightless birds have descended from flying ancestors*

After *Archaeopteryx*, bird fossils are extremely rare up until the Eocene although a few are found in the Cretaceous. Most come from America, the best known being the gull-like *Ichthyornis* and *Hesperornis*, which are often depicted with bills of small, sharp teeth. Recently, this attribute has been questioned, at least for the *Ichthyornis* fossil, whose jaws may have become confused with those of small dinosaurs found abundantly in the same deposit. However, there is firm evidence for teeth in the bill of *Hesperornis*, which was also of interest for having lost all power of flight. Its wings were either absent or much reduced, having only one small flimsy bone within them. The legs were well developed for swimming and therefore placed well back on the body. This must have made it difficult for the bird to walk on land. Where and how it emerged to lay its eggs is a mystery – such extreme and inflexible adaptations to aquatic life are not seen in any living bird.

*Hesperornis* was something like a modern diver or loon, and other Cretaceous birds included plausible ancestors for the flamingoes and the cormorants. That these are all waterbirds is no coincidence, for only they had a good chance of being preserved. In general, fossils are less readily formed on land than in water where they can quickly become covered by silt and mud. For birds, whose delicate, hollow bones are easily dispersed and destroyed, fossilization on land is extremely unlikely.

Nonetheless, from the Eocene onward, more and more birds are found, and representatives of nearly half the living orders are known. The diversity of bird forms appears to have increased dramatically, perhaps facilitated by the demise of the dinosaurs, and a rival group of flying reptiles, the pterosaurs. In the hiatus left by the dinosaur extinction, some birds developed into massive flightless forms, such as the carnivorous *Diatryma* which stood 2.1m tall. These birds were the dominant land carnivores until ousted by the mammals. Plant-eating giants such as the moas outlasted them, and even survived until a few hundred years ago in New Zealand, where they were free from mammalian competition.

### Extinct giants

*There are 47 known extinct species of the group of flightless birds known as ratites. Some were the largest birds ever known. Notable among them were the plains-dwelling elephant birds of Africa and Europe, which include the stout-limbed Aepyornis titan, found in Madagascar. It stood 3m tall, may have weighed 450kg, and was probably Sinbad's roc – the legendary bird in the tales of the "Thousand and One Nights", which carried off elephants in its claws.*

*Fossil remains indicate that these birds were hunted to extinction by man. Its eggs are still occasionally found buried in sand on the seashore or in loose soil beside lakes. Measuring as much as 33cm and with a volume of about 9 liters including the food and protective layers, they are the largest single cells in the animal kingdom.*

*Of equally if not more recent extinction were the 13 moa species of New Zealand, the largest of which matched the elephant birds in stature. The moas had no natural enemies until the arrival of immigrant Polynesians (Maoris). Radiocarbon dating suggests that the final extinction of the group only occurred in the 17th century.*

▲ ► *After Archaeopteryx, no fossil birds are known for over 30 million years. Ichthyornis (above) was a bird of the oceans that covered what are now the Great Plains of North America. It was just 20cm high, had a strong "keel" to its sternum (breastbone) and therefore probably had well-developed flight muscles and powers of flight. From the same region and period, the much larger Hesperornis (right) was unable to fly, having reverted to flightlessness from a flying ancestor.*

▼ *The number of birds increased dramatically after the disappearance of the dinosaurs. Some were small flying species like the majority of birds today. Others were flightless giants like Diatryma (below) which fed on mammals of Europe and North America.*

▶ The brown kiwi of New Zealand has taken flightlessness to the extreme. The tiny wings are buried among the feathers and the tail feathers have disappeared. The kiwi hen's egg is a quarter of her own weight. It sustains the developing embryo for 65-85 days and even after hatching the chick continues to feed on the yolk sac. The kiwi is relatively small and could probably not have developed in the presence of large mammals.

▶ Last of the giants, the moas were exterminated only in the 17th century. Thirteen species of these giant plant eaters are known – some over 2.5m tall. They formed part of the biggest expansion of the flightless ratites, which took place in quite recent times, from 1.5 million years ago, in New Zealand.

## A flightless group

The ostrich, rheas, emu, cassowaries and kiwis – all long-legged, bulky, flightless birds – are collectively known as ratites. The name derives from these birds' flat or raft-like sternum (Latin rata: raft); flying birds, with their deep, keeled sternum to which the flight muscles are attached, are sometimes known as carinates (Latin carina: keel). Ratites are not as closely related as their similar appearance suggests, but do share a common ancestor, which was once distributed throughout Gondwanaland, the southern part of Pangea (▶ page 124). With the breakup of Gondwanaland 100 million years ago, the ancestral ratite was separated into South American, African and Australasian populations, which began to diverge into the forms we see today. The greatest radiation took place in New Zealand, where there were no large mammals to compete with the birds.

In the 19th century there was great controversy over the status of the ratites. Because they lacked a sternal keel, it was thought that ratites evolved from primitive birds which had never developed the power of flight. Today, however, the ratites are regarded as secondarily flightless – their ancestors had the power of flight.

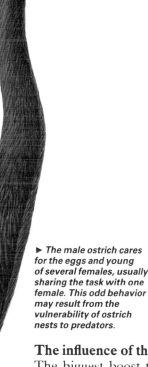

▶ The male ostrich cares for the eggs and young of several females, usually sharing the task with one female. This odd behavior may result from the vulnerability of ostrich nests to predators.

## The influence of the ice ages

The biggest boost to the evolution of new bird types came with the advent of the ice ages in the Pleistocene period, which embraces the last two million years of fossil history. While the glaciations undoubtedly caused widespread extinctions, they also led to a wholesale geographical redistribution of birds. In both hemispheres, small pockets of land were isolated by a mosaic of ice, and this created perfect conditions for the evolution of new species and races.

The differentiation of the treecreepers *Certhia* illustrates this oft-repeated process. It is believed that during one of the glacial periods a population of common European treecreepers *Certhia familiaris* was isolated, probably on the Iberian peninsula, and there evolved into the short-toed treecreeper *Certhia brachydactyla*. When the climate improved, and the two populations were reunited, their physical characteristics and ecology had diverged sufficiently to enable them to coexist as separate species.

## Managing without teeth

*Teeth are useful for breaking up food but they are also heavy. Some Cretaceous birds (such as Hesperornis, page 114) still had teeth but by the Eocene these had disappeared, sacrificed to more efficient flight. Presumably most birds at that time ate fish, insects and other food that did not require chewing. Today many birds eat seeds, and they must make up for their lack of teeth by using stones to pulverize their food. The stones are swallowed and stored in the gizzard, whose muscular action grinds the food between them.*

*In most other birds the sharp tip of the bill is adequate for breaking up food, but substitutes for teeth are known. Two fossil birds, Osteodontornis and Odontopteryx, from the Eocene and Miocene, had bony outgrowths of the jaws that were superficially similar to teeth. Among living birds, the mergansers or goosanders have serrations along the edge of the bill that help them to keep hold of slippery fish.*

*The bills of birds show a remarkable variety. Some bills clearly serve an important function in display, as in the brightly colored bills of male puffins in the breeding season. However, most bill shapes reveal adaptation to diet. The long slender bill of the hummingbird gives it access to its food in the nectaries of flowers, while the "pouch" in the pelican's lower bill holds its "catch" of fish. Finches have stout conical bills for cracking seeds. Birds of prey have a hooked upper bill for tearing flesh. Mallard duck bills are fringed for filter-feeding on duckweed, while skimmers use their longer lower mandible for scooping up fish (◗ page 169). The long slender bills of most waders are for probing in mud or sand. The crossed mandible tips of the crossbill help them extract seeds from fir cones.*

## Nest building

*Many other animals build nests but none can compete with the skill and effectiveness of birds. At their most complex, birds' nests may be knotted macramé-style from grasses, as in the weaverbirds, or made from two leaves "sewn" together with grass by the aptly named tailorbirds. Ovenbirds and swallows shape neat domed or cup-shaped nests from soft mud, while swifts catch floating feathers and other scraps while in flight, then stick them all together with their gluey saliva. The need for a nest stems from the birds' almost unique biology, shared only with the egg-laying mammals. By combining endothermy with egg-laying, they are committed to keeping their eggs at a warm, even temperature to ensure their development. The nest is a vital accessory, helping to insulate the eggs from heat or cold, as well as providing a firm base on which the bird can sit during incubation.*

▲ **Compound nests of the social weaver in an acacia in southwestern Africa. These extraordinary structures may incorporate 50-100 separate nests. Numerous pairs build their nests close together, then work collectively all year round to build and maintain a shared "roof" over the whole collection. Each individual nest has an entrance obstructed by grass stalks to impede any predators.**

▶ **Lacking teeth, a great gray shrike uses its hook-tipped upper bill and the thorn-spike which is the site of its "larder" (or in this case, freezer), to tears up its mouse prey.**

# Mammals

**16**

*Early mammals and their origins...Reproduction – and the three groups of living mammals...Giants, predators and omnivores...The defenses of the herbivores... PERSPECTIVE...Skin glands...The duck-billed platypus "hoax"...The opportunistic opossums...The Pleistocene extinctions...Flying mammals...Evolution and the changing continents*

Mammals are the dominant form of life on Earth today, and have been so for the past 65 million years. But they have been around for much longer than that. When their era of supremacy began, mammals already had a long history, stretching back 150 million years. During much of that period, they had been represented by small, unobtrusive animals, probably nocturnal and largely eclipsed by the monumental success of the dinosaurs. Before the Age of Reptiles drew to a close, the mammals had already begun to diversify, but it was only with the extinction of the dinosaurs that mammals finally came into their own.

The first true mammals were small shrew-like beasts such as *Megazostrodon*, and they probably looked rather similar to some of the very advanced mammal-like reptiles that were also alive at that time. The mammal-like reptiles of the Permian and Triassic record a remarkably detailed sequence of stages in the acquisition of mammalian characters (◀ page 106). Paleontologists call *Megazostrodon* a mammal because it had crossed some important thresholds in evolution. The lower jaw was made of only one bone, the dentary, instead of several separate bones, and the joint between jaw and skull was completely mammalian (◀ page 107). *Megazostrodon* was almost certainly covered in hair, and it was therefore fully endothermic, or "warm-blooded". The dinosaurs dominated the land, and hunted during the day, and the early mammals were probably forced to hunt at night, when the ability to control their temperature and generate heat physiologically would have been advantageous.

▲ *A Cape fox vixen suckles her cubs. The mammary glands of modern mammals help get the young off to a head start by providing the necessary nutrients. They are thought to have evolved from sweat glands.*

### Milk, sweat and smells

Two principal characteristics of mammals are homeothermy and the nurturing of the young with milk. Both of these utilize special glands in mammalian skin, which have, in the course of evolution, been adapted for various purposes. At their simplest these glands produce a largely watery substance – sweat. In many mammals, though not all, this is used to cool the body down by evaporation, so helping to maintain a steady temperature, regardless of changes in the environment. From these simple skin glands, more specialized versions have evolved, which produce a thick secretion loaded with fats, proteins and sugars – in other words, milk. It is possible that this development took place among mammal ancestors living in an arid environment. They may have produced copious amounts of sweat from certain areas of the body, to provide their young with drinking water. Later the secretion could have come to include more and more nutrients.

A third characteristic of mammals is also related to the skin glands – their intrinsic smelliness. Being nocturnal and secretive, early mammals probably adopted smells as a convenient means of communicating with each other and, for most, smell is still the most important social signal. (Humans are unusual in having a poor sense of smell, so these messages tend to pass us by.) The scent glands which produce the smells are, like mammary glands, derived from sweat glands.

◀ *A cheetah marks its territory by spraying scent from an anal gland. Most mammals declare their territory in this way, and social animals transfer scent to other members of the group, so that there is a recognizable group smell to aid recognition. A cat rubbing itself against its owner's legs is depositing scent from a gland on the side of the head.*

## The monotremes

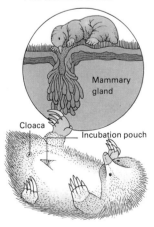

▲ **The spiny anteater's egg is coated with sticky mucus that keeps it in the rudimentary pouch. The egg hatches after a week; the young is 1.25cm long.**

### The monotremes

The living monotremes are a very small group, consisting of the duck-billed platypus of Australia and two species of echidnas from Australia and New Guinea. When a specimen of the duckbilled platypus was sent to England in the early 19th century, zoologists were certain it was a hoax. Someone had apparently stitched the beak of a large duck onto an otter's body. However, the platypus really does have a broad beak and no teeth: it sieves through mud on the bottom of ponds for small aquatic animals. The broad paddle-like limbs are used for swimming (hence the otter-like appearance) and for burrowing. Echidnas, or spiny anteaters, are superficially quite different from the platypus. They resemble large hedgehogs but with strange, tubular snouts, and they feed on ants and termites.

The superficial oddities of these animals are the result of specialization to particular ecological niches, and they tend to obscure the really bizarre characteristic of these animals: both the platypus and the echidnas lay eggs. The female platypus incubates her eggs at the end of a long burrow, whereas the echidnas have a rudimentary pouch on the belly in which the single egg is kept. On hatching, the young are small and underdeveloped, and those of the spiny anteater stay in their pouch for a while. They feed on milk, which simply oozes out of the mother's belly, there being no nipple, although the persistent sucking of the young on the mother's skin creates "pseudonipples".

The monotremes are a puzzle to paleontologists, because some features of their skulls – especially the inner ear, with its three tiny bones derived from the reptilian jaw – are remarkably modern. These features place them with other living mammals, but this implies that the egg-laying habit survived very late in mammalian evolution. Alternatively, if monotremes are an offshoot of more primitive mammalian stock, the complex arrangement of the ear must have evolved independently, but in exactly the same way as in other living mammals, which seems unlikely. This is a puzzle which can only be solved by the discovery of more mammalian fossils.

During the Jurassic and Cretaceous, the early mammals evolved along several lines, and, while most were small, unobtrusive creatures, some of them became as big as cats. However, they were apparently not able to compete with the dinosaurs, and they never became common. In fact, fossils of Mesozoic mammals are so rare that many of the species are known only from a few teeth.

In the early Cretaceous when the dinosaurs were in their prime, some new kinds of mammals came on the scene, and these were the ancestors of the modern mammals. All other primitive Mesozoic mammals died out with the dinosaurs, or shortly after.

## Beyond the egg

The modern mammals, or therians, are divided into three groups: the monotremes, marsupials and placentals (or eutherians) – on the basis of their reproduction. The monotremes lay leathery-shelled eggs like those of a reptile, but feed the young on milk. On hatching, the young monotreme is at a very early stage of development, and this is also true of marsupial mammals, such as the kangaroos, and opossums. The marsupials give birth to grub-like embryos, which crawl through the mother's fur into a pouch where they continue to develop while feeding on milk. Among placentals – generally considered the most advanced mammals – the young are not born until they are much further developed, and they are sustained in the womb by a nutritive organ, the placenta. The placenta is a derivative of the allantoic membrane seen in the amniotic egg (◀ page 103) and it forms a selective barrier. The blood supplies of the mother and of the developing embryo pass close together in the placenta but do not mix. Nutrients and oxygen pass into the embryo, and waste materials and carbon dioxide pass out. The placenta acts as an immunological barrier and prevents the embryo from being treated as a foreign body by the mother's immune system. Because the placenta feeds the developing embryo, birth can be delayed until development is well advanced: some young mammals can stand and run within hours of birth. But all are fed on milk after birth, for periods from a few days to over a year. The production of milk is an important feature, common to the reproductive strategies of all three groups of mammals.

◀ *A female platypus with young, in her burrow. The tiny young feed on milk for five months. Instead of sucking on a pseudonipple as echidnas do, they lap it up from the mother's fur.*

▲ *A young kangaroo can continue suckling after it has left the pouch, until it is about a year old. The milk it gets has a different composition to that which the resident young receive.*

## The marsupial mammals

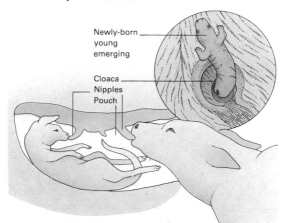

Newly-born young emerging

Cloaca
Nipples
Pouch

▲ *The kangaroo licks her fur to make it wet before giving birth, so that the grub-like baby can crawl through it to the pouch. There it remains for eight months.*

## The placental mammals

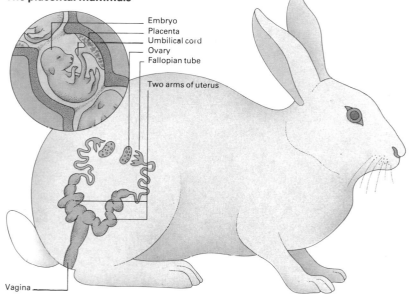

Embryo
Placenta
Umbilical cord
Ovary
Fallopian tube

Two arms of uterus

Vagina

▶ *Developing inside the mother's uterus may have contributed to the placentals' success, but it is not clear what advantages there are to this strategy.*

*For several million years all mammals remained fairly small, living on a diet of plants or invertebrates*

## Modern mammals

The first therians date from the early Cretaceous and by late Cretaceous times marsupials and placentals can be distinguished. Both radiated into several lines in the late Cretaceous, and especially in the early Tertiary, after the dinosaurs became extinct.

The early marsupials were, for the most part, small opossum-like creatures. They originated in the Americas and spread through North America to Europe, Africa and Asia, and through South America to Antarctica and Australasia, then a single landmass. Later the marsupials died out in most parts of the world, but they survived and radiated in Australia and in South America, owing to the isolation of these continents (♦ pages 124-125).

Of the placental mammals, the primates were one of the early groups to expand, although they looked more like mice then, and filled rodent-like niches in the trees. For several million years all mammals remained fairly small, with a diet of plants or invertebrates. The dominant large carnivores were still the crocodiles, and giant flightless birds such as *Diatryma* with terrifying hooked beaks. But larger carnivorous mammals then appeared and replaced these archaic predators. At the same time squirrel-like rodents developed and expanded, replacing most primates as arboreal plant-feeders. Rodents have the advantage that their teeth continue growing throughout life, so they are better equipped to deal with abrasive plant foods. This was only a temporary setback for the primates however, and the survivors of the rodent take-over later went on to produce the bush babies, galagos, lemurs, monkeys and apes.

## The Eocene world

Toward the end of the Eocene, 40 million years ago, the mammals of the world would not have looked totally unfamiliar to modern eyes. Shrews and hedgehogs, having survived from dinosaur times, continued to flourish, and rabbits and bats appeared at about this time. Miniature horses, no larger than dogs, but recognizably horse-like, trotted about. Other animals were utterly unlike those we know today, however, including the gigantic lumbering *Uintatherium* whose grotesque head bore a multitude of knobbly bones. These and many other large herbivores later became extinct, because of changes in the climate and vegetation.

Most of the large carnivores living at that time also became extinct later, and they included such oddities as *Andrewsarchus*, a heavily-built dog-like animal which measured over 5m from toe to tail. But in the trees were the forerunners of today's carnivores – small, long-bodied animals, known as miacids, which looked rather like the living civets and weasels. Modern civets are similar to the ancestors of the cats and hyenas, while the weasels are thought to resemble the ancestor of the dogs and their allies – the other major group of living carnivores. The dog group diversified a great deal subsequently to give rise to bears, coatis, raccoons, pandas, badgers and wolves.

The first animals with hoof-like nails, instead of claws, appeared in the Eocene, and from then onward, larger and larger hoofed plant-eaters appeared. Quite early on the hoofed mammals, or ungulates, split into two distinct groups: artiodactyls (even-toed ungulates) and perissodactyls (odd-toed ungulates). The modern artiodactyls include the antelopes, deer, giraffes, goats, pigs, hippopotamuses, camels and llamas, while the perissodactyls are today represented by the horses, zebras, tapirs and rhinoceroses.

▲ *The four-eyed opossum, a South American marsupial.*

### The American opossums

*Although most modern marsupials live in Australasia, a few species of rat opossums and opossums survived in South America, which likewise had a long period of isolation. One species – the Virginia opossum – later moved into North America, and has spread as far north as Canada. The American opossums owe their success to an ability to digest virtually any sort of food. This indiscriminate diet contributed to their survival 65 million years ago, when they flourished in the post-dinosaur age. Today they raid garbage cans and scavenge on bodies of animals killed on roads.*

▲ *An African civet, a relative of the cats and hyenas.*

▲ ► *Perissodactyls were initially much more successful than artiodactyls; most were small forest-dwellers like today's tapirs (above), and they died out as the forests waned. Giraffes (right) are specialized, tree-feeding artiodactyls.*

*As early herbivores began feeding more extensively on grass they may well have maintained and even created open grassland*

▲ **Two zebra put on an extra turn of speed as a cheetah closes in on them. The "arms race" between predators and prey (◆ page 234) has resulted in extraordinary achievements among the mammals. The cheetahs can move at 110km per hour.**

◀ **Like many mammals, duiker antelopes are secretive, and largely nocturnal, relying on smell for communication. Here a duiker deposits scent from a gland beneath the eye.**

*Moenitherium*
38 million years ago

*Trilophodon*
26-2 million years ago

*Platybelodon*
12-7 million years ago

*Mammithera imperator*
2 million years ago

## Pleistocene extinctions

*At the end of the ice ages, 10–15,000 years ago, large numbers of mammals died out. In fact it is estimated that 200 genera became extinct. Many of these were very large species – the ice age "megafauna". There is great controversy at present over the cause of these extinctions.*

*The "Pleistocene overkill" hypothesis suggests that the extinctions were caused by early people who were spreading worldwide and who had learned efficient new hunting skills that allowed them to tackle much larger animals. During the retreat of the last glaciers in North America, the extinction rates rose dramatically, and the highest rates, between 11,000 and 10,000 years ago, correspond to an expansion of human populations. Mammoths and woolly rhinoceroses became extinct, while camels and horses disappeared from the New World. Imperial mammoths and giant ground sloths vanished from South America at about the time that humans arrived there.*

*An alternative theory suggests most of the extinctions were caused by environmental stresses connected with the retreat of the ice sheets.*

◄ *The trend for increasing size, shown here by the elephants, is common in mammals. The peak, which now seems to be past, was the ice age megafauna. It included giant species of rhinoceros, deer, beaver, warthog and ape, as well as the imperial mammoth.*

*Loxodonta africana
(modern African elephant)*

## Chewing the habitat into shape?

The two groups of ungulates, the artiodactyls and perissodactyls, proceeded to evolve in parallel. Both developed more robust, hard-wearing teeth for grinding plant foods, and a digestive system employing bacteria to break down that most indigestible of food-stuffs, cellulose (♦ page 172). Some members of the two groups also tended to grow taller, with more elongated legs for faster running. With this elongation, went the loss of "fingers" – from five to one in the horses, and from five to two in the antelopes and their relatives. Not all became more nimble and long-legged however, some grew larger and more stolid – such as the rhinoceroses and hippos.

These evolutionary developments in the herbivores accompanied changes in the world's climate, which gradually grew drier so that the forests gave way to grassland. Adapting to the new environment, many herbivores – particularly the ancestors of the antelopes and horses – began to exchange leaves and soft fruits for a diet of grass, developing the necessary teeth and digestive equipment for dealing with this much more abrasive plant material. Some biologists believe that, as these early herbivores began feeding more extensively on grass, they in turn became an agent of change: grazing itself started to have an effect on the environment. Grasses differ from other plants in having their growing points near the ground – so when nibbled they rapidly regrow from the base, whereas trees and shrubs are killed or severely stunted. Consequently, grazing animals maintain, and perhaps even create, grassland because they prevent all other plants from making headway, particularly shrubs and trees.

Whether it was caused solely by climate changes, or in part by the action of grazing animals is still debated, but there certainly was a steady change from forest to grassland during the Miocene. With the loss of tree cover, the grazers had more to eat, but became more susceptible to predators in this open habitat. The stealth, concealment, and solitary existence of forest animals were no longer useful, and the survivors were those who could make a run for it. As the herbivores grew faster and longer-legged, so did the carnivores, and a biological "arms race" developed.

## Bigger – and brighter

While the horses and antelopes were becoming fleeter of foot to escape predators, other herbivores took a more defensive option and developed thick hides and a sturdy physique. The modern rhino and buffalo are relics of this trend, but they would have been dwarfed by *Baluchitherium*, which stood over 5m at the shoulder and weighed about 16 tonnes. As these large, heavy herbivores evolved, a few predators became specialized to prey on them, notably the saber-toothed cats, whose long, stabbing teeth could penetrate the thickest hides. Saber-tooths eventually specialized in hunting mammoths and they disappeared at the end of the ice ages, along with their prey.

For many mammals, there was also a steady increase in intelligence, and it is this that has led to their great success. They are able to learn much faster than other animals, and take a more calculated approach to the business of survival. In some mammal species, cunning and adaptability are the key to success, particularly among predators that stalk their prey, or omnivorous opportunistic animals like rats and bears. For other mammals, greater intelligence is linked with tightly knit social groups, where survival is a matter of cooperation, as in cetaceans and primates.

# Evolution and the Changing Continents

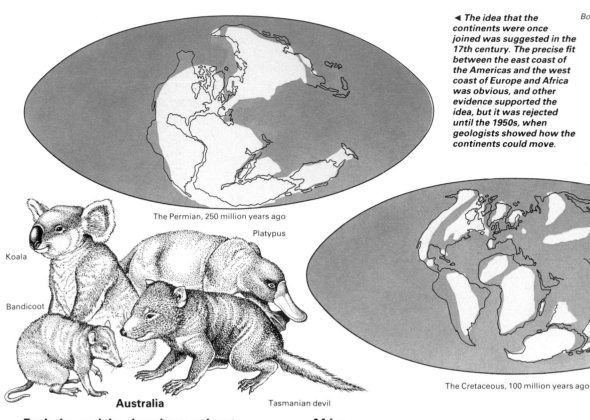

Borhyaena

Giant anteater

◀ The idea that the continents were once joined was suggested in the 17th century. The precise fit between the east coast of the Americas and the west coast of Europe and Africa was obvious, and other evidence supported the idea, but it was rejected until the 1950s, when geologists showed how the continents could move.

The Permian, 250 million years ago

Platypus

Koala

Bandicoot

Australia

Tasmanian devil

The Cretaceous, 100 million years ago

## Evolution and the changing continents
The evolution of the mammals, more than that of any other animal group, has been fundamentally affected by continental drift and changes in sea level. The supercontinent of Pangea that had existed in Permian and Triassic times, began to break up during the Jurassic. By the Paleocene, when mammals were beginning to diversify, the continents were moving apart toward their present positions. Animal communities became isolated, and much of the diversity of the present-day mammals is due to these events.

## Australia
Marsupials reached Australia before it broke away from Antarctica, but the more advanced placentals were too late. Free from the competition that ousted their kind elsewhere, marsupials enjoyed a 50-million-year period of evolutionary enterprise in Australia (◆ page 126). Eventually Australia's northward drift brought it close to Southeast Asia. Lowered sea levels, especially during the ice ages, allowed some exchange of small fauna: a few mice and rats invaded Australia, and some monotremes and marsupials ventured northward into New Guinea. Bats also came south, and early human settlers brought in dogs, which escaped and are now known as dingos. Rabbits and other introductions came much later, with European colonization. The marsupials have not all withstood these invasions but many have done so, showing that they can now compete with placental mammals. The egg-laying monotremes, which also survived only in Australasia, are likewise exhibiting remarkable resilience. A long period adrift from the rest of the world has let a successful group of animals emerge from this primitive stock.

## Africa
A combination of factors kept Africa largely isolated from Europe and Asia from the end of the Cretaceous until the Miocene. Early mammals were already there however, and they evolved into several unique lines. Among the first were the hyraxes, which came in a great many shapes and sizes, including a giant hyrax, the size of a rhinoceros. Today only the diminutive conies and dassies remain. Distantly related to the hyraxes were the elephants, which also had their origins in this period of Africa's isolation, as did an extinct grazer, Arsinotherium, a lumbering, two-horned creature, which has no near relatives. The insectivores also produced a unique family, known as the elephant shrews.

Although the primates originated in Europe or North America, they died out there, probably due to the expansion of the rodents, and survived only in Africa and South America. Those in Africa developed differently from their American cousins, giving rise, for example, to the ground-dwelling baboons, and, in a much later period, to the apes, and ultimately to the human species.

## Madagascar
Lying close to the African mainland in the Cretaceous, Madagascar moved away to an insular existence during the Paleocene. It took with it archaic primates which gave rise to the lemurs, mouse lemurs, indris and aye-aye. Elsewhere in the world, most of these early primates died out in the face of competition from the more intelligent and adaptable monkeys. The only primitive primates to survive outside Madagascar are the lorises and tarsiers – small, specialized, nocturnal animals that inhabit the forests of Africa and Asia.

◀ The faunas of Australia and Southeast Asia have intermingled slightly, but there is still a distinct barrier between them, due to a deep-water channel near the Celebes. This was identified by Alfred Russel Wallace, co-discoverer of natural selection, and is still known as "Wallace's Line".

▲ During its period of isolation, South America produced a unique set of animals. Fossils of many extinct forms were found by Charles Darwin during his Beagle voyage. Comparison with living species, such as sloths and anteaters, helped to convince him that evolution had occurred.

▶ ▼ Africa did not have such a long period of total isolation as South America, so its unusual animals are fewer. But the lemurs of Madagascar are a unique reminder of the earliest primates. Sadly, forest destruction now threatens many species with extinction.

## Madagascar

Lemur

**South America**

Giant
ground sloth
(*Megalosaurus*)

*Macrauchenia*

Capybara

Armadillo

Coati

## South America

High sea levels kept South America largely isolated
from North America for much of its history,
although there were temporary links, via chains of
islands, which allowed some very early ungulates
to move into South America. These evolved into
unique creatures like Macrauchenia. Archaic
placentals also gave rise to another South
American original, the edentate order. Represented
today by sloths, anteaters and armadillos, the
group also included in the past the massive
armadillo Glyptodon which was almost 4m long,
and the giant ground sloth, which stood 6m tall.
But there were no placental carnivores and these
developed instead from marsupial stock. A dog-like
marsupial called Borhyaena preyed on
Macrauchenia and its relatives.

During the Oligocene, the sea level fell, exposing
a chain of islands again, and a few porcupine-like
rodents were able to invade from North America.
They diversified to produce the typical South
American rodents of today – chinchillas, guinea
pigs, capybaras and coypus. Members of the
raccoon family and early primates also moved
south, later developing into the coatis and the New
World monkeys respectively. Like the rodents,
these monkeys evolved in parallel with those
elsewhere but remained distinctly different from
them. Finally, in the late Pliocene, a full land bridge
was established, and North American mammals
arrived in force. Faced with this sort of advanced
competition as well as climatic changes, the home-
grown ungulates like Macrauchenia died out, along
with the marsupial carnivores. But many of the
unusual animals survived; some were successful
enough to advance northward, so that armadillos
and opossums are now found in North America.

The Eocene, 50 million years ago

The Pleistocene ice ages, 40,000 years ago

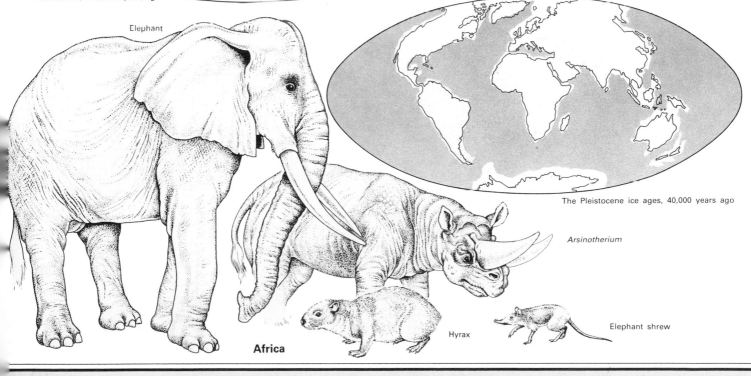

Elephant

*Arsinotherium*

Hyrax

Elephant shrew

**Africa**

# Marsupials and Placentals

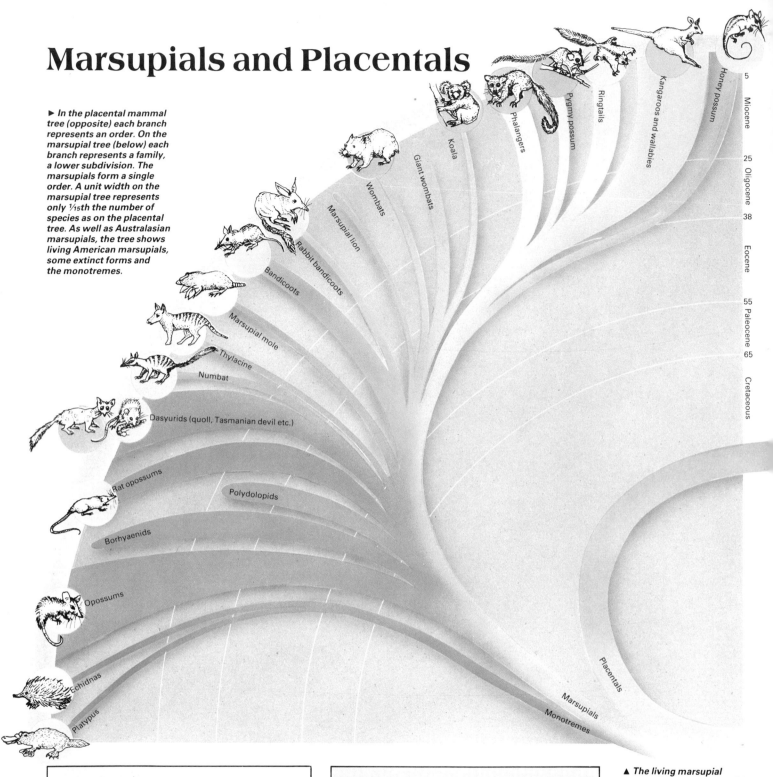

▶ In the placental mammal tree (opposite) each branch represents an order. On the marsupial tree (below) each branch represents a family, a lower subdivision. The marsupials form a single order. A unit width on the marsupial tree represents only 1/15th the number of species as on the placental tree. As well as Australasian marsupials, the tree shows living American marsupials, some extinct forms and the monotremes.

Miocene — 5
Oligocene — 25
— 38
Eocene
— 55
Paleocene
— 65
Cretaceous

Honey possum
Kangaroos and wallabies
Ringtails
Pygmy possum
Phalangers
Koala
Giant wombats
Wombats
Marsupial lion
Rabbit bandicoots
Bandicoots
Marsupial mole
Thylacine
Numbat
Dasyurids (quoll, Tasmanian devil etc.)
Rat opossums
Polydolopids
Borhyaenids
Opossums
Echidnas
Platypus
Placentals
Marsupials
Monotremes

### Close parallels
Parallel or convergent evolution of placentals and marsupials has produced a number of species that have striking similarities. For example, the marsupial mole and the various placental moles (members of the insectivore order) all have enlarged forelimbs for digging, and vestigial eyes; their body shape is almost identical. The thylacine, a marsupial, and the members of the eutherian wolf and dog family, look remarkably similar. The quoll, a smaller carnivorous marsupial belonging to the dasyurid group, is a parallel of the civets, small cat-like predators. The prosimians, members of the primate order which includes lemurs and bush babies, are mirrored by the ringtails and phalangers, marsupials that feed on insects and tree gum. Ant-eating species, too, are similar: the numbat, an ant-eating marsupial, and the giant anteater of South America, both have a tubular snout and a long sticky tongue.

### General resemblances
There is a superficial resemblance between the small marsupial "mice", members of the dasyurids, and placental mice, which are rodents. But placental mice are largely seed-eaters, whereas the marsupial mice are carnivorous, and much fiercer – more like the placental shrews. There are few seed-eating species among the marsupials, possibly because many Australian plants have seeds that are distributed by ants – ants tend to remove the seeds to their nests, thus putting them out of reach of seed-eating mammals. Burrowing rodents that eat roots find their ecological parallel in the marsupial wombats. When the extinct marsupials are considered, some further parallels emerge. There were "marsupial lions" that strongly resembled large cats, and a fossilized "marsupial bear". The marsupials went through a phase of producing giant species, just as the placentals did.

▲ The living marsupial mammals have developed in virtual isolation in Australasia, while the placental mammals were evolving elsewhere. This has resulted in two independent mammal faunas. There are 3,750 species of placental mammal, but only 250 of marsupial, simply because their distribution is more limited. Placentals have had a wider variety of habitats to exploit so they are inevitably more varied.

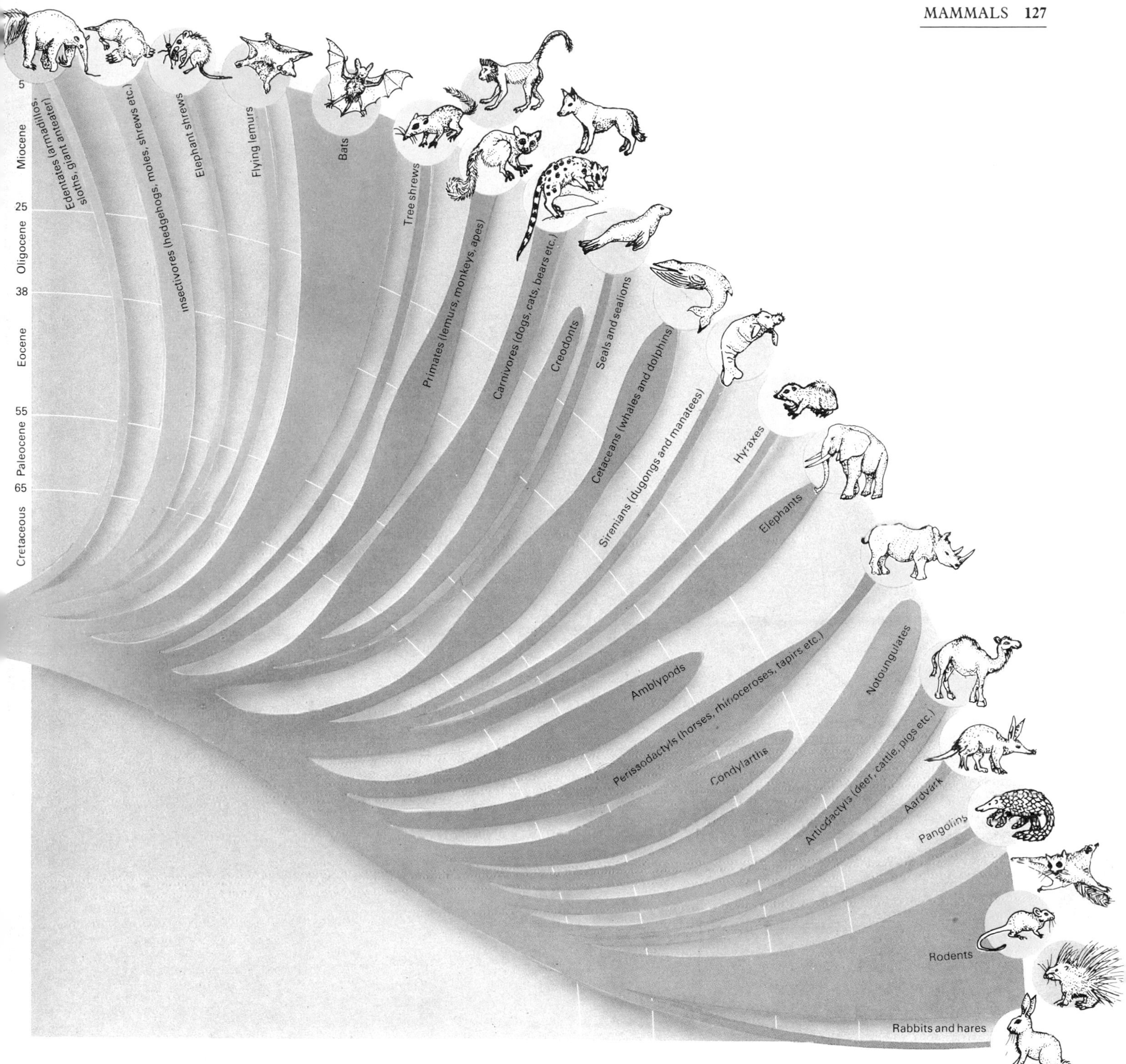

Miocene

Edentates (armadillos, sloths, giant anteater)

Insectivores (hedgehogs, moles, shrews etc.)

Elephant shrews

25

Oligocene

Flying lemurs

38

Eocene

Bats

Tree shrews

55

Paleocene

Primates (lemurs, monkeys, apes)

65

Cretaceous

Carnivores (dogs, cats, bears etc.)

Creodonts

Seals and sealions

Cetaceans (whales and dolphins)

Sirenians (dugongs and manatees)

Hyraxes

Elephants

Amblypods

Perissodactyls (horses, rhinoceroses, tapirs etc.)

Condylarths

Notoungulates

Artiodactyls (deer, cattle, pigs etc.)

Aardvark

Pangolins

Rodents

Rabbits and hares

▲ Comparisons between marsupials and placentals are of great evolutionary interest. Most striking are the close parallels, where two animals have the same sort of diet and way of life, and look astonishingly alike. But these are relatively few. Many groups show a general resemblance and some have a few characters in common, but differ in other ways. Several are unique. Overall, the differences outweigh the similarities, but since these two sets of mammals have evolved independently, from different stock, this is hardly surprising.

**Characters in common**
There are a number of groups of marsupials and placentals that have some features in common but not others. The kangaroos and wallabies fill the same niches as the deer, antelope and other grazing mammals. They all chew tough plants, and their teeth are remarkably alike. Bacteria aid digestion of cellulose in both groups, and the stomach is similarly compartmentalized to accommodate bacteria. However, their methods of moving about are very different. Two marsupial families – the pygmy possums and ringtails – include gliding forms. In appearance these are remarkably like the flying squirrels, of the rodent order, and the flying lemurs. However, the marsupial gliders largely feed on insects, tree gum, nectar and pollen, while the placental species are more strictly vegetarian. Flying squirrels eat nuts, leaves, buds and bark; flying lemurs eat leaves, buds and flowers.

**Unique groups**
The placentals boast three groups of sea-going mammals – whales and dolphins, seals and sealions, dugongs and manatees – whereas there are none among the marsupials. Also unique to the placentals, are the true fliers – bats. They managed to invade Australia from Asia by air, so filling this niche. Other placentals with no obvious parallel include elephants, and higher primates – monkeys and apes. Armored animals like armadillos and pangolins are not seen among marsupials, and nor are prickly ones like hedgehogs and porcupines – although there are examples among the monotremes. The marsupials have no truly unique animals, though the eucalyptus-eating koala is certainly unusual, and the nectar-eating honey possum has no real equivalent. Some small placental mammals, such as the dormouse, sometimes eat nectar and pollen, but none specialize in this diet, except the nectarivorous bats.

### Conquering the air...

One of the most specialized and remarkable mammalian groups – the bats – appeared very early in the period of mammal expansion, over 50 million years ago. But they were not early enough. Birds had then been around for 100 million years and there were no vacant niches for flying animals – not in the daylight hours anyway. The only slots that bats could fill were nocturnal ones. Birds, like their reptile ancestors, are largely dependent on sight for getting about and even today very few can fly in total darkness. Mammals had evolved nocturnal senses during the Age of Reptiles, when dinosaurs dominated the Earth by day: most relied on a highly sensitive nose and excellent hearing. The insectivores had probably begun to emit high-pitched (ultrasonic) noises for communication, as shrews do today, and from this it was a short step to evolving echolocation, in which the echoes of those ultrasonic squeaks were interpreted for information about the outside world – the first radar system. A simple form of this system is believed to operate in modern shrews, but it was when the insectivores took to the air that echolocation really came into its own.

The main food sources open to bats were those insects that had become nocturnal as an escape from bird predation. In the temperate regions, insect-eating bats (Microchiroptera) are the only types found. The tropics, however, offer other nutritional possibilities – fruit, nectar or pollen – which fruit bats (Megachiroptera) exploit. They often feed at dusk, and are larger than microchiropterans, with huge eyes and a less sensitive form of radar using clicks audible to humans. They can also afford to be slower-flying and achieve wingspans of up to 1·5m.

It is among the microchiropterans that an interesting diversification can be observed. In the tropics are found four species that catch fish, three that suck blood (vampire bats), eight that prey on small mammals (false vampires) and a few that catch frogs. This could perhaps be the start of a new line of development for the bats, an adaptive radiation (◀ page 16) that is just beginning.

▼ **Manatees superficially resemble whales but evolved independently. Horny nails on the flippers recall their terrestrial past.**

▲ **Having wings instead of front legs means that large bats cannot easily move about on the ground, but some run quite fast, and a few even dig burrows.**

### ...and the sea

Sea-going mammals have arisen independently no less than three times in the course of mammalian evolution. The most specialized are the cetaceans (whales and dolphins) which are so divorced from their terrestrial past that they die if beached, the larger ones being crushed by the pull of gravity on their massive bodies. These creatures mate and give birth in the water, as do the second group, the dugongs and manatees, slow-moving herbivorous mammals that inhabit estuaries, lagoons and rivers.

The third and least specialized group, the seals and sealions, emerge onto land to breed, and have retained their hindlimbs, external ears (in sealions), sensory whiskers and other typically terrestrial features. Little is known about the origins of any of these groups, although it is thought that the whales emerged in the swampy coastal waters of Africa, during its period of isolation.

# The Chemistry of Life

## 17

*The chemistry of living cells...Sugars, the fuel of life...
Saturated and unsaturated fats...Amino acids, building
blocks of protein...Enzymes, catalyzing reactions in the
cell...Using energy...DNA and RNA, reproducing the
cell...PERSPECTIVE...Some basic chemistry...The spark
of life...The metabolic jungle...How muscles work...
Discovering the structure of DNA*

In 1897, two German pharmacists, Hans and Eduard Buchner, were
trying to prepare a yeast extract for medicinal use. Having made their
cell-free extract, they needed to preserve it, without using toxic compounds, so they turned to sugar, the common "preservative" of the
kitchen. The combination of their yeast extract and the sugar produced surprising results: overnight the mixture frothed and foamed,
blowing the cork from its container. Against all expectation, fermentation had occurred. The accepted doctrine of the time, formulated in
1860 by Pasteur, was that only living things could perform fermentation. Pasteur was partly right – only living things have the innate
ability to perform fermentation. But what the Buchners had discovered was that the chemical processes could continue *outside* the cell.

Experiments with muscle tissue subsequently showed that many of
the chemical processes occurring in animals were identical to those
found in yeasts. This pointed to the fundamental unity of life, which
all further biochemical research has confirmed. Moreover, biochemists have established that living things are composed of exactly
the same atomic building blocks as the rest of the universe, and that
the reactions involved obey the normal laws of chemistry. Yet the
chemistry of life is distinctive enough to be dubbed "biochemistry".

## Some basic chemistry

An **element** is the term applied to substances that
cannot be decomposed into simpler substances by
chemical reactions. The matter of the universe is
composed of 92 naturally occurring elements, from
hydrogen, the lightest, to uranium, the heaviest.
Scientists have assigned each element a chemical
symbol – thus O is the symbol for oxygen, H for
hydrogen, Na for sodium. An **atom** is the smallest
fragment of a chemical element that retains the
properties of that element and can take part in
chemical reactions. Atoms are believed to consist
of a tiny nucleus containing protons, which carry a
positive electrical charge, and neutrons, which are
uncharged. The number of protons in the nucleus
defines which chemical element the atom is. The
nucleus is associated with a number of electrons,
which bear a negative electrical charge. In an atom
the number of electrons equals the number of
protons, but in an electrically charged **ion**, there is
either a surfeit or a deficit of electrons.

It is the interactions of the outermost electrons in
an atom that are responsible for the chemical
behavior of matter. Since most atoms do not have
stable electron configurations, they undergo
chemical reactions in which they join, or "bond"
with one or more other atoms to achieve molecules
with more stable outer electron shells.

**Covalent bonding** occurs when two atoms share
electrons. If they share one pair of electrons (one
provided by each partner) they are said to have a
**single bond**. Thus a molecule of hydrogen contains
two hydrogen atoms (1), and is shown by the
chemical formula $H_2$, or the structural formula H-H,
where – represents a single bond. Atoms may also
share two pairs of electrons in a **double bond** as in
a molecule of oxygen (2), written as $O_2$ or O=O.

When two hydrogen atoms share electrons with
an oxygen atom, the result is a molecule of water
(3), written as $H_2O$ or H-O-H, indicating that each
hydrogen atom has a single bond to the oxygen
atom, but that the hydrogen atoms are not bonded
to each other. Water is an example of a chemical
**compound** – a substance consisting of two or more
different elements combined in a fixed ratio.

Although hydrogen and oxygen share their
outermost electrons in the water molecule, they do
so rather unequally, the electron being pulled more
toward the oxygen atom. Thus the oxygen has a
slight negative charge and the hydrogens a slight
positive charge. The molecule is said to be "polar".

Another form of bonding, known as **ionic**, does
not involve any sharing of the electrons. Instead
there is a complete transfer of one or more
electrons from one atom to the other. This gives
ions which attract each other because of their
opposite charges. Salt (4) is the ionic bonding of a
sodium ion ($Na^+$) with a chlorine ion ($Cl^-$).

Another type of bond is the hydrogen bond, in
which atoms in different molecules (or atoms that
are in different parts of one large molecule) "share"
a hydrogen atom. Hydrogen bonds are weak and
are readily formed or broken but they have a
specific length and orientation; this feature is very
important in helping to determine the three-
dimensional structure of large molecules such as
proteins (♦ page 134).

## Covalent bonding

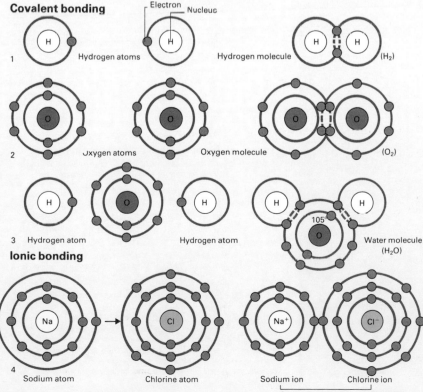

Electron  Nucleus

1  Hydrogen atoms          Hydrogen molecule          ($H_2$)

2  Oxygen atoms          Oxygen molecule          ($O_2$)

3  Hydrogen atom          Hydrogen atom          105°          Water molecule ($H_2O$)

## Ionic bonding

4  Sodium atom          Chlorine atom          Sodium ion          Chlorine ion

Sodium chloride molecule (NaCl)

**Hydrogen bonds and the structure of water**

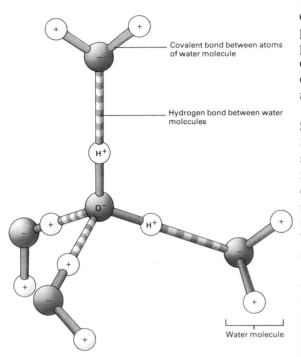

Covalent bond between atoms of water molecule

Hydrogen bond between water molecules

Water molecule

▲ *Water makes up about 70 percent of a cell, and living organisms make great use of its distinctive characteristics. Because of their polarity, water molecules form hydrogen bonds with one another, and these keep water liquid (rather than gaseous) at a wide range of temperatures, which gives living organisms great stability. The polarity of water molecules also attracts them to ions and to other polar molecules, and they cluster around them so that they become "dissolved" in water. Most of the reactions in a cell occur in an aqueous solution.*

One important feature of biochemistry is its dependence on enzymes. These are protein molecules which act as catalysts in the cell, bringing other molecules together and making reactions between them take place much faster than they would normally. Enzymes, like other proteins (◆ page 134), are made up of amino acids, and these are one of the four major classes of organic molecules occurring in all living organisms. The others are *sugars* (see below), *lipids* (◆ page 132) and *nucleotides* (◆ page 138).

**Sugars: the power source**

Some of the most numerous molecules in living organisms are the sugars or saccharides, also called "carbohydrates". They play a major role as food molecules in the cell, being broken down to produce energy. Monosaccharides, such as glucose, are the simplest type of sugar. These monosaccharide rings can link up to form a two-ringed sugar (a disaccharide) such as sucrose, the familiar sugar that we eat. The single rings can also join up to form very much larger "polysaccharide" molecules with thousands of monosaccharide units.

The various kinds of simple sugars can join up in several different ways to create an enormous variety of chemically distinct structures. One important role for long-chained polysaccharides is to serve as energy reserves – glycogen in animals and starch in plants. Glycogen is stored in the liver and can be broken down to give glucose. It provides a quick-release energy source, that keeps us going between meals – only fasting for longish periods requires our fat reserves to be broken down. The starch stored by plants is what makes potatoes, rice, bread and pasta sustaining. Although starch does not taste sweet, it is made up of long chains of sugar molecules.

But sugars have yet more roles in the cell, for example as building materials. Cellulose, which gives plants their rigidity, and chitin that forms the outer casing of insects' bodies, are both polysaccharides.

**The spark of life**
*The belief that life was fundamentally different from non-life led to the division of chemistry into two disciplines, inorganic and organic. The latter concerned itself solely with substances derived from living things. Since these substances were all based on chains or rings of carbon atoms, organic chemistry was also the chemistry of carbon. It was believed that organic compounds had special chemical characteristics and could only be made by living things, but in 1828 Fredrick Wohler disproved this by synthesizing urea from an inorganic compound, ammonium cyanate. Thereafter, organic chemistry became simply the study of carbon compounds. Despite Wohler's discovery, and that of the Buchner brothers, "vitalism" took a long time to die. Many people wanted to believe that the chemistry of life was somehow different, and as late as the 1940s there were scientists who thought that DNA would turn out to have some unique chemical basis. Watson and Crick's discovery of the double helix with its conventional chemical bonds disappointed them.*

◀ *Insects such as pondskaters are able to walk on water thanks to its high surface tension. This is produced by the hydrogen bonds between the water molecules which effectively create a "skin" at the water's surface. The high surface tension of water is vital to many physiological processes, particularly the transport of water in plants.*

## The distinctive chemistry of life

Life on Earth is based on carbon, an element that has unusual properties making it particularly well suited to such a role. Carbon is unique among elements in its ability to form large, stable molecules. In pure forms, atoms of carbon can bond to one another in two ways, either forming extensive two-dimensional lattices (graphite) or tetrahedral crystals of great strength (diamonds). But by virtue of its small size and complement of electrons, carbon can also form strong bonds with other atoms, such as oxygen, hydrogen and nitrogen, and in organic molecules it can create very long chains or rings of enormous diversity. At least one and a half million carbon compounds exist. It is thanks to this versatility of carbon that life as we know it has evolved.

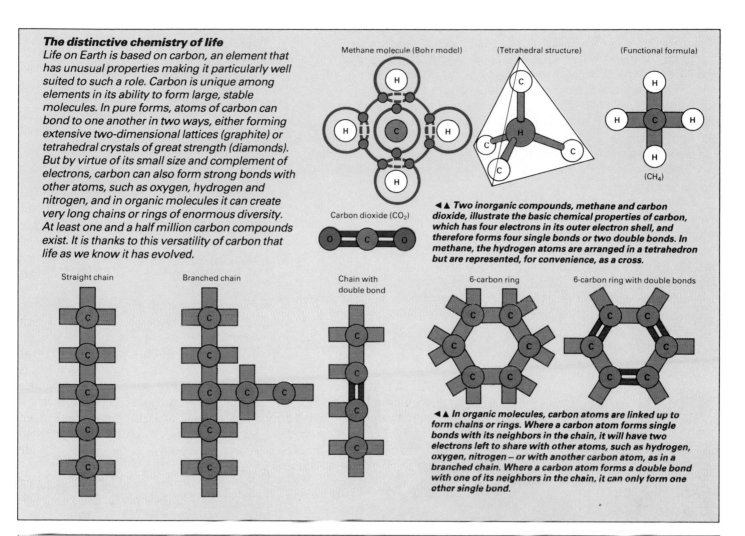

Methane molecule (Bohr model)    (Tetrahedral structure)    (Functional formula)

$(CH_4)$

Carbon dioxide $(CO_2)$

◀▲ Two inorganic compounds, methane and carbon dioxide, illustrate the basic chemical properties of carbon, which has four electrons in its outer electron shell, and therefore forms four single bonds or two double bonds. In methane, the hydrogen atoms are arranged in a tetrahedron but are represented, for convenience, as a cross.

Straight chain    Branched chain    Chain with double bond    6-carbon ring    6-carbon ring with double bonds

◀▲ In organic molecules, carbon atoms are linked up to form chains or rings. Where a carbon atom forms single bonds with its neighbors in the chain, it will have two electrons left to share with other atoms, such as hydrogen, oxygen, nitrogen – or with another carbon atom, as in a branched chain. Where a carbon atom forms a double bond with one of its neighbors in the chain, it can only form one other single bond.

## Sugars

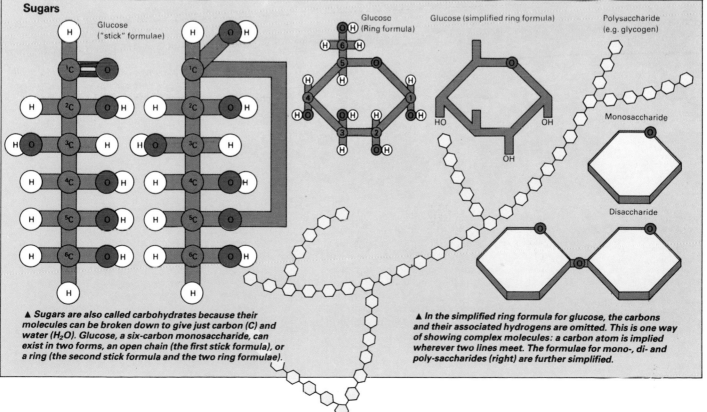

Glucose ("stick" formulae)    Glucose (Ring formula)    Glucose (simplified ring formula)    Polysaccharide (e.g. glycogen)

Monosaccharide

Disaccharide

▲ Sugars are also called carbohydrates because their molecules can be broken down to give just carbon (C) and water ($H_2O$). Glucose, a six-carbon monosaccharide, can exist in two forms, an open chain (the first stick formula), or a ring (the second stick formula and the two ring formulae).

▲ In the simplified ring formula for glucose, the carbons and their associated hydrogens are omitted. This is one way of showing complex molecules: a carbon atom is implied wherever two lines meet. The formulae for mono-, di- and poly-saccharides (right) are further simplified.

## The versatile lipids

Lipids form a second class of small organic molecules that are essential to life in many ways. They are all made up largely of hydrogen and carbon, with few polar groups attached – or none at all in some cases. Thus they are hydrophobic – insoluble in water. Most abundant are the fatty acids, which have an ambivalent nature – largely hydrophobic but with a hydrophilic head. This ambivalence is preserved in the phospholipids where it makes cell membranes possible (♦ page 133). Fatty acids, in the form of triglycerides, are also good storage molecules because they yield twice as much energy as the equivalent weight of glycogen.

Another important group of lipids are the steroids, which are all made up of four interlocked carbon rings, with different side-chains attached, giving each its particular properties. Steroids include the sex hormones, such as testosterone, another hormone, cortisone and vitamin D, which is responsible for transporting calcium into the bones. The much-maligned cholesterol is also a steroid, and it has a vital role in stabilizing membrane structure – 95 percent of body cholesterol is in the membranes, and the body synthesizes it to supply these needs. However, on a rich diet, cholesterol in food boosts the supply, and this may lead to the blood becoming overloaded with it, and thus to fatty deposits in the arteries.

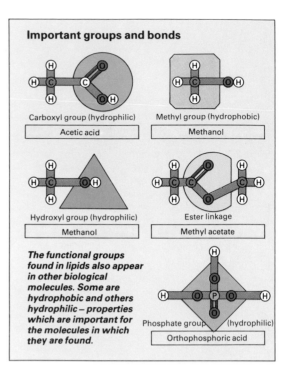

**Important groups and bonds**

Carboxyl group (hydrophilic)
Acetic acid

Methyl group (hydrophobic)
Methanol

Hydroxyl group (hydrophilic)
Methanol

Ester linkage
Methyl acetate

*The functional groups found in lipids also appear in other biological molecules. Some are hydrophobic and others hydrophilic – properties which are important for the molecules in which they are found.*

Phosphate group (hydrophilic)
Orthophosphoric acid

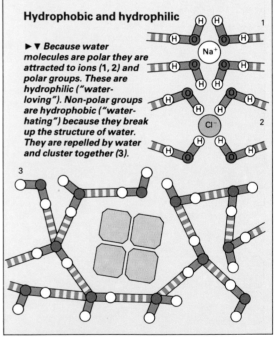

**Hydrophobic and hydrophilic**

► ▼ *Because water molecules are polar they are attracted to ions (1, 2) and polar groups. These are hydrophilic ("water-loving"). Non-polar groups are hydrophobic ("water-hating") because they break up the structure of water. They are repelled by water and cluster together (3).*

▲ *Carotenoids are responsible for most of the red, orange and yellow colors seen in nature. More importantly to humans, carotenoids can be converted to vitamin A, the source of our visual pigment, rhodopsin. The old saying that "carrots help you seen in the dark", is not quite correct, but they are a good source of vitamin A – and a deficiency of this vitamin causes "night blindness".*

### The colors of life

Whenever yellow, red or orange colors occur in plants or animals, a group of lipids called carotenoids are likely to be responsible. These compounds are universally distributed and in plants and bacteria they help in photosynthesis by gathering light energy and channelling it to chlorophyll, the main photosynthetic pigment. Carotenoids are also found in bacterial cells, which they protect from light-damage.

The carotenoids in leaves are not obvious most of the time, because the green of chlorophyll predominates. But before their leaves fall, most plants, particularly trees, resorb chlorophyll to conserve the magnesium it contains. It is then that the carotenoids become evident. The progression from yellow through orange to red, that is seen in dying leaves and ripening fruit, is characteristic of these pigments. Simple chemical transformations produce these changes, and as the changes are progressive, the colors always go in the same order. Freak varieties of vegetables, such as yellow tomatoes, are caused by a mutation which knocks out the last step in this pathway. Blood oranges and pink grapefruit have re-acquired later steps, absent in the normal variety.

## Fatty acids

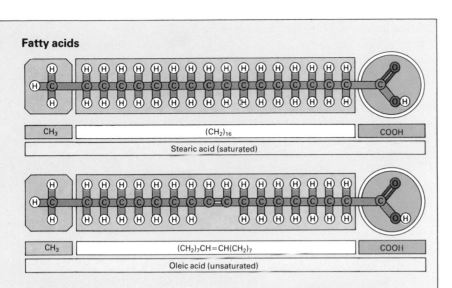

| CH₃ | (CH₂)₁₆ | COOH |

Stearic acid (saturated)

| CH₃ | (CH₂)₇CH=CH(CH₂)₇ | COOH |

Oleic acid (unsaturated)

## Triglycerides

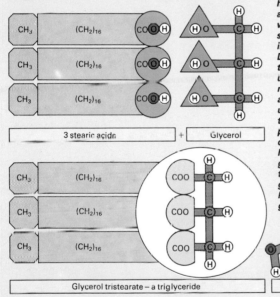

| 3 stearic acids | + | Glycerol |

Glycerol tristearate – a triglyceride

Water

▲ ◀ *Fatty acid chains having only single bonds are said to be "saturated" with hydrogen; they are straight and pack together in stable arrangements. Double bonds put kinks into the chain which make unsaturated fatty acids more fluid. The relative amounts of saturated and unsaturated fatty acids help to determine membrane properties. A hydrocarbon chain of fatty acid is hydrophobic, the carboxyl group is hydrophilic. In triglycerides each carboxyl group is bound to another hydrophilic molecule, glycerol.*

## Phospholipids

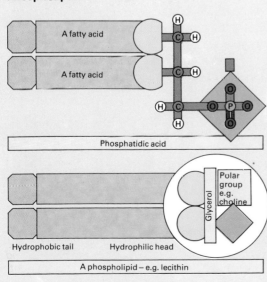

Phosphatidic acid

| Hydrophobic tail | Hydrophilic head |

A phospholipid – e.g. lecithin

◀ *Phospholipids, like triglycerides, consist of fatty acids bound by their carboxyl groups to a hydrophilic moiety. Phospholipids basically consist of two fatty acids and a phosphate group bound to an alcohol, usually glycerol. This gives phosphatidic acid, which then binds to another polar group to give the phospholipid. In lecithin, a common phospholipid, the polar group is choline – (CH₃)₃NHCH₂CH₂OH – a short-chain alcohol. It becomes linked to the phosphate via its hydroxyl group. The polar head group of the phospholipid, though shown as spherical in the diagrams (left and right), is in reality quite elongated.*

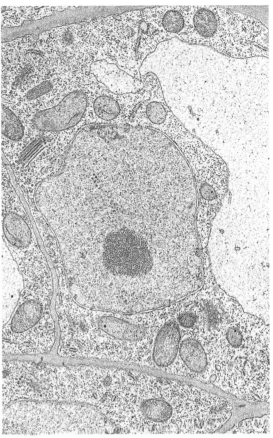

▲ ▼ *An electron micrograph of a typical plant cell. It is enclosed by a membrane, and has many membrane-bound organelles within it (◊ page 157). These membranes are made up of various lipids but principally of phospholipids such as lecithin. If these phospholipids are purified and placed in water, they spontaneously form a surface film and/or globular micelles, because the hydrophobic tails of the molecules are repelled by water. In a cell membrane (shown diagrammatically at the bottom), the molecules form a bilayer for the same reason.*

## Lipid aggregates

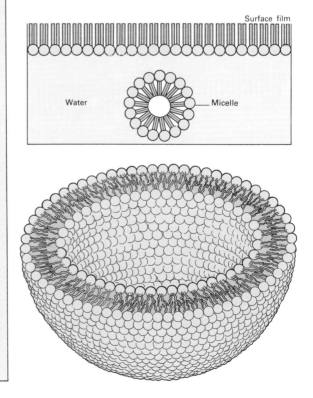

Surface film

Water — Micelle

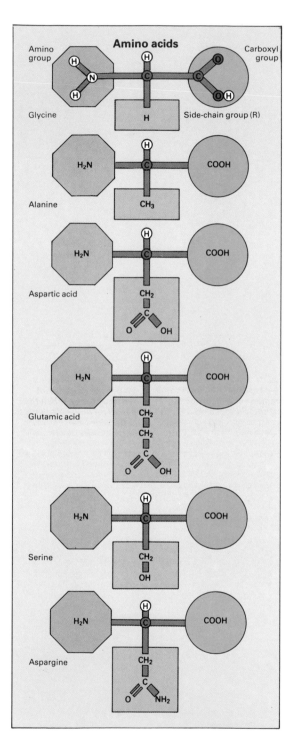

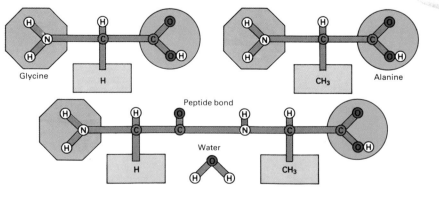

## Amino acids: the building blocks of protein

Proteins do almost everything in the body, from catalyzing reactions (as enzymes), fighting off foreign invaders (as antibodies), storing and transporting oxygen (as hemoglobin and myoglobin) to forming muscle, skin, hair and a variety of other structural tissues. They exist in a multitude of forms, but almost all are constructed from a basic set of just 20 common amino acids. These amino acids are joined together in various combinations to form the long chains that are proteins; shorter chains of amino acids are called polypeptides.

All amino acids share a carboxyl group and an amino group, both linked to the same atom of carbon. The nature of the "side chain", also bonded to this carbon atom, distinguishes one amino acid from another. It is probably no coincidence that the four amino acids that are easiest for a chemist to make – glycine, alanine, aspartic acid and glutamic acid – are very abundant in proteins. They were probably the first amino acids to be formed in the ancient seas.

Another striking feature of present-day proteins is that they are all made up of amino acids linked by a "peptide" bond between the carboxylic acid of one amino acid and the amino group of the next. Somehow living organisms settled on this linkage, in preference to any of the other ways that amino acids can join up – via their side-chains, for example. By always linking amino acids through their central carbon atom, a uniform backbone for protein molecules was established.

The order of amino acids in a protein is of immense importance because that sequence determines how the side chains will interact with one another to create the three-dimensional shape of the protein. It is the shape or conformation of a protein that ultimately determines its function in the living organism.

Shape is important to all proteins, but particularly to enzymes, which act as biocatalysts, controlling the metabolic processes of the cell by initiating and regulating certain reactions. Like ordinary chemical catalysts they speed up reactions without being consumed in the process. But enzymes are supreme among catalysts in their specificity and efficiency. They can speed up most reactions by a factor of a million. Without them, biochemical reactions could not happen at the low temperatures at which life proceeds.

Enzymes are able to coordinate the body's metabolism because they do not catalyze reactions indiscriminately. Thanks to their unique three-dimensional shape, determined by the sequence of amino acids, enzymes are highly specific – most will catalyze only one reaction. (The sort of enzymes that go into washing powders are an exception to this, chosen for their lack of specificity.) As a consequence of this, many different enzymes are required. A bacterial cell needs at least 2,000 enzymes to carry out all its metabolic reactions.

◄► *There are 20 common amino acids and they all have a carboxyl group at one end and an amino group at the other. These join up in a peptide bond (right). As the bond is formed, a molecule of water is produced. What distinguishes one amino acid from another is the side chain, attached to the central carbon atom. Some are hydrophobic and therefore tend to bury themselves in the center of the protein molecule to avoid contact with water. Others are hydrophilic, and some may bear a negative or positive charge, which makes them attract or repel other charged amino acids. Two amino acids (methionine and cystine) contain sulfur and these can form strong "disulfide" linkages with other sulfur-containing amino acids in the chain. All these factors affect the shape that the protein adopts.*

► This protein contains 416 amino acids, of which 4 are shown. This diagram is based on a model of the protein in which each atom is represented by a small plastic ball – the model stands 2.5m high.

◄ Sections of beta sheet (indicated by broad arrows) are formed by two or more strands of the protein chain lying alongside one another, and hydrogen bonds forming between the carboxyl groups and adjacent amino groups.

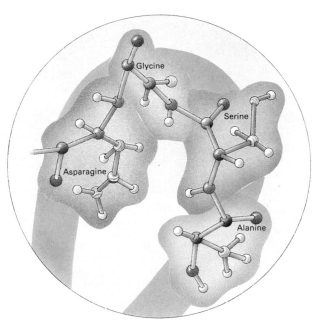

Glycine
Serine
Asparagine
Alanine

Covalent bond
Hydrogen bond
Carbon
Oxygen
Nitrogen
Hydrogen
Side chain

◄▼ The shape or "conformation" of a protein molecule is determined by the sequence of the amino acids that go to make it up. Most proteins contain some regions of α helix and β sheet; these are rigid structures that make up the "body" of the protein. Some amino acids favor the formation of β sheets or α helices. For example, alanine is a common component of β sheets, and glutamic acid is a strong helix former. But the question of why β sheets and α helices tend to form in some parts of the molecule and not other parts is a very complex one, and a great many different factors are thought to be involved in the process.

◄ The protein shown here is an enzyme, phospho-glycerate kinase. It has two parts, known as domains, and its activity depends on a hinge mechanism between them. When the substrate molecule binds to the enzyme it changes the conformation, eventually influencing the hinge region. The change in the hinge region causes the two domains to rotate onto each other. The substrate is then in a suitable environment for the reaction to proceed.

▼ Section of α helix are indicated by cylinders. They are held together by hydrogen bonds between carboxyl and amino groups. This one has 9 amino acids.

*Enzymes organize the cell's metabolism, while other types of protein make up muscles, tendons, skin and claws*

### The metabolic maze

*Even the simplest cells are a metabolic maze of astonishing complexity. Any small molecule participates in a variety of metabolic pathways and is acted on in diverse ways by many different enzymes. But the upshot of all this is a cell which operates efficiently, and shows surprising stability, because it is regulated by an elaborate network of control mechanisms.*

*The most basic sort of control occurs at the genetic level, where a metabolite can turn a gene on or off ( ◆ page 26). A similar type of control is applied to the enzymes themselves by way of inhibitors. Sometimes, for instance, the first enzyme in a chain of reactions is inhibited by the end product, so production ceases when levels of the product are high. This is known as feedback regulation. Enzymes can also be switched on by particular chemicals known as activators.*

*A few crucial enzymes can also shift the metabolism of a cell from, say, degrading glucose, to synthesizing it using fatty acids or amino acids. Such mechanisms enable our bodies to keep our brains supplied with glucose even during prolonged periods without food. The pathways are carefully controlled (activated and inhibited by key compounds) so that each occurs only in the appropriate circumstances.*

### How to baffle an enzyme

*Enzymes can, it seems, do almost anything. This is a mixed blessing for living organisms, because enzymes can be used against them by other creatures. Plants, in particular, must build up tissues that fungi and animals cannot easily break down. Cellulose, the cell wall polymer, is quite difficult to digest ( ◆ page 173) but lignin, the crucial ingredient of wood, is even more resistant to enzymatic attack. Its only enemies are a few types of fungi, and the fact that these have not rampaged through the world's forests suggests that eating lignin is not an easy option.*

*The way in which lignin resists attack throws light on how enzymes work. The basic constituents of the lignin polymer are rings of carbon atoms, but these are joined together in a random way, rather than following a regular repeated pattern as in most polymers. It is the randomness that defeats enzyme action: their structural precision, which is what makes them such powerful and specific catalysts, is a severe limitation when faced with an irregular molecule like lignin.*

### Enzyme deficiencies

*Mutations ( ◆ page 25) can change the amino acid sequence of proteins. When an amino acid that is crucial to maintaining the enzyme's conformation, or one that is part of the active site, changes, the enzyme's effectiveness will be impaired. The effect is often lethal, but not always. A defective enzyme on the pathway leading to the pigment melanin, results in albinism – a lack of pigment in the skin and hair. Siamese cats have a defective enzyme that only fails to perform at certain temperatures – if kept cool it can function normally. This is why Siamese cats only have dark pigment at the body's extremities, where temperatures are lower.*

Two molecular features give enzymes their special powers. The shape of the molecule allows only the substrate, and certain other specific molecules, to bind to it. The substrate molecule binds to the enzyme's "binding site", within which is the "active site", where catalysis occurs. The enzyme does its job by putting the reactants in a chemical milieu where the reaction is energetically much more favorable than it would otherwise be. When the reaction is complete, the end products break away from the enzyme.

Many enzymes require help from a non-protein in order to do their job. The helper is called a cofactor and it can range from a metal ion to a complex organic molecule such as adenosine triphosphate, or ATP ( ◆ page 138). These larger molecules, or "coenzymes", mostly function as carriers, bringing to the reaction an essential component such as hydrogen, a phosphate, a carboxyl or a methyl group. In other reactions, the same coenzymes act as acceptors for these same groups.

It is difficult to overemphasize the central role that enzymes play in the life of organisms. A living creature needs to be able to break down complex molecules to extract energy, and synthesize other molecules needed for the repair and reproduction of cells. The total of all the reactions within it is known as its metabolism, and enzymes are the biological molecules that control these reactions. In all living organisms, long chains of reactions, known as metabolic pathways, have evolved. In a pathway devoted, say, to the breakdown of sugar to release energy, each reaction is catalyzed by a particular enzyme, and the end product of one reaction is the starting point of the next. Modern cells function via a bewildering network of such pathways.

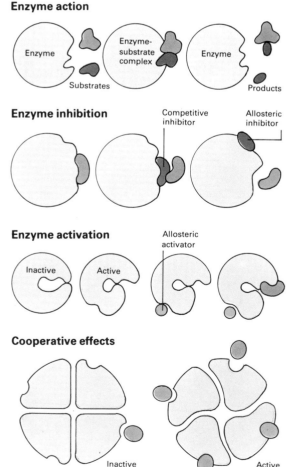

**Enzyme action**

Enzyme — Substrates

Enzyme-substrate complex

Enzyme — Products

**Enzyme inhibition**

Competitive inhibitor

Allosteric inhibitor

**Enzyme activation**

Inactive — Active

Allosteric activator

**Cooperative effects**

Inactive

Active

*An enzyme's binding site has a very specific fit for its substrate or substrates. Competitive inhibitors are usually similar to the substrate. They can therefore occupy the binding site, preventing access by the substrate. Allosteric inhibitors attach themselves to the enzyme, but not at the binding site. They produce their effect by changing the shape of the enzyme, and thus distorting the binding site so that the substrate no longer fits. Allosteric activators control enzymes that have two possible shapes – one of which is active, the other inactive. Normally, the inactive form is much more stable, so that at any one time 99% of the molecules will be in this conformation. The addition of the activator makes the active form stable, and the reaction can then proceed. Cooperative effects are seen in enzymes made up of two or more subunits, where the substrate itself stabilizes the active form. The subunits adopt the same conformation, so if substrate binds to one, making it change to the active form, then its neighbors are also activated.*

## Structure of elastin

▲ *Elastin is made up of relatively unstructured polypeptide chains that can stretch out when pressure is applied to them (below) and then coil up when the pressure is removed (top). Elastin forms a rubbery matrix around distensible organs like the lungs.*

### Structural proteins

Apart from their importance as enzymes, proteins have many structural roles in the body – and outside it, as in the silk proteins produced by arthropods (♦ page 86). Three important proteins in vertebrates are keratin, collagen and elastin.

Keratin is an important component of feathers, fur, scales, claws, nails and various other structures, such as rhinoceros horn. It has two forms, α keratin and β keratin. In α keratin, each molecule contains many α-helices (♦ page 135). It is further coiled into a helix with other molecules, to produce a protofibril, and several of these are packed together to make up a single keratin fibril. The α-keratin is elastic because the α helices can easily be broken down into a more elongated structure based on β-sheets – this is β keratin. When the protein needs to contract, the β keratin can revert to α keratin.

Collagen is a much more rigid molecule than keratin, due to its inelastic triple-helix, and the staggered arrangement of the protein molecules in a microfibril. The arrangement of the fibers in layers, like plywood, gives additional reinforcement. Collagen is the major component of cartilage, bones, tendons and teeth.

Another important structural protein is elastin, a remarkably flexible material that surrounds organs like lungs and arteries, which undergo changes in shape and size. Elastin consists of relatively unstructured polypeptide chains. They can open out when pulled, and then coil up loosely when the tension is removed. Strong cross-linkages between the protein molecules give elastin its integrity.

### Structure of collagen

Microfibril

Fibril · Fiber

Tropocollagen molecule

Glycine · Various amino acids, often proline and hydroxyproline

▲ ◄ *A false-color scanning electron micrograph of collagen fibers (yellow ribbons) and red blood cells, surrounding striated muscle fiber. The protein chains that make up collagen (below) have an unusual amino acid composition. Glycine accounts for one third, and the remainder is made up of proline and two rare amino acids – hydroxyproline and hydroxylysine. Three such protein chains, each containing about 1,000 amino acids, are twisted together in a triple helix: a tropocollagen molecule. Each molecule has a distinct head and tail end where the helical arrangement breaks down. The tropocollagen molecules are staggered at intervals equal to ¼ their length in the microfibril, which appears banded due to their head and tail regions. Microfibrils make up the collagen fibrils, and these are bundled together again to make up the collagen fibers.*

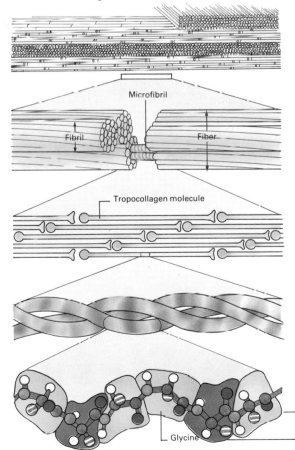

*DNA has been described as the "brains" of the cell*

It is particularly during biosynthesis, when living organisms build complex molecules out of simpler starting materials, that the uniqueness of life – and the remarkable powers of enzymes – are striking. Reactions that join simpler molecules into something more complex never occur spontaneously: energy has to be put into a system to make such things happen. During biosynthesis, living organisms are apparently going against the grain of the universe, where, as the second law of thermodynamics states, disorder tends to increase. Living things seem at first glance to be in violation of this basic principle of physics, but they do toe the line in the end; they exist as ordered entities only because they increase the disorder of the world at large by releasing heat. Heat increases the random motion, and hence disorder, of molecules.

As a corollary to all this, any chemical reactions that lead to an increase in disorder, or less "free energy", are energetically favorable. If free energy decreases markedly, because the reaction produces much smaller and more stable molecules, then it will have a strong tendency to happen – explosives are a striking example of such reactions. Conversely, if the reaction results in a large increase in free energy, it will never happen – *unless* it is coupled with a reaction so energetically favorable that the net result is a decrease in free energy. This is just the strategy that living organisms adopt.

The energy to drive biosynthetic reactions is provided through the ingenious deployment of enzymes. The enzymes couple the synthesis of the desired compound, which is energetically unfavorable, to a reaction that is energetically very favorable, usually the breakdown of ATP, the energy currency of the cell. The net result is a decrease in free energy, and the second law of thermodynamics is obeyed.

## Nucleotides: carriers of the genetic information

The fourth group of small organic molecules so distinctive to life are the nucleotides. These are the building blocks of the nucleic acids – DNA (deoxyribonucleic acid) and RNA (ribonucleic acid). DNA and RNA are similar chemically, differing principally in the sugar that forms, with phosphate, the "backbone" of the molecule.

In most organisms, it is DNA that is the stuff of heredity. It makes up the genes that an organism inherits from its parents, and these tell the cells which proteins to make. Each gene – a short stretch of DNA – directs the production of a particular protein in the cell. And proteins, in the form of enzymes (◀ page 136), initiate and regulate all the chemical reactions within the cell.

The information for building proteins is encoded in the sequence of bases in the nucleic acid. Proteins are made from sequences of amino acids, and the important task is to assemble those amino acids in the correct order – this, in turn, determines the protein's conformation, and its enzymatic or other function. A living cell translates the base sequence in a stretch of DNA into a sequence of amino acids, which are then joined up to form the protein. As there are thousands of different kinds of protein, it seems at first sight as if DNA is quite inadequate to contain a blueprint for all of them. The only variables are the bases, and there are just four of them: cytosine, guanine, thymine, and adenine. However, with four bases to choose from, there are 64 different ways of arranging them in sets of three. And as there are only about 20 amino acids in nature, the four bases can be arranged, in threes, to provide a code for all the amino acids. Each sequence of three bases coding for an amino acid is called a codon.

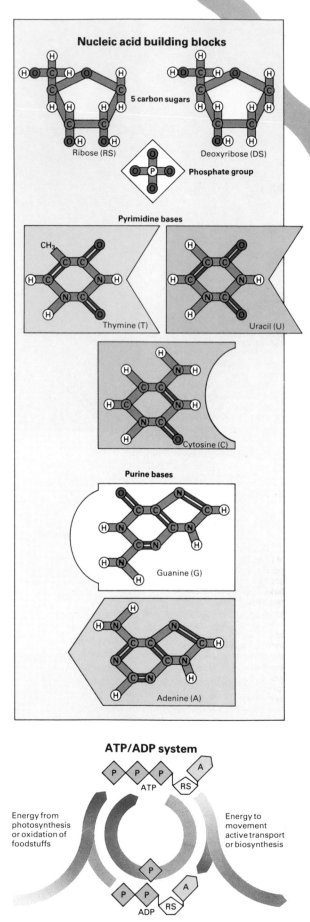

Nucleic acid building blocks

5 carbon sugars

Ribose (RS)   Deoxyribose (DS)

Phosphate group

Pyrimidine bases

Thymine (T)   Uracil (U)

Cytosine (C)

Purine bases

Guanine (G)

Adenine (A)

ATP/ADP system

ATP   RS

Energy from photosynthesis or oxidation of foodstuffs

Energy to movement active transport or biosynthesis

ADP   RS

**DNA**

**RNA**

Guanine

Cytosine

Adenine

Thymine

Guanine

Cytosine

Adenine

Uracil

▼ *Absolutely fundamental to life is the ability of the bases in one strand of DNA to pair in a consistent way with bases in another strand. G forms hydrogen bonds with C, and A with T. This "base-pairing" is the essence of heredity because the affinity of the bases for their partners enables nucleic acids to be self-replicating. Nucleotides can link up along an existing strand of DNA to form a complementary "negative" strand of DNA. G on one strand will be represented by C on the other and A by T. In a second round of copying, with the complementary strand acting as the template, the original sequence is reproduced.*

◄ *Cells replicate their DNA before they divide and so pass on their genetic information. The production of a strand of RNA from DNA (transcription) proceeds in just the same way, except that uracil is substituted for thymine.*

Guanine

Cytosine

Adenine

Thymine

CH₃

◄ *Each nucleotide is made up of a sugar, a phosphate group, and a nitrogenous base. The latter are of two types, purines and pyrimidines. In DNA and RNA, the pairs consist of one purine and one pyrimidine, so they are all the same length. As well as making up DNA and RNA, nucleotides have other roles in the cell, principally as coenzymes, such as ATP (see below), NAD, FAD and coenzyme A.*

◄ *Most coenzymes have multiple roles within the cell, operating in various different pathways. Adenosine triphosphate (ATP), for example, can donate a phosphate group and/or energy to a variety of reactions. Its "alter ego" adenosine diphosphate (ADP), accepts phosphate groups and energy. ATP features so often in biochemical reactions that it has been called the "energy currency of the cell.*

**How muscles work**
*How is food energy transformed into movement by the muscles? The answer lies in two proteins, myosin and actin, which, chemically speaking, interact in quite a simple way. Myosin is a very long molecule with a globular head. It is also an enzyme which binds an ATP molecule and splits it into ADP and phosphate. This releases energy which changes the shape of the molecule – the head flexes backward, toward the tail. Actin has a much more passive role – it makes the myosin release its endproducts (ADP and phosphate) so the reaction can occur again.*

*The molecules of myosin are bundled together like golf clubs with their heads sticking out all round. Packed around them are filaments, composed of actin. Contraction occurs because the myosin heads repeatedly break down ATP molecules. Each time this happens the myosin head binds to the nearest actin, undergoes its change of shape, releases its endproducts and then breaks away from the actin again. This creates a tiny movement, as if the myosin was pulling itself along the actin. Repeating the process up to ten times a second, and with thousands of myosins all pulling together, gives a muscular contraction.*

**DNA replication**

Parent DNA

New strand

Daughter DNA

Daughter DNA

## Protein synthesis

Most of the DNA in the cell is found within the nucleus. But proteins are formed in specialized structures in the cytoplasm, known as ribosomes. A series of intermediary molecules, called messenger RNA, transfer the information contained in the DNA to the ribosomes, and ensure that the instruction is carried out. If DNA is the "brains" of the cell, messenger RNA is its "nervous system", carrying vital messages out to the cytoplasm.

Messenger RNA (mRNA) is formed alongside the DNA helix, just like an additional DNA strand, and is a template of one of the DNA strands. Messenger RNA travels out of the nucleus, and carries its genetic message to the ribosome. There, a second form of RNA, which is known as transfer RNA (tRNA), brings individual amino acids to the messenger RNA. Each transfer RNA fits its amino acid into a position denoted by a codon on the messenger RNA, thus building up a protein. There is a third kind of RNA making up the ribosomes, and called ribosomal RNA (rRNA). It may be purely structural, or it may have a role in organizing protein synthesis, but as yet this is poorly understood.

◄ *Replication of the DNA double helix*

▼ *The ribosome starts at one end of the mRNA molecule and works along it. Three bases, making up a codon, pair up with three bases on the transfer RNA molecule, the anticodon. Each tRNA brings with it an amino acid, and this joins onto the growing polypeptide chain. Enzymes known as aminoacyl-tRNA synthetases are responsible for pairing the tRNA molecules up with the "right" amino acid molecules: there is only one specific enzyme for each type of tRNA.*

▶ *A space-filling model of the DNA molecule. Such models include all the atoms and show them filling up all the spaces within the helix – more realistic than the diagrams shown so far. The structure of DNA was elucidated by model-building.*

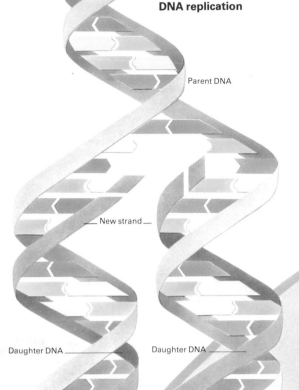

Translation site

Ribosome

Translation

Movement of ribosome

Messenger RNA

Nuclear pore

Growing polypeptide chain

▶ *The ribosome is a complex structure made up of RNA and various enzymes. These control the process of translation but the exact details are unknown. There are two grooves in the ribosome, one for the mRNA and one for the growing protein.*

▶ *Transcription occurs inside the nucleus and involves one strand of the DNA being copied into RNA. An enzyme is needed to transcribe DNA into RNA. In eukaryotes the mRNA must pass through pores in the nuclear membrane. Before it does so, RNA processing may occur – for example, introns can be removed (♦ page 28).*

Codon

Transfer RNA

Cell cytoplasm

Enzyme (RNA polymerase)

Enzyme

Amino acid

Nuclear membrane

DNA template

Amino acid attachment site

Cell nucleus

Transcription

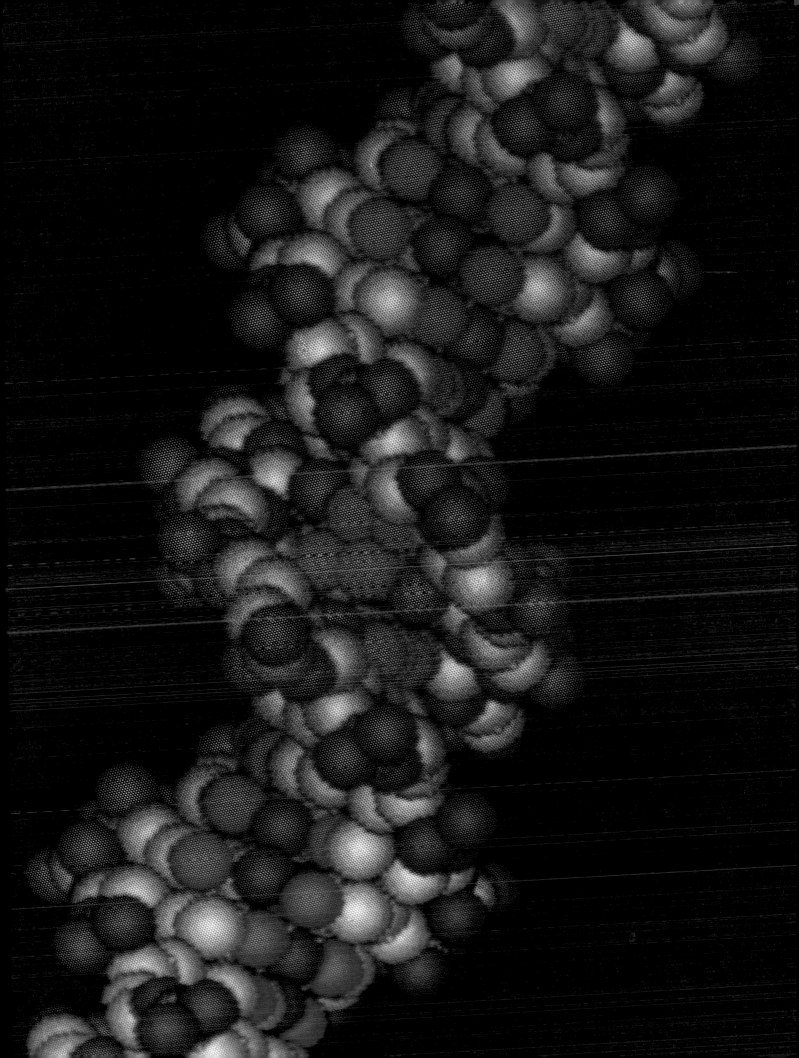

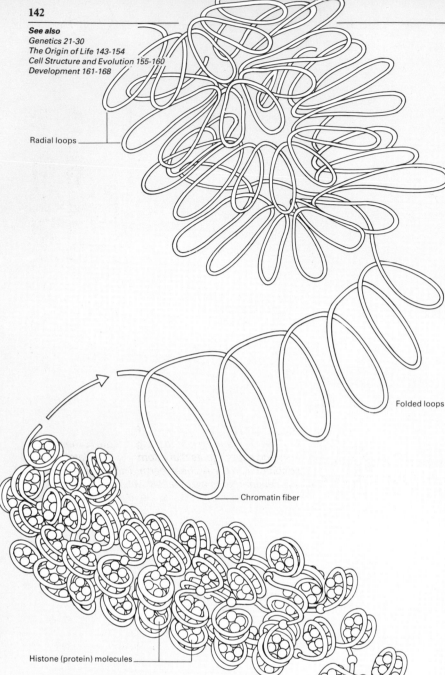

Radial loops

Folded loops

Chromatin fiber

Histone (protein) molecules

Spacer region

Mononucleosome

DNA helix

### Watson and Crick

The discovery of the structure of DNA in 1953 will probably be remembered as the most significant biological breakthrough of the 20th century. It explained the mechanism of heredity and was the first step toward direct manipulation of the genes – the basis of modern biotechnology or "genetic engineering". Several pieces of evidence led to the discovery. Firstly, it had been shown, in 1944, that DNA carried genetic information from one bacterial cell to another. Then there were X-ray photographs of DNA crystals that pointed to a helical structure, but it could have involved two, three or even four chains. Chemists had shown that the polynucleotide chains had a sugar-phosphate backbone, with the bases added on, but no one knew whether the backbones were at the center of the helix or on the outside. Analysis of the DNA from various organisms revealed that the amounts of adenine and thymine were always about the same, as were the amounts of guanine and cytosine, but the significance was not clear at first.

The only way these strands of evidence could be pulled together was by model-building. Watson and Crick were essentially theorists, who used experimental data from many different sources to build a plausible model of DNA. When they had done so, it became clear how such a structure functioned genetically. The strict pairing of guanine with cytosine, and adenine with thymine was the basis of a self-replicating molecule. But working along the strands of the helix, there were no such rules: any base could occupy any site, and this gave the scope for an infinitely variable message. Subsequent research revealed that the genetic code was based on sets of three bases – the codons – and the code was eventually cracked.

▼ The American-born James Watson (b. 1928) and the Englishman Francis Crick (b. 1916), of the University of Cambridge, employed Pauling's technique of model-building to pull together the disparate strands of evidence about DNA. Together with Maurice Wilkins, who also worked on DNA, they were awarded the Nobel Prize in 1962.

### Chromosome structure

In recent years a great deal of progress has been made in understanding the chromosome's structure, which is much more complex than anyone expected. The structure has been revealed by unraveling the chromosome chemically and then studying the products with an electron microscope. It turns out that each chromosome contains 10,000 times its own length of DNA, and to achieve this compression the DNA is folded and looped in a very complex way.

The DNA helix is firstly wrapped around bundles of eight histone (protein) molecules to create a mononucleosome. This gives a string-of-beads effect (technically called an oligonucleosome) that can be seen in some electron micrographs. Extra histone molecules are attached to the DNA in the spaces between each mononucleosome. This "necklace" is then coiled up to give a chromatin fiber. Next, chromatin fibers are folded into loops, and this looped structure is then coiled again in radial loops to give the chromosome. This is 500 times fatter than the original DNA helix.

*The "biotic soup" of the early Earth...Which came first – cells, enzymes or genes?...The triumph of life – making food work...The oldest pathways for breaking down food...Harnessing the Sun...The oxygen revolution... PERSPECTIVE...The simplest cell...Ways of fermenting... Survivors from the dawn of life...The versatility of blue-green algae...Defenses against oxygen...Doing without the Sun*

▲ Stanley Miller, at work in the early 1950s.

Life on Earth probably began 3,500-4,000 million years ago, in the late Hadean or early Archean eons. We know almost nothing about its origins. Yet most researchers agree that the first step in the creation of life from non-life was a process of "chemical evolution". Simple biological molecules arose spontaneously from inorganic molecules under the peculiar conditions prevailing on the young Earth.

Earth was then a violent place, with torrential rains, lightning and erupting volcanoes. Much of the Earth's crust was probably covered by warm, shallow, slightly salty water. The Earth's atmosphere was also different from that of the present day. It contained virtually no free oxygen ($O_2$) and no ozone ($O_3$). In today's atmosphere, a layer of ozone in the upper reaches protects us from most of the harsh ultraviolet radiation which the Sun emits. At that time the Earth must have been subjected to a level of radiation which would now prove lethal to most living things.

Although it is agreed that oxygen was lacking, exactly which gases *were* present in the ancient atmosphere is a matter of debate. Earlier suggestions that methane and ammonia were prevalent have given way to the idea that nitrogen, carbon dioxide (or carbon monoxide), hydrogen and water vapor predominated.

In these seemingly inhospitable conditions, the generation of the organic molecules that form the basis of life proved possible. At first glance, the idea that complex organic molecules such as amino acids, formed spontaneously through natural geochemical processes is surprising. Today only living organisms (and organic chemists) can create such compounds. Their synthesis requires special conditions, notably the absence of oxygen. But organic compounds are still formed in outer space, and in experiments that attempt to simulate conditions on the ancient Earth. From simple starting materials arise the fundamental molecules of life.

### Creating the precursors of life
The best evidence about the origin of life comes from the experiments that attempt to simulate conditions on the Archean earth. The pioneer of such experiments was Stanley Miller, of the University of Chicago, who showed that it is surprisingly easy to create organic compounds starting from a few simple inorganic molecules.

In a sealed network from which oxygen was excluded, Miller mixed the gases he assumed were ejected into the primeval atmosphere by volcanoes – methane, ammonia and hydrogen. He heated water to form steam, and added energy in the form of an electrical spark or ultraviolet radiation – simulating the lightning and harsh rays of the Sun. In a matter of days, this simple apparatus generated various amino acids and other organic molecules.

Since Miller's time, many researchers have performed similar experiments, with various sources of energy and mixtures of gases. As long as the starting mixture includes a carbon-containing gas, a source of nitrogen, water and some hydrogen, a wide range of small organic compounds arise.

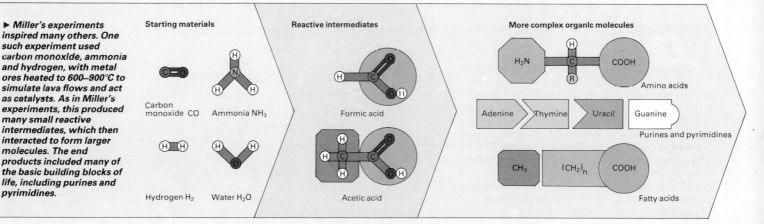

► *Miller's experiments inspired many others. One such experiment used carbon monoxide, ammonia and hydrogen, with metal ores heated to 600–900°C to simulate lava flows and act as catalysts. As in Miller's experiments, this produced many small reactive intermediates, which then interacted to form larger molecules. The end products included many of the basic building blocks of life, including purines and pyrimidines.*

Starting materials

Carbon monoxide CO    Ammonia NH₃

Hydrogen H₂    Water H₂O

Reactive intermediates

Formic acid

Acetic acid

More complex organic molecules

H₂N    C    COOH    Amino acids

Adenine  Thymine  Uracil  Guanine — Purines and pyrimidines

CH₃  (CH₂)ₙ  COOH — Fatty acids

*No one knows how life progressed from the "biotic soup" to the first replicating cells*

### A giant step for life

*Over many thousands, perhaps millions, of years, organic molecules must have been accumulating in the seas of the world, forming the so-called "biotic soup" or "organic soup". The next step in the evolution of life – and a truly giant step – was the organization of these organic chemicals into cells with the ability to replicate and pass on genetic information to their progeny. How this occurred is a complete mystery. We do not even know which came first: the cell (that is, some sort of physical packaging of biomolecules), the enzymes (the protein molecules that make biochemical reactions happen), or the genes (which store the instructions for making proteins).*

### Cells first?

*One theory of the origins of life was suggested in the 1920s by A.I. Oparin. He proposed that some sort of cell came first, enzymes second, and genes third. The theory was based on an analogy with coacervates, small droplets formed by certain large molecules, which spontaneously coalesce in water under the right conditions. Oparin argued that life could have begun when complicated populations of molecules accumulated in such droplets. Enzymes arose next to organize the molecules into metabolic cycles, and genes appeared last.*

### Genes first?

*In the 1970s, a new theory about these crucial steps in the origin of life was proposed, in which genes came first, then enzymes, and finally cells. This theory has attracted supporters because the crucial aspect of life is the capacity for inheritance. The theory suggests that an RNA with the ability to replicate itself appeared first. The notion is that, in the biotic soup, polynucleotides (nucleic acids) competed, so to speak, for raw materials to make copies of themselves. Those that came to predominate were the ones which could replicate themselves more quickly and more accurately than their fellows, and produce more stable copies. Particular proteins, in turn, may have been able, by chance, to enhance the replication of polynucleotides with particular sequences of bases, thus acting as primitive enzymes. But how early life could have made the huge leap to the genetic code – the correspondence between the sequences of bases in nucleic acids and the sequence of amino acids in proteins – is entirely mysterious.*

### Enzymes first?

*Recently, Freeman Dyson of Princeton University has argued for the plausibility of the "enzyme-first" theory. He points out that amino acids (the building blocks of enzymes) are easier to synthesize than nucleotides (the building blocks of DNA and RNA) and that it makes more sense for the "hardware" – the proteins – to come before the "software" – the genes. Dyson proposes that the earliest genetic material was RNA, not DNA, something on which the various theories agree. But he suggests that RNA made its appearance as a parasitic disease, an accidental by-product of the metabolism of a closely-related molecule, adenosine triphosphate or ATP (♦ page 139).*

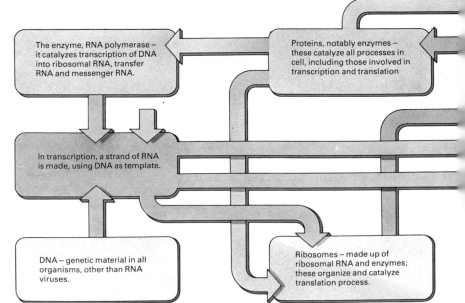

The enzyme, RNA polymerase – it catalyzes transcription of DNA into ribosomal RNA, transfer RNA and messenger RNA.

Proteins, notably enzymes – these catalyze all processes in cell, including those involved in transcription and translation

In transcription, a strand of RNA is made, using DNA as template.

DNA – genetic material in all organisms, other than RNA viruses.

Ribosomes – made up of ribosomal RNA and enzymes; these organize and catalyze translation process.

### A chicken-and-egg problem

*Although the "genes-first" theory of the origin of life is attractive, there are real problems associated with it. Living cells make RNA only with the help of enzymes and another nucleic acid that acts as a template. If RNA was the original living molecule, it would have to have made copies of itself without enzymes or a template. Attempts to make RNA behave in this way in the laboratory have failed.*

*Manfred Eigen, a proponent of the "genes-first" theory, has taken a solution of nucleotide monomers and coaxed them to join up to form a long molecule (polymer) of RNA that can replicate. But to achieve this he found it necessary to add a polymerase enzyme, extracted from a living virus.*

*Another chemist, Leslie Orgel, has shown that nucleotide monomers can, under certain conditions, join up to form RNA without any polymerase enzyme, but only if they are given an RNA template to copy. This is an advance – it shows how early RNA molecules could possibly have reproduced themselves without enzymes. But it seems to rule out RNA forming spontaneously in the first place; there could have been no template when the very first RNA molecule was formed.*

*There is a further problem (although this affects all the theories, not just the "genes-first" hypothesis) in explaining how the relationship between RNA and proteins originated. In the process of translation whereby proteins are produced (♦ page 140), it is the order of bases on the messenger RNA that determines the order of amino acids in the protein. But there is no inherent attraction between the codons on the mRNA and the amino acids – translation occurs via a code, and in order to interpret that code, both a transfer RNA molecule and a synthetase enzyme (a protein) are needed. Since the synthetase enzyme itself is a product of translation, it is very difficult to imagine how the system could have originated.*

### The simplest cells

*Mycoplasmas are the smallest entities capable of an independent existence and may be the nearest surviving thing to the first cells. They contain enough DNA to manufacture about 750 different proteins. Some researchers speculate that a living organism with fewer genes would not be able to reproduce; others estimate that the first cells only needed 50 genes. Many mycoplasmas are now parasites or live harmlessly in the digestive tract.*

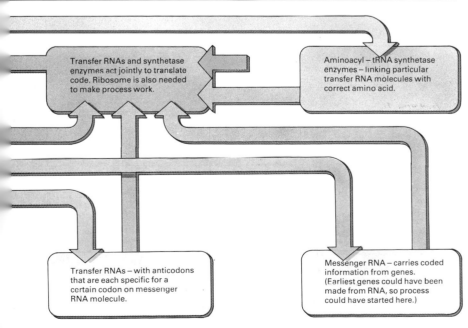

Transfer RNAs and synthetase enzymes act jointly to translate code. Ribosome is also needed to make process work.

Aminoacyl – tRNA synthetase enzymes – linking particular transfer RNA molecules with correct amino acid.

Transfer RNAs – with anticodons that are each specific for a certain codon on messenger RNA molecule.

Messenger RNA – carries coded information from genes. (Earliest genes could have been made from RNA, so process could have started here.)

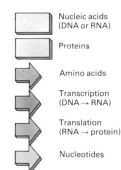

Nucleic acids (DNA or RNA)

Proteins

Amino acids

Transcription (DNA → RNA)

Translation (RNA → protein)

Nucleotides

◄ **How did the relationship between DNA (or RNA) and proteins begin? The basis of all life today is the ability of DNA and RNA to produce specific proteins. But they do this via a code, and the translation of that code requires two principal factors, a synthetase enzyme and a transfer RNA, as well as the help of the ribosomes. It is very difficult to imagine a simple version of the system from which the translation mechanism seen today could have evolved.**

*Glycolysis is an ancient biochemical pathway that we still use today*

## The triumph of life: making food work

The earliest cells lived by breaking down the organic molecules available in the "biotic soup". Their food was still being created by the geochemical processes that were at work on the ancient Earth – the same processes that had forged the constituents of the very first cells themselves.

Like living animals, they were able to salvage and store the energy trapped in the chemical bonds of these food molecules. They could then use this energy to drive the synthesis of molecules such as nucleic acids which the cell needs to reproduce. The ability of living organisms to capture chemical energy and use it for their own ends is a major triumph of life, and is performed in virtually the same way in all living things.

Cells manage to trap the energy liberated from food molecules by a series of enzyme-controlled reactions, which create the energy-rich molecule, ATP (◊ page 139). Rather like a rechargeable battery, the ATP molecule serves as a short-term store for energy. When needed, it can drive the synthesis of macromolecules, power the contraction of muscles, or provide the energy for transporting vital substances across cell membranes.

One of the most widespread pathways for the breakdown of food is glycolysis. It is the chain of reactions that breaks down glucose in the absence of oxygen, and it occurs in all higher organisms, and most bacteria. All the vertebrates, including humans, exploit anaerobic glycolysis to produce energy virtually instantaneously – long before the lungs and circulatory system have time to deliver an extra ration of oxygen to the muscles. We can lift weights and sprint for buses thanks to the anaerobic bacteria that invented glycolysis thousands of millions of years ago.

Glucose is a six-carbon sugar and glycolysis effectively splits it in two, so that the end product is two three-carbon molecules called pyruvate. In organisms living without molecular oxygen, this pathway is the cell's major source of ATP. What happens to the pyruvate next depends on the organism. In the muscles of higher animals, pyruvate is converted to lactate (◊ page 147), while slightly different reactions occur in bacteria and yeasts, resulting in other organic compounds. Such reactions are known as fermentation, and they have proved immensely useful in producing bread, cheese, yoghurt, beer, wine, and a variety of other foodstuffs.

### Oxidation without oxygen

*One difficulty in discussing the biochemistry of the earliest cells is that oxygen dominates both our present-day world and the language of chemistry. Breaking down food involves what are called "oxidation" and "reduction" reactions, but not all oxidation involves oxygen. Indeed, in the early history of our planet, there was no free oxygen. An example of a typical oxidation reaction today is the burning of methane ($CH_4$)("natural gas"), which combines with molecular oxygen ($O_2$) to form carbon dioxide ($CO_2$) and water ($H_2O$). Oxidation, in its broader meaning, denotes any reaction in which electrons are removed from an atom. Reduction – its opposite – means the addition of electrons to an atom. Food is made up of carbons and hydrogens that are relatively rich in electrons, and so are in a reduced state. As a molecule of food is broken down, or oxidized, it releases energy.*

▶ *Glycolysis splits glucose molecules in two, and harvests energy from them. For every molecule of glucose broken down, four molecules of ATP are generated directly, but two of these are simply "repayments" for the ATP invested initially. The NADH generated has reducing power and can feed directly into the electron transport chain (◊ page 153), generating three more molecules of ATP. Thus the overall yield of glycolysis is five ATP molecules per molecule of glucose. This ATP is used to power muscles (◊ page 139) or for a variety of other reactions that require energy input.*

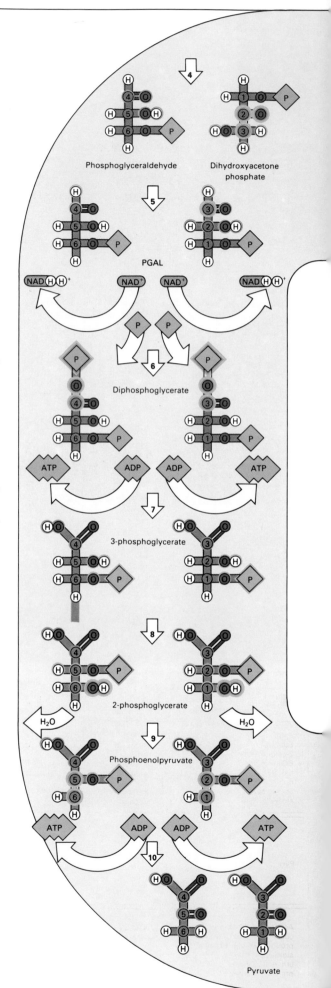

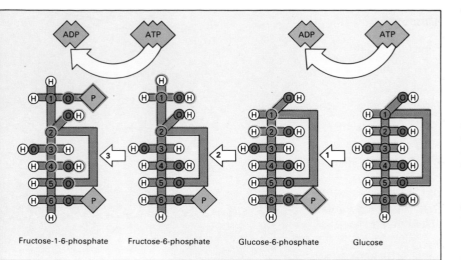

Fructose-1-6-phosphate    Fructose-6-phosphate    Glucose-6-phosphate    Glucose

**Glycolysis**

1 Phosphate group added to glucose molecule. This uses ATP, but energy will be recouped later.
2 Reorganization step.
3 Another phosphate group added.
4 Sugar molecule split.
5 The two 3-carbon molecules produced by split have same composition and differ only in structure. One is converted to other form.
6 Energy released by splitting 6-carbon sugar was stored in PGAL molecules. Now transformed into high-energy phosphate bond (by addition of inorganic phosphate), and NADH. NADH can feed into electron transport chain (♦ page 153) to yield more ATP.
7 Energy in new phosphate bond harvested, with creation of ATP from ADP.
8 9 Reorganization steps
10 Energy originally invested (in steps 1 and 3) recouped by formation of ATP.

○ Atoms involved in next step
○ Atoms involved in previous step
(NAD+) Nicotinamide adenine dinucleotide

Ethanol ("alcohol"), a 2-carbon compound, plus CO$_2$, is produced in plant tissues and by some fungi, notably yeasts. Yeasts are used in baking and to make alcoholic drinks.

Lactic acid, a 3-carbon compound, is produced by animal muscles, various protozoa, fungi and several kinds of bacteria. Lactic-acid bacteria make cheese, yoghurt etc.

▲ **For sudden bursts of muscular activity, as in weight-lifting, we rely solely on energy liberated anaerobically (without oxygen) by glycolysis.**

Pyruvate

KREBS' CYCLE

Acetic acid, a 2-carbon compound, plus CO$_2$ gas, is produced by some bacteria, starting from pyruvate or ethanol. Commercial end-product is vinegar.

Acetone (3-carbons), butanol (4-carbons) and other products are generated by *Clostridium* bacteria through a complex fermentation process. Once used industrially.

◄ **Fermentation involves adding electrons to pyruvate and can generate a variety of products. Shown here are those that are commercially useful.**

### Ways of fermenting

The ancient ability to generate energy without oxygen – anaerobic glycolysis – has been retained even by creatures who are dependent on oxygen. In animal muscle, glycolysis begins with the release of glycogen, the energy storage compound (♦ page 130). Enzymes convert the glycogen into glucose, which is then broken down to pyruvate by the glycolysis pathway. In the process, five molecules of energy-rich ATP are formed.

The power this system generates per unit time far exceeds that available through oxygen-consuming processes. But anaerobic metabolism in the muscle cannot go on for very long. The sprinter tires far earlier than the marathon runner, who is running on oxygen. The disadvantage of anaerobics lies in the endproduct of glycolysis. When oxygen is present, pyruvate is broken down completely by the Krebs' cycle (♦ page 152), to give easily removed endproducts – water and carbon dioxide. The oxygen acts as an electron acceptor and this produces water. In anaerobic conditions, the cells must find an alternative place to deposit the spare electrons, and naturally enough, they use pyruvate, which is accumulating as fast as the electrons. Reducing pyruvate (in animals) gives lactic acid, and this organic acid tends to build up in the muscle, although some of it is carried away in the blood. As concentrations of lactic acid in muscle rise, so fatigue sets in.

Yeasts have the same trouble, at least in human hands. They normally respire aerobically, using oxygen. But when trapped in a brewer's vat, the carbon dioxide produced during the aerobic process builds up. Instead of suffocating, as an animal would, the yeast switch to fermentation. They convert sugars into pyruvate, and then use it as an electron-acceptor, a reaction which produces carbon dioxide and ethanol – the alcohol humans drink. Their ability to be so adaptive has made yeast highly prized by human tipplers for at least 10,000 years. But ethanol is a waste product for yeast, as lactic acid is for humans. When the concentration of ethanol reaches some 12 percent, the yeast themselves are poisoned. Hence no naturally fermented drinks, such as wine and beer, have more than 12 percent ethanol.

Fermentation in yeasts also gives us leavened bread. The carbon dioxide produced by the yeast causes the dough to rise; the ethanol produced as well is driven off by the baking process.

Bacterial fermentation is also important. The lactic acid bacteria give us yoghurt, butter and cheese, and related bacteria are responsible for producing sauerkraut and silage. At one time the chemical industry also relied on fermenting bacteria to produce the industrial solvents acetone and butanol. Large-scale production of acetone by this means was established in World War I, when enormous quantities were needed to make munitions. Both products are now produced largely from petroleum, but microbial fermentation is growing in popularity again, as an obvious source of renewable energy. Brazil is currently exploiting the powers of yeast to convert sugar cane and cassava into ethanol, creating "green petrol" to fuel motor cars.

*In the primeval famine, bacteria found several new ways to sustain themselves –
using light or inorganic molecules for energy*

## Harnessing the Sun

The bonanza of free food in the biotic soup could not last. Microorganisms were busily consuming the organic molecules, but these
molecules were produced by relatively slow geochemical processes,
and now they were being used up faster than they could be replen-
ished. As supplies dwindled many microorganisms must have died
out. In the primeval famine that followed, some bacteria circum-
vented the food shortage by inventing a method of building sugars
from the carbon in carbon dioxide. Life on Earth today depends on
this metabolic process, which was invented more than two billion
years ago.

Carbon dioxide was plentiful in the early atmosphere, but the carbon it contains is in an oxidized and inert state, making it difficult to
utilize. What organisms must do to make the carbon more reactive is
reduce it – that is, give it a larger share of electrons, by bonding it to
hydrogen atoms. The process of building complex organic compounds from carbon dioxide is known as "fixing" carbon dioxide.

But it is no easy task. Fixing carbon dioxide requires a great deal of
energy and reducing power. Some of the anaerobic bacteria came up
with a solution to both problems: use the energy in light from the Sun
to create both ATP – the energy currency – and NADPH – reducing
power. The microorganisms that achieved this were relatives of living
cells known as green sulfur bacteria. These tiny creatures were the
first organisms to develop a way of trapping the Sun's energy to create
organic molecules – a process that now feeds almost all life. This
revolutionary process is known as photosynthesis.

The ancestors of the present-day green sulfur bacteria used the
energy from sunlight to transfer electrons and hydrogen ions from
hydrogen sulfide ($H_2S$), a gas that was plentiful at that time. This
light-powered reaction creates NADPH, which then has sufficient
reducing power to fix carbon dioxide. The waste product of this
process is sulfur – and the evolution of these creatures is marked by
the deposition of organic carbon and sulfur in sediments dating from
the Archean era.

The whole reaction is dependent on having a molecule that can trap
light energy, and the molecule that all bacteria, algae and plants use is
chlorophyll. When chlorophyll absorbs a photon of light, an electron
is excited to a higher energy state and this electron can be induced to
leave the excited chlorophyll and pass to an electron acceptor. This
leaves the chlorophyll with a positively charged "hole" that has a high
affinity for electrons. The hole is filled by an electron whipped from
the electron donor – in this case, hydrogen sulfide.

Carbon fixation also requires appreciable amounts of energy to
drive enzymatic reactions, and the early anaerobic bacteria devised a
way of using electrons from the excited chlorophyll to generate ATP.
This process, known as cyclic phosphorylation, comes into action if
levels of NADPH are high.

The green sulfur bacteria changed the world, by making new
sources of carbon and nitrogen available to heterotrophic bacteria that
fed upon them. Hence they inspired a flurry of evolutionary activity.
But even more importantly, they may have been the ancestors of the
cyanobacteria, which release oxygen as a byproduct of photosynthesis. These cyanobacteria are among the most ecologically significant life form ever to have evolved. For the waste product of their
metabolism – oxygen – was to create a major crisis for living organisms that led to a revolutionary change in ways of living.

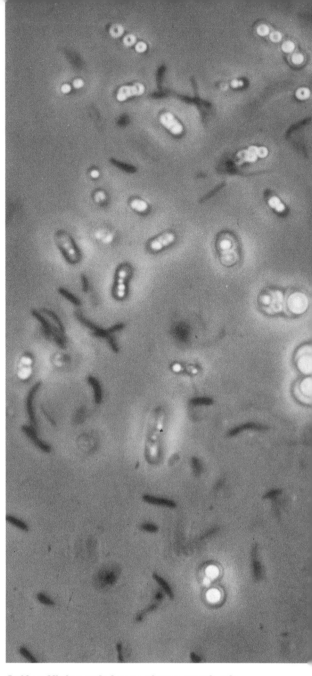

***Self-sufficiency is born: chemosynthesis***
*The most significant new life-forms to emerge from
the primeval famine were undoubtedly the
photosynthetic bacteria. But even before they
appeared, other groups of bacteria had devisd their
own solution to the problem of getting nutrients
and energy in novel ways. Many broke their
dependence on the fast-disappearing organic
molecules, to become chemosynthetic autotrophs
– creatures able to generate energy from chemical
reactions involving inorganic molecules.*

*The methanogenic bacteria were probably the
pioneers in this field. These bacteria are curious
forms of life that use carbon dioxide to oxidize
hydrogen. Three thousand million years ago the
young Earth spawned many volcanoes, thus
guaranteeing ample supplies of both these gases.
These microorganisms are called methanogenic
bacteria because they generate methane, or natural
gas, by this reaction – which also produces water
and releases energy. Some methanogenic bacteria
can switch to using organic acids – such as
formate, methanol and acetate – as food when the
opportunity arises – a reminder of their past,
because such molecules would have been plentiful*

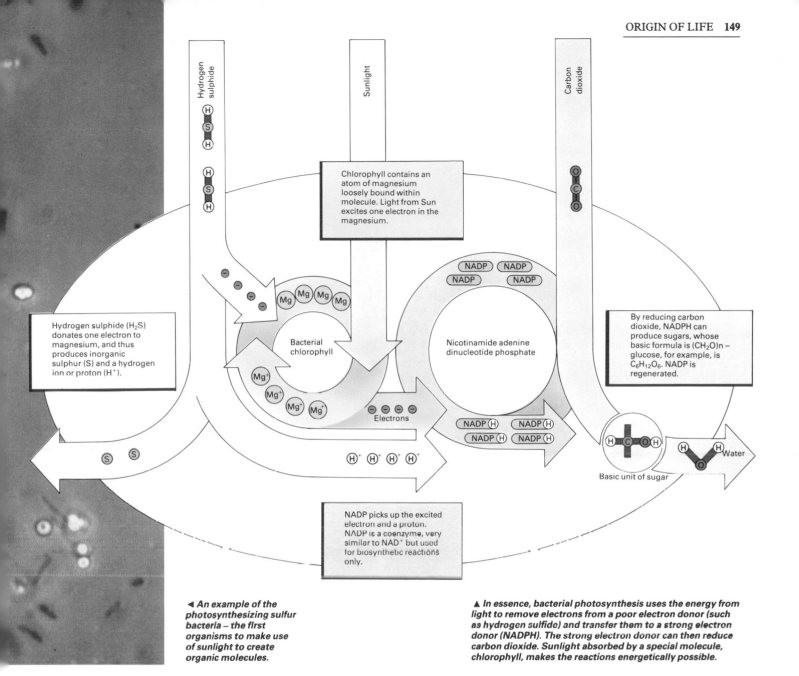

Hydrogen sulphide

Sunlight

Carbon dioxide

Chlorophyll contains an atom of magnesium loosely bound within molecule. Light from Sun excites one electron in the magnesium.

Hydrogen sulphide ($H_2S$) donates one electron to magnesium, and thus produces inorganic sulphur (S) and a hydrogen ion or proton ($H^+$).

Bacterial chlorophyll

Nicotinamide adenine dinucleotide phosphate

By reducing carbon dioxide, NADPH can produce sugars, whose basic formula is $(CH_2O)n$ – glucose, for example, is $C_6H_{12}O_6$. NADP is regenerated.

Electrons

Basic unit of sugar

Water

NADP picks up the excited electron and a proton. NADP is a coenzyme, very similar to $NAD^+$ but used for biosynthetic reactions only.

◄ *An example of the photosynthesizing sulfur bacteria – the first organisms to make use of sunlight to create organic molecules.*

▲ *In essence, bacterial photosynthesis uses the energy from light to remove electrons from a poor electron donor (such as hydrogen sulfide) and transfer them to a strong electron donor (NADPH). The strong electron donor can then reduce carbon dioxide. Sunlight absorbed by a special molecule, chlorophyll, makes the reactions energetically possible.*

in the biotic soup. Apart from these unusual appetites, the ancient origins of these cells is also suggested by the peculiar RNA found in their ribosomes (♦ page 37).

Not surprisingly, these survivors from the dawn of life are obligate anaerobes. That is to say, molecular oxygen is very toxic to them, and they are obliged to live in environments that are strictly free of oxygen: in sewage sludge, or deep in bogs, where they produce "swamp gas". Occasionally spontaneous ignition of this swamp gas (methane) may sometimes be seen as an eerie flame-like phosphorescence on the surface of marshes and swamps – the origin of myths about marshland spirits, called Will o'the wisp or Jack o'Lantern.

This first try at self-sufficiency was of limited application in the long run, but organisms soon went on to develop new and better ways of growing their own food. The problem with the methanogenic bacteria's solution was that their source of energy – hydrogen – later disappeared from the environment. What was needed was a reliable, abundant source of energy, and there was an obvious one just waiting to be tapped – the light from the Sun.

▲ *Will o' the wisp, the spontaneous ignition of "swamp gas".*

*The cyanobacteria, more than any other living organisms, have made the Earth what it is today*

## The oxygen revolution

The cyanobacteria tackle the most difficult, but most rewarding, chemical task. They practice photosynthesis but use water as a source of electrons and hydrogen ions, which takes ten times more energy than extracting them from hydrogen sulfide. This energetic disadvantage is outweighed by the fact that water is superabundant, whereas hydrogen sulfide is not. This final innovation meant that sugars could be synthesized from the most abundant of raw materials: water, carbon dioxide and light. Cyanobacteria could only achieve this by adding a second light-activated reaction (known as photosystem 2) to the photosynthetic pathway already perfected by the green sulfur bacteria (photosystem 1). The combination of these two photosystems produced enough energy to break down the stable water molecule into its elements and use it to reduce carbon dioxide.

Splitting water in this way generates oxygen as a waste product and this gas began to accumulate in the Earth's atmosphere, entirely due to the prodigious activities of the cyanobacteria. Gradually, over millions of years, the cyanobacteria pushed the amount of oxygen in the atmosphere up until it reached 21 percent, its present level. This created an enormous problem for other living organisms. All were adapted to life without oxygen – they metabolized anaerobically. For many, the appearance of oxygen must have spelled extinction, but a few were able to retreat into environments where oxygen could not reach them and these are bacteria we now describe as "obligate anaerobes". Others must gradually have adapted to the new gas, and thus evolved into the aerobic organisms of today.

### In praise of cyanobacteria

*Cyanobacteria (once known as blue-green algae) are incredibly versatile. Not only can they fix carbon dioxide via photosynthesis in the manner of plants (thus producing oxygen), but some can revert to bacterial-style photosynthesis as well. They can also fix atmospheric nitrogen, and are able to live with or without oxygen.*

*Cyanobacteria also show an ability to differentiate – structurally modify their cells in response to the environment – to a degree found nowhere else in the bacterial world. If nitrogen is limited, they develop heterocysts – cells that specialize in fixing nitrogen. When conditions are really bad, they form akinetes – propagating bodies more resistant to adverse condition. Besides this structural versatility, cyanobacteria seem to be particularly good at establishing symbiotic relationships with other organisms. No other group of microorganisms has formed such a wide range of partnerships. Cyanobacteria link up to mutual benefit with everything from fungi, green algae, mosses, ferns and flowering plants, to sponges, shrimps and mammals.*

*People too make use of cyanobacteria. Spirulina from Mexican and Taiwanese lagoons is now marketed in the US and Japan as a health food and much research is focused on their potential as natural fertilizers. In some parts of India, for instance, rice fields are inoculated with cyanobacteria, to enrich the soil with nitrogen.*

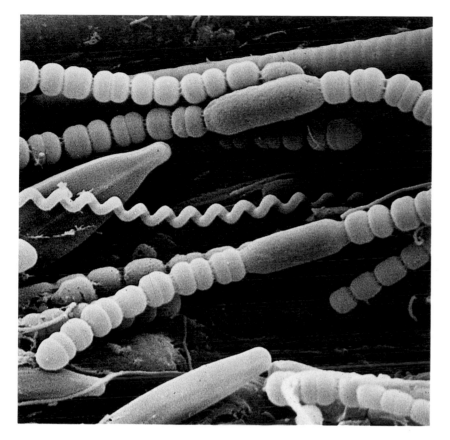

◄ Ancient rocks in the eroding badlands of Arizona. The reddish-brown bands contain ferric (iron) oxide – familiar as "rust". Its deposition is thought to mark the build up of oxygen in the atmosphere as a result of photosynthesis by cyanobacteria.

▲ Cells of three different species of cyanobacteria – Anabaena (bead-like), Spirulina (corkscrews), and Microcoleus (tubes). The cells are magnified 480 times. Like bacteria, these cells are prokaryotes (♦ page 156) but with complex internal membranes.

▼ Present-day stromatolites in Shark Bay, Australia. Here the cyanobacteria are free from grazing animals, so they create dense mats which trap tiny chalk particles from the sea water washing over them, and eventually calcify into stromatolites.

### On the trail of ancient algae

The cyanobacteria ruled the Earth 2,500 million years ago. The Proterozoic era, which began then and lasted for some 2,000 million years, was truly the age of cyanobacteria. They colonized virtually every habitat on earth and changed the history of life by releasing oxygen into the atmosphere.

Although they are microorganisms, the cyanobacteria have left substantial fossil remains in the rocks. Known as stromatolites, they are large columnar structures made largely of calcium carbonate and as impressive as the coral reefs of modern seas. Paleontologists once doubted that bacteria could have created such massive pillars of rock. But in the late 1950s, similar structures, created by living communities of cyanobacteria, were discovered in Shark Bay in Western Australia. In this particular spot, the water in the lagoon is so salty that it inhibits the growth of large organisms that normally graze upon the cyanobacteria. So the slow-growing cyanobacteria can still flourish in sufficient numbers to create dense filamentous mats. These become filled with tiny particles of chalk from the water washing over them. In the seas of 2,000 million years ago, predators were a thing of the future, so the cyanobacteria could have led the same sort of untroubled existence. The origin of the fossil stromatolites has been confirmed by microscopic examination. When thin sections are cut from the fossils, the filaments and spherical single cells of the ancient cyanobacteria are visible.

Cyanobacteria probably evolved before the Proterozoic, in the Archean era, but few rocks from this time remain undamaged by subsequent high temperatures and pressures. And the fossil remains that are found in such ancient rocks cannot reveal precisely when the bacteria developed their revolutionary ability to use water in photosynthesis and thus generate oxygen. The earliest bacterial fossils date from some 3,800 million years ago. By 3,500 million years ago life was already abundant and diverse; the bacteria were a variety of shapes and sizes and some of the fossils dating from this period could be cyanobacteria. But indirect signs from the chemical composition of sedimentary rocks suggest that they probably evolved somewhat later.

The most obvious of these signs are the huge bands of oxidized iron which first appear in rocks dating from about 2,500 million years ago. The sudden appearance of oxidized iron suggests that oxygen was being pumped into the environment at this time. Initially, the free oxygen produced by the cyanobacteria would have gone to oxidize iron in the ocean, various minerals on land, and volcanic gases such as hydrogen sulfide and hydrogen. When all these had been oxidized, oxygen gas would have begun to build up in the atmosphere, probably about 2,300 million years ago.

The world they had created was not kind to the cyanobacteria. By the end of the Proterozoic, 570 million years ago, they were in decline, though they have survived to this day in reduced numbers. The cause of their demise seems to have been the very organisms – some of them voracious grazers – that the oxygen had allowed to evolve.

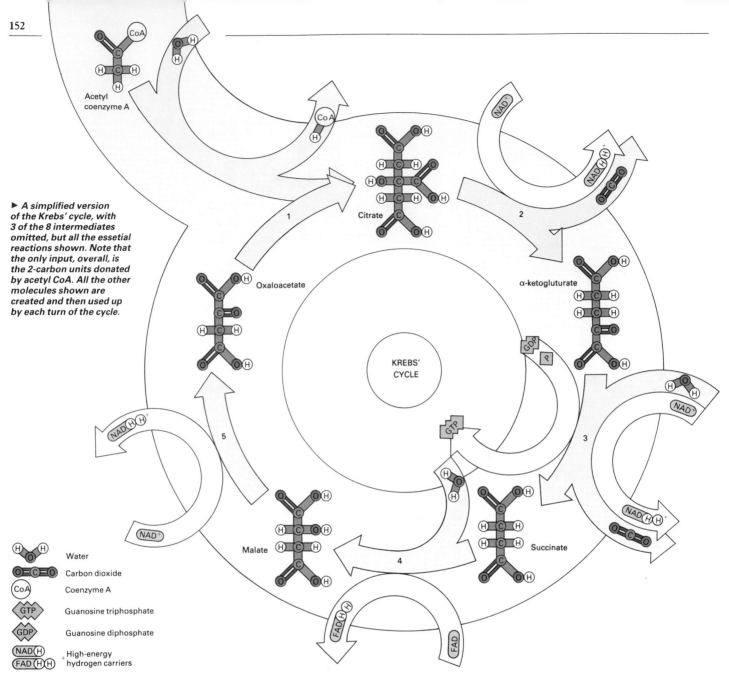

► A simplified version of the Krebs' cycle, with 3 of the 8 intermediates omitted, but all the essetial reactions shown. Note that the only input, overall, is the 2-carbon units donated by acetyl CoA. All the other molecules shown are created and then used up by each turn of the cycle.

Water
Carbon dioxide
Coenzyme A
Guanosine triphosphate
Guanosine diphosphate
High-energy hydrogen carriers

**Krebs' cycle**

1 Acetyl CoA donates its acetyl (2-carbon) group to oxaloacetate. An ionized water molecule is involved in reaction – H⁺ ion goes to CoA and OH⁻ to citrate.

2 2-step reaction – citrate reorganized, then carboxyl group split off to form carbon dioxide gas. Hydrogen atoms removed and energy harvested in form of NADH. This can feed into electron transport chain (◆ page 153) to yield ATP.

3 2-step reaction – another carboxyl group removed and more energy harvested, as NADH and GTP. The latter can react with ADP to produce an ATP molecule, which can then be used by cell.

4 2-step reaction – more energy harvested and hydrogens removed.

5 Again energy harvested and hydrogens removed. At same time molecule reorganized to give oxaloacetate again.

**Fixing carbon...**

The "carbon-fixation cycle" is the process by which photosynthesizers make sugars. The central reaction combines a molecule of carbon dioxide with a five-carbon sugar to form two molecules of a three-carbon compound. The reaction is catalyzed by a large protein known as ribulose bisphosphate carboxylase. This enzyme works remarkably slowly; it handles about three molecules of its substrates per second, compared to the thousand or so molecules that most enzymes process in that time. So the cell synthesizes vast quantities of this enzyme, making it probably the most abundant enzyme in the world.

Some of the three-carbon products are later used to regenerate the five-carbon sugar. This is achieved by a complex set of reactions, which are delicately balanced and controlled, so that there is always an adequate supply of the five-carbon sugar on hand to participate in more "fixes" of carbon dioxide. The remaining three-carbon products are converted into a variety of products that the cell needs, including fatty acids, other lipids, amino acids, starch and sugars.

**...and nitrogen**

One of the problems confronting living organisms is the need for nitrogen, which is essential for building proteins and nucleic acids. In the atmosphere of the young Earth, ammonia ($NH_3$) or nitrogen gas ($N_2$) was incorporated into organic molecules formed in the shallow seas (◆ page 143). But once the violent climate of the young Earth settled down, and the complex nitrogen compounds were used up, very little more became available. Today, some nitrogen is still fixed (that is, incorporated into more complex molecules) during electrical storms, but not enough to sustain the life of the planet.

Most of the nitrogen in living things today has been endlessly recycled – returned to the earth as living organisms die or excrete waste products, only to be taken up again by plants, and then pumped back into the food chain via plant-eating animals. But inevitably the cycle is not completely efficient. Some nitrogen compounds are lost in the cycle and these losses must be made good.

The irony of it all is that nitrogen is an abundant element, making up almost 80 percent of the

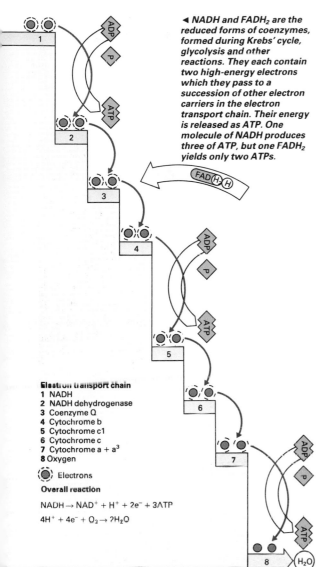

◄ NADH and FADH$_2$ are the reduced forms of coenzymes, formed during Krebs' cycle, glycolysis and other reactions. They each contain two high-energy electrons which they pass to a succession of other electron carriers in the electron transport chain. Their energy is released as ATP. One molecule of NADH produces three of ATP, but one FADH$_2$ yields only two ATPs.

**Electron transport chain**
1 NADH
2 NADH dehydrogenase
3 Coenzyme Q
4 Cytochrome b
5 Cytochrome c1
6 Cytochrome c
7 Cytochrome a + a$^3$
8 Oxygen

⊙ Electrons

**Overall reaction**

$NADH \rightarrow NAD^+ + H^+ + 2e^- + 3ATP$

$4H^+ + 4e^- + O_2 \rightarrow 2H_2O$

Earth's present atmosphere. But raw nitrogen is useless to most living organisms, being a stubbornly inert and unreactive gas. The ability to fix nitrogen gas is confined to a handful of bacteria, all of which reduce it to ammonia.

Some of the present-day bacteria capable of this feat, such as Azotobacter, live in the soil and are aerobic, but the majority are anaerobic. Clostridium is one such anaerobe, responsible for the deadly food poisoning, botulism, as well as the disease tetanus, or lockjaw. The clostridia, ancestors of the present-day Clostridium, are believed to be among the most ancient of bacteria.

Other microorganisms in the genus Rhizobium enter into a symbiotic relationship with plants. They live in specialized nodules in the roots of legumes (plants such as clover, peas and beans) and convert nitrogen from the atmosphere into the amino groups of amino acids. They rely on plants to provide them with a secure, oxygen-free environment. The plants provide this by means of leghemoglobin – a molecule very similar to the hemoglobin in the blood of animals – which traps any free oxygen in the root nodule.

## Learning to live with oxygen

Oxygen is not the innocuous substance humans, as well-adapted aerobes, tend to think. It is extremely reactive and can disrupt the delicate balance of reactions inside a living cell. Even after millions of years of life with oxygen, living organisms can still be poisoned by high concentrations of oxygen: just breathing rapidly (hyperventilating) makes people feel dizzy, and a few whiffs of pure oxygen are fatal. To the anaerobic microorganisms, the arrival of oxygen was an unmitigated disaster, and many must have disappeared. Others, such as the ancestors of the anaerobic bacteria that survive today, coped by hiding away from oxygen.

But oxygen could benefit life – if only it could be tamed. If a cell could somehow control the way oxygen reacts, the organism could use the reactivity of oxygen to oxidize food, more completely than is possible through anaerobic glycolysis. By harnessing oxygen, a creature could thus extract much more energy from its food.

The cunning response to the oxygen threat was the evolution of "respiration": the ability to use oxygen to oxidize food, and channel the energy released into the synthesis of ATP. Today the vast majority of all organisms, including bacteria, can perform this biochemical feat. Life has indeed succeeded in taming oxygen.

Respiration begins in special structures in the cell known as mitochondria, often with the end product of glycolysis, pyruvate. Inside the mitochondrion, pyruvate encounters a complex of enzymes that rapidly convert it to a molecule known as acetyl coenzyme A (acetyl CoA). This crucial intermediary then enters a cycle of reactions known as the citric acid cycle, or Krebs' cycle, after its discoverer, Hans Krebs (b. 1900). Acetyl CoA is also produced by the degradation of spare amino acids, not used in protein synthesis, and by the breakdown of fatty acids – thus, energy from fat in foods, and that stored in fat layers in the body, can also be channeled into the Krebs' cycle.

The Krebs' cycle effectively dismembers acetyl CoA into carbon dioxide and hydrogen. Much of the hydrogen is transferred to carriers – NAD+ or FAD – and forms high-energy bonds with these molecules. It is these hydrogen carriers that channel energy into the final respiratory pathway: the electron transport chain. Here, energized electrons are passed along a chain of electron carriers, losing energy at each step.

Many different electron carrier molecules of the electron transportation chain are embedded in the inner membrane of the mitochondrion. Each successive carrier in the chain has a higher affinity for electrons – that is, a greater tendency to bind them than its predecessor. So the electrons fall into progressively lower energy states as they proceed down the chain. The electrons are finally transferred to oxygen, which has the greatest affinity for electrons of all. As the electrons pass down the chain and lose energy, this is harvested in the form of ATP molecules.

By binding to oxygen, the electrons give it a negative charge and, as positively-charged protons (hydrogen ions) from the surrounding solution rush in to neutralize the charge, the oxygen is reduced to water. This reaction is comparable to burning hydrogen in air to produce water – in normal circumstances, an explosive and violent reaction. What the electron transport chain does is to release the energy in a gradual step-by-step way, so that it can be harnessed. Because the energy released is used to synthesize ATP, the entire process is called oxidative phosphorylation.

### Doing without the Sun

*The free food in the biotic soup was long ago used up and now photosynthesis feeds almost all living things – apart from a few methanogenic bacteria and their kind, all life on Earth today depends ultimately on the Sun. Even animals that live in total darkness – in caves, or in the ocean's depths – are part of a food chain that starts with a plant.*

*Or so it was thought until 1977, when exploration of the ocean floor in deep trenches near the Galapagos Islands revealed communities of bacteria and animals, clustered around hydrothermal vents. These are places where the Earth's crust is particularly thin. Sea water seeping down through the crust, close to the Earth's molten core, is superheated and forced up again as it tries to boil. Hot, and loaded with dissolved minerals, it spews into the icy waters of the ocean's abyss.*

*Among other things, the vent water contains hydrogen sulfide, and feeding off the hydrogen sulfide fountain is a thriving community of chemosynthetic bacteria, which obtain energy by oxidizing hydrogen sulfide to give inorganic sulfur. The water is thick with these bacteria, and they nourish many filter-feeding species. Some of the smaller filter-feeding creatures are preyed on by fish, blind crabs or other predators, and together they make up a unique food-chain, independent of the Sun. The community around the vent is a world apart, surviving on a food source created by the Earth's thermal energy.*

**▼ A luminescent comb-jelly. Today, most animals that are luminescent use their ability for signaling purposes, or to deter predators by startling them. The light is produced by a variety of methods, most of which involve the reduction of oxygen. The molecules involved may originally have served to mop up oxygen in the cell.**

**▶ Beardworms, of a previously unknown species, were found around deep-sea hydrothermal vents, where a whole community of bacteria and animals lives independently of the Sun. Beardworms have chemosynthetic bacteria living symbiotically within the red tissues at their tips and supplying them with nutrients.**

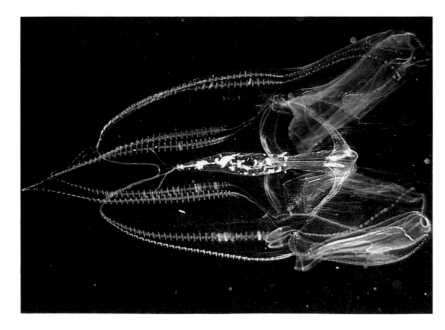

### Defenses against oxygen

*Early anaerobes may have synthesized some molecules, which are now very important to life, simply in order to protect themselves against the onslaught of oxygen. Some enzymes, for instance, can break down the reactive free radicals of oxygen, such as the superoxide radical ($O_2^-$). Other molecules may have originally been made to soak up some of the toxic oxygen. Porphyrins, found today in chlorophyll, hemoglobin and many other molecules, may have first been created to protect organisms from oxidation. Isoprenoids, another large class of molecules which includes vitamin K, phytol involved in photosynthesis, and the carotenoid pigments (♦ page 132), could similarly have acted as oxygen traps. All require oxygen in the final steps of their synthesis. Steroids and their relatives (♦ page 132) might have been synthesized simply because they react with oxygen. Even bioluminescence, the light emitted by creatures as diverse as bacteria, fungi and insects, may originally have evolved as a mechanism for detoxifying oxygen.*

# Cell Structure and Evolution

*Development of the cell membrane...Animal, plant and bacterial cells compared...Bacteria-like organisms – the ancestors of more complex structures... PERSPECTIVE...How many kingdoms?...A strange symbiosis...Green animals – photosynthesis in organisms other than plants*

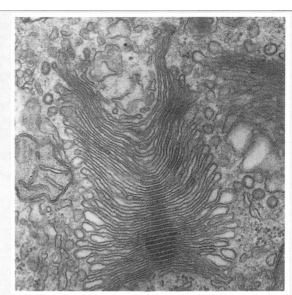

▲ *The Golgi body, a structure found in higher cells.*

An essential stage in the early evolution of life was the development of the membrane: a barrier that could enclose the living molecules and segregate them from the general chemical free-for-all of the biotic soup (◀ page 144). Exactly how membranes came about is unknown, but in all living organisms today they are made up of phospholipids, or similar molecules, arranged in a bilayer (◀ page 133). This bilayer is selectively permeable: that is, it will let some molecules through but keep others out. This selectivity is enhanced by protein molecules, embedded in the membrane, which can facilitate the diffusion of particular molecules or even pump them into the cell (▶ page 170). But membranes can have other uses, besides enclosing the cell contents. They can help the cell organize its affairs by providing a flat surface to which enzymes are bound at specific points. Thus the enzymes of a particular metabolic pathway can be arranged alongside one another, so that the molecules they process can pass along from one to another with maximum efficiency. To make more surface area available for this task, the outer membrane of some bacterial cells is extended into the cell and arranged in multiple folds. In several bacterial groups, infolded membranes known as mesomes are thought to carry respiratory enzymes, or to be involved in controlling cell division. Similarly, infolded membranes occur in photosynthetic bacteria, where they are known as thylakoids and carry the photosynthetic machinery. Some bacteria also have simple membrane-bound structures that do not appear to be extensions of the cell membrane, such as gas vacuoles, which help them to stay afloat.

### The cell membrane

*All cells are delimited by a selectively permeable membrane. The precise nature of the cell membrane is unknown as it is extremely thin, but the most widely accepted idea of its structure is the fluid-mosaic model. This proposes that the cell membrane is a fluid bimolecular layer of lipids with their hydrophobic tails facing inward and their hydrophilic polar heads outward to form the internal and external surfaces of the membrane. Proteins are believed to occur at intervals, some embedded in the lipid bilayer, others loosely associated with the polar ends of the lipid molecules. The inner and outer halves of the membrane are not identical. Proteins in the inner half may be anchored to the cytoskeleton (▶ page 157) and help to maintain the cell's shape. Linked to some outer proteins and lipids are carbohydrate chains, which may play a part in cell-to-cell contact.*

### The cell membrane

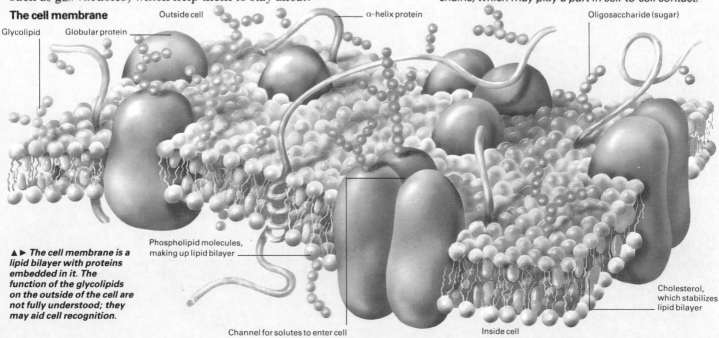

Glycolipid | Globular protein | Outside cell | α-helix protein | Oligosaccharide (sugar)

Phospholipid molecules, making up lipid bilayer

Channel for solutes to enter cell | Inside cell | Cholesterol, which stabilizes lipid bilayer

▲ ▶ *The cell membrane is a lipid bilayer with proteins embedded in it. The function of the glycolipids on the outside of the cell are not fully understood; they may aid cell recognition.*

*Eukaryotic cells are 10 times the size of bacterial cells, thanks to their complex internal structure*

Although simple membranous structures are found within many prokaryotic cells, it is only in the eukaryotic cell that the full potential of membranes is realized. There the genetic material is enclosed by a double thickness of membrane, called the nuclear envelope, which divides the nucleus from the rest of the cell. The complex layers of the endoplasmic reticulum help control the movement of important substances around the cell and offer an anchorage point for many biosynthetic enzymes, as well as ribosomes needed for protein synthesis. The Golgi body, or Golgi apparatus, provides the eukaryotic cell with a packaging service for some of the synthesized molecules, wrapping them in a sphere of membrane. Among the Golgi body's products are secretory vacuoles, which move to the cell membrane and are released from the cell. They may contain digestive enzymes, mucus, neurotransmitters, or a variety of other products that the cell needs to secrete. Several other membrane-bound structures of eukaryotes contain enzymes of various kinds. The lysosome, for example, contains powerful digestive enzymes that can coalesce with vacuoles containing food, taken in by phagocytosis (◆ page 170). Lysosomes have also been described as "suicide bags" because they can destroy the cells in which they are found, for example during the development of the embryo, where pre-programmed death of certain cells is a necessary part of differentiation.

In addition to these structures, all eukaryotic cells (with the exception of degenerate parasitic forms) have membrane-bound organelles known as mitochondria, which house the respiratory enzymes of the Krebs' cycle and electron transport chain (◆ page 152). Internally, the mitochondrion is divided up by infolded membranes, known as christae, and it is these which carry the enzymes. The strangest thing about mitochondria, however, is that they contain a little DNA, some ribosomes, transfer RNA molecules and other items needed to synthesize protein. Although they only produce a tiny fraction of their own proteins, and rely on the cell's nuclear DNA for the rest, the presence of this protein-making equipment is intriguing. Furthermore, the mitochondria are not put together by other cell organelles, but reproduce themselves by binary fission – suggesting that they could have been derived from independent organisms.

### A fundamental difference

*In 1937, a French biologist, Edouard Chatton, suggested that there was a fundamental division in the living world, between complex cells that had a membrane-bound nucleus and various cell organelles (notably mitochondria and chloroplasts), and a simpler group of cells that lacked these structures. The former group he called eukaryotes, or "true nuclei", and the latter prokaryotes, or "pre-nuclei". The prokaryotes he identified as the bacteria and "blue-green algae" (now called cyanobacteria), while the eukaryotes account for the rest of the living world, including animals, plants, fungi and protozoa. This fundamental division has been confirmed by subsequent research, and many other items can be added to the list of differences. Eukaryotes have various other membrane-bound organelles. Their genetic material, DNA, is closely associated with proteins and, when the cell divides, it appears as multiple structures called chromosomes. Prokaryotes just have a simple, circular DNA, with fewer proteins attached.*

*The cytoplasm of eukaryotes is also more structured than that of prokaryotic cells, and is said to possess a "cytoskeleton". This can produce movement within the cell, give it a definite shape, and organize the transport of vital molecules. It consists of a network of protein filaments – the microtrabecular lattice – in which are suspended, not only the cell organelles, but also microfilaments and microtubules of protein.*

*A further difference lies in the flagella and cilia of eukaryotes, which are made up of many protein tubules in a characteristic "9 + 2 arrangement" (◆ page 160). The flagella of prokaryotes are much simpler, being composed of a single protein fibril. They are also made of a different protein. Several other chemical differences exist between the two groups, with the prokaryotes showing a much greater diversity of metabolic processes (◆ page 149). Some can live without oxygen, which eukaryotes, apart from a few parasites, cannot do.*

## Mitosis

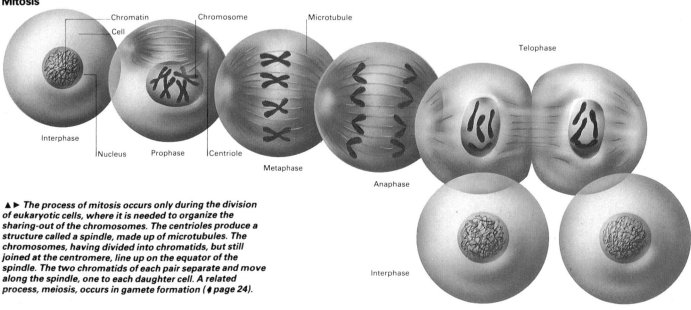

▲ ► **The process of mitosis occurs only during the division of eukaryotic cells, where it is needed to organize the sharing-out of the chromosomes. The centrioles produce a structure called a spindle, made up of microtubules. The chromosomes, having divided into chromatids, but still joined at the centromere, line up on the equator of the spindle. The two chromatids of each pair separate and move along the spindle, one to each daughter cell. A related process, meiosis, occurs in gamete formation (◆ page 24).**

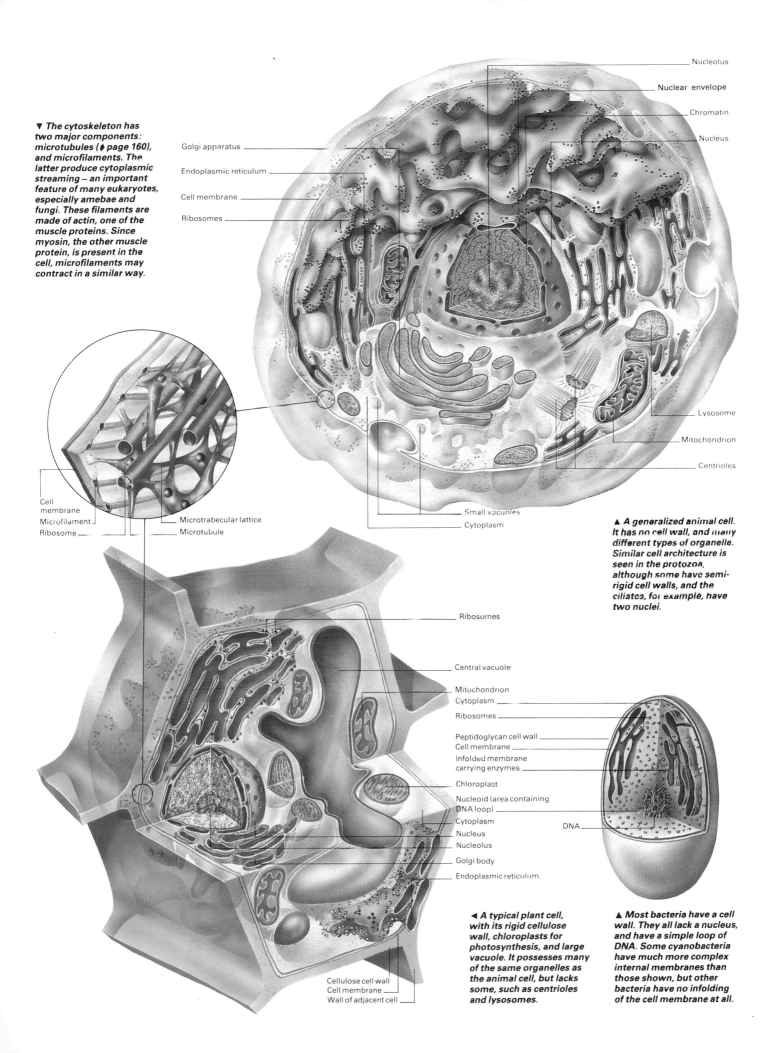

▼ *The cytoskeleton has two major components: microtubules (◆ page 160), and microfilaments. The latter produce cytoplasmic streaming – an important feature of many eukaryotes, especially amebae and fungi. These filaments are made of actin, one of the muscle proteins. Since myosin, the other muscle protein, is present in the cell, microfilaments may contract in a similar way.*

Golgi apparatus

Endoplasmic reticulum

Cell membrane

Ribosomes

Nucleolus

Nuclear envelope

Chromatin

Nucleus

Lysosome

Mitochondrion

Centrioles

Small vacuoles

Cytoplasm

Cell membrane
Microfilament
Ribosome
Microtrabecular lattice
Microtubule

▲ *A generalized animal cell. It has no cell wall, and many different types of organelle. Similar cell architecture is seen in the protozoa, although some have semi-rigid cell walls, and the ciliates, for example, have two nuclei.*

Ribosomes

Central vacuole

Mitochondrion
Cytoplasm
Ribosomes
Peptidoglycan cell wall
Cell membrane
Infolded membrane carrying enzymes
Chloroplast
Nucleoid (area containing DNA loop)
Cytoplasm
Nucleus
Nucleolus
Golgi body
Endoplasmic reticulum

DNA

Cellulose cell wall
Cell membrane
Wall of adjacent cell

◀ *A typical plant cell, with its rigid cellulose wall, chloroplasts for photosynthesis, and large vacuole. It possesses many of the same organelles as the animal cell, but lacks some, such as centrioles and lysosomes.*

▲ *Most bacteria have a cell wall. They all lack a nucleus, and have a simple loop of DNA. Some cyanobacteria have much more complex internal membranes than those shown, but other bacteria have no infolding of the cell membrane at all.*

The mitochondria and chloroplasts could be "stowaways" in the eukaryotic cell

Exactly the same sort of autonomy seen in mitochondria is shown by chloroplasts, the cell organelles responsible for photosynthesis in plants, algae and some protozoa. They, too, have their own DNA and reproduce by fission. Moreover, chloroplasts bear a striking resemblance to cyanobacteria. This has led to the hypothesis that the first eukaryotic cells evolved by a process of endosymbiosis.

The suggestion is that the original eukaryotes did not develop mitochondria and chloroplasts *de novo*, but were invaded by bacteria which formed symbiotic relationships with them. Photosynthetic prokaryotes, principally cyanobacteria, are proposed as the ancestors of chloroplasts, and aerobically respiring bacteria as the forerunners of mitochondria. These cells gradually lost their independence and became integral parts of the host cell. The similarity between the mitochondria of animals, plants and fungi suggests that all these groups have a common ancestor. This ancestor could have been an anaerobic bacterium which was saved from extinction as oxygen levels rose (◀ page 150) thanks to an invasion by an aerobic bacterium. Plants could subsequently have evolved from this main stock. The fact that chloroplasts of red algae resemble cyanobacteria, and those of green algae resemble the related *Prochloron* suggests that this happened at least twice (◀ page 46).

### Endosymbiosis: history of an idea

The notion that some of the structures found in the cells of animals, plants and fungi are the descendants of simpler bacteria-like organisms that once invaded the cells is now accepted by many biologists. But until very recently, most researchers regarded the theory of endosymbiosis as fanciful.

The hypothesis that the cells of higher organisms evolved "suddenly", through endosymbiotic associations, arose in the 19th century, when microscopes became powerful enough for the organelles of cells to be clearly seen. In the 1880s a German botanist, A.F.W. Schimper, noticed that certain chloroplasts looked rather like free-living "blue-green algae" (cyanobacteria) and divided in a similar way. He suggested that the chloroplasts of the plant cells might be related to the cyanobacteria. In 1890 another German, R. Altmann, suggested that mitochondria arose from a symbiotic association. Two decades later the Russian biologist K.C. Mereschkowsky elaborated these ideas into his "theory of symbiogenesis". But these notions were ignored or rejected, as biologists stuck to the view that the cell of higher organisms evolved through the gradual accumulation of advantageous mutations.

The fact that the modern theory of endosymbiosis has now won wide acceptance owes much to the writings of Lynn Margulis of Boston University. Furthermore, advances in molecular biology and electron microscopy have at last provided the data that could critically test the hypothesis, and it has been found that the ultrastructure and biochemistry of the mitochondria and chloroplasts do indeed bear a striking resemblance to certain bacteria. Most biologists now accept that mitochondria and chloroplasts are the products of endosymbiosis, but a further claim, that spirochete bacteria were ancestral to the cilia and flagella of eukaryotic cells, remains highly contentious (▶ page 160).

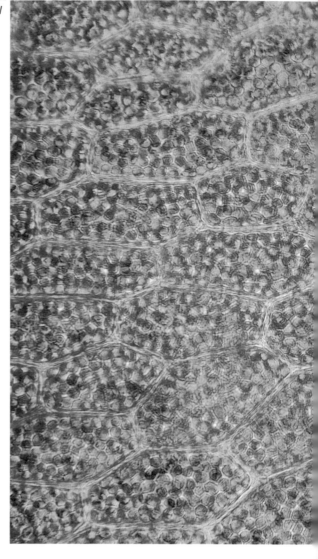

► The surface of a moss leaf, showing the chloroplasts, which perform photosynthesis, packed into each cell.

▼ The giant clam is a filter-feeder, but it also obtains nutrients from unicellular algae living in its mantle's protruding edge.

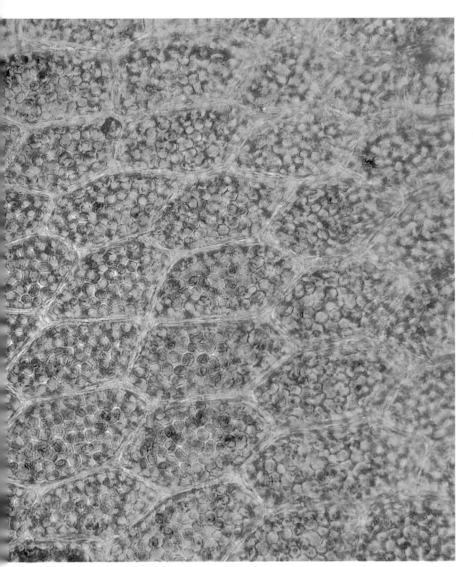

### Green animals

The idea that endosymbiosis could have produced the chloroplasts of eukaryotic plants is partly supported by the many analogous relationships observed in the living world today. A whole range of animals, protozoans and fungi have photosynthetic organisms living within their tissues and supplying them with food. The list includes clams, sea slugs, tunicates, nematodes, paramecia and the group of fungi known as lichens. In some the photosynthetic partner is a single-celled alga (a eukaryote), in others a cyanobacterium.

This sort of relationship has been particularly well studied in the green paramecium, which has many algal cells in its tissues. If these are removed, it needs a supply of nutrients in order to live, whereas the alga can survive quite well alone. When reintroduced to the algal cells, the paramecium absorbs them, but does not digest them. They grow and divide, until the number the paramecium normally carries is reached. Then they stop multiplying. Thereafter, if the paramecium takes in algal cells it digests them. Somehow it "knows" that it has enough symbiotic algae, and is able to regulate their reproduction – perhaps a first step on the road to full control and total interdependence, as seen in modern plant cells.

Similar parallels do not exist for mitochondria because almost all eukaryotes have them already. The need to "reinvent" mitochondria has not arisen, as it has with chloroplasts.

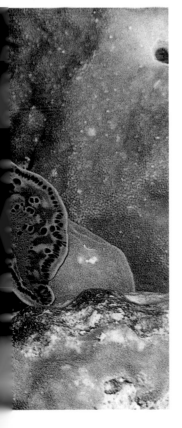

### How many kingdoms?

Linnaeus recognized two major kingdoms, the Animalia and the Plantae. Organisms that are mobile and ingest food he identified as animals, while those that are immobile and make their own food by photosynthesis he called plants. Fungi were put with plants, on the assumption that they had once had photosynthetic powers but had lost them. Later, Ernst Haeckel (1834–1919) proposed a third kingdom, the Protista, for bacteria, protozoa and other organisms that were not clearly plants nor animals, and had a simple form of organization. Haeckel proposed that the slime molds, fungi and algae should be put into this group, but later changed his mind, and the word "protist" subsequently came to be used to denote single-celled organisms only.

In 1956, a four-kingdom system was suggested by Herbert Copeland (1902–1968). The bacteria and cyanobacteria he placed in the Kingdom Monera, on the basis that they are prokaryotes, whereas members of the other three kingdoms are all eukaryotes. The next two kingdoms accounted for the animals and plants, but, like Haeckel, Copeland did not include the multicellular algae – seaweeds and the like – in the plant kingdom. Instead he placed them in a rather unnatural group, the Kingdom Protoctista (sometimes confusingly called the Protista). This also included the single-celled algae, the protozoa, the slime molds and the fungi. Copeland justified this grouping on the basis that all organisms included had a unicellular or simple form of organization, without differentiation into specialized tissues, as seen in higher animals and plants. A refinement of Copeland's classification was the five kingdom system, suggested by R.H. Whittaker (1924–1980). Whittaker gives the fungi (including slime molds) a kingdom of their own, and he classes the higher algae as plants, thus leaving his Kingdom Protista as a more homogeneous group than Copeland's with only unicellular or colonial organisms. These include the protozoa, the dinoflagellates (treated as algae in this book), and the hypochytrids (considered as lower fungi in this book).

A five-kingdom system is now becoming widely accepted, though not always as Whittaker envisaged. Some scientists prefer Copeland's definition of the Protoctista, though with all the higher fungi and some of the lower fungi removed to the Kingdom Fungi. In this system, the Protoctista can be defined in a purely negative way. It includes organisms that are not bacteria (because they are eukaryotic), not animals (because they do not pass through a blastula stage during development), not plants (because they do not develop from an embryo), and not fungi (because they have one or more flagella at some stage in their life cycle, and do not produce spores).

This kingdom is the least satisfactory of all and in an effort to sort it out, new systems with 10, 13, 17 or even 20 kingdoms have been suggested. None of these fully resolves the problem, however, for, as Whittaker reflected: "There is no good way to separate the lower and higher eukaryotic organisms, there are only different choices with different difficulties."

## A controversial theory

If the chloroplasts and mitochondria of living eukaryotes could have developed through endosymbiosis, then why not other structures? The additional candidates proposed for inclusion in this hypothesis are the flagella, cilia and centrioles, all of which are composed of protein mictrotubules. The idea that these structures could have evolved through endosymbiosis is an intriguing one but, as yet, entirely conjectural. Microtubules are made of a special protein, tubulin, whose compact dumbbell-shaped molecules are arranged in a tightly packed spiral, to create a hollow tube. These tubules run through the cytoplasm of eukaryotes, and are used for internal transport, being particularly important in large cells, such as the motor neurons of the central nervous system. These can be up to a meter in length (◆ page 198), and to carry proteins and other vital supplies from the cell body to its extremities requires microtubules which run the whole length of the axon. In all cells, regardless of size, microtubules are also important during mitosis (◀ page 156) and meiosis (◀ page 24). Their role in these vital processes is to form the spindle, which controls the division of the chromosomes between the daughter cells. Microscope observation of animal cells has shown that the microtubules of the spindle are synthesized by the centrioles.

The centrioles have a distinctive structure, consisting of nine bundles of three microtubules each, arranged in a circle. One interesting discovery is that this same arrangement of microtubules appears in the basal bodies of the flagella and cilia. And a similar pattern is seen in the flagella and cilia themselves, with nine pairs arranged around a central pair (◆ page 211). (This is often called a "9 + 2 formation", and the eukaryotic flagellum a "9 + 2 flagellum", or "9 + 2 undulipodium", to distinguish it from the simple single-protein-filament flagellum of bacteria.) Occasionally, centrioles left over after mitosis have been observed migrating to the cell surface, developing a flagellum, and becoming basal bodies, so the link between these structures is fairly clear. But whether it actually reflects the contribution of symbiotic spirochetes to the eukaryotic cell millions of years ago, as has been claimed, remains a matter for debate. There is little other evidence to support the idea.

### Bacterial oarsmen

*One of the most extraordinary relationships known in the living world occurs in the protozoan* Myxotricha pardoxa. *Itself a symbiont, living in the gut of a wood-eating termite,* Myxotricha *has three bacterial associates of its own. One is internal and helps it to digest the wood particles obtained from the termite's gut. The other two live on the surface of the cell. The first is rod-shaped and rests in hollows on the surface. Its function is unknown. The second is a spirochete – a corkscrew-shaped bacterium – that moves the protozoan about. Hundreds of these spirochetes beat in a coordinated way to produce a smooth gliding motion. How their activities are controlled by the host remains a mystery, but they have led to the suggestion that the flagella and cilia of eukaryotic cells could have arisen by a similar sort of symbiotic relationship.*

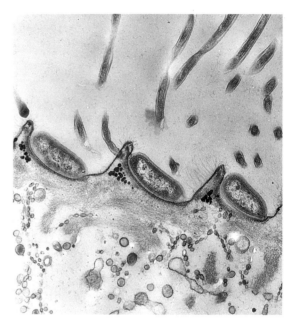

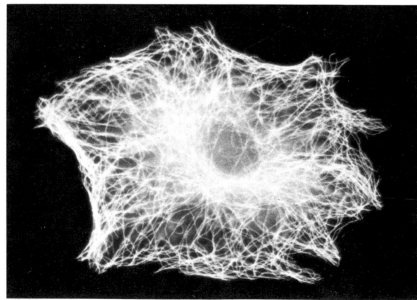

◀ *The cytoskeleton of a eukaryotic cell. This picture was taken by preparing fluorescent antibodies, specific for the proteins of the cytoskeleton.*

▲ ▶ ▼ *The surface of* Myxotricha *carries two types of bacteria, spirochetes (1), which move it about, and rod-shaped cells (2) whose function is unknown.*

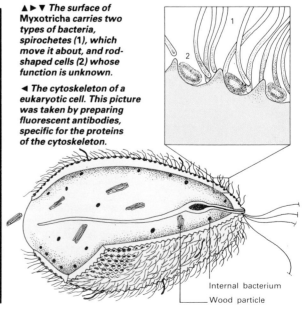

Internal bacterium

Wood particle

*The fertilized egg – the source of billions of cells...
The developing egg – the frog example...The triggers
of development...Cell "fate maps" timing genes...
PERSPECTIVE...The mother's influence...Embryo
development – reliving the past?...How cell
movements are traced...Losing limbs in self-defense...
Regeneration and cancer*

Blue whales, giant redwoods, humans, corals and earthworms all have one thing in common: they can all breed sexually, and when they do so, their offspring must begin life as a single fertilized egg cell. In multicellular organisms the development of the body's form – the process known as morphogenesis – often involves a great amount of cell division and specialization. In a vertebrate, for example, there can be hundreds of cell types and billions of individual cells. But all this cellular diversity is coded for by the DNA in a single, tiny cell – the fertilized egg. This DNA also codes for the mechanisms by which the body grows and develops, and even for the way it later reacts and behaves. Many animals show a wealth of instinctive behavior, such as the cuckoo's knowledge of its migration route or a weaverbird's ability to create its complex nest. All this knowledge and skill must ultimately be carried in their genetic material.

Quite how instinctive behavior is chemically coded for is still far from being explained, and even the question of how a complete organism is produced from a single cell as yet has no satisfactory answers. However, some of the processes that are involved in morphogenesis are now understood, following the study of the very earliest stages of development.

### A triumph of miniaturization

The problem of how organisms develop from such simple beginnings was neatly sidestepped in the 18th century by the theory of "preformation".

Preformationists held that all development was simply a matter of growth, and that inside every egg cell lay a tiny but complete organism, ready to grow into an adult. To back this up, early microscopists claimed to have observed "homunculi", or tiny humans in sperm cells, and made drawings of them. Considering the limited power of the microscopes of the time, these observations were extraordinarily detailed. Preformation implies that organisms are made up like Russian dolls. Every homunculus would have to have homunculi within it, on an even smaller scale, and so on ad infinitum. Some believed that the human race would come to an end when its stock of preformed homunculi finally ran out. But not all early biologists were convinced of the validity of the theory. The "observations" made by the preformationists could not explain how some animals – like frogs and birds – could be seen to develop from an initial state which was quite clearly without any bodily structures. And many felt that preformation did not answer the question of how development occurs – it merely moved the question further back in time. The homunculists never successfully answered these criticisms, and eventually the idea of preformation was abandoned.

▼ *This female Australian shield bug guards her eggs until the young hatch out. While she protects her clutch, each egg undergoes one of the most complex series of transformations in the living world – the change from a single fertilized cell to a complete adult organism, containing many thousands of cells.*

*The number of cells in a frog's egg increases 10,000 times in a few hours after fertilization*

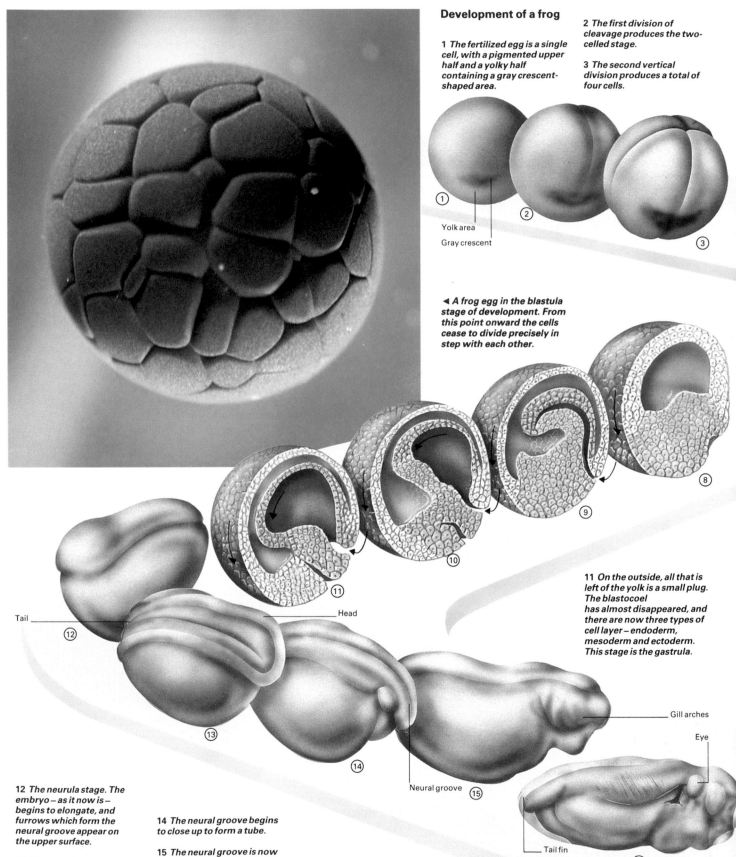

### Development of a frog

**1** *The fertilized egg is a single cell, with a pigmented upper half and a yolky half containing a gray crescent-shaped area.*

**2** *The first division of cleavage produces the two-celled stage.*

**3** *The second vertical division produces a total of four cells.*

Yolk area

Gray crescent

◄ *A frog egg in the blastula stage of development. From this point onward the cells cease to divide precisely in step with each other.*

**11** *On the outside, all that is left of the yolk is a small plug. The blastocoel has almost disappeared, and there are now three types of cell layer – endoderm, mesoderm and ectoderm. This stage is the gastrula.*

Tail

Head

Gill arches

Eye

Neural groove

Tail fin

**12** *The neurula stage. The embryo – as it now is – begins to elongate, and furrows which form the neural groove appear on the upper surface.*

**13** *The neural groove deepens on the upper surface. The head area becomes clearly visible.*

**14** *The neural groove begins to close up to form a tube.*

**15** *The neural groove is now completely sealed into a tube. The gill arches have become visible behind the head.*

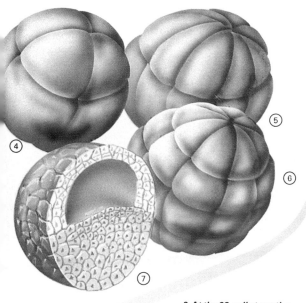

**4** *A third division – this time horizontal – cuts all the cells in two to produce eight cells.*

**5** *Two further vertical divisions produce a total of 16 cells.*

**6** *At the 32-cell stage the egg is known as a morula.*

**7** *The divisions become less organized. By this stage the egg is a sphere of cells (a blastula) rather than a solid ball, because an internal cavity – the blastocoel – has developed. The gray crescent has almost disappeared.*

**8** *A pore appears in the yolky area, and the pigmented cells begin to divide and expand towards it.*

**9** *The pigmented cells move in through the pore to create a new internal layer.*

**10** *As cell division continues, the yolk begins to be used up. The pigmented cells now cover most of the surface.*

**16** *The young tadpole now has rudimentary eyes and a tail fin. The internal organs are almost complete.*

**17** *Development of the tadpole is complete.*

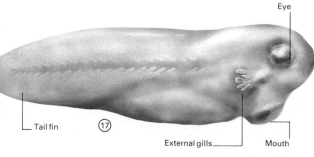

Eye

Tail fin

External gills

Mouth

## The developing egg

In sexually reproducing organisms, development begins only after fertilization, when the full complement of genetic material from both parents is present. Once fertilization has occurred, profound changes start to take place as the egg's DNA begins to program an enormously complex but carefully controlled sequence of development. These changes have been best studied in animal eggs, especially those of aquatic organisms, which are often semi-transparent.

After fertilization, an animal egg initially remains the same size while the process of cleavage divides the original single cell into a ball of hundreds, and ultimately thousands, of daughter cells. All vertebrate and echinoderm eggs undergo "radial" cleavage, in which the daughter cells divide along radii of the egg. Most invertebrate eggs undergo "spiral" cleavage, in which daughter cells lie diagonally opposite each other. This important difference in the way early development is programmed splits the animal kingdom into two groups – the protostomes and deuterostomes (◀ page 88) – and these go on to develop in different ways.

The development of the eggs of the frog *Xenopus laevis* has been carefully mapped out. The cleavage divisions initially take about 30 minutes each, a typical amphibian rate, and about 20 times faster than the average rate for a mammal. Six hours after fertilization, rapid division produces a fluid-filled sphere, or blastula, made up of about 10,000 cells. The stage is now set for gastrulation, a series of cell movements which completely alters the blastula's shape. If the blastula is imagined as a partially inflated rubber ball, gastrulation is, in effect, like pushing the ball in on one side, so that the sides that were originally opposite come close together. In animals with eggs that contain little yolk, this is exactly what happens. In animals like *Xenopus*, whose eggs have a yolk mass, the movements are more complicated. The new cavity is squashed almost flat by the yolk at first, but as the yolk is used up, and more and more "outside" cells move into the interior, the cavity opens up. Gastrulation is a key process because it changes the hollow sphere of cells into a gastrula with three distinct layers of tissue – ectoderm, the external layer of tissue, endoderm, the internal layer, and mesoderm, the new layer between them. In *Xenopus*, ten hours after fertilization, the gastrula contains about 30,000 cells, but despite this tremendous activity and continual protein synthesis it is still no bigger than the original egg.

Once the process of gastrulation is complete, the separate tissue layers begin to develop rudimentary structures. During the process of neurulation, which occurs in all vertebrates, the primordial nerve tissue appears and the body begins to show a distinct head-to-tail orientation. In *Xenopus* 24 hours after fertilization, neurulation has occurred and the basic plan of the body, with all the main divisions, has been laid down. The development of mammal embryos is similar to that of amphibians but with a few important differences. Cleavage is much slower, and because development takes place inside the mother's womb, the embryo has to have structures which enable it to implant and grow there.

Throughout the early development of the egg and embryo, cells are constantly moving as well as dividing. Some detach themselves and migrate to new sites, while others adhere to adjacent cells and pull them into different configurations. The whole process of development involves a remarkable degree of coordination among thousands and sometimes millions of cells.

*Embryological research reveals the mechanisms that lie behind the process of development*

### Techniques in embryology

*Most embryological studies have been carried out on the developing eggs of amphibians, birds and echinoderms, although mouse eggs are sometimes used as well.*

*To establish how a group of cells moves around during development, they must be made distinguishable from their neighbors. "Vital dyeing" is a technique pioneered by Wilhelm Vogt in which a harmless coloring agent is used to stain groups of cells. As the stained cells divide and move, the color travels with them.*

*As well as tracing cell movements, embryologists have learned much through artificially separating or mixing groups of cells. In one technique, the initial single egg cell is divided with a needle or cord to see how the halves develop when they are separated. This technique led to the discovery that some zones in the cytoplasm, like the gray crescent of frog eggs, play a part in the control of development. Moving whole groups of cells reveals how they relate to their neighbors. If embryonic cells of three different tissue types (endoderm, mesoderm and ectoderm) are mixed up, they reorganize themselves into their correct positions, showing that they are able to recognize each other chemically. Cells from different embryos of the same species can also be mixed together and they too seem to organize themselves correctly, because they form a viable "mosaic" embryo. If the cells have different genotypes – for instance, genes for different fur color in mice – they will unite to form a patchwork mouse.*

*Grafting is the transfer of large groups of cells from one site on the embryo to another, the main technique used in work on induction and regeneration. The Spemann–Mangold experiment – a classic piece of research of the 1930s – used grafting to show that parts of one developing embryo can initiate an extra embryo when grafted onto another, producing two joined organisms.*

### The "gray crescent" experiment

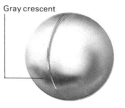

Gray crescent

Gray crescent

Crescent divided equally

Crescent in one half only

Normal tadpole

Abnormal cell mass

Normal tadpole

Normal tadpole

### Vital dyeing

► *In a technique known as vital dyeing, pieces of agar (a jelly-like substance) containing harmless dyes are used to stain groups of cells. This allows the cell clusters to be tracked during development so that their eventual position in the embryo can be mapped out exactly.*

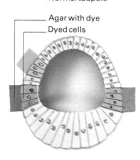

Agar with dye
Dyed cells

► *The development of bird embryos is influenced by the large amount of yolk in the egg. The embryo is initially an elongated disk of tissue lying on the upper surface of the yolk. Blood vessels radiate from the embryo to extract nutrients from the yolk. By the time the chick is fully developed, the yolk has completely disappeared. A domestic chick embryo is shown here at 26 hours, 48 hours, 4 days and 7 days.*

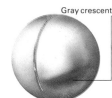

◄ *This experiment, in which frog eggs are divided by a fine cord, shows what effect the "gray crescent" has on development. In the egg on the left, the gray crescent is shared between the two halves of the egg. The result is two normal tadpoles. In the egg on the right, the gray crescent is only in one half. The half containing the crescent produces a normal tadpole, whereas the half without the crescent produces a mass of undifferentiated cells. This shows that the gray crescent is vital to frog development.*

▼ *If cells from the fertilized eggs of mammal parents are mixed, they will form a mosaic egg. In some cases, this egg will develop to produce a viable embryo. By mixing cells with visibly different characteristics – for example, different fur color in mice – the distribution of the descendant cells can be seen in the adult body.*

## The blueprint for development

How do cells know what to become, and when is their fate decided? These are the two fundamental questions in embryology. The second is the easier of the two to answer because the timing of development is relatively simple to test. The most obvious possibility is that every cell's developmental fate is fixed right at the beginning by the egg's genetic blueprint, and this is indeed true of many invertebrates. The nematode worm *Caenorhabditis elegans*, for example, has 959 somatic cells (body cells as opposed to gamete cells) in the adult – the total is always exactly the same. From the moment the egg undergoes its first division until the worm reaches adulthood just three days later, the development plan is always identical. (If, after the second cleavage, one of the four cells is taken away, only three-quarters of a worm is produced.)

A "fate map" can be drawn showing what structures the dividing cells will give rise to, because they always divide in exactly the same way to produce the different parts of the body. This pattern of development is shown by all protostomes, that is the arthropods, annelids, mollusks, nematodes and flatworms. However, insects have semideterminate eggs. Here the fate of individual cells is not fixed until development is underway. By contrast, the eggs of deutero-

### The mosaic egg

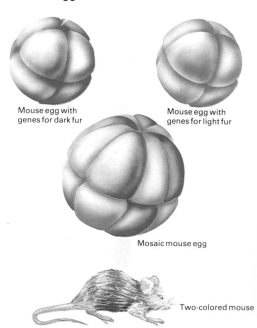

Mouse egg with genes for dark fur

Mouse egg with genes for light fur

Mosaic mouse egg

Two-colored mouse

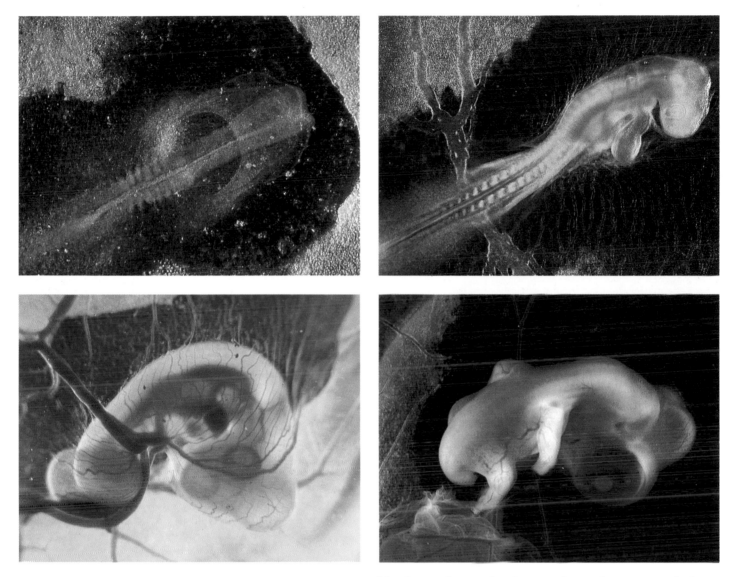

## Maternal influence

*Although the nucleus of a fertilized egg contains genetic information from both parents, the mitochondria and the cytoplasm are produced by the mother alone. This means that the mitochondrial genes and the cytoplasmic genetic information contained in messenger RNA molecules ( ◊ page 140) is entirely maternal. The mitochondrial genes code for a few mitochondrial proteins only, but the messenger RNA in the cytoplasm is capable of controlling the developmental process of the whole cell. The unfertilized eggs of some invertebrates can be prompted into starting development even if their nuclei are removed. Although this never progresses very far, it does show that the RNA from the mother alone is able to direct the process. Some eggs have a distinct polarity – in frog eggs, for example, the upper half is pigmented, while the lower half contains the yolk. These halves, the production of which is directed by the mother's genes, go on to develop in different ways. In some snails, the direction of coiling of the shell is controlled by the mother alone, via messenger RNA produced before fertilization.*

stomes – echinoderms, lower chordates and vertebrates – are indeterminate. If a cell is lost at an early stage, the loss can be made good without any effect on the organism, indicating that the fate of individual cells is not fixed until fairly late. Furthermore, extra cells introduced artificially into the embryo can sometimes be incorporated without disrupting development. Plants are even more flexible, being indeterminate as embryos, and also very variable when mature.

As cells divide during development, there must be mechanisms which switch some of their genes on and off, making them differentiate, that is, adopt just one particular shape and function. Differentiation is not a case of cells losing part of their genetic information and expressing whatever characteristics are left. This can been demonstrated by removing the nucleus from a frog's egg and replacing it with the nucleus of a differentiated cell, for example one taken from the intestine of a tadpole. The experiment does not work with adult frog nuclei, but with tadpole nuclei the egg will sometimes begin development, eventually producing a completely normal frog. Similarly, a single differentiated cell from a mature plant can sometimes be cultured to produce a whole new plant. These are examples of totipotency – an ability which most animal cells lose at an early stage, but which many plant cells retain throughout their life.

*As an organism develops, its cells react to each other in complex ways to produce the body's shape*

## The triggers of development

The question of how the genes are turned on and off during cell differentiation is difficult to answer. A single cell can contain up to 50,000 genes, and it is highly unlikely that they are switched on and off individually. Evolution tends to produce much more economical methods than this. The control of development is more likely to operate on whole groups of genes, and so far research has revealed it in action both at the single-cell egg stage, and later, as the embryo takes shape.

When the egg is still just one cell, some control factors are quite easy to pick out. Many eggs are internally asymmetrical. The elliptical eggs of the fruit fly *Drosophila*, for example, have "pole plasm" at one end of the egg, and this transforms the cells which develop from that end into those which eventually produce gametes. Experiments with other types of egg have shown that many have similar substances, unevenly distributed in the egg, which can later activate different parts of the genome, so that the cells develop in a particular way. This has been confirmed by experiments which stir up the cytoplasm inside sea squirt eggs: development becomes erratic because the chemical determinants are not in their usual places in the cytoplasm.

Another way in which development is triggered is through cell-to-cell contact, or induction. It is well established that cells can recognize each other, and it has recently been shown that cell adhesion molecules (CAMs) bind them together in an organized way. But as well as recognizing each other, cells can also influence what goes on inside their neighbors through the process of induction. During induction, the inducing cells communicate in some way – as yet not identified – with the induced cells and switch on part of their genome. Induction is a very important process in development. Many skin structures, including hair, scales, feathers and the lens of the eye, are produced from the outer layer of tissue, the epidermis. But it has been shown by grafting experiments that it is the layer of tissue underneath the epidermis which determines where these structures will be produced. Inducing agents from the dermis are responsible for producing the hairline on the human scalp, for example, and the pattern of feather buds on the back of a young bird.

▲ *This northern leaf-tailed gecko from Queensland, Australia, has a regenerated tail. The animal's shape makes it unclear to a predator which part is the head, and so the attack may well be launched at its tail. If this happens, the tail detaches, and the gecko escapes. In many reptiles, shed tails wriggle vigorously after separation from the body, providing a further distraction while the owner makes its getaway. The ability to regenerate a limb or tail has been lost in most higher animals.*

### Regeneration
Although most animal cells lose their developmental flexibility at an early stage, some adult cells retain it and can undergo a radical change of character during the process of regeneration, when part of the body – usually a limb – is lost. The ability to regenerate large parts of the body is well known in invertebrates like flatworms, insects and starfish, but in vertebrates it is chiefly restricted to reptiles and amphibians. These animals are able to regenerate their limbs and tails, and some of them use this ability as a defense mechanism: in a process known as autotomy, they actually shed parts of their bodies when attacked. Regeneration of damaged or shed body parts requires controls very much like those that operate in embryo development: cells must divide and differentiate into the right type at the right place, and they must do so in step.

Experiments have shown that there are chemical communication systems in the body by which cells acquire positional information, and by which their division is either provoked or suppressed. After loss of a limb or part of an organ, cells are stimulated to develop in such a way that the original pattern of this chemical information is restored. The mechanism is self-regulating: it always acts to restore the status quo.

It is not clear why the ability to regenerate parts of the body varies so widely. Although humans cannot regenerate limbs, they can regenerate some internal structures. The liver has great regenerative powers if part of it is removed, and in this case it is known that chemicals in the blood regulate how fast liver cells divide. When the organ is intact, these chemicals prevent it from growing. But when part of the liver is lost, the control chemicals are reduced, and regeneration begins.

Regeneration can also go wrong. In its least harmful form, this can lead to doubling up of regenerated limbs or to benign growths. But if tissue regeneration starts when it is not required, and if the dividing cells then "metastasize" or spread through the body, the result can be cancer – one reason why regeneration is an important area of biological research.

## Triggering development

▼ ▶ *Induction is the process by which one group of cells triggers the development of another group. On this page, three examples of induction in vertebrate development are shown.*

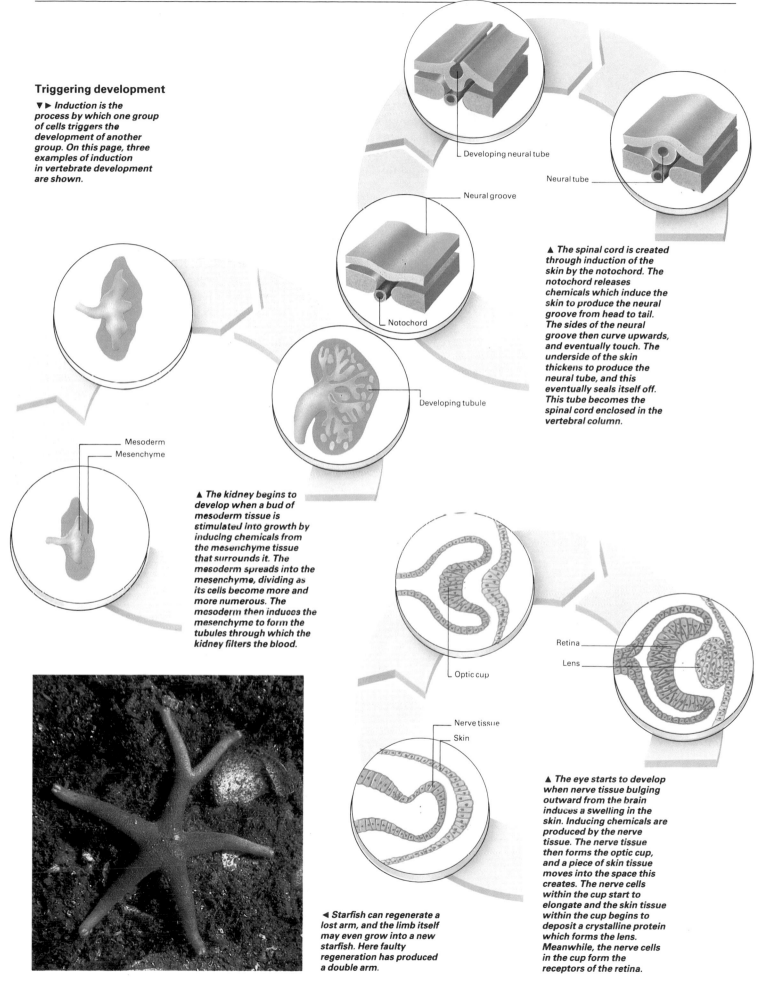

Developing neural tube

Neural tube

Neural groove

Notochord

Developing tubule

▲ *The spinal cord is created through induction of the skin by the notochord. The notochord releases chemicals which induce the skin to produce the neural groove from head to tail. The sides of the neural groove then curve upwards, and eventually touch. The underside of the skin thickens to produce the neural tube, and this eventually seals itself off. This tube becomes the spinal cord enclosed in the vertebral column.*

Mesoderm
Mesenchyme

▲ *The kidney begins to develop when a bud of mesoderm tissue is stimulated into growth by inducing chemicals from the mesenchyme tissue that surrounds it. The mesoderm spreads into the mesenchyme, dividing as its cells become more and more numerous. The mesoderm then induces the mesenchyme to form the tubules through which the kidney filters the blood.*

Retina
Lens

Optic cup

Nerve tissue
Skin

◀ *Starfish can regenerate a lost arm, and the limb itself may even grow into a new starfish. Here faulty regeneration has produced a double arm.*

▲ *The eye starts to develop when nerve tissue bulging outward from the brain induces a swelling in the skin. Inducing chemicals are produced by the nerve tissue. The nerve tissue then forms the optic cup, and a piece of skin tissue moves into the space this creates. The nerve cells within the cup start to elongate and the skin tissue within the cup begins to deposit a crystalline protein which forms the lens. Meanwhile, the nerve cells in the cup form the receptors of the retina.*

## Reliving the past?

*The German biologist Ernst Haeckel (1834–1919) proposed that the development of an embryo relived the complete evolutionary development of its species, or that "ontogeny recapitulates phylogeny". He saw this as the explanation for the similarities between human embryos and various adult animals, including fish and reptiles, explaining that these were all stages through which at some time our species had passed. The theory encouraged some scientists into highly imaginative interpretations of their observations. In 1860 the French anatomist Etienne Serres, on examining a deformed human fetus, declared it to have died in the "molluskan" stage of development. His evidence for this was that it had gill-like blood vessels and no head. Such fervor did not help the theory, and gradually it fell into disrepute. Today, the idea of recapitulation in its original form is largely dismissed. Haeckel maintained that embryos recapitulate the adult forms of their ancestors, undergoing their entire evolutionary history before stopping at the point ordained for them. What actually happens during development is that embryos of related species share similar early stages, but each develops the initial plan in different ways. Human embryos, for example, pass through a stage when they have branchial arches homologous to the gill arches of fish. But these are not gills, merely the rudimentary structures from which some vertebrates develop them.*

## Chronogenes and homeoboxes

Although processes like induction explain how development can be triggered, they themselves also must be initiated in some way. Chromosomal studies of developing embryos have shown at least two control mechanisms which can be traced right back to DNA.

The first of these are chronogenes, which were discovered in the nematode, *Caenorhabditis elegans*. These genes determine when groups of cells begin to differentiate. If a chronogene mutates, it upsets the programmed series of cell divisions. In a nematode, where development is completely determinate, correct timing in cell differentiation is crucial. If just one cell fails to keep in step, the body will show abnormalities. Frequently the mutations halt development completely, and so are lethal.

More recently some genes have been found to share a short, similar sequence of DNA called the "homeobox". About 10 or 15 copies of the sequence appear in the genomes of species as distantly related as nematodes, fruit flies, mice and humans. These genes containing the homeobox may be master genes in development, controlling groups of other genes that are important in the positioning of cells in the embryo. The genes which contain the homeobox produce proteins that bind specifically to the DNA of other genes and probably control them during development. The 60-amino-acid protein chain that the homeobox produces differs by only one amino acid between the fruit fly and the frog *Xenopus*. This extremly small degree of difference in the amino acid sequence is a clear indication that the protein is of critical importance in the developmental process (◀ page 20).

◀ *The process of development is a continuing one, and is not restricted to the egg stage. A dragonfly nymph initially lacks wings and reproductive organs, but by the time it enters its final molt, seen here, these have been developed and are ready to function after the nymph's skin is shed. In more advanced insects, the larva is completely different from the adult, and there is a total reorganization of the body when it develops into an adult (◀ page 83). This complete metamorphosis mirrors many of the processes which occur during the development of an embryo.*

# Sustaining Life

**Raw materials and energy...Breaking food down...
Different methods of digestion...Taking in gases...Salt
and water...Expelling wastes...Maintaining a balance...
PERSPECTIVE...Animals and plants...Breathing
techniques...Parasites...Waste disposal...Feeding the
young...A question of size**

All living things need to take in supplies of various chemicals in order to survive, grow and multiply. These chemicals are needed for two main purposes. Firstly, they provide the *raw materials* needed to build new cells and maintain the ones already formed. Secondly, they are often used as a source of *energy*, to power many of the chemical processes upon which all cells depend.

Some of the required supplies are gases. Oxygen, for example, is needed by most organisms to "burn" foods to supply energy (◀ page 153), and plants need carbon dioxide gas as a raw material for photosynthesis. Gases enter the cell by the process of diffusion, but other supplies are consumed as solids, and many more come dissolved in water, which is itself an essential commodity needed by all life. The cell has various means of absorbing these substances.

The general term for the chemical supplies needed by living things, other than water and gases, is "nutrients". The term "food" is usually restricted to organic nutrients (ie. carbon-based molecules produced by other organisms) such as sugars, proteins and fats, which are needed by animals, fungi and most protozoa, but not by plants.

Living organisms are made out of one or more cells, and all cells are bounded by a fatty membrane that forms a barrier between the cells and the environment outside. So, for all life, the problem of obtaining supplies involves getting these supplies through the cell membrane. There are three main ways for this to be achieved, known as diffusion, active transport and endocytosis (◀ page 170).

**Animals and plants – a basic difference**
The supplies needed to sustain living things vary widely, depending on the organisms concerned.

Plants are known as autotrophs ("self-feeders") because they can make all of the chemicals they need from a supply of simple inorganic nutrients: water, carbon dioxide gas, and simple minerals such as nitrates, phosphates and sulfates. Many bacteria are also autotrophs, and some, like plants, use the energy of sunlight to convert their simple raw materials into all the various components of the living cell. There are also some bacteria that use inorganic chemicals, rather than light, as their power source.

All animals and fungi are classed as heterotrophs ("other-feeders") since they cannot survive on inorganic nutrients alone. Their most fundamental need is for a supply of preformed organic food, such as carbohydrate or fat, and a supply of protein (or the amino acids that make up proteins). They get these supplies by eating the bodies or body-products of other organisms.

In the course of evolution, most heterotrophs have also come to require other preformed molecules from their diet – there is no point in retaining the ability to synthesize a compound that is freely available in your diet. Many of these essential substances are described as "vitamins", but these substances really have little in common, except that human cells need them only in small amounts and cannot make them for themselves. Other animals also have a need for vitamins, though not necessarily the same ones that humans require. A number of the vitamins serve as coenzymes, which means that they become bound to particular enzymes and allow them to work properly (◀ page 136).

▼ *African skimmers, feeding at dusk. In these birds, the lower half of the bill is considerably longer than the upper half, enabling them to lift fish from just below the surface – a good example of a special adaptation for getting food.*

*Nutrients must cross the membrane that surrounds all cells*

### How cells eat

There are three main methods by which nutrients and other substances can enter cells: diffusion, active transport and endocytosis.

Any nutrient molecules that can pass through the cell membrane itself, or enter through channels spanning the membrane, can simply "diffuse" into a cell provided there is more of the nutrient outside the cell than inside it. Diffusion takes place because of the constant random movement of molecules, ions and atoms. If there is more of some nutrient outside a cell than inside, for example, then this random movement will inevitably make the molecules pass into the cell more often than they pass out. Some chemicals can enter cells by diffusion even though they cannot cross the membrane directly or pass through membrane channels. Instead they rely on "carrier proteins" to bind them and carry them across the membrane. This is known as "facilitated diffusion". It is very specific, whereas simple diffusion is fairly non-specific, except that it excludes large molecules. Water is taken up into cells largely by a process known as "osmosis", which is really just a form of diffusion: water molecules diffuse from a dilute solution into a less dilute one.

Active transport can concentrate a particular solute inside the cell. It relies on proteins embedded in the cell membrane which are believed to bind to nutrient molecules outside. These proteins then either rotate, or change shape, or actually move across the membrane so that they can release their nutrient cargo into the cell. Active transport allows cells to gather up nutrient molecules and ions that cannot simply diffuse into the cell. However, unlike diffusion and osmosis, it uses up energy, in the form of ATP.

Endocytosis is the uptake of food and nutrients by the invagination of the cell membrane, and is the least specific of the three processes. It includes phagocytosis ("cell eating") and pinocytosis ("cell drinking"). In phagocytosis, small lumps of food are taken in by membrane-coated vesicles, known as food vacuoles. These fuse with lysosomes, which contain powerful digestive enzymes. In pinocytosis, liquids are taken into the cell in smaller vesicles. Most cells practice pinocytosis, while phagocytosis is restricted to certain specialized cells, such as amebae.

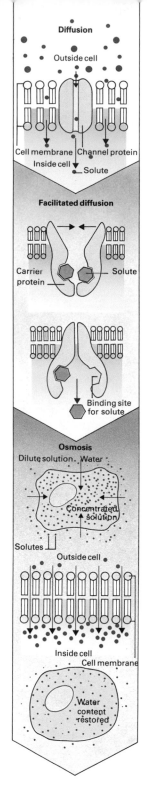

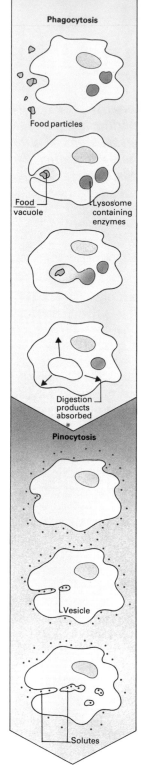

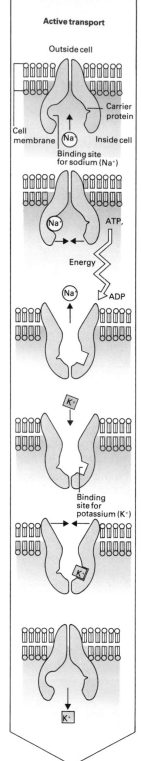

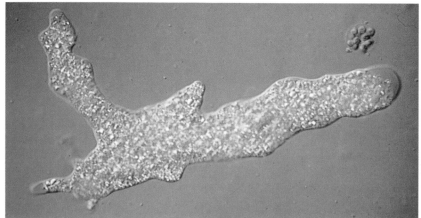

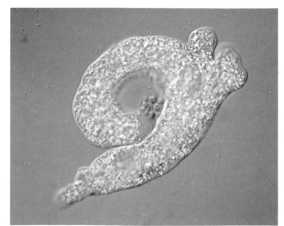

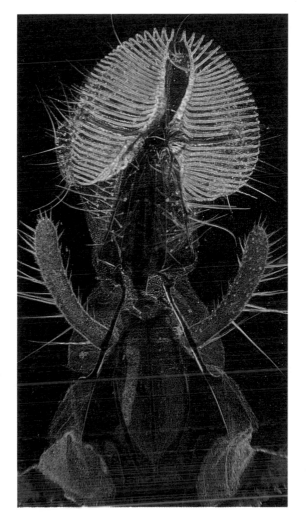

◄ The three main methods of absorption into the cell. The active transport diagram shows a membrane pump that is present in most cells – it forces potassium ions into the cell, while pumping sodium ions out.

▼ A giant ameba feeding on the colonial alga Pandorina, by phagocytosis.

▲ Digestion does not always take place inside the body. House flies feed by pouring digestive enzymes out onto their food, and then mopping up the nutrient-rich liquid produced. Their mouthparts, shown here highly magnified, have branching grooves and tubes which soak up the liquid by capillary action.

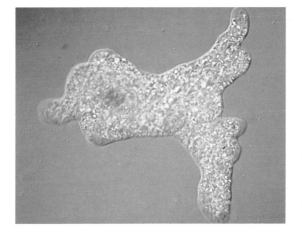

## Digestion

Before they can be useful to an organism, most foodstuffs will need to be broken down into smaller units and chemically altered so that they can be absorbed by the cells. This process is known as digestion.

The best example of digestion is the complex mechanical and chemical processing that goes on inside a higher animal's digestive tract (its mouth, stomach and intestines). But even fungi and single-celled organisms may need to alter some of their food and nutrient supplies in ways that could be described as digestion. For example, some bacteria release enzymes that break down foods found in the environment into simpler substances. Fungi, too, release digestive enzymes that can break up organic materials – such as bread, wood, seeds or the leaves of plants – into forms suitable for uptake by their cells. A few unusual types of plants also have something akin to digestion – those that are parasitic on other plants, and those that trap and "eat" insects, for example ( ◀ page 61).

The most complex digestive process occurs within the digestive tracts of animals, however. For most vertebrates, it begins with chewing up the food in the mouth, mincing it into small pieces and exposing it to powerful enzymes secreted along with saliva. Partly digested food then moves down to the stomach, where it generally meets a strongly acid environment and further enzymes, whose main job is to break up proteins into small peptides and amino acids.

Further extensive digestion, particularly of fats, takes place in the duodenum, the first short section of the small intestine. Here the food meets a battery of enzymes, alkali and other chemicals released from the liver, gall bladder, pancreas and intestinal wall. After this onslaught, the food is almost fully digested and it passes into the intestine. Although it may meet further digestive secretions here, the main activity is the uptake of digested food into the absorptive cells lining the intestine.

In some animals, the shape of the digestive tract, and the enzymes and other secretions it produces, are highly specialized. Grazing animals that employ bacteria to break down cellulose for them are a good example ( ◀ page 172) and many other animals show equally remarkable adaptations to their chosen diet. Spiders, for instance, secrete special enzymes that liquify their tough insect prey, while clothes moths and their relatives produce digestive enzymes that only attack wool and fur proteins. Burrowing animals, like earthworms and lugworms, are also very specialized. They have highly distensible intestines to allow them to take in huge quantities of sand or earth. Most of it is indigestible, and specialized cells engulf the precious food particles, passing these to wandering cells, known as amebocytes, that are responsible for digestion. The system is rapid, processing each mouthful in a mere 15 minutes. And it needs to act swiftly, since the animal must eat up to six times its own weight of sand or soil a day in order to get enough nutrients.

In contrast to these specialized feeders, some animals are generalists, feeding on whatever is available. Their digestive tract, like that of humans, is equipped to cope with a variety of foods. Other animals change their diet with the seasons, and their digestive apparatus follows suit. The bearded tit, a small European bird, switches from insects in summer to seeds in winter, developing a thick, muscular gizzard to help it break down the seeds, and losing it again in the spring. A similar seasonal change is seen in some other birds, such as the common starling.

*Mammals cannot live on grass without the help of bacteria that digest cellulose*

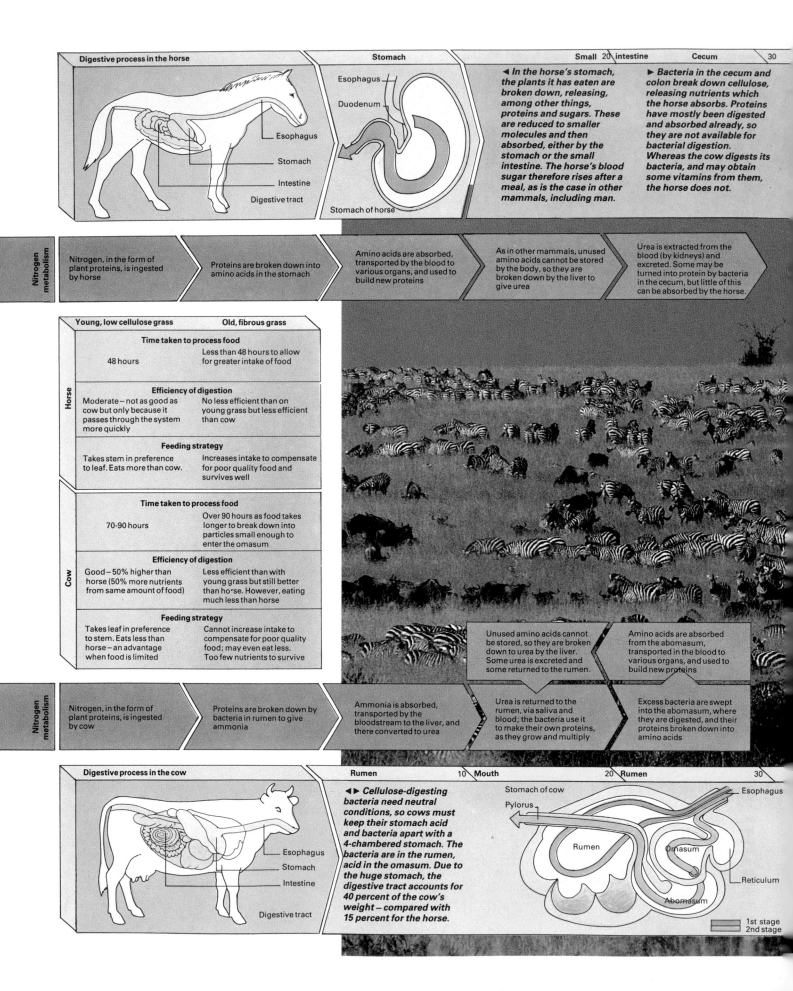

**Digestive process in the horse**

Esophagus
Stomach
Intestine
Digestive tract

**Stomach**

Esophagus
Duodenum

Stomach of horse

**Small** 20 **intestine**   **Cecum**   30

◄ *In the horse's stomach, the plants it has eaten are broken down, releasing, among other things, proteins and sugars. These are reduced to smaller molecules and then absorbed, either by the stomach or the small intestine. The horse's blood sugar therefore rises after a meal, as is the case in other mammals, including man.*

► *Bacteria in the cecum and colon break down cellulose, releasing nutrients which the horse absorbs. Proteins have mostly been digested and absorbed already, so they are not available for bacterial digestion. Whereas the cow digests its bacteria, and may obtain some vitamins from them, the horse does not.*

**Nitrogen metabolism**

| Nitrogen, in the form of plant proteins, is ingested by horse | Proteins are broken down into amino acids in the stomach | Amino acids are absorbed, transported by the blood to various organs, and used to build new proteins | As in other mammals, unused amino acids cannot be stored by the body, so they are broken down by the liver to give urea | Urea is extracted from the blood (by kidneys) and excreted. Some may be turned into protein by bacteria in the cecum, but little of this can be absorbed by the horse. |

| | Young, low cellulose grass | Old, fibrous grass |
|---|---|---|
| **Horse** | **Time taken to process food** | |
| | 48 hours | Less than 48 hours to allow for greater intake of food |
| | **Efficiency of digestion** | |
| | Moderate – not as good as cow but only because it passes through the system more quickly | No less efficient than on young grass but less efficient than cow |
| | **Feeding strategy** | |
| | Takes stem in preference to leaf. Eats more than cow. | Increases intake to compensate for poor quality food and survives well |
| **Cow** | **Time taken to process food** | |
| | 70-90 hours | Over 90 hours as food takes longer to break down into particles small enough to enter the omasum |
| | **Efficiency of digestion** | |
| | Good – 50% higher than horse (50% more nutrients from same amount of food) | Less efficient than with young grass but still better than horse. However, eating much less than horse |
| | **Feeding strategy** | |
| | Takes leaf in preference to stem. Eats less than horse – an advantage when food is limited | Cannot increase intake to compensate for poor quality food; may even eat less. Too few nutrients to survive |

Unused amino acids cannot be stored, so they are broken down to urea by the liver. Some urea is excreted and some returned to the rumen.

Amino acids are absorbed from the abomasum, transported in the blood to various organs, and used to build new proteins

**Nitrogen metabolism**

| Nitrogen, in the form of plant proteins, is ingested by cow | Proteins are broken down by bacteria in rumen to give ammonia | Ammonia is absorbed, transported by the bloodstream to the liver, and there converted to urea | Urea is returned to the rumen, via saliva and blood; the bacteria use it to make their own proteins, as they grow and multiply | Excess bacteria are swept into the abomasum, where they are digested, and their proteins broken down into amino acids |

**Digestive process in the cow**

Esophagus
Stomach
Intestine
Digestive tract

**Rumen** 10 **Mouth** 20 **Rumen** 30

◄► *Cellulose-digesting bacteria need neutral conditions, so cows must keep their stomach acid and bacteria apart with a 4-chambered stomach. The bacteria are in the rumen, acid in the omasum. Due to the huge stomach, the digestive tract accounts for 40 percent of the cow's weight – compared with 15 percent for the horse.*

Stomach of cow
Pylorus
Rumen
Omasum
Esophagus
Reticulum
Abomasum

1st stage
2nd stage

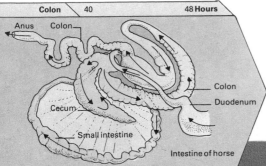

Colon 40     48 Hours

Anus — Colon
Colon
Cecum
Small intestine
Colon
Duodenum
Intestine of horse

◄ The horse has a greatly enlarged cecum and colon where its fermenting bacteria live. The enlargement of the colon also allows absorption of the fermentation products. Although the site of fermentation is different in the cow, the bacteria are very similar.

## A subtle difference

What an animal eats, and how it digests it, has far-reaching effects on its way of life. The cow and the horse, for example, have very similar diets, and both use bacteria in the gut to help them break down cellulose. However, the horse harbors the bacteria in its intestine, while the cow, a ruminant, has them in the stomach. This difference affects the range of foods that can be eaten, the ability to survive poor conditions, their nitrogen metabolism, water needs and even body size and shape.

It is often stated that ruminants are much better at digesting cellulose than non-ruminants. This is clearly an over-simplification, however. Unlike a cow, a horse can thrive on old, fibrous grass that is high in cellulose, because the cow's specialized digestive tract places a limit on the amount of food eaten, so it cannot compensate for a poor food by eating more. But on a diet of young grass, the cow grows faster. The reasons are not clear, but unusual nitrogen metabolism may be a factor.

Cows, like other vertebrates, can synthesize some amino acids but must obtain the remainder – "essential" amino acids – pre-formed from their food. If any of these are in short supply they limit the use that can be made of other amino acids. And because they cannot store amino acids in their bodies, any that are not used immediately are broken down to give the waste product, urea. In the cow, almost all the nitrogen it eats is utilized, because the bacteria in the rumen can turn urea back into protein, which is then digested in another part of the stomach. Without the help of bacteria, mammals cannot make use of urea, and, as it is toxic, they must excrete it. Since ruminants need to excrete very little urea they produce much less urine and therefore need less to drink.

◄ Zebra and wildebeeste regularly feed together on the African grasslands. They take the same sort of plants, but the zebra (a close relative of the horse) eats the high-cellulose stalks on the tops of the plants, whereas the wildebeeste, a ruminant like the cow, takes the less fibrous leaves from lower down. Thus the wildebeeste is somewhat dependent on the zebra to eat down the top layer of the herbage for it, so that it can forage successfully.

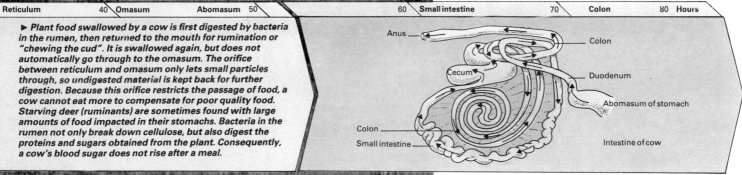

Reticulum 40   Omasum    Abomasum 50        60   Small intestine    70    Colon     80 Hours

Anus
Colon
Cecum
Duodenum
Abomasum of stomach
Colon
Small intestine
Intestine of cow

► Plant food swallowed by a cow is first digested by bacteria in the rumen, then returned to the mouth for rumination or "chewing the cud". It is swallowed again, but does not automatically go through to the omasum. The orifice between reticulum and omasum only lets small particles through, so undigested material is kept back for further digestion. Because this orifice restricts the passage of food, a cow cannot eat more to compensate for poor quality food. Starving deer (ruminants) are sometimes found with large amounts of food impacted in their stomachs. Bacteria in the rumen not only break down cellulose, but also digest the proteins and sugars obtained from the plant. Consequently, a cow's blood sugar does not rise after a meal.

▲ The ring of branched "tentacles" on the back of this sea slug are actually gills, used to obtain oxygen.

▼ Fish gills (top) and mammalian lungs (below) have a large surface area to maximize gas exchange.

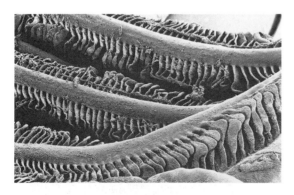

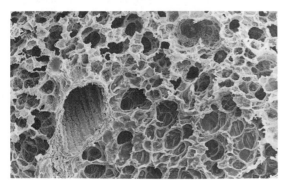

## Getting gases

With the exception of the anaerobic bacteria (◀ page 149) and a few parasites, all living organisms need oxygen, but they get it in a variety of ways. Many animals, including ourselves, breathe air into lungs, which are basically air-filled cavities surrounded by a dense network of blood vessels. The surface area of the lung is increased by various means to expand the area available for gas exchange. In vertebrates, the lung branches and forms many small sacs, known as alveoli, while in land snails the lung has a corrugated surface. The "lung books" of scorpions consist of many thin leaves of tissue, like the pages of a book, contained in a pit on the surface of the body. In all these structures, there is a layer of moisture lining the lungs, and oxygen from the air becomes dissolved in this. It then diffuses into the cells of the lung's surface, and from there it generally passes to the bloodstream, which carries it to all parts of the body.

The inner surface of an animal's lung needs a covering layer of moisture in order to work properly, because its cells cannot efficiently absorb oxygen directly from the air – the gas must be dissolved in water. This requirement probably reflects the fact that all life originally evolved in the sea. In order to colonize the land, animals needed to develop cavities within the body where their oxygen-collecting cells could be kept moist, but without the loss of too much precious water from the tissues.

Provided animals have their own "private sea", however, obtaining oxygen from air is easier than extracting it from water. Whereas the atmosphere is 20 percent oxygen, there is rarely more than 10 percent in water, and often much less. Moreover, oxygen diffuses much less

quickly through a body of water than through the equivalent body of air, so an aquatic animal must be able to maintain a good flow of water around the oxygen-collecting cells. These are usually located on filamentous or feathery structures known as gills. In fish, the gills consist of many thin gill filaments containing blood vessels. The oxygen dissolved in water diffuses into the cells of the gill filaments, and on into the blood vessels.

Insects do not have lungs or gills, and although they do have a circulatory system, it only plays a minor role in transporting oxygen. Instead, their bodies contain a branching network of fine air tubes called "tracheae". These branch further into smaller and smaller "tracheoles" that ramify throughout the body and carry air directly to every cell. At the end of the tracheoles the oxygen simply dissolves in the moisture surrounding the cells and then diffuses into the cells themselves.

Air enters the insect tracheal system through tiny openings called "spiracles" found all over the body. To reduce moisture loss, these can be closed by special valves when the insect is less active and therefore needs less oxygen. Some larger insects pump air in and out of their tracheal systems using muscular contractions of the body, but in most cases the air just diffuses in and out.

Tracheae have evolved independently more than once, being found in some arachnids as well as insects, so they must represent a very efficient system. One problem, however, is that the size of the creatures with tracheae is limited, since air could not diffuse quickly enough to reach the center of a large body. This is part of the reason why insects are generally quite small.

▼ *Originally land animals, the water spiders take a reservo of air with them in silken "diving bells".*

▲ *Flatworms have no gills or blood system. A flat body allows good oxygen uptake and distribution.*

*Oxygen has become indispensable to most living organisms*

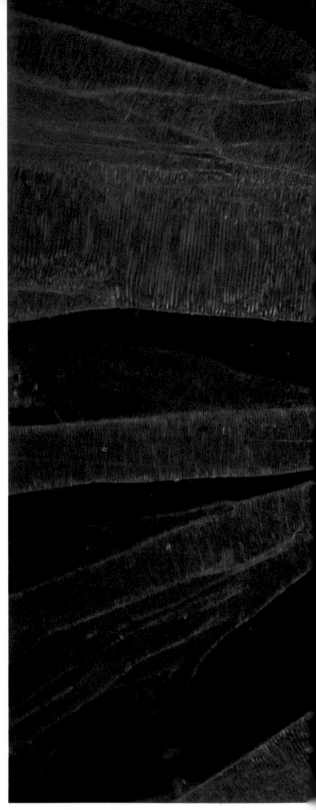

▲ *Swamp cypresses are relatives of the giant redwoods, adapted to growing in water-logged conditions. Swamp water is poor in oxygen, and the trees have special aerial roots to boost the supply of air to their roots. These knobbly projections contain spongy tissue through which air can easily flow.*

◄ *The stomata of a pea leaf. When the guard cells swell up they bow outwards and the central slit opens.*

### How plants breathe

Like animals, plants need supplies of gases: carbon dioxide as a raw material for photosynthesis, and oxygen for respiration. Land plants obtain these gases through small pores in their leaves known as stomata, which can be opened or closed by the swelling or shrinking of special guard cells. Oxygen and carbon dioxide dissolve in the layer of moisture surrounding the plant cells within, and from here they can diffuse into the cells. The stomata also allow waste gases, such as surplus oxygen produced during photosynthesis, or carbon dioxide produced at night when respiration is occurring but photosynthesis is not, to diffuse out of the plant.

► *The mudskippers of tropical mangrove swamps emerge at low tide to feed. They obtain oxygen in several different ways while on land. Firstly, they gulp water into the gill chamber before leaving the sea, and can extract oxygen from this with their gills. When it becomes oxygen-depleted, they replace it with water from a puddle. In addition, they can breathe through their skin, or through the membranes of their open mouths.*

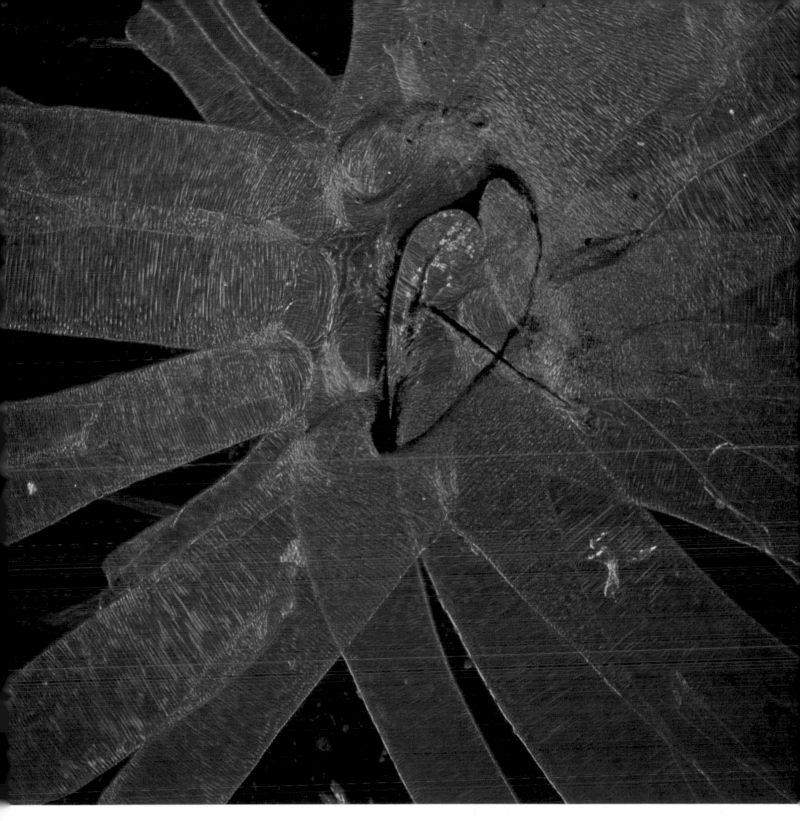

### Breathing through the skin

Many small invertebrates have no specialized breathing organs such as lungs or gills. Instead they rely on oxygen absorbed through the skin, (which must be kept moist to work efficiently) and excrete their carbon dioxide by the same route. In earthworms, for example, blood vessels lie just beneath the skin, and oxygen diffuses into them from the atmosphere.

Even animals that have specialized organs for breathing may still fulfil some of their oxygen requirement by absorption through the skin. In humans, only about one percent of our oxygen is obtained in this way, but among amphibians, skin breathing can account for up to 90 percent of gas exchange. The use of the skin as a "third lung" improves an amphibian's ability to adapt to changeable environments. By diverting the blood supply from the lungs to the skin it can take advantage of well-oxygenated water and breathe mainly through its skin, during a dive, for example. If, on the other hand, it finds itself in poorly oxygenated water it can increase the blood flow to the lungs and concentrate on gulping air at the surface. Some amphibians have extensions to the skin, in the form of folds or finger-like projections, and these probably increase its propensity for gas-exchange.

▲ The tracheal tubes that radiate from a single spiracle in a caterpillar. These tubes are the start of a ventilation system that carries oxygen throughout the caterpillar's body, and removes carbon dioxide waste. The larger tubes, shown here, are reinforced by rings of chitin, the material that makes up the exoskeleton. As they penetrate further into the body, the airways become smaller and more delicate, so as to reach every cell.

# Parasites

## Parasites

The tapeworms are a group of flatworms (◀ page 68) that live out their lives in the intestines of vertebrate animals, attaching themselves to the wall of the gut by hooks and suckers. They have no mouth or gut: their food is all around them in the gut contents of their host, and they absorb it directly. In most species, the body is made up of separate units, called proglottids, that superficially resemble the segments of annelids. Each produces eggs and sperm, and when the eggs have been fertilized the proglottid breaks free and is deposited with the host's feces. A tapeworm can produce 100,000 eggs every day, although only a tiny proportion of these survive to maturity, due to the difficulties encountered in infecting a new host. The process of infection often involves an intermediate host, called a vector. For the most widespread human tapeworm, pigs are the intermediate host.

Tapeworms are typical endoparasites – that is, they live inside the body. Animals such as fleas and lice, which live on the host's outer surface, are termed ectoparasites. In general, the adaptations of endoparasites are more extreme than those of ectoparasites, but both show similar trends. The feeding apparatus is modified for a parasitic way of life, and often greatly reduced, because their food is abundant and predigested. Indeed, a few endoparasites even lose some of the metabolic processes involved in obtaining energy from food. The parasite that causes sleeping sickness in humans passes one stage of its life cycle in the blood, and this stage lacks both the Krebs' cycle and the electron transport chain (◀ page 152).

Breathing apparatus, excretory organs and certain sense organs are also lost in many endoparasites. In fact, the loss of organs and tissues can transform parasites to such an extent that their ancestry is difficult to make out. One parasite found in sea cucumbers consists of little more than a tube attached to its host at one end. The tube contains a short alimentary canal and a long coiled gonad which produces both eggs and sperm. There are no other organs at all, and in the 19th century this creature was assumed to be a part of the sea cucumber. But study of the larvae produced by its eggs showed it to be a gastropod mollusk.

Another feature seen in the tapeworm, and common to many parasites, is the heavy commitment to reproduction. The huge number of eggs produced are an attempt to overcome the odds against transmission to a new host. In the wild, these odds are generally very high, but when the host species becomes crowded together, as in humans and their domestic animals, the odds fall. Then the parasite's massive reproductive capacity poses a serious threat to the host population.

### The tapeworm

Proglottids

Hooks on head

Head

▲ A dead caterpillar covered by the pupae of an ichneumon wasp. These wasps lay their eggs inside the caterpillar, where the grubs later feed on blood and fat. They then chew their way out, killing the caterpillar, and pupate.

▶ The trypanosomes, which cause sleeping sickness, among red blood cells. These are protozoans, and are related to the photosynthetic euglenoids. Some stages in their life cycle have lost basic respiratory pathways.

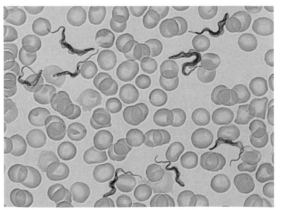

▲ A cat flea obtaining its meal of blood. To avoid being damaged by the host's scratching, fleas have tough, laterally-flattened bodies, and no wings. The lack of flight is partly compensated for by their impressive jumping ability.

▶ Strictly speaking, parasitism is a relationship between two individuals of different species, but the males of some deep-sea angler fish are often said to be "parasites" of the female. They draw all their nutrients from her.

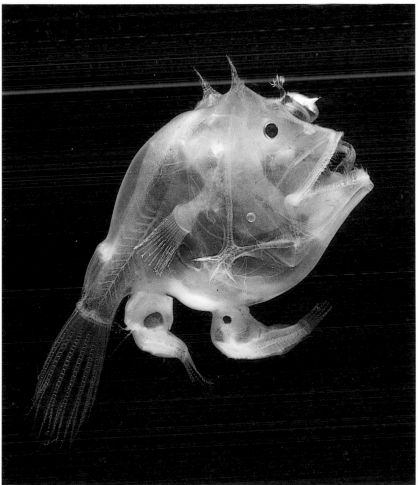

◀ A pair of the blood flukes that cause bilharzia in humans.

### Defining terms

A parasite can be defined as an organism that lives in or on another organism (the host) and is metabolically dependent on the host. The degree of dependence varies, and there is no clear demarcation between parasitism and other forms of relationship such as commensalism, nor between parasites and predators. In general, however, a predator has a lower rate of reproduction than its prey, while parasites reproduce much more prodigiously than their hosts. Often parasites are defined as organisms that harm their hosts, but this is not necessarily the case.

### The ultimate parasites

Viruses and disease-causing bacteria are conventionally described as pathogens but they are, in effect, very small parasites. Indeed, viruses have been described as "the ultimate parasites" because they consist of little more than the genes required for their own reproduction.

Once inside the host cell, they hijack the machinery for transcription and translation (◀ page 140) to produce further copies of their genes. Thus they show complete metabolic dependence on their host.

### Types of relationship

Parasitism is just one form of symbiotic relationship, that is, a close association between two organisms of different species. Another common type of symbiosis is mutualism, which is defined as a close association that benefits both parties. The relationship between a ruminant, such as the cow, and the bacteria in its gut (◀ page 140) is a mutualistic one. In some cases of mutualism, the partners cannot live without each other, while in others they can.

A looser type of relationship, in which only one partner benefits, is commensalism. Usually, this involves one partner feeding on surplus food obtained by the other – picking up the crumbs from its table, so to speak, but not greatly affecting its welfare. Often the commensal can survive fairly well alone, but it is likely that parasitic relationships evolve from commensal ones by a process of increasing dependence.

Many relationships fall outside these definitions because neither partner gains any sustenance from the other. In the plant world, many climbers rely on larger, sturdier plants to give them support, while some plants, called epiphytes, grow on the branches of trees but draw no nutrients from them. A few plants, such as the bromeliads of tropical forests, are specialized for an epiphytic way of life, but many ferns, mosses and small flowering plants can grow epiphytically in the right conditions. Transport is another benefit that small organisms can derive from larger, more mobile species. The remoras, often seen stuck to large fish by suckers on their heads, are not parasites but simply "hitchhikers". Relationships such as these are less restricted than mutualism or commensalism, in that different species can act as the "host".

*Balancing the diet is crucial to an animal's survival*

◄ A common European toad capturing a beetle larva. Its sticky protrusible tongue takes only a tenth of a second to flick out and back again. Toads, like many predators, only respond to moving prey. By ensuring that their food is alive and healthy they reduce the risk of being infected with parasites or pathogens.

▲ Mineral salts, such as calcium, sodium and potassium, are vital to all living organisms. Macaws feed on fruits and seeds, and while this diet provides an adequate supply of energy and protein, it is lacking in certain minerals. This deficiency is made up by the birds eating small quantities of rock or soil containing these minerals.

## Salts and water

The chemical reactions of living cells will only work properly in the correct chemical environment. Two of the most important components of that environment are water and compounds known as "salts". These "salts" can be made up of various ions, such as sodium, chlorine, potassium and calcium – whereas the everyday stuff we call salt, is pure sodium chloride (that is, it contains sodium ions and chloride ions only). Ions are important because they carry an electric charge – either a negative charge (anions) or a positive charge (cations). Ions can be concentrated to create an overall positive or negative charge within cells, and manipulation of ions by the cell is an important part of life – as in the conduction of nerve impulses for example (▶ page 198). The balance between the amount of water that cells contain and the amounts of various essential salt ions must always be kept just right, because too much or too little can be fatal.

Creatures that live in seawater probably have fewer problems in this respect than most other organisms. The balance of water and ions in seawater does not change much, and the cells of most marine creatures require an internal environment very similar to that of the sea outside. (So too do terrestrial animals – another indication of our marine origins.) Many seafish, however, tend to lose too much water in their urine. They compensate for this by drinking all the time and by actively excreting the chloride and other ions contained in the seawater from special secretory cells in their gills. Seabirds that live on a diet of salty fish have a similar problem and have evolved special glands, located near the eyes, to excrete the excess salts.

Desert animals have particular problems in conserving both salts and water, and they show very specialized adaptations to their environment. The kangaroo rat of North American deserts, for example, never perspires, excretes a highly concentrated urine and absorbs virtually all the water out of its food.

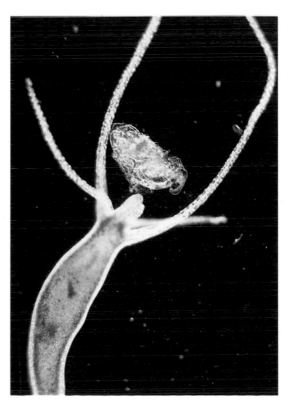

▶ A hydra ejecting undigested food. Its simple digestive system has just one opening, which takes food in as well as expelling waste. More advanced animals have a "one-way" digestive system with two openings, mouth and anus. This allows specialization of different parts of the system for various aspects of digestion.

◀ A feral pigeon drinks from a water fountain. Water is a key component of living cells and therefore vital to all forms of life. And it often contains minerals, dissolved from rock, which are also important for metabolism. But not all animals need to drink – some can obtain enough moisture for their needs from the sap of plants or the body fluids of animal prey.

### Waste disposal

*In addition to taking up supplies, all organisms must get rid of unwanted and possibly poisonous wastes. There are two main categories of waste disposal: "defecation" and "excretion". Defecation is the elimination of materials which have been eaten but cannot be digested, while excretion refers to the removal of chemical wastes from the cells of an organism – wastes produced by the metabolic activities of the cells, together with basic supplies that have been taken up in excess, such as salts and water. The important point is that they have been inside the cells, not just in the digestive tract.*

*The main waste products of animal metabolism are water and carbon dioxide, produced by aerobic respiration, and various nitrogen-rich chemical wastes, produced by the breakdown of protein. (Sometimes "excretion" is used to refer solely to nitrogenous waste disposal.) The carbon dioxide and some of the water is generally excreted from the lungs, gills or tracheae. However, in very small, simple animals, it can be lost by direct diffusion out of the body. Salts can be released to the outside in urine or sweat, or from specialized salt-secreting glands.*

*Nitrogenous waste is lost in the form of simple compounds like ammonia, uric acid, urea, allantoin, or guanine. Ammonia simply diffuses out of the body, while urea must be excreted to the outside dissolved in water, as urine. Uric acid, allantoin and guanine need less water than urea to flush them away, since they are less toxic, and they can even form a solid crystalline deposits.*

*Ammonia is the easiest compound to make, but has the disadvantage of being the most toxic. It is the usual excretory product in aquatic invertebrates, where the surrounding water washes it away easily, and in some insects which produce ammonia gas. But most terrestrial animals have turned to uric acid, or, less commonly, urea. Uric acid is found in birds for example, and enables them to excrete nitrogen while still in the egg, without the toxicity problems that ammonia or urea would create. Guanine, used by spiders, and allantoin, used by some insects, are also water-saving products. Only mammals and some fish rely on urea, which requires good water intake.*

*The range of organs used for excretion is truly remarkable. In vertebrates, the kidneys are the main excretory organs, responsible for filtering nitrogenous waste, water and salts from the blood as it circulates through them. Insects collect chemical wastes in fluid-filled tubes, known as Malpighian tubules, which extend throughout the body and actively remove nitrogenous wastes from the blood. They then excrete these wastes via excretory pores, or via the anus, having first resorbed much of the water. The mollusks have a different system again, with the kidneys being intimately linked to the heart. The pressure created by the heart's contractions forces some of the fluid out through the heart wall, which is slightly leaky and acts as a filter. This fluid drains out of the pericardial cavity into the kidneys, where it passes through spongy tissue containing many blood vessels. These selectively resorb some of the water and salts and the rest drains away to form urine.*

*Some birds can produce "milk" to feed their young*

### A question of control

The problems organisms have in getting supplies are only part of the larger problem of getting the right supplies in the right amounts and keeping things that way. All organisms face quality and quantity control problems as they go about getting supplies. Humans need salt, for example, but too much of it will kill us. All organisms and cells need water, but again too much can kill. Cells need supplies of mineral ions (salts), but their relative proportions must be very strictly controlled for the cells to survive and work properly.

At the level of individual cells, quality and quantity control is essentially performed by the cell membrane and whatever proteins are embedded in it. Evolution has equipped all cells with suitable membrane proteins to allow them to gather the supplies they need and reject or remove those they do not. Some proteins pump in particular ions, for example, whereas others pump ions out. Some proteins let certain supplies enter a cell by facilitated diffusion or active transport, but then stop that entry when suitable levels have been reached. So the proteins of the cell membrane set up a series of highly selective and controllable "gates" that let material in or out as appropriate.

Much more tricky control problems have to be solved by large multicellular organisms, however. The whole process of taking in food and digesting it is a huge and complex challenge to the body's control systems. First of all what makes animals want to eat, when their bodies need more food supplies? The response is very complex and involves several different mechanisms, but basically, when glucose levels in the blood are low, impulses reaching the brain stimulate the desire to eat.

Once food has been digested it is taken up into the blood capillaries lining the small intestine. From there, it goes first to the liver. The liver is one of the major quality control organs of the body. Its cells contain enzymes to convert toxic substances into harmless forms, and to modify the raw uptake products into a mixture more suitable for passage through the body. The liver can be thought of as a massive central processing unit, screening and modifying the supplies extracted from food.

Feedback mechanisms also control gas, water and salt intake. In mammals, lack of oxygen stimulates a muscular reflex which results in an extra-large breath being taken – in other words, a yawn. Lack of water, or too much salt leads to more water being resorbed from the urine to compensate. The amount of water in the blood is sensed by osmoreceptor cells in the brain. When blood becomes too concentrated, these cells stimulate the brain to release "anti-diuretic hormone", which travels to the kidneys (through the bloodstream) and makes water resorption increase.

These are just a few examples of a great many complex and extremely sensitive ways in which a mammal's body controls the quality and quantity of the supplies that it gathers up from the world outside. Other organisms all have their own batteries of complex control systems, specialized to meet their own particular needs.

▲ Some foods do not give a balanced diet. Plant sap, for example, contains sugar, minerals and protein, but the protein component is very small. Aphids feeding on plant sap must take in an excessive amount of sap, selectively absorb the proteins, and deposit most of the sugar as a waste product – honeydew. This feeding strategy has led to a curious mutualistic relationship with ants, which feast on the honeydew, and at the same time ward off the aphids' predators. The aphids retain the honeydew for the ants, only releasing it when their abdomens are stroked by the ants' antennae.

◄ A seal, having just given birth, eats the placenta. This behavior is widespread in mammals and probably serves to replenish the mother's body with vitamins and minerals.

► A male emperor penguin feeds its young chick on "milk". For penguins, the production of milk allows breeding to take place in winter, and at a safe distance from the open sea. The male incubates the egg alone during the long antarctic winter and then feeds the newly hatched young on "milk", fueled by stores of fat that were laid down many months before. Meanwhile the female spends the winter feeding at sea, returning in the spring to assist with the care of the chick.

Plants are also equipped with many adaptations to control their salt and water needs. The rate at which they lose water can be carefully controlled by opening and closing their stomata. Many desert plants have very few stomata, and these are hidden within deep rifts, so that water losses can be kept to the absolute minimum. This may be accompanied by the possession of a thick waterproof covering over the leaves.

Plants may also have to dispose of, or at least inactivate, salts that they have absorbed in excess. In many plants, crystals of calcium oxalate are found in the leaves, and these are believed to be dumps for excess calcium. Salt marsh plants, and others that live in brackish conditions, have had to find ways of coping with excess salt, which is inevitably absorbed by the plants' roots. Mangroves concentrate the salt in certain leaves which are then dropped, while the Australian saltbrush expels salts from time to time by the bursting of "bladders", which contain special cells that gather up salts from the rest of the plant body. Single-celled creatures, such as protozoa, have their uptake and excretion of salts controlled directly by proteins in their membranes. They get rid of excess water by forming a large watery "vacuole" within them, which then bursts open at the cell surface and expels the water.

**Feeding the young**
*The food that an adult animal eats is not necessarily suitable for its young. Some solve this problem by feeding (or being fed) on a different diet in their early stages. But others have tackled the problem in a different way, with the parents consuming extra food and producing a nutritious secretion on which the young can feed. All mammals do this, providing milk for their offspring (♦ page 117), but this adaptation is not confined to mammals. Many other animals produce a milk-like substance to feed their young. Pigeons, for example, eat hard seeds which must be ground with stones in the gizzard as a prelude to digestion. Clearly, this would be difficult for a tiny nestling, and anyway the seeds contain too little protein to sustain rapid growth. Other seed-eating birds can switch to catching insects for their young, but pigeons are too slow and ponderous for this strategy. The answer to the problem is "milk", in this case formed by layers of nutrient-rich cells being shed from the crop, normally a storage organ for food that has just been swallowed. "Milk" for the young is also produced by a few other birds, including flamingoes and emperor penguins.*

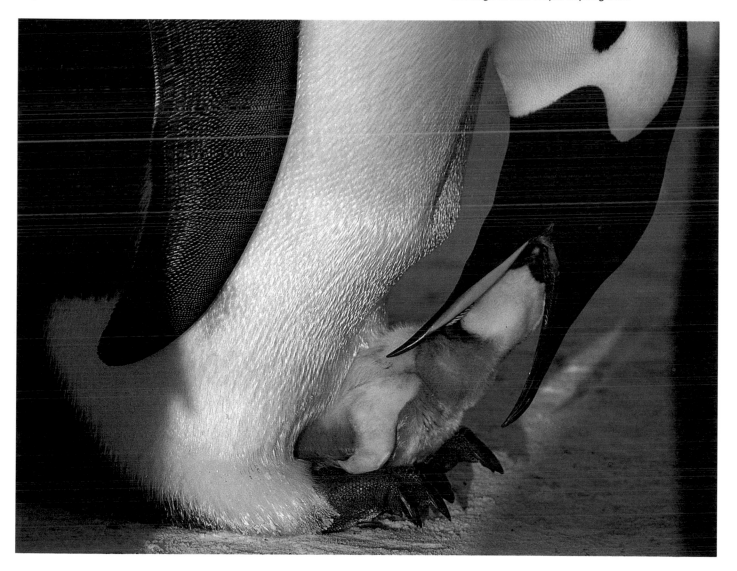

## Problems of size

*As any object increases in size, the ratio of its volume to its surface area begins to grow. So as organisms got larger, the increase in volume rapidly outpaced the increase in surface area. Not only was it increasingly difficult for supplies to be distributed to all parts of the body, but the reduced surface area was unable to take up enough supplies for the needs of the body within.*

*Evolution has produced various solutions to these problems. Firstly, the surfaces involved in collecting supplies became highly folded, or ruffled, or branched, to provide a greater surface area through which supplies could be collected. Secondly, organisms developed a variety of circulatory systems which could transport supplies around their bodies, and gather up wastes.*

*In the simplest sort of system, the circulatory fluid, or "blood", is pushed round the body as a side-effect of the animal's muscular movements. But above a certain size, a muscular pump, the heart, is needed to drive the blood around the body.*

*In mammals, the heart takes in blood from the veins, and then pumps it out along arteries. Blood arriving at the heart is rich in carbon dioxide gas and is pumped from the heart to the lungs where the carbon dioxide diffuses out and oxygen diffuses in. The oxygen-rich blood then flows back to the heart, to be pumped at high pressure along the arteries that take it to all to parts of the body.*

*The continual branching of the arteries eventually yields many tiny vessels or capillaries, which are distributed throughout the tissues. Oxygen and nutrients pass out through the capillary walls into the cells, while carbon dioxide and other chemical wastes pass in. After a short distance, the capillaries join up again into the veins that take the blood back to the heart. Other capillaries run alongside cells lining the small intestine and these absorb nutrients and water from the digestive system.*

*The circulatory system of mammals is known as a "closed" system, since the blood is always confined within blood vessels. Some invertebrates have have a similar system, but many have an "open" circulatory system, where the blood is not always within vessels, and can wash around inside the animal's hemocoel cavities ( ◆ page 74). Open circulatory systems do have some sort of a heart, but the vessels carrying blood from the heart and bringing it back to the heart are not joined up.*

*Because oxygen has only a limited solubility in water, its transport requires special carriers – oxygen-binding proteins, such as the hemoglobins found in the red blood cells of vertebrates. Various arthropods and mollusks use a blue copper-containing protein called "hemocyanin" to carry their oxygen supplies, while some worms use a green protein called "chlorocruorin".*

*Plants also have circulatory systems, made up of two main types of transport vessels known as xylem and phloem. The xylem transports water and minerals from the roots upward to all the other parts of a plant, while phloem transports sap, containing food molecules and other substances (such as plant hormones), either upward or downward, as required.*

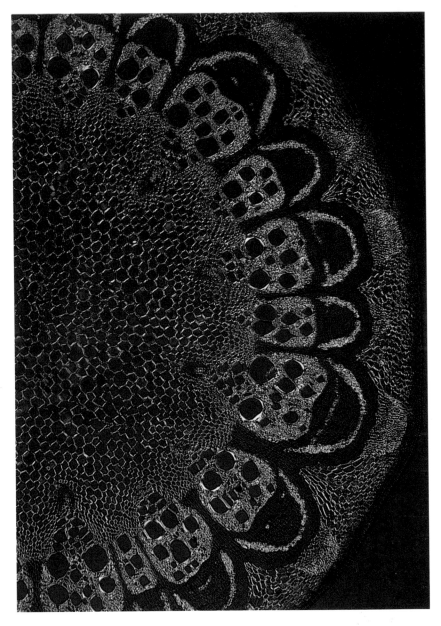

**Intestinal villi**

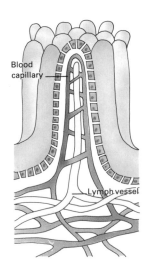

Blood capillary

Lymph vessel

**Plant root hairs**

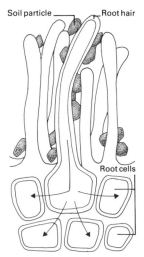

Soil particle — Root hair

Root cells

▲ *A cross-section of a plant stem viewed under polarized light. The many openings are part of the transport systems that conduct water and sap around the plant.*

◄ *The intestinal villi of mammals and the root hairs of plants are both devices for increasing surface area – hence their similar appearance under the microscope. But internally they are quite different. Each villus is a complex structure, with lymph vessels and blood capillaries for rapid transport of the nutrients it absorbs. The root hair is a single elongated cell and the minerals and water it takes up pass into the root by diffusion and osmosis.*

*Energy "cash-flow"...Controlling temperature in hot conditions and cold...What happens in hibernation... Supercooling of body fluids...Tolerance of temperature extremes...PERSPECTIVE...Warm-blooded and cold-blooded...Size and temperature control...Temperature control in dinosaurs...Metabolic shutdown...Chilling to preserve living tissue*

Energy is one of life's essentials. Living organisms must expend it whenever they grow, make a movement, or actively transport substances around their bodies, and it is constantly used up by the chemical processes occurring in their cells. They meet these high costs of living by extracting energy from food molecules and storing it in adenosine triphosphate (ATP), and other high-energy molecules (◀ page 139). Over half the energy locked in food molecules is captured as ATP, the rest being lost in the form of heat.

The energy flowing in and out of a living body can be viewed rather like cash flowing in and out of a bank account. For animals, the intake of energy must equal the sum of the following: production of new tissue, plus work done on the environment, plus the energy discarded in urine and feces, plus the energy lost as heat during metabolism. Scientists can measure these items of expenditure and income and draw up an "energy budget" for the animal concerned.

### Hot and cold

*Animals can be classed into two groups: those that hold a steady temperature by generating heat internally (the homeotherms, endotherms, or "warm-blooded" animals) and those that do not (the poikilotherms, ectotherms or "cold-blooded animals"). Of living creatures, only the mammals and birds are homeotherms. The term "cold-blooded", though widely used, is rather misleading, because poikilotherms can be just as warm, or warmer, than homeotherms when external temperatures are high. The distinction between these two groups is not a hard and fast one. Some mammals, notably the sloths, have a variable, low body temperature, which drops at night. Combined with a slow, ponderous life-style, 17 hours of sleep a day, and reduced muscles, this allows them to survive on a low-calorie diet of leaves. Additionally, there are many small mammals and birds, including bats, tits and hummingbirds, that cool down substantially at night. On the other hand, poikilotherms have ways of warming themselves up above the ambient air temperature. Many lizards, for example, bask in the sun, while a hawkmoth's thorax may be 35°C warmer than the outside world, because of the heat released by muscular effort. Shivering is used to boost its temperature and the fur on the body serves as insulation.*

▼ *A sloth moves slowly along, carrying her offspring.*

One significant entry in any animal's energy budget is the heat lost during metabolism. Most creatures allow this valuable commodity to escape into the outside world. But some, notably the homeotherms, harness metabolic heat and use it to control the temperature of their bodies. They do this principally by having a layer of insulating material – feathers, fur or fat – to keep in the body's heat. But they also burn off some extra food molecules when external temperatures are particularly low, to generate extra heat. Their ability to regulate their body temperature frees homeotherms from the adverse effects of environmental changes. Such fluctuations are not particularly important to animals that live in the relatively constant environment of the ocean, but they make a good deal of difference in shallow waters or on land, where the temperature oscillates daily, and covers a vast range – as much as 100°C – with the changing seasons.

The speeds of many enzymatic processes are halved if the temperature drops by 10°C, so keeping warm is valuable. There is also much to be gained by insulating the body from disruptive rises in temperature in hot environments. What homeotherms achieve is a constant internal milieu that allows sustained activity at the peak of performance. But internal constancy can be an expensive habit, especially in cool climates. Mammals need to eat between 5 and 10 times more food than comparable reptiles to fuel the fires that keep body temperature at about 37°C. Consequently, they must shunt food through their digestive system ten times faster. They are able to capture the goodness from their fast-moving food only because their intestines are longer and equipped with more villi (◀ page 184) providing a much larger surface area for nutrient absorption.

▲ Daily temperature fluctuations are greatest in the desert. The Namib lizard is only active at temperatures of 27–40°C, and this confines its activities to just two hours, each morning and evening. Here, it reduces its body temperature by lifting two legs off the hot sand. Early in the morning, however, it warms itself up by lying on the sand with all four legs off the ground, absorbing heat through its belly.

◄ *Lions resting in the shade to escape the midday sun. Homeotherms (birds and mammals) have various physiological means of controlling their body temperature but, like poikilotherms, they also rely on behavioral strategies for temperature control. When there is no shade, lions sometimes lie on their backs, exposing their white undersides. This might perhaps help them to keep their temperature down, because a white surface absorbs less radiant heat (from the Sun's rays) than a dark surface.*

▼ *A sooty tern with its chick, trying to keep cool despite the lack of shade on their nesting ground. By spreading its wings, it shades the core of the body and allows heat to escape by convection from its flanks. Like other birds, terns also pant to keep cool, the rate of breathing rising from about 100 to as many as 300 breaths per minute. In pigeons, the panting response is initiated by thermoreceptors in the spinal cord. Some birds also pant while flying, to dissipate excess heat generated by their muscles.*

## Keeping warm and keeping cool

A homeotherm can keep its body temperature at a steady level largely due to part of the brain called the hypothalamus, which monitors the temperature of the body and brings about responses that compensate for any change. In the warm, a homeotherm must allow surplus heat to escape into the environment. Four routes are open. Any water that evaporates from the lungs, mouth or skin, helps to cool the body down. In addition, the processes of radiation (direct emision of heat from the body's surface), convection (loss via air currents) and conduction (by direct contact) have parts to play.

Hot humans perspire through their 2·5 million sweat glands. These secretions cool the body as they evaporate. But not all mammals sweat, and birds cannot afford to because it would ruin the aerodynamic properties of their plumage. Instead they resort to panting, which has much the same effect. Another important cooling device is the diversion of blood into vessels that run close to the surface of the skin, where heat can be dissipated by radiation and convection. The flow of blood in these vessels increases as much as 100-fold when the need is greatest. Insulating coverings, such as fur and feathers, can usually be flattened in the warm so that they only trap a thin layer of air and do not impede the loss of heat.

In very hot and dry environments, water is a commodity that homeotherms can ill afford to waste on sweating or panting. Camels have solved these problems by a combination of measures. They can function unusually well at a range of temperatures, and allow their body temperature to fluctuate by as much as 6 or 7°C. So, instead of fighting to lose heat, they warm up to 41°C by day and then cool down to about 34°C at night, thereby conserving around five liters of water.

A warm-blooded animal can use food-energy to generate heat

In cool conditions, all homeotherms must conserve heat. They force blood to flow away from the skin's surface and they minimize evaporation. They also fluff up fur or feathers so as to trap a thick layer of air. Humans feel their hairs erecting and goose pimples forming – signs of a past when we had a layer of hair worth the name. The final ploy is to generate warmth by increasing metabolism. Unprotected humans must react in this way as soon as the temperature drops below 28°C, but the arctic fox is so well insulated that it need not turn up its metabolic fires until the outside temperature reaches −40°C.

Homeotherms produce heat by two methods: they exercise their muscles (as poikilotherms may also do), either by shivering or by conscious efforts, and they increase the general level of metabolism – a process called non-shivering thermogenesis. One such source of heat is eating, due to the so-called specific dynamic action (SDA) of food. This is a rise in metabolic rate (of up to 30 percent, depending on diet) that occurs just after feeding. What accounts for the SDA is still a matter of dispute, but it may be due to the metabolic costs involved in synthesizing proteins, and breaking down and storing food.

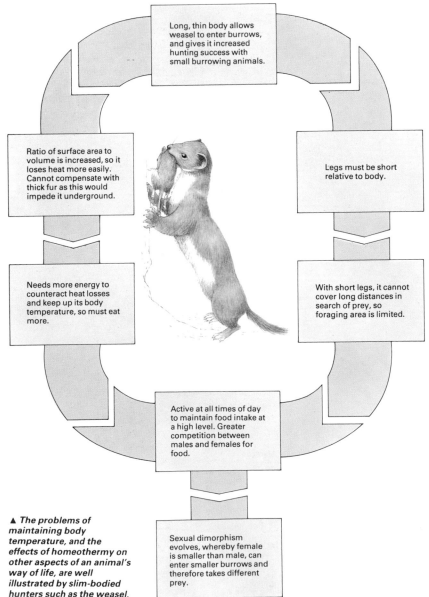

Long, thin body allows weasel to enter burrows, and gives it increased hunting success with small burrowing animals.

Ratio of surface area to volume is increased, so it loses heat more easily. Cannot compensate with thick fur as this would impede it underground.

Legs must be short relative to body.

Needs more energy to counteract heat losses and keep up its body temperature, so must eat more.

With short legs, it cannot cover long distances in search of prey, so foraging area is limited.

Active at all times of day to maintain food intake at a high level. Greater competition between males and females for food.

▲ The problems of maintaining body temperature, and the effects of homeothermy on other aspects of an animal's way of life, are well illustrated by slim-bodied hunters such as the weasel.

Sexual dimorphism evolves, whereby female is smaller than male, can enter smaller burrows and therefore takes different prey.

◄ *In cold weather, birds stand on one leg to reduce heat losses.*

► *Fur on an elephant hawkmoth conserves the heat it generates by muscle movements.*

▼ *Poikilotherms are at risk when the external temperature falls, because when they become too cold certain physiological processes grind to a halt. If, having consumed this rat, the python becomes chilled, its internal temperature may be so low that the digestive enzymes will not work properly. The food will then rot inside the snake and kill it. This is why captive snakes find a warm place to sleep off a meal.*

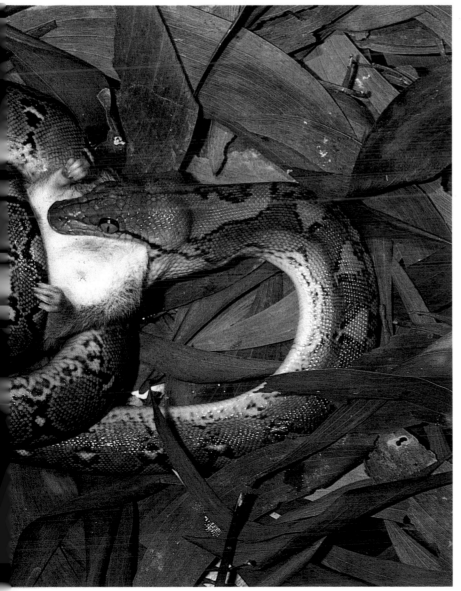

### The size factor

Size has an important bearing on loss of heat through the skin. Compared to larger mammals, a small creature like a shrew has a much greater surface area relative to the volume of its body. Hence it tends to lose heat rather rapidly and must keep stoking its internal fires with an endless supply of food. Shrews eat their own weight in food each day, while elephants take an amount equal to less than five percent of their body weight.

The absolute amount of metabolic fuel burnt by mammals rises with increasing body size, but at a faster rate than the surface area of their bodies. So, in complete contrast to the shrews, the elephant, hippopotamus and rhinoceros face the problem of how to dispose of excess metabolic heat, especially in hot climates. In evolutionary terms, their solution has been to rid themselves of furry insulation and reduce their coat to a few sparse hairs.

### Were the dinosaurs warm-blooded?

In the early 1970s, some biologists suggested that the dinosaurs might have been homeothermic. Another extinct group of reptiles, the pterosaurs, were certainly warm-blooded (♦ page 105), and since birds are believed to be descended from dinosaurs, it is possible that their ancestors had already evolved homeothermy, before birds appeared. Many dinosaurs were obviously vigorous and agile, particularly the carnivorous forms such as Tyrannosaurus. Modern reptiles have to warm up for a very long while in the sun before they can begin to be this active. On the other hand, the climate was generally warmer in the Cretaceous. Most biologists now believe that the dinosaurs were not true homeotherms, although the larger ones were "warm-blooded" in a way. Just because most of them were so huge, they would have had a fairly constant body temperature, as large crocodiles do: their great bulk means that they have a low surface-area-to-volume ratio, and thus they heat up and cool down much more slowly than a smaller reptile.

*Effective insulation allows some mammals to survive at −50°C*

## Hibernation

Some homeothermic animals face severe difficulties in the extreme cold of winter, because a high metabolic rate puts impossible demands on their ability to find food. Birds can migrate to warmer climates, but many small mammals, especially rodents, insectivores and bats, must hibernate when the going gets tough. Among the birds, there is only one hibernator, a species of nightjar called the poorwill, found in the western USA. But many other species, such as hummingbirds and swifts, can become torpid for a few hours at a time.

Mammals entering hibernation often let their temperature fall to within one or two degrees of the outside temperature. Their metabolic rate plummets to between 1/30th and 1/100th of its former level, while vital functions become dramatically slowed. The heartbeat may be reduced to 3–4 times per minute, and breathing to an average of one breath every two minutes. Both may be quite irregular.

However, such animals do not behave as though they were poikilotherms, since their condition is strictly controlled. Should the temperature fall to a level that threatens life, many species wake up. Others, such as the European hedgehog, switch on their system of regulation to ensure that their internal temperature stays a few degrees above freezing.

Hibernators are able to bring about their own arousal by producing heat. Most seem to do this every few days throughout the winter, for reasons that have yet to be explained. Brown fat is a prime mover in the arousal of mammals, but shivering is also important. Careful distribution of blood ensures that heat goes first to the front end of the body, where the brain, heart and lungs lie. Meanwhile the rear waits its turn for warmth.

## Biological antifreeze

Homeothermic animals – hibernators included – avoid the worst ravages of cold by keeping their bodies at a temperature above freezing. But plants and poikilothermic animals have no such protection. They are frequently exposed to temperatures below the freezing point of their tissues. That spells danger, because ice is a killer, its crystals puncturing delicate cell walls and membranes as they form.

However, water does not always freeze when the temperature drops below 0°C. Ice forms only if molecules of water come together around a particle called a nucleator, which can be a tiny embryonic ice crystal, or a small speck of dust or dirt from the atmosphere. Until nucleation takes place, the water is said to be in a supercooled state. The extent to which water can be supercooled before it freezes can be increased by the presence of solutes.

Several plants, mites, insects and fish, make use of these properties. The antarctic mite *Alaskozetes antarcticus* is exposed to temperatures as low as −25°C, yet it survives, simply because it is able to remain supercooled, even at a temperature of −30°C. Every fall, the mite makes a substantial quantity of a solute, glycerol, which acts as an antifreeze, and increases its power of supercooling. Since food in the gut is a potential source of nucleators, the mite must also refrain from eating throughout the winter.

Some plants and insects, and a few rather unusual frogs, do tolerate the freezing of their bodies, but they mostly do so by restricting ice to the fluids outside their cells. Many produce their own nucleators, whose job is to bring about freezing in a controlled fashion and in the right places – in the fluid of the circulatory system, for example.

▲ *Crabeater seals resting on sea ice. In returning to the sea, mammals faced the problem of insulation. Whales and dolphins, which spend all their lives in the water, have dispensed with fur and have a thick layer of fat instead. Seals and sealions have both fur and fat.*

▼ *A hibernating dormouse curls up to reduce surface area.*

► *The arctic fox can withstand temperatures of −50°C or even lower. It has furry soles to its feet, a short muzzle and small ear flaps to reduce heat loss. The proportions of its head make an interesting contrast to desert-dwelling foxes, such as the fennec fox, whose ear flaps may be as long as its head. They probably improve its hearing ability, but also serve to increase heat loss.*

### Nature's electric blanket: brown fat

Brown fat is a mammalian tissue that specializes in heat production. Deposits of this material, which is quite unlike normal (white) fat, are particularly widespread in hibernating and newborn animals. Pads of the tissue have been likened to electric blankets, for their job is to warm the body, for example, when an animal is emerging from hibernation. Cells of brown fat oxidize sugar without producing ATP and this yields substantially more heat than normal oxidation. Brown fat may play a role in some non-hibernating adult animals too, because it can burn off surplus food and help prevent obesity. In humans, it has been suggested that some individuals have more – or more active – brown fat than others. But while human babies are well provided with brown fat, the importance of the tissue in human adults is still a matter of debate.

*See also*
Mammals 117-128
The Origin of Life 143-154
Sustaining Life 169-184

## Life at the limits

What are the extremes of temperature at which active life is still possible? The ubiquitous insects have pushed life close to its thermal limits. At one end of the spectrum are midges and grylloblattids that remain active on glaciers or snow at temperatures as low as −16°C. At the other extreme is the firebrat, a wingless insect related to the silverfish, that inhabits bakeries and fireplaces, and can tolerate a temperature up to 50°C, and midge larvae that reside in hot springs and can withstand water temperatures of 49–51°C. While the firebrat is immobilized if the temperature drops below a relatively mild 12°C, the cold-adapted insects are paralyzed by the warmth of a human hand. The biochemistry of each is tailored to fit its own particular range of temperatures and is disrupted by any major change.

Certain bacteria are even more resistant to temperature extremes, and can thrive at temperatures as low as −20°C or below. The upper limit for bacteria is likewise very high, but cannot be stated exactly as it is still being vigorously debated. Some bacteria living in the deep ocean, at places where the heat of the molten core is felt, are adapted to a scalding 105°C. (Water does not turn to steam at such temperatures owing to the high pressures of the deep ocean.) Even more remarkably, bacteria from deep-sea hydrothermal vents (◀ page 154) are reported to flourish at 250°C, although this claim is disputed. Such heat-loving bacteria apparently find 75°C too cold for comfort and will stop growing at this "low" temperature – one which kills many ordinary bacteria.

Exactly what factors limit the range of temperature over which an insect can be active, or a bacterium can prosper, are still not known with certainty. A range of different structures and processes within the body are probably involved. The membranes around and within the cell, which are composed of lipids (◀ page 133), change in consistency as the temperature rises and falls, and this may affect cell processes. Alternatively, metabolic imbalances could arise if the enzymes that control cellular chemistry are affected to different extents by changes in temperature. At more extreme temperatures, actual damage to the enzymes and other metabolic machinery may set in. Evasion of these problems must loom large in creatures with extreme tolerance of high or low temperatures. In particular their enzymes and membranes must be adapted to work at a range of temperatures that most organisms find debilitating. Even more dramatic adaptions must play a part in highly thermophilic bacteria, with exceptionally heat-stable enzymes and membranes presumably being involved.

### Suspended animation

*Hibernating mammals seem quite inactive, but their metabolism continues to tick over. Some invertebrates and plants can go one better, surviving a complete shut down of metabolism. They include mosses, water bears, rotifers and nematodes, plus a few insects and crustaceans. All live in habitats where they are exposed to the threat of severe drying. When such conditions set in, they lose most – perhaps all – of their water, and enter a state called cryptobiosis.*

*Scientists have known about these abilities ever since Antonie van Leeuwenhoek discovered them in 1702, but the question of metabolic shutdown has occasioned fierce argument over the years, for some have thought it impossible. No one can be certain that cryptobiotic creatures are completely inert, but experiments on the nematode* Ditylenchus dipsaci *do seem fairly conclusive. When the worm is in a state of cryptobiosis, scientists can detect no metabolic activity, even with the aid of the most sensitive techniques that would register a metabolic rate equal to 1/10,000th of normal.*

*How do organisms survive cryptobiosis? Slow drying is a factor, and many have ways of reducing the rate of water loss. Nematodes coil their bodies, and tardigrades form barrel shapes, thus restricting the surface area from which water can evaporate. Slow drying probably allows them to reorganize their cell contents in an orderly fashion.*

*The membranes that surround a cell and make up its internal components, such as mitochondria, are particularly prone to damage when water leaves the cell. Some cryptobiotic animals make a sugar called trehalose, which, by replacing water in the cell, may prevent injury to their membranes. Even if they are damaged slightly, repair mechanisms can restore them to full working order when water reappears. Mitochondria, for example, often appear damaged in the early stages of rehydration, but later return to normal.*

*Through cryptobiosis, organisms can survive for decades, perhaps centuries, and tolerate extraordinary conditions. Cryptobiotic tardigrades and rotifers survive temperatures as high as 151°C and as low as −272°C. The cryptobiotic larva of the insect* Polypedilum vanderplanki *revives after a day spent immersed in pure alcohol.*

### The immortal dream

*Part of the interest of cryptobiosis lies in its potential as a method of long-term storage for living tissues. However, the most practical method does not rely on desiccation, as practiced by tardigrades and nematodes, but on chilling to −196°C, the temperature of liquid nitrogen. Metabolism comes to a complete standstill under such extreme conditions. The technique, already used for storing a range of tissues from spermatozoa to shoot tips, would be of immense value if it could be extended to human organs destined for transplants. Researchers are currently working toward this goal, but the idea of preserving whole bodies in this fashion remains a dream.*

◀ *Grylloblattids live high up on mountain snow fields.*

# Coordination

## 23

*Communication between cells...Chemical messengers...
Local communication...Action at a distance...
Hormones...The nervous system in simple animals...
Developed nervous systems...The brain...PERSPECTIVE...
Cell recognition...Endocrinology, a young science...
Hijacking a messenger system...Plant hormones...Giant
neurons for jet propulsion...Studying nerves*

The teeming billions of cells that make up a living body cannot afford to act in isolation. On the contrary, they must coordinate their activities if they are to survive and prosper. But domestic harmony demands a constant exchange of information. As a result, cells come equipped with a wide repertoire of channels of communication. One fundamental aspect of coordination is cell-to-cell recognition. For this purpose, cells carry an array of molecules on their surfaces which proclaim their identities, allowing them to recognize one another and act accordingly. Cellular recognition on contact can take two forms. In the first, complementary molecules on the surfaces of a pair of interacting cells fit one another, as a key fits a lock. In the second mechanism, cells carrying similar receptor molecules are united by a molecular "bridge" that is capable of binding to both parties.

A second fundamental element in overall coordination is cell-to-cell communication, which keeps cells in touch with their immediate neighbors. In animals, this is done by passing messages through openings known as gap junctions, which act as communicating doors between cells. Each gap junction is a collection of minute channels lined with special protein molecules. Through these openings small molecules and ions (electrically charged atoms) can pass – including those that play a crucial role in linking cells, so that they behave in concert.

Plant cells are equally communicative. Although each cell of a plant is surrounded by a thick cell wall, small perforations in the wall ensure that the cell makes contact with its neighbors, via narrow bridges of cytoplasm called plasmodesmata.

### The nervous cell
Coordination in living things depends on electrical and chemical communication, but from what beginnings did such systems evolve? This is at present an impossible question to answer, although single-celled creatures may provide some clues. When a Paramecium, for example, swims into an obstacle, it moves backward, and then swims off in a new direction. The internal events that accompany the response show interesting parallels with our own nerve cells (see below).

Unicellular creatures also communicate chemically. Such an interaction underlies the process of conjugation in protozoa, which can only occur between individuals of different mating types. Chemicals shed into the water, or borne on the cell's surface, provide the necessary information on pedigree. These messages are read by receptors on the surface of the other cell.

Some biologists believe that interactions of this type could have been the forerunners of cell recognition and communication in multicellular animals. This might explain why yeast cells signal to one another with a compound that resembles one of our hormones, why the cells of certain protozoa contain insulin, and why some amebae have receptors for human neurotransmitters.

### Cell recognition
An example of cell recognition using a molecular bridge comes from sponges. If a sponge is broken into its component cells, some of those cells will reaggregate and regain an ordered structure. Even more impressively, if cells from certain sponges of different species are mixed together, they only link up with others of the correct type. Such recognition depends on a large molecule called an aggregation factor (AF), which is released by disintegrating sponges. Reaggregation happens in two stages. Each cell bears specific receptors – proteins known as baseplates – which bind to the AF appropriate to its species. Then, molecules of AF join together, in the presence of calcium ions, to reunite the cells.

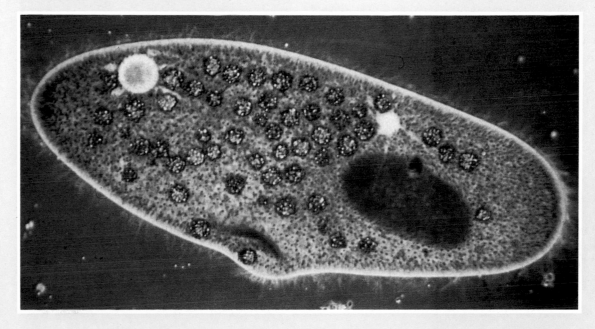

◀ A Paramecium *moves about through the combined efforts of its hundreds of tiny, thread-like cilia, which must beat in coordinated waves. If it swims into an obstacle, the beat of the cilia is reversed and the* Paramecium *moves backward. It is interesting that electrical events are involved in the response, as in nerves, and the actual change in direction is brought about by the movement of calcium ions into the cell. Calcium ion influx also plays an important part in the firing of nerve synapses, and in stimulating muscle cells to contract (▶ page 199). These and other parallels with single-celled organisms may point to the evolutionary origins of the nervous systems of more advanced organisms.*

Plasmodesmata are much wider than gap junctions, but they serve similar functions. They allow plant cells to respond to electrical events in nearby cells and offer a route for the rapid movement of important substances, such as nectar, around the plant.

In addition to the channels of communication offered by gap junctions, animal cells can pass messages to one another by secreting chemicals into their surroundings. These chemicals rapidly activate other cells in the vicinity, but have purely local effects because they are attacked by special enzymes soon after they are released.

Histamine is perhaps the best known of such local chemical messengers since it plays a part in human allergic reactions. Cells known as mast cells contain packets of histamine, which they release in response to infection or injury. Once released, histamine relaxes the walls of blood vessels and hastens the flow of blood to the affected area. It also helps the body's white blood cells to reach the inflamed zone, by making blood vessels more leaky. Unfortunately, certain types of pollen, and other irritants, sometimes cause the same reaction in humans – with highly unpleasant results. Hay fever, asthma and allergic rashes are all caused by the mast cells overreacting to essentially harmless substances.

Another well known group of local messengers are the prostaglandins. In humans, these chemicals are manufactured from fatty acids in a range of body tissues and have various functions, ranging from contraction of muscle in the womb during childbirth, to slowing the secretion of acid in the stomach, and controlling excretion of water and ions in the kidney. But production of prostaglandins is not limited to the mammals. They play a part in ovulation in fishes, while in the gastric brooding frog – an amphibian that rears its tadpoles in its stomach – they help staunch the normal flow of gastric acid. Invertebrates, notably corals, also produce prostaglandins.

## Action at a distance

In addition to emitting short-range signals, the cells of animals and plants have evolved methods of transmitting messages over relatively long distances. In animals, such communication takes two forms. One depends on the electrical messages carried by the nervous system, which is fast and specific in its effects. The other relies on the release of chemical mediators called hormones, which spread throughout the body, and exert their effects on distant cells. This system is slower, but its effects are prolonged and wide-ranging. However, the distinction between the nervous and hormonal systems is often blurred. Many chemicals traditionally seen as hormones double as neurotransmitters (♦ page 198) in the nervous system, and some nerves, when stimulated, release hormones into the bloodstream in a process called neurosecretion.

Hormones perform a wide range of regulatory tasks in animals. They feature in all but the most lowly life forms, but have been studied most intensively in insects, crustaceans, worms, mollusks and vertebrates. A hormone-like substance controls the regeneration of head and tentacles from a beheaded *Hydra*, while insects deploy hormones to regulate the intricacies of metamorphosis, as well as to control everyday physiological processes, such as excretion of waste products. The hormones of vertebrates affect growth, the onset of sexual maturity and reproduction, as well as the day-to-day operation of liver, gut, kidneys and much else besides. In short, they work hand-in-hand with the nervous system to regulate the body's affairs.

**A young science**
*The study of hormones belongs to the 20th century. Even the word "hormone" itself was not coined until 1905. One of the pioneers in this field was the German anatomist Arnold Berthold (1803–1861), who reversed the effects of castration in a cockerel by reimplanting a testis. Thanks to this experiment and others, the idea of internal messengers was gradually accepted in the 19th century but endocrinology proper dates from the early 1900s, with the work of physiologists such as Ernest Starling (1866–1927) and William Bayliss (1860–1924). They studied the mechanisms that control the flow of digestive juice from the pancreas when acidic, half-digested food leaves the stomach. In 1902, they carried out a crucial experiment on a dog, cutting through all the nerves serving the relevant section of the gut. They found that the dog's pancreas went on secreting when stimulated by acid. When an extract from the wall of the intestine was injected into the dog's blood stream, the pancreas again began to secrete. They deduced that a chemical messenger was released by the intestinal wall into the blood and traveled to the pancreas via the bloodstream.*

▼ *Among vertebrates, some of the most obvious effects of hormones are on reproductive behavior. Male robins, for example, show a number of behavioral changes in spring, including more prolonged singing, and an increasingly aggressive response to other birds entering their territory. Similar changes are seen in other bird species, and they are related to rising levels of testosterone in the blood.*

▲ In red deer, the rutting behavior of males includes roaring, lip-curling, wallowing in peat bogs, frequent urination and fighting. This behavior is not seen in castrated males but can be restored by implantation of the hormone testosterone.

► Most female mammals are only sexually receptive when ovulating, and the males must be stimulated to mate at that time. In the female baboon, hormonal changes cause swelling of the genital area and changes in odor which attract males.

### Sex hormones — and how they work

Some of the best-studied hormones are those that control sexual reproduction in vertebrates, such as estradiol (also called "oestrogen") and testosterone. These all belong to a class of lipid substances known as steroids (◆ page 132). The steroid hormones work by infiltrating cells and affecting the workings of the DNA in their nuclei. The first stage is the formation of chemical links with special receptor proteins (perhaps as many as 10,000 per cell) inside target cells. Once the receptor protein has been activated by the hormone, it becomes able to bind to DNA, affecting the transcription of genes (◆ page 140) and hence the types of proteins made by the cell. Steroids often act less rapidly than other mediators, but their effects are long-lasting and profound.

*Plants also have hormone-like substances*

### Purifying hormones

Because hormones are effective in such small quantities it is very difficult to obtain adequate amounts for study. Thyroxine, for example, was first isolated in 1914 by Edwin Kendall (1886–1972), an American biochemist. He began with three tons of pigs' thyroids and ended with 33g of thyroxine. Scientists working in the 1930s and 1940s, on hormones of the adrenal glands, dissected out 100kg of glands from 20,000 cattle. Only 26g of that mass was biologically active and this yielded about 300mg of each of 29 substances.

### Plant hormones

Plants also produce hormones, although they differ from most animal hormones in that they are neither released from, nor aimed at, special glands. Until recently, just five classes of plant hormone were recognized: auxins, cytokinins, gibberellins, ethylene and abscisic acid. Each has a wide range of roles – for example, ethylene (a gas) hastens the ripening of fruit and plays a part in responses to injury, while auxin encourages the growth of shoots and roots, but delays the ripening of fruit and the senescence of leaves.

One recent development, that promises to shed light on plant hormone action is the discovery of regulatory substances called oligosaccharins – short-chain sugars that have been split off from the plant cell wall by enzymes. They exert dramatic effects on plant tissues. In the laboratory, they can induce cultured tissue of tobacco to develop either as flower buds or as shoots and leaves. Some scientists think that plant cells may release oligosaccharins when stimulated by hormones. Auxins, for example, may induce cells to issue various oligosaccharins, each specific in its effects.

▼ **The axolotl normally spends its whole life in the larval form (◊ page 101). In captivity, however, it can be induced to develop into an adult by treatment with the hormone thyroxine.**

► **Cranes have elaborate dance displays which help to synchronize the reproductive states of the pair and induce the female to lay, by stimulating hormone secretion.**

Thyroxine is a typical example of a hormone. It is widespread among the vertebrates; for example, tadpoles need it if they are to turn into frogs. In mammals, the thyroid gland in the neck secretes a daily ration of thyroxine into the blood. Thyroid hormone prompts tissues to increase their metabolic rate and so consume more oxygen; it increases the uptake of carbohydrates from the gut; it reduces blood cholesterol and it is necessary for correct growth and development.

Secretion of thyroid hormone is under the control of a gland called the anterior pituitary, which is situated just under the brain. This gland releases a thyroid-stimulating hormone (thyrotropin), which travels in the blood to the thyroid, where it prompts the secretion of thyroxine. Thyrotropin itself is under the control of another blood-borne internal secretion (thyrotropin-releasing hormone or TRH), which comes from a set of nerve cells in an area of the brain called the hypothalamus. Various controls ensure that levels of the hormone remain appropriate to need. For example, a rise in the amount of thyroxine in the blood inhibits release of both thyrotropin and TRH, thereby preserving the status quo.

Any communication network is susceptible to interference from organisms of other species, which can turn the internal messages to their own ends. One species of parasitic fluke infects an ant, later transferring to a grazing animal, such as a sheep. The flukes invade the ant's brain, where they influence its behavior. As a result, the ant spends much time perched atop grass stems – in just the right place to be eaten by grazers.

Communications can also be intercepted by parasites. For example, three parasites of the common European frog time their reproduction to coincide with the tadpole season by responding to the frog's hormone changes. They are then well placed to infest the new generation of hosts.

Coordination by hormones is also prone to disruption. For example, plants often contain substances that mimic the sex hormones of vertebrate herbivores, and can disrupt their reproductive physiology. Whether such substances have evolved for defense against grazers, or whether they have other roles is not yet clear.

Plants also produce chemicals that mimic the insect hormones, ecdysone (molting hormone) and juvenile hormone, which jointly control molting and metamorphosis. Plants such as the common yew produce quite large quantities of ecdysone-like substances. Many insects can render these ecdysones harmless by chemical means, however, suggesting that the "arms race" between plant and insect is still in progress.

Researchers discovered juvenile hormone in plants by accident, when laboratory insects reared in dishes lined with a certain kind of paper were unable to metamorphose. They traced the problem to a chemical in fir trees used to make the paper.

▼ *Certain rainforest fungi that infect ants influence the nervous system and thus modify the behavior of their hosts, causing them to climb to the top of a tree. The ant then dies and the fungus produces fruiting bodies, as shown here. From the tree-top position it has gained by influencing the ant's behavior, the fungus is ideally situated to disperse its spores on the breeze.*

## Flight or fight

Thyroid hormone, like the sex hormones, has a relatively long-term effect, which it achieves by entering cells and binding to special receptors. These in turn bind to DNA and influence the types of protein manufactured by the cell and hence its metabolism. But not all hormones exert their effects by infiltrating cells, and some have much more short-term effects achieved by influencing enzymes themselves. Such hormones generally bind to receptors on the cell's outer surface and rely on a "second messenger" to pass their message on to the cell's interior. One such hormone is epinephrine (adrenaline), responsible for the "flight or fight" response to stress. An important part of this response is the mobilization of glucose from reserves of glycogen. When epinephrine binds to its receptor, it starts a cascade of chemical changes. The receptor operates via an intermediary to activate an enzyme, adenylate cyclase, which then makes a chemical called cyclic adenosine monophosphate (cAMP). This substance acts as the second messenger, which sparks off the chemical reactions that produce glucose from stored glycogen.

*Nerves are superb biochemichal "machines" that depend on specialized proteins for their precise action*

## Living on your nerves

With the exception of the sponges, virtually all multicellular animals are equipped with nervous systems. Moreover, all such systems work along similar lines. They employ specialized nerve cells, which are devices for conducting electrical messages around the animals' bodies. A typical neuron consists of a cell body and a variable number of projections, one of which – the axon – may be a meter or more in length. The cell carries messages in the form of transient electrical disturbances, which rush along the axon at speeds of up to 100 meters per second. These electrical disturbances are known as "action potentials".

The speed at which an action potential moves along a nerve cell varies with the diameter of the cell, its temperature and the amount of insulation around it. The fast nerves of the squid rely on size for their speed, and they need a diameter of more than half a millimeter to transmit at 25 meters per second, but vertebrates have evolved a different ploy for fast conduction. Many of their axons are wrapped in an insulating layer of membranes known as a myelin sheath, separated by small gaps called the nodes of Ranvier. The action potential shoots from one node to the next, and thus achieves speed without a massive diameter. For example, a frog's nerves have the same rate of conduction as a squid, but with axons that are 65 times thinner.

Nerve cells communicate with one another at special junctions called synapses. At some synapses, the cells are in direct contact via gap junctions (◀ page 193) and their messages are passed on by electricity. This very fast communication system is useful where rapid responses, such as escape reactions, are required. But the majority of synapses are not like this. Instead, the cells are separated by a gap, called the synaptic cleft, across which they communicate by chemicals known as neurotransmitters. Chemical synapses are a little slower than electrical ones, but they have certain advantages. They allow a greater flexibility of response, because the presynaptic cell can influence the postsynaptic cell in many different ways, such as producing a long-term modification in the way it reacts (not shown here).

### Proteins – the basis of nerve action

*Nerve action depends on highly specialized proteins which make up ion channels in the neuron's membrane. Each ion channel is a group of protein molecules. Like many proteins, they have more than one shape or conformation and certain conditions make them change shape. When the proteins of an ion channel adopt one shape it makes the channel open, whereas the other shape closes the channel. There are two basic types of channel in the neurons: ligand-gated and voltage-gated. In the former, the binding of a specific molecule (the "ligand" – in this case, the neurotransmitter) to the proteins makes them change shape. In the second type, a change in voltage is responsible – this is probably due to charged amino acids on the protein's surface, making one shape stable in, say, a negatively charged milieu, but unstable in a positive one.*

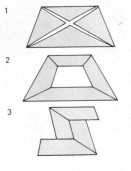

1
2
3

◀ *The axon hillock and nodes of Ranvier have special sodium channels (1) that open in response to positive charge (2) admitting sodium ions. They then go into a closed-and-inactive form which cannot open (3). Once the cell's negative charge has been restored they revert to a closed-but-ready-to-open form (1). This prevents the nerve cell from going into a spasm of firing.*

Myelin sheath
Node of Ranvier

▼▶ *In this diagrammatic representation of a human motor neuron (a nerve that causes a muscle cell to contract), the axon has been greatly shortened. It can be up to a meter long.*

Axon
Axon hillock

Cl⁻

Surface of postsynaptic cell
Synaptic vesicle
Neurotransmitter molecule
Ion channel (closed)
Synaptic cleft
Presynaptic cell

▼◀▶ *The neuron receives impulses from a great many synapses, of which just three are shown here. Each synapse releases neuro-transmitters of a particular type, which bind to specific ion channels – each kind of ion channel has a different effect on the neuron. There are thousands of ion channels on the dendrites and cell body.*

◀ *Synapse from a neuron that is not firing. No neurotransmitter molecules are available, so the ion channels remain closed.*

Nucleus

Cell body

▶ *Synapse from an excitatory neuron that is firing. The neurotransmitter binds to the ion channel, making it open up. It is negatively charged, so only admits cations: sodium (Na⁺), potassium (K⁺), or calcium (Ca⁺⁺). They rush in, due to the negative charge in the cell.*

Ca⁺⁺
K⁺
Na⁺

▲ *Synapse from an inhibitory neuron. It opens up ion channels which only admit negative ions – largely chloride (Cl⁻). They enter, despite the negative charge within, because chloride concentration in the cell is very low. This influx helps keep the cell negatively charged.*

Dendrite

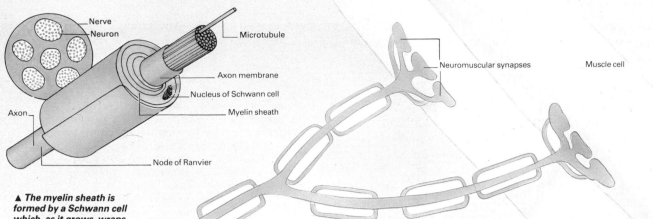

Nerve
Neuron
Microtubule
Axon membrane
Nucleus of Schwann cell
Myelin sheath
Axon
Node of Ranvier

Neuromuscular synapses

Muscle cell

▲ The myelin sheath is formed by a Schwann cell which, as it grows, wraps itself around the axon to form up to 100 layers of insulating membrane.

► The action potential is transient because after a few milliseconds, the automatic closure of the sodium channels prevents more sodium ions coming into the cell. The membrane pumps can then work to restore the negative potential. In some nerves, this process is accelerated by other channels that open just after the sodium channels, to let potassium out of the cell.

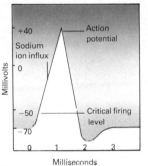

+40
Sodium
ion influx
0
Millivolts
−50
−70
Action
potential
Critical firing
level
0    1    2    3
Milliseconds

## How a nerve impulse is produced

The cytoplasm of neurons (like most cells) is negatively charged, due to a membrane pump that forces sodium ions out of the cell and potassium ions in ( ◀ page 170). Other channels let potassium leak out of the cell (which it does because it is concentrated inside) and the overall effect is an exodus of positive ions, producing a negative potential inside.

Nerve impulses are transient disturbances of this negative potential. They originate in the neuron's cell body, as a result of excitatory impulses from other neurons, which open up ion channels to admit positive ions. A motor neuron has many hundreds of synapses from other nerve cells impinging on its dendrites and cell body. Some come from sensory neurons in the skin or muscles and provide instant feedback. Other neurons bring signals from the brain or spinal cord. Each synapse makes its own contribution to the overall charge of the cell body. As well as excitatory synapses, there are inhibitory synapses, which admit negative ions.

When excitatory signals outweigh inhibitory ones, the cell body becomes more positively charged, and at a certain point an action potential is fired. This starts at the axon hillock as special sodium channels open in response to positive charge. The first few to open admit sodium ions, causing a rise in positive charge that open more channels, and so on, in a cascade effect. The cells' cytoplasm conducts the electric charge and, when it reaches the first node of Ranvier, another action potential is fired. Action potentials are generated repeatedly along the axon.

Na⁺

Na⁺

Na⁺

Node of Ranvier (calcium ion channels here)

Na⁺

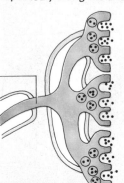

◀ When the action potential reches the axon terminal, voltage-gated ion channels open to admit calcium ions, which trigger the release of the neuro-transmitter. This opens ion channels in the muscle cell membrane, causing an inrush of positive ions. They in turn release calcium ions from vesicles within the muscle cell, and this makes the muscle fibers contract.

*The giant nerve fibers of the squid first allowed the details of nerve action to be studied*

### Jet propulsion and giant nerve fibers

*The cephalopod mollusks move about by jet propulsion (♦ page 210), producing a powerful jet of water by contracting the mantle cavity. The system depends upon simultaneous contraction of muscles all over the mantle – otherwise it would only bulge in one place while contracting in another. So the nerve impulses triggering the muscles must arrive simultaneously, despite the fact that some parts of the musculature are much more distant than others. Lacking the myelin sheaths of vertebrates, the squids have solved this problem by increasing the diameter of the nerve fibers – large nerves conduct more rapidly than small ones. Some of the nerves running to the more distant parts of the mantle can be as much as 1 mm in diameter. The discovery of these giant nerve fibers permitted a range of hitherto impossible experiments, because ultrafine metal electrodes could be placed within individual nerves. The findings from such experiments, carried out in the 1950s by Alan Hodgkin (b. 1914) and Andrew Huxley (b. 1917), form the basis of our understanding of how nerves work.*

*Today, much smaller nerves can be studied, by means of the microelectrode, a glass tube drawn out to a fine point, less than a thousandth of a millimeter across. The tube contains a solution of salts that conducts electricity, so it acts like an electrode. Scientists can impale a tiny nerve cell on the tube and record its electrical activity.*

### Studying nerves

*Although today's researchers use an array of elaborate techniques to study nerve cells directly and locate neurotransmitters, their work builds on a foundation of careful microscopic studies that was laid at the end of the 19th century. In 1873 the Italian biologist, Camillo Golgi (1844–1926) invented a stain that revealed nerve cells in microscopical sections, by precipitating silver salts inside them. The technique was later called "the find of the century", because it allowed scientists to document the shapes and dispositions of neurons.*

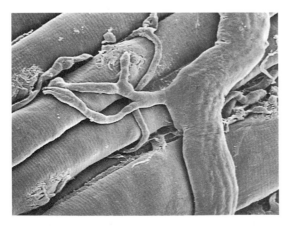

▲ **A scanning electron microscope picture of a neuro-muscular junction, where an axon terminal branches and synapses onto a muscle cell.**

▶ **A shoal of squid, moving by jet propulsion. The demands of this system of movement led to the evolution of giant nerve fibers, up to 1mm thick.**

### Neurotransmitters

In recent years, a great many different neuro-transmitters have been discovered, and over 60 are now known in humans alone. Exactly why so many different transmitters are needed is not yet clear, but they may allow the nervous system to control the body in a more subtle and complex way.

Not all neurotransmitters act by opening ion channels. Some, such as dopamine, are slower to act and have longer-lasting effects. They work by sparking off a sequence of biochemical reactions in the post-synaptic cell. Like certain homones, these substances pass their signals on to secondary messengers, such as cyclic AMP, which can have profound effects on a cell's behavior.

Dopamine is one of a group of neurotransmitters known as modulators, that seem, among other things, to alter the responsiveness of circuits in the brain. For, example, certain modulators can reduce sensitivity to pain, and it is believed that acupuncture may work by prompting the nervous system to release these natural pain-killers.

▲ A spotted flycatcher seizing a moth in flight. This bird, like many others, depends on split-second reactions and precise muscular coordination to capture its prey, and its way of life would not be possible without a complex and highly sophisticated nervous system.

▼ A strawberry poison-dart frog from the rainforest of Costa Rica. Its skin secretes a toxin that is used by South American Indians to make curare for their poisoned arrows. When injected beneath the skin, this toxin causes paralysis by competing with acetylcholine – the neuro-transmitter found at most nerve-muscle junctions.

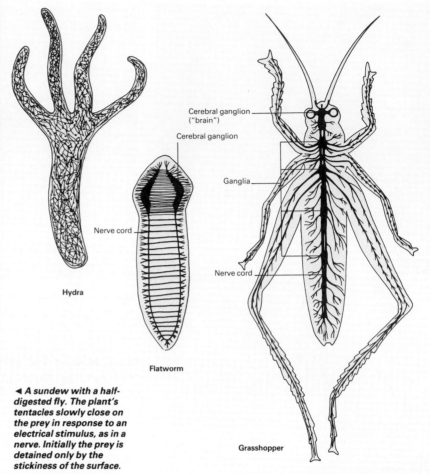

Cerebral ganglion ("brain")

Cerebral ganglion

Nerve cord

**Hydra**

Ganglia

Nerve cord

**Flatworm**

**Grasshopper**

◄ *A sundew with a half-digested fly. The plant's tentacles slowly close on the prey in response to an electrical stimulus, as in a nerve. Initially the prey is detained only by the stickiness of the surface.*

▼ *A sea anemone feeding on a shrimp. Cnidarians, with their simple nervous systems, can only catch fast-moving prey like shrimps because they have stinging cells that discharge automatically on contact.*

▲ ► *In the hydra, individual neurons making up the nerve net are shown. In the other diagrams, only the main nerves are shown, and in the cat a great many nerves have been omitted for clarity.*

## The sensitive plant

Plants have never evolved nerves. Since they are rooted to the spot, as it were, fast reactions are seldom advantageous. But plants do occasionally pass information from cell to cell by means of action potentials. Insect-eating plants, like the sundews, use such skills, as does the sensitive plant, Mimosa pudica, whose leaves collapse when touched.

If an insect brushes against one of the sundew's tentacles, the tentacle begins to bend inwards. But it cannot match the speed of movement seen in animals – the tentacle takes about three minutes to complete its movement. Only the extreme stickiness of the leaf surface detains the insect while this slow imprisonment occurs.

This act of aggression is controlled by action potentials, which are generated in response to the insect's struggles and which travel down to the tentacle's base. There they induce cells to change shape, and this produces movement in the tentacle. A similar system enables the leaves of Mimosa to react to touch. Special cells transmit action potentials to structures called pulvini, whose activities bring about the collapse of the leaf.

The action potentials of plants move more slowly (at about two or three centimeters per second) and last longer (10–30 seconds in the sundew) than their animal equivalents, but the effect is much the same: an all-important message is transmitted by a wave of electricity.

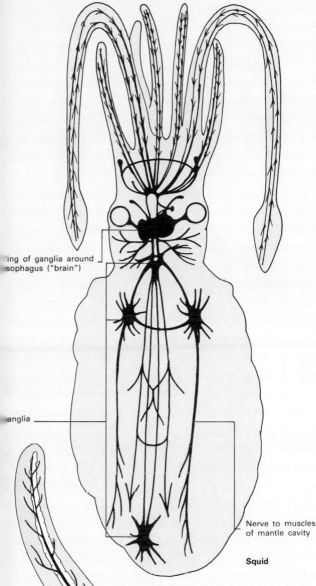

ring of ganglia around
sophagus ("brain")

ganglia

Nerve to muscles
of mantle cavity

**Squid**

## The nervous system

The humblest creatures with a nervous system are the cnidarians – the jellyfish, sea anemones and their allies. These animals are equipped with a net of nerve cells, dispersed throughout the body. Impulses can travel around the net in all directions and along many different routes, although there are often "through-conducting pathways", which convey important messages at a faster rate. In general, however, conduction is slow, and often localized – only strong nervous impulses affect the whole animal. Nevertheless, this type of nervous system is adequate for creatures that are radially symmetrical and need to move only slowly. Despite their sluggishness, predatory cnidarians are able to capture fast-moving animals, thanks to specialized stinging cells (nematocysts) which are discharged automatically on contacting prey. These provide a quick response and immobilize the prey long before the cnidarian's tentacles have begun to move.

Most other animals have gone in for a more highly structured "central nervous system" where thousands, or millions, of neurons make multiple contacts with their fellows. In such systems, the neurons run alongside each other in nerves, and their cell bodies are grouped together in swollen areas, known as ganglia, where information is exchanged and responses are coordinated. In vertebrates, and many invertebrates, the whole system centers on nerve cords, made up of many separate but interlinked nerves. There may be a single nerve cord running the length of the body, as in vertebrates, or a pair of cords linked by regular cross-connections, resembling the rungs of a ladder. Whatever the differences in detail, the basic system is the same in all cases: messages are conducted along specialized high-speed links, both towards the central nervous system from sensory organs, and away from it to specific targets, such as muscles or glands.

Any animal that moves around at reasonable speed needs to have a front end which always goes forward first, and which carries the major sensory organs. Inevitably this produces a tendency for the ganglia at the front end to become enlarged, and assume overall control of the animal's activities. Through being near the sense organs, this "cerebral ganglion" can effect a coordinated response to incoming signals with the least possible delay.

◄ *The nerve net of* **Hydra** *is the most primitive type of nervous system. The flatworm shows more centralization, with a ladder-like nervous system, and distinct cerebral ganglia. Insects have a more centralized system still, and a well-developed brain. But there are also ganglia in each segment, which have a great deal of autonomy. For example, wing and leg movements can be produced by the thoracic ganglia alone. Cephalopod mollusks such as the squid also have a highly developed nervous system, but it is not based on one central nerve cord, and its brain is a ring of ganglia around the esophagus. The process of encephalization is most highly developed in vertebrates, such as the cat.*

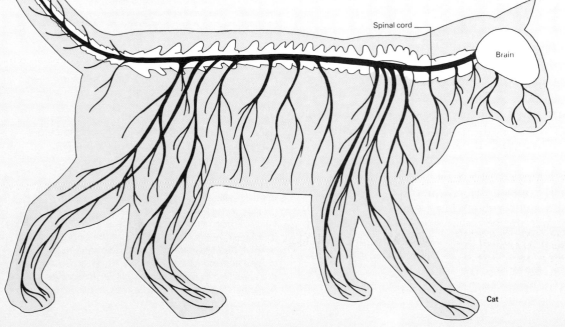

Spinal cord

Brain

**Cat**

## The brain

Increased development of the cerebral ganglia – a process known as "encephalization" has occurred independently in the evolutionary history of many different animal groups. In some, notably the vertebrates, the process has continued to produce a large and complex brain which is responsible for much of the animal's behavior. Our own brain contains about 10 billion cells, linked by an estimated 10,000 billion synapses, and not suprisingly, it is the least understood part of the body. However, the specialization of different areas for different tasks is quite well documented. Some centers in the brain are involved in the task of interpreting information received from sense organs, each area being devoted to a specific sense organ, while others control bodily movements. In addition to these sensory and motor areas, there are areas devoted to the regulation of physiological events, to sexuality, to emotions and to motivation. Much information about the vertebrate brain has come from electrical recordings made by implanting electrodes into various animals.

But complex human abilities, such as memory, language, judgement and conceptual thought, are much more difficult to study. An important technique focuses on specific defects caused by damage to certain areas of the brain. For example, the various regions involved in speech have been studied by these methods, and separate areas identified, some involved in word recognition or association, others in the actual mechanics of speech. Interestingly, these areas are not arranged together on the brain, but are some distance apart.

The workings of memory have proved particularly difficult to study. Scientists have traditionally pursued three ideas: memories could be stored as patterns of electrical activity, they could be encoded chemically in the structure of large molecules, or they could be the result of changes in and around the all-important synapses of the brain. Many scientists now favor some version of the third idea. For example, some recent experiments show that the nature of certain synapses can be altered by progressive unmasking of receptor sites for neurotransmitters. The understanding of memory has benefited from the study of lower animals, such as the sea hare, a gastropod mollusk. This beast shows a simple reflex of withdrawing its gill when a structure called the siphon is touched. Repeated stimulation dulls the response, but this process of "habituation" can be broken by an electric shock or other painful stimulus, which sensitizes the animal for some time. These processes are simple forms of learning, and experiments have shown that changes in the ion channels around the synapse between sensory nerve and motor nerve are responsible. Habituation makes the calcium channels at the tip of the sensory axon admit less calcium when an action potential arrives. This reduces the amount of neurotransmitter released, with the effect that the gill-withdrawal response becomes muted. By contrast, sensitization blocks potassium channels in the axon. These normally let potassium ions out of the neuron after the action potential has passed, and help to restore the resting (negative) charge inside the cell more quickly. Blocking them, therefore, makes the action potential last longer. That, in turn, allows more calcium to enter the cell, where it causes more neurotransmitter to be released across the synapse, amplifying the effect of the sensory neuron's signal. This change in the ion channels is produced by another neuron, known as the facilitator, which synapses onto the sensory neuron, and produces its effect via the release of the widely used "messenger" substance, cyclic AMP.

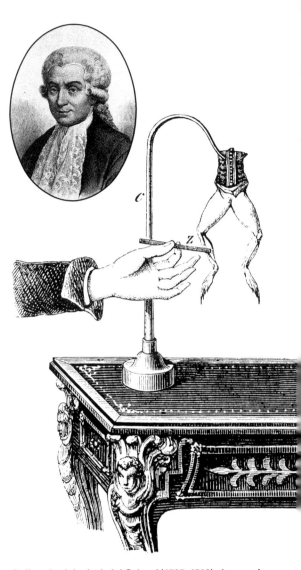

▲ *Italian physiologist Luigi Galvani (1737–1798) pioneered the study of electrical phenomena in animals. His famous experiments on frogs' legs, in which he persuaded muscles to twitch by a variety of methods (including electrical stimulation using the current generated by a flash of lightning striking a lightning conductor), paved the way for modern neurophysiology.*

### Reflexes

*Simple nervous reactions called reflexes are seen even in creatures with a central nervous system and a well-developed brain. They rely on them for routine nervous control of the body. In humans, the well-known knee jerk reflex, in which a tap below the knee produces a straightening of the leg, depends on just two neurons. The sensory nerve cell responds to the stimulus of the tap and carries its message to the spinal cord. Here it synapses directly with the motor nerve that causes the muscle to twitch and the leg to kick. Reflexes may involve more than two neurons, and some are even mediated by the lower brain, but the important point is that they operate as self-contained circuits, whose action is determined by the way the neurons are wired up to one another. Nevertheless, in humans, at least, some reflexes can be brought under conscious control with practice.*

# Movement

## 24

*The three mechanisms of movement...Types of muscle...Elasticity – the perfection of the flea... How microorganisms move...PERSPECTIVE...Insect flight...Recording movement...The effects of size... Unique rotary mechanisms*

Although movement is a characteristic of all living matter, it plays its major role in the life of animals. All animals use movement both to exploit their external environment, and to control their internal medium. They employ three different mechanisms to do so, namely ameboid motion, the beating of cilia and flagella, and the contraction of muscle. All three have features in common, in that they depend on similar contractile proteins and a similar source of energy, but there are many differences beween their modes of operation.

The contraction of vertebrate muscle, achieved by actin and myosin, is the best understood of these mechanisms ( page 139). All vertebrate muscle has the same basic action, but there are two types, "smooth" and "striated". Smooth muscle is used where long, slow contractions are needed to control internal activities, for example in the walls of the intestines and blood vessels. Striated muscle (so called because of its striped appearance under the microscope, which is produced by the very regular overlapping arrangement of actin and myosin molecules within it) is used for all movements associated with the skeleton. Heart muscle is also striated, but is highly specialized for rhythmic pumping activity.

Even within skeletal muscles there are different types of fibers, specialized for different tasks. "Tonic" (or "slow-twitch") fibers contract slowly, and can maintain low-force contractions for long periods. They are red in color as they contain a large supply of myoglobin, a protein which is similar to hemoglobin and which stores oxygen within the muscle. Tonic fibers give only a small contraction when stimulated, but if they are stimulated often their response increases. They are ideal for the job of maintaining body posture.

By contrast, "twitch" (or "fast-twitch") fibers contract rapidly, but generally fatigue easily. They contain only small amounts of myoglobin, so they are pale or white in color, and are often used anaerobically. They give an "all or none" response to stimulation, and are particularly suited to short bursts of rapid movement.

In practice, the muscles of mammals usually contain a mixture of both types of fiber, the mix balanced to the precise function of the muscle. But in some fish which swim constantly, such as tuna, the red and white fibers are found in separate blocks of muscle. When cruising at a steady pace they use only the red muscles. If a short burst of high-speed swimming is needed, the fish brings the white muscle blocks into operation. Several species of fast-swimming squid have a comparable arrangement, their swimming muscles being organized into layers of white and red muscle.

With the exception of heart muscle, which has its own inherent rhythm, and some insect flight muscles, all these types of muscle follow the rule that one nerve impulse results in one contraction. They are therefore called synchronous muscles.

**Synchronous flight**

◄▼ *Synchronous flight muscles operate the wings directly, the outer muscle pulling the wing down, and the inner one pulling it back up, via a lever. They cannot beat as fast as asynchronous muscles.*

Synchronous flight muscle

Exoskeleton of thorax

**Asynchronous flight**

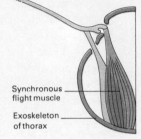

◄▼ *Asynchronous flight muscles work by changing the shape of the thorax. The inner muscle bands, shown here in cross section, contract horizontally, shortening the thorax.*

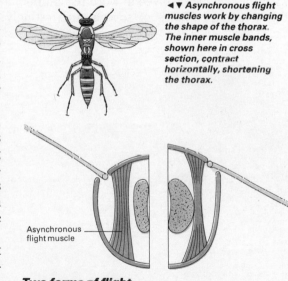

Asynchronous flight muscle

### Two forms of flight

*Some insects fly with such rapid wing beats (of up to 1,000 cycles per second) that the normal triggering mechanism will not cope. They include the bees, wasps, flies and beetles, all of which have flight muscles with a unique way of sustaining rapid contractions. Known as asynchronous or fibrillar muscles, their most significant feature is that if they are stretched by an outside force, this stimulates their contraction. Within the insect's thorax, two groups of these muscles work in opposition to each other. The groups contract in turn, distorting the exoskeleton of the thorax and thereby causing the other set to stretch. Thus the contraction of one set indirectly stimulates the contraction of the other. This sets up a rhythmic distortion of the thorax which in turn moves the wings. Just one nerve impulse every 40 cycles is sufficient to keep the oscillation going.*

*The cheetah could break the speed limit on most roads, at 110 kilometers per hour*

### The eye of the camera

Although much has been learnt about how animals move by studying their anatomy, the most useful tools for investigating locomotion are photography and cinematography. Two men who are considered pioneers of the motion picture were in fact applying the art to the study of animal movement. They were the French physiologist Étienne Marey (1830-1904) and an English photographer Eadweard Muybridge (also 1830-1904).

Marey developed a hand-held device known as a photo-gun, whereas Muybridge used a battery of cameras alongside a horse-racetrack with the shutter of each camera triggered by a trip wire running across the track. As a horse ran along the track, it triggered each camera in turn.

With the development of high speed cinematography these devices have been superseded, and it is now possible to analyze exremely rapid movements. By looking at film of a flea jumping, which was shot at 3,500 frames per second, biologists have worked out just how it can jump 50 times the length of its own body. The camera has helped give an understanding of many other movements too, ranging from the beating of cilia to the running of the cheetah.

▼ *Muybridge's sequence pictures of horses showed that all four legs leave the ground once during each stride. The cheetah, by contrast, has two airborne movements per stride, one with legs outstretched. Its low weight and flexible spine give it the edge over the horse, despite the fact that the horse has longer legs. The cheetah takes 7 strides for every 5 strides by the horse, and can travel 60 percent faster.*

### Movements compared

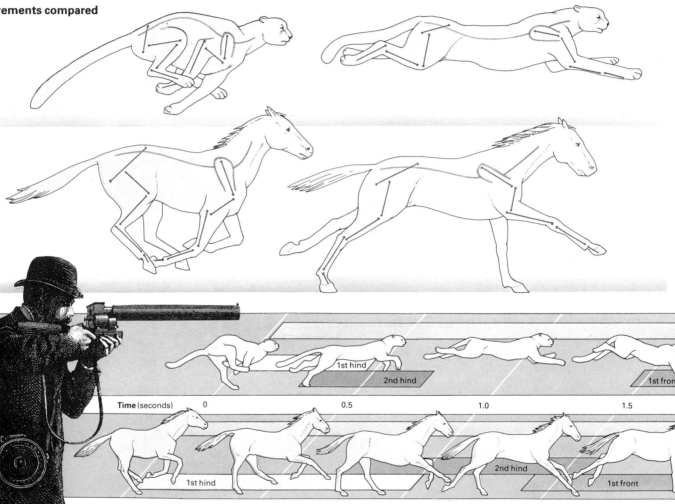

| Time (seconds) | 0 | 0.5 | 1.0 | 1.5 |

◀ *Étienne Marey was a physiologist who studied animal motion. He developed a device called a "fusil photographique" (photo-gun) which would take a series of 12 photographs in one second, on a revolving plate.*

▶ *An elastic tendon in the horse's leg stores energy for more efficient running. Impact with the ground stretches the tendon, and its contraction, as the foot leaves the ground, gives extra impetus to the leg.*

### Tendons in a horse

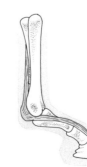
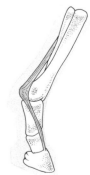

Tendon

## Legs compared

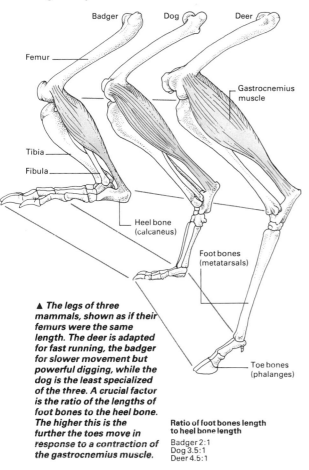

Badger  Dog  Deer

Femur

Gastrocnemius muscle

Tibia

Fibula

Heel bone (calcaneus)

Foot bones (metatarsals)

Toe bones (phalanges)

▲ The legs of three mammals, shown as if their femurs were the same length. The deer is adapted for fast running, the badger for slower movement but powerful digging, while the dog is the least specialized of the three. A crucial factor is the ratio of the lengths of foot bones to the heel bone. The higher this is the further the toes move in response to a contraction of the gastrocnemius muscle.

Ratio of foot bones length to heel bone length
Badger 2:1
Dog 3.5:1
Deer 4.5:1

## Skeletons and joints

Muscle can be effective only if it can pull on some form of fairly rigid skeleton. This can be inside the body, or on its surface, and it can be made of bone, cartilage, shell or any other nonflexible material. Even a fluid-filled tube will serve as a skeleton if the fluid is under sufficient pressure to make it rigid. Such fluid-filled or "hydrostatic" skeletons are found in annelids and echinoderms.

Hydrostatic skeletons have an inherent flexibility, but other skeletons, whether internal or external, need to be articulated by means of flexible joints. They form a system of levers and pulleys, the skeletal elements which form the limbs pivoting at the joints, and being pulled by muscles. These elements are held together by means of extremely tough but elastic materials which allow restricted movement only. Vertebrate bones are connected by means of ligaments made of the fibrous protein collagen (♦ page 137), while insects use a rubber-like protein called resilin.

Many types of movement use elastic materials to store energy. A running vertebrate uses a great deal of energy in repeatedly accelerating and decelerating its limbs. Stretched tendons (the links between muscles and bones) have elastic properties and can store this energy. When they recoil, energy is released. This occurs in the Achilles tendon of a human runner, just before the foot leaves the ground, helping to lift it clear. The same tendon in kangaroos reduces the work done by the leg muscles when bounding by about 40 percent. The flea uses elasticity to perfection. Its enormous leap is powered not by muscle at all, but by releasing energy from compressed resilin, rather like a catapult. Resilin is as near to the ideal as one can get in rubber-like materials, and can deliver 97 percent of its stored energy. Unlike muscle, it works just as effectively at low temperatures as at high ones, which is undoubtedly an advantage to the flea.

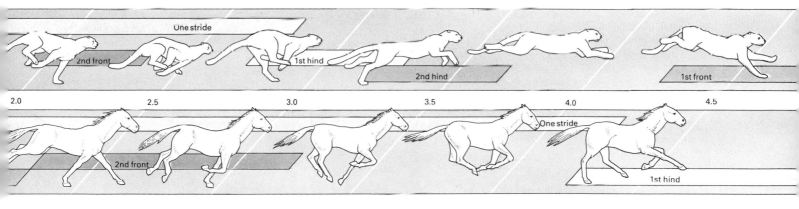

One stride

2nd front

1st hind

2nd hind

1st front

2.0   2.5   3.0   3.5   4.0   4.5

2nd front

One stride

1st hind

## A joint on a spider's leg

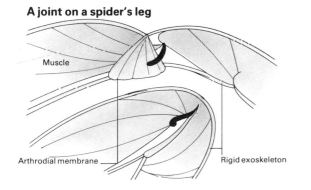

Muscle

Arthrodial membrane

Rigid exoskeleton

◄ Arthropods have a rigid external skeleton made of protein and chitin (♦ page 79) which, like the vertebrates' internal skeleton, provides something solid for the muscles to pull against. A more flexible covering, the arthrodial membrane, replaces the exoskeleton at the joints. In the joint shown here, linked rings of arthrodial membrane fan out as the spider's leg is extended, then telescope together as the joint is bent.

### "Clamming up"

Joints are usually operated by two sets of muscles working in opposition to each other, so that movements may be reversed. Some muscles, however, work singly, and are opposed by the action of elastic materials.

The two halves of a bivalve mollusk shell, for example, are closed by the contraction of a very strong muscle, called the adductor muscle. This works in opposition to a pad of elastic protein adductin, which is situated at the hinge of the shell. When the muscle relaxes this pad of adductin releases its stored energy, which makes the two halves of the shell spring open.

*Whether walking, burrowing, swimming or flying, efficient movement demands special adaptations*

### The effects of size

The blue whale may weigh over 100 tonnes, and a single-celled ciliate only 0·1µg. Both share the same environment, the sea, and both are swimmers, but the laws of physics create quite different problems for movement at these two extremes of size. The forces which act on a body in a fluid depend on the way the fluid flows over it, and this in turn depends to a great extent on the linear dimensions of the body. When moving through a fluid, an organism drags some of the fluid along with it, and the viscosity of the fluid causes even more fluid to be dragged along as well. For a small slow-moving organism like a ciliate, the effects of viscosity are paramount. The action of a cilium beating in water is rather like that of an oar in molasses. For larger, faster swimmers like fish and whales, the effects of viscosity are minimal, and the resistance of water is the main force to be overcome.

Viscosity is also an important consideration for very small flying animals like the fruit fly. Air, like water, is viscous, and the same principle applies, so the wings of a fruit fly, for example, are less effective at generating lift than those of larger insects, due to the drag caused by a thick boundary layer of air. The problem becomes so acute at very small size that one minute wasp, Encarsia, which weighs only 0·03mg, employs a special mechanism to generate lift. It holds its wings upright and clapped together behind its back, then rapidly flings them open. By doing so about 400 times per second it creates a circular vortex of air which provides sufficient lift for it to hover.

At the other end of the size spectrum, the resistance of air creates enormous stresses for a large flapping wing, and yet bones strong enough to withstand these stresses would make the animal too heavy to fly. The largest airborne animal that ever lived was a pterosaur, Quetzalcoatlus, whose remains were discovered in 1975. Given its enormous wingspan of 10m, it seems unlikely that Quetzalcoatlus was an active flier. It was probably a gliding animal, depending on thermals to get aloft.

▲ A frog leaps vertically from its pond. These amphibians are specialized for jumping. As well as long well-muscled legs they have a shorter, more compact body than other amphibians, such as newts, and they have also lost their tails.

◀ Millipedes are specialized for burrowing, and thus have short legs, making them stronger than the centipedes. Wave-like movements of the legs pass along the body, and because many limbs are pushing together, they can propel the animal forward through the soil with considerable force.

▶ A lacewing becomes airborne. Taking off is one of the most demanding aspects of flight.

*The squid and cuttlefish "invented" jet propulsion five hundred million years ago*

## Jet propulsion of the squid

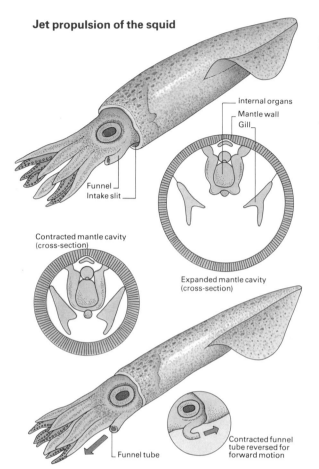

Internal organs
Mantle wall
Gill
Funnel
Intake slit

Contracted mantle cavity
(cross-section)

Expanded mantle cavity
(cross-section)

Funnel tube

Contracted funnel
tube reversed for
forward motion

◄ **The principle of jet propulsion in cephalopods, such as the squid, is simple. They first enlarge a muscular-walled cavity, the mantle cavity, which fills up with water entering through narrow intake slits. The funnel, which was previously closed, then opens, while the intake slits close. Muscles in the mantle cavity wall contract, forcing a narrow jet of water out through the funnel – the only way it can leave. Because the funnel opening is small, the jet of water is very powerful, and sends the animal shooting off in the opposite direction. The whole procedure of expansion and contraction is repeated rhythmically to maintain swimming momentum. The muscle contractions are stimulated by nerve cells with remarkably thick axons, allowing nerve impulses to travel very quickly (♦ page 200).**

▼ **The "movement" of a stinkhorn fungus fruiting body, photographed at hourly intervals. It reaches its full size, of 10–20cm, in a mere four hours. This is achieved by expansion of the basal tissues, initially compact and fleshy, into a spongy, hollow stalk.**

### Jet propulsion

*Five hundred million years ago the cephalopod mollusks took up jet propulsion, and have since developed it to become the fastest-moving invertebrates. Squid have been recorded leaving the ocean's surface, to escape predators, at 55 kilometers per hour, although their usual swimming speed is only about 20–30 kilometers per hour. Cephalopods propel themselves by ejecting a powerful jet of water from a tube known as the funnel. When swimming rapidly, they in fact move backward – a rather odd arrangement that recalls their ancestry from shelled cephalopods (♦ page 78). However, the funnel is flexible and and can be bent around through 180°, so that they can move forward too.*

*Jet propulsion is not confined to the cephalopods, although, interestingly enough, it has only been developed in aqueous environments, never in air. A dragonfly larva, Aeschna, swims by squirting water from its rectum. Scallops can attain sufficient speed to escape from starfish by rapidly closing their hinged shells, so that two jets of water are forced out, one each side of the hinge.*

### Plant movements

*Plants and fungi have no use for locomotion, but other types of movement do occur. In plants, there are two main types of movement, tropic and nastic. Tropisms are movements whose direction is directly related to the direction of a stimulus such as light, gravity, touch or certain chemicals. They initially help to orientate the plant correctly in space, with roots and stem both growing in the right direction. Nastic movements are those whose direction is independent of the direction of the stimulus which has caused them. Such movements are hinge-like, and are often responses to changes in light intensity, humidity or temperature. The opening of a flower when brought into a warm room is a thermo-nastic movement.*

*Both tropic and nastic movements can be brought about by growth differences on different sides of an organ, the concentration of growth hormones being greater on the one side than on the other. This is the mechanism which causes the flower-opening mentioned above.*

*The most dramatic plant movements of all, however, are the result of changes in turgor, the internal water pressure of plant cells. If the leaflets of the sensitive plant, Mimosa, are knocked or wounded, they respond by rapidly folding together, as water rushes out of the cells at their hinged joint. If there is no further stimulation, water gradually flows back into the cells and after 15–20 minutes the leaves return to their normal position.*

*The closing of the two halves of the leaf of a Venus's flytrap, after stimulation by an insect, depends on a similar mechanism. In this case there is a rapid increase in turgor in the cells on the underside of the midrib. Recovery, however, is much slower, to enable the plant to digest its meal. Similar mechanisms exist in other insectivorous plants, such as sundews.*

*It is also possible that contractile proteins play a part in plant movements, as in animals, but far less attention has been paid to their study in plants.*

## Ciliary and flagellar movement

Many protozoans and other single-celled eukaryotes move about by means of thin, hair-like projections from the cell surface, known as cilia and flagella. Some bacterial cells also have a process called a flagellum, but it is quite different from the flagellum, or undulipodium, of eukaryotic cells. It consists of just a single filament of protein, and moves in an entirely different way, the force being generated at the base, not in the flagellum itself (♦ page 212). The structure and mechanism of eukaryotic cilia and flagella are identical, but cilia are short (up to 15μm), and are often found in great numbers, while flagella tend to be much longer (100–200μm), and are usually found singly or in pairs.

Cilia have a rapid lashing movement, bending only at their base during their active stroke. This is followed by a recovery stroke in which the bend spreads along the cilium from base to tip. Flagella generate a wave along their length, or just at the tip, which usually travels in the opposite direction to that of the animal's movement. The wave does not just travel passively along the length of the flagellum, but originates at the parts which are moving.

Each cilium or flagellum consists of a set of protein microtubules (♦ page 160), arranged in a circle of nine pairs, called *doublets*, around a pair of single tubules at the center. Adjacent doublets are connected by two sets of regularly spaced protein side-arms, and a set of protein "spokes" connects each doublet to the central pair.

The mechanism of ciliary bending is not fully understood, but it seems to depend on the sliding action of the doublets relative to each other. As a cilium bends, the doublets on the inside of the curve slide away from the base of the cilium, toward the tip. They slide past the doublets on the other side, which remain fixed in position. One set of side-arms, made of the protein dynein, is believed to initiate this sliding by hydrolyzing ATP – a similar process to that which occurs in the proteins of mammalian muscle. The other set of side-arms limits the extent of the sliding, and further accessory proteins are responsible for its regulation.

Cilia and flagella are by no means confined to protozoans. The flagellum finds a role in propelling the sperm cells of animals and many lower plants, while the ability of cilia to move fluids is used in the internal organs of all metazoan animals, apart from arthropods and nematodes. In mammals cilia occur in the Fallopian tubes, where they help transport the ova, and also in the respiratory tract, removing mucus-trapped debris from the airways. One of the many harmful effects of tobacco smoke is to paralyze these cilia.

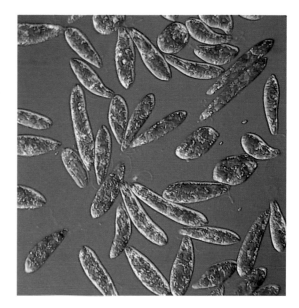

▲ ▶ ▼ *The cilia and flagella of eukaryotic cells have a distinctive structure made up of protein microtubules, and enclosed by an extension of the cell membrane. They are thought to bend by the microtubules actively moving past each other, in a similar way to muscle proteins (♦ page 139). The main difference between cilia and flagella is that the latter occur in ones or twos, are longer, and generate a wave-like movement that runs the full length of the flagellum, as in* Euglena *(above). Cilia, as seen in* Paramecium *(below left), are much more numerous, and have a beating movement.*

### Flagellar motion

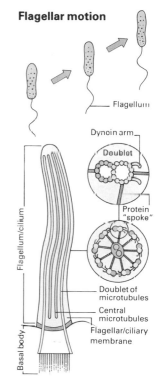

Flagellum

Dynein arm

Doublet

Protein "spoke"

Flagellum/cilium

Doublet of microtubules

Central microtubules

Flagellar/ciliary membrane

Basal body

### Ciliary motion

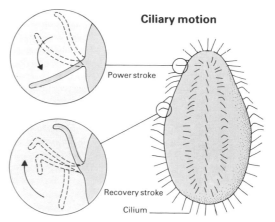

Power stroke

Recovery stroke

Cilium

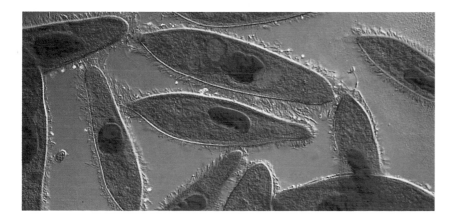

### The puzzling spirochetes

*The spirochetes are a group of long, slender, corkscrew-shaped bacteria that have a unique form of locomotion, paralleling the swimming movements of aquatic worms. The spirochetes have a semiflexible cell wall, which allows them to change their body shape. Between the cell wall and the cell membrane, is a band of parallel protein fibers, the axial filament, which appears to be derived from a set of bacterial flagella that have become internalized and secured at both ends. The number of separate fibers varies from two to 100, depending on the species. Somehow this axial filament produces the characteristic swimming action of the spirochetes – a complex set of movements in which the bacterium retains its tightly coiled shape but undergoes all sorts of contortions – wriggling, spinning, boring and looping its way through the liquid in which it lives.*

*How the axial filament produces these movements is still not understood, but presumably it rotates at the base, just as ordinary bacterial flagella do. The advantage of spirochete movement over the normal method is probably greatest when the viscosity of the external medium is high.*

### Spirochete movement

Fibres of axial filament

▲▶ *The axial filament powers the spirochetes' peculiar "swimming" movements. It is probably derived from a set of bacterial flagella, but how it works is not known.*

Nucleoid
Inner membrane
Cell wall
Cytoplasm
Axial filament

### Bacterial wheels

*Despite the great variety of movement systems in the living world, rotary mechanisms seem to be almost entirely absent. In higher animals, the problems of creating a rotary joint and supplying it with nerves and blood have clearly defeated the ingenuity of evolution. However, recent research has shown that there are indeed some organisms showing true rotary movement, albeit on a microscopic scale. These are bacteria, and the parts that rotate are flagella – whip-like threads of protein that extend from the bacterial cell wall.*

*The power to drive the flagella comes from a ring of proteins in the inner membrane. A gradient of $H^+$ ions across this membrane somehow causes the protein ring to spin round at up to 6,000 revolutions per minute. The flagellum is linked to this ring of proteins, but passes straight through the cell wall, so that its movement is not inhibited by it. Energy is needed to maintain the rotation, of course, and it is supplied in the form of ATP which powers the membrane pumps that maintain the $H^+$ gradient.*

### Ameboid movement

Many protozoans, and some other single cells, move in ameboid fashion, by constantly changing shape. Their cytoplasm flows forward in the direction of movement, forming what look like stubby legs, called pseudopodia, which are continually extended and retracted.

This type of movement, which appears so simple, is still not fully understood. It seems to depend on the ability of cytoplasm to make transitions between two states. In an amebal cell, an inner core of fluid endoplasm is surrounded by a layer of viscous gel-like ectoplasm. As the endoplasm streams toward the tip of a pseudopodium it congeals into ectoplasm, while elsewhere in the cell, ectoplasm is reverting to endoplasm. Cell biologists now believe that endoplasm is squeezed out of a pseudopodium by contraction of microfilaments made of the protein actin, found in abundance just below the cell membrane (◀ page 157). Actin is one of the contractile proteins found in muscle, and the mechanism of contraction may be the same.

### Ameboid movement

▶ *The amebae have given their name to "ameboid movement". A refinement of this gives them an effective way of feeding, by engulfing food particles (◀ page 171).*

Vacuole    Nucleus

Point of contact

Plasmasol or endoplasm (liquid)
Plasmagel or ectoplasm (solid)

Plasmagel turning to plasmasol, and contractions of actin filaments creating pressure

Plasmasol turning to plasmagel

New point of contact

### The rotary flagellum

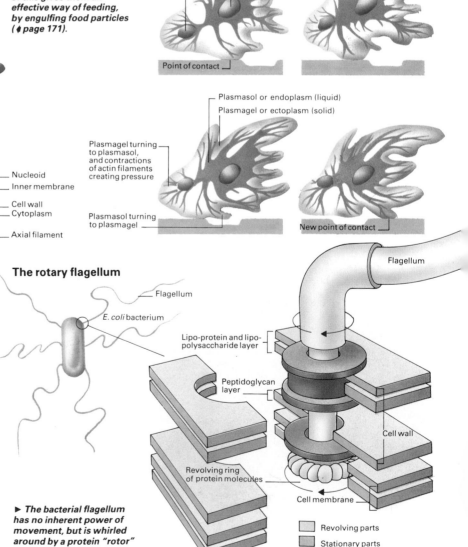

Flagellum

*E. coli* bacterium

Flagellum

Lipo-protein and lipo-polysaccharide layer

Peptidoglycan layer

Revolving ring of protein molecules

Cell wall

Cell membrane

▶ *The bacterial flagellum has no inherent power of movement, but is whirled around by a protein "rotor" at the base.*

☐ Revolving parts
☐ Stationary parts

# Senses

## 25

*How bacteria monitor their world...Sensory adaptation...What animals sense...Chemistry of sensation...Special adaptations of the eye...The senses of predators...Mental maps...PERSPECTIVE... Sensing magnetic fields...How animals navigate... Vibrations...Internal clocks...Ultrasound... Chemical messengers*

Even the humblest creatures monitor the world with the help of senses. Bacteria, for example, are attracted by certain chemicals dissolved in the surrounding water, such as sugars and amino acids, while they are repelled by others. The process is called chemotaxis. Senses like this must have been among the first to appear in evolution, for the earliest organisms living in the "biotic soup" (◀ page 144) would have needed to direct their motion toward food molecules and away from noxious chemicals.

The movements of a bacterium such as *Escherichia coli* depend on rotation of the whip-like threads known as flagella. When the flagella rotate counterclockwise, the cell moves forward, but every so often the flagella do an about-turn and spin clockwise, whereupon the bacterium experiences a sort of random motion called tumbling. Attractive chemical stimuli suppress tumbles and keep the bacterium on course, while unpleasant ones increase their frequency, thereby making a change of course more likely. This simple sensory response is accomplished with the help of a series of special molecules. These detect the original stimulus at the cell's surface and convey messages to the internal motors that power the cell's flagella.

An *E. coli* bacterium exposed to a steady level of a chemical attractant soon becomes insensitive to it, whereupon the rate of tumbling returns to normal. This important effect, which is called sensory adaptation, is caused by chemical modification of one of the proteins involved in the sensing process. Once the bacterium has adapted, only a rise in the concentration of the attractant will suppress tumbles. Eventually the cell adapts to that level too, and begins tumbling again. In this fashion, the bacterium tends to move up a gradient of concentration until it reaches the source of the chemical. Sensory adaptation ensures that it responds to changes rather than constancy – a fundamental property of all sensory systems.

## Ulterior motives

*Certain anaerobic bacteria can sense the Earth's magnetic field and align themselves on a north–south axis. However, their real interest is not in magnetism itself, but in gravity, which they cannot sense directly. Their strategy works because the lines of the Earth's magnetic field are inclined at an angle to the surface of the globe. In the northern hemisphere, bacteria are drawn towards magnetic north, and that response leads them downward – away from damagingly high levels of oxygen and toward the anoxic mud that is their normal home. Because of the nature of the Earth's magnetic field, bacteria from the southern hemisphere should turn toward magnetic south to achieve the same effect, and they have in fact been found to do this. The sensitivity of these bacteria to magnetism depends on a chain of tiny particles of magnetite (a magnetic oxide of iron) which they carry in their cells. This structure can turn them toward magnetic north or south in the manner of a compass needle.*

*Like magnetic bacteria, many other organisms respond to one type of stimulus simply because it is a reliable guide to some other feature of their environment. Such ulterior motives lie behind a plant's responses to gravity. The Earth's gravitational pull is of little direct interest to plants, but it points their roots toward water deep in the soil, and can guide shoots up toward the light.*

*In roots, the response begins in cells known as statocytes, which contain tiny grains of starch. If a seedling is laid on its side, the starch grains in the statocytes settle under gravity. This effect is eventually translated – by as yet unknown steps – into a change in hormone levels. As a result, the uppermost surface of the root grows faster than the lower surface and the root tip turns downward.*

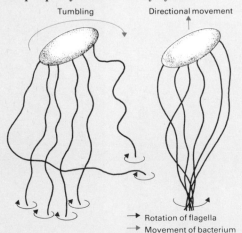

Tumbling    Directional movement

◀ **The simple response of Escherichia coli to chemical stimuli.**

▶ **Crustaceans such as the crayfish detect gravity with organs known as statocysts in their antennules. The statocyst is a chamber lined with sensory hairs, and containing grains of sand. These settle under gravity's pull, and the hairs record their position. If the sand is replaced with iron filings, and a strong magnet held above the crustacean, its perception of gravity is reversed and it will swim upside down.**

→ Rotation of flagella
→ Movement of bacterium

*Many animals have sensory powers that are unknown in human beings*

## A range of senses

Detection of chemicals plays an important part in the lives of advanced animals, as it does in bacteria, but in their quest for knowledge of the outside world, living things have learned to respond to a much greater array of stimuli. Many organisms are sensitive to light, or other forms of electromagnetic radiation, and perception of mechanical stimuli is also widespread. For example, organisms frequently respond to various vibrations such as sounds, as well as to touch, sustained pressure, acceleration and gravity. Knowledge of atmospheric humidity is potentially useful, while an awareness of temperature helps animals avoid dangerous extremes of heat or cold. Sensing the Earth's magnetic field provides cues that assist with navigation. Electrical fields are also full of information. Some fish find their way in murky waters by detecting disturbances in an electrical field that they themselves create. Others locate prey by monitoring the electrical activity of their victim's muscles. Organisms must also keep track of events taking place inside their own bodies. Damage to the tissues is registered as "pain", and an important group of mechanoreceptors regulate bodily movements by responding to the internal state of muscles. Other internal receptors monitor the composition of blood and other body fluids ( ◀ page 182).

## How do senses work?

In complex animals, sensing is the job of receptor cells, whose structure is often highly specialized. For example, visual cells contain stacks of membranes that house light-sensitive pigments, while cells that detect sound or other vibrations often bear special movable hairs. Their task is to transform a stimulus of a certain kind into an electrical signal suitable for sending to the central nervous system. Eventually that signal appears in the form of a train of impulses in a sensory nerve, the frequency of which reflects the strength of the stimulus.

How do cells achieve the initial phase of "transduction" – the generation of an electrical charge in response to a stimulus? Scientists have made a special study of one sort of visual cell in the eye's retina, known as the rod. It contains a pigment called rhodopsin, which changes its structure when it is struck by light. This change, to an "excited" state, sparks off a series of events. First, excited molecules of rhodopsin activate a protein called G-protein. This is then able to activate a second protein – an enzyme called a phosphodiesterase (PDE). The job of PDE is to break down a small messenger molecule called cyclic guanosine monophosphate (cGMP), which seems to influence the electrical charge inside the cell.

The rod's internal charge is governed by movements of ions through channels in its outer membrane ( ◀ page 199) and cyclic GMP appears to hold certain channels open as long as the cell is unilluminated. When light arrives, cyclic GMP is broken down, the channels close and the cell's voltage changes. That, in turn, influences the next cell in the chain that carries the message to the brain.

Although this chemistry may seem somewhat circuitous, it has an important advantage: amplification of the original signal. Every excited molecule of pigment activates several molecules of G-protein, each of which goes on to influence PDE. Scientists calculate that absorption of light by a single pigment molecule breaks down 10,000 molecules of cGMP in a tenth of a second. Rods have much in common with other receptors. G-proteins, for example, appear to be at work in the nose as well as in the eye.

▲ *The thin silvery line on the side of this dace is its lateral line, a sensory organ found in all fish, and in the larvae of amphibians. It detects water movements and pressure, by means of movable sensory hairs contained in a jelly-like matrix within cup-shaped structures (the cupulae). Hundreds of these cups link up to form the lateral line.*

▼ *A section through the retina of a mammal's eye, showing the two types of visual cell: rods and cones. The latter are specialized for color vision, and are less sensitive to low light intensities than the rods. Many nocturnal animals lack cones altogether. In diurnal animals they are generally concentrated in the fovea ( ◀ page 218).*

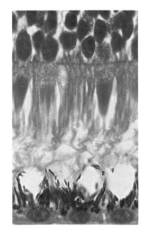

### Feeling vibrations

Our own sense of hearing is designed to detect airborne vibrations, but many creatures are sensitive to vibrations carried by other media. Males of a certain type of spider, which lives on banana plants, use vibrations to locate their mates. When the male detects the scent of a female, he vibrates his abdomen and legs. The plant transmits these movements, and the female picks them up – probably via her sensitive slit sensilla. She then issues a reply. The male eventually reaches the leaf upon which she is ensconced by monitoring vibrations of the plant's various leafstems and selecting the most promising direction.

Another activity in which vibrations are useful is the detection and capture of prey. Sand scorpions of the species Paruroctonus mesaensis hunt in the dark with immense precision, even when their insect victims are burrowing through the sand. Tests have revealed that the scorpion uses sensory hairs and slit sensilla on its legs to detect its prey. Just as we locate sounds by comparing time of arrival at each ear, the scorpion pinpoints its victim by monitoring differences in the time that the vibrations arrive at each of its eight legs.

### Pheromones

Smell plays an intriguing role in communications between members of the same species. Of special importance are signaling chemicals called pheromones, which can be divided into two main types. Primer pheromones influence the physiology of the receiver, often over a long time scale. For example, a pheromone in the urine of male mice can induce abortions in pregnant females who are not familiar with these males. By contrast, releaser pheromones exert more immediate effects on behavior. In mammals, they are often important in sex attraction and the marking of territorial boundaries.

The importance of smell can even extend to the recognition of individuals by their odorous "signatures" – distinctive personal smells under genetic control. Mice, for example, can discriminate between their fellows on the basis of smell. Those most closely related smell most alike, and since mice prefer to mate with a partner whose smell differs from their own, the result is that they avoid inbreeding. As tracker dogs can distinguish individual humans by scent, we may also have personal odorous signatures.

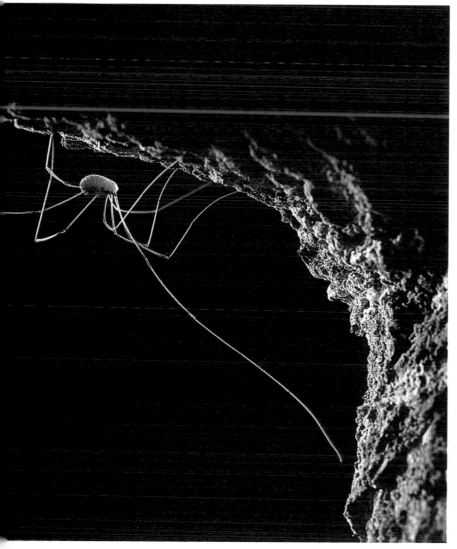

◄ A harvestman cautiously feels its way along a tree branch. One leg is greatly elongated for sensory purposes, and covered with touch-sensitive hairs. These are present on its other legs as well, but are more numerous on the elongated leg, which the arachnid uses much as an insect might use its antennae.

▼ Many female moths attract their mates by means of releaser pheromones, and, to detect these chemicals, the males are equipped with antennae of remarkable sensitivity, with up to 10,000 receptors each of which can respond to a single molecule of pheromone. Shown here are the antennae of the male atlas moth.

*A bee may see a flower in a completely different way from us*

▲ ▶ *A flower photographed under "visible light" (above) and ultraviolet light (right). Many flowers have patterns of lines leading to the nectaries which we cannot normally see, but which become obvious under ultraviolet illumination. These are probably useful to insects with their ultraviolet vision.*

▶ *Lions seen at night with the aid of an image intensifier, which magnifies each photon of light received to levels that the human eye can detect. Such pictures show that there is enough light at night to see quite clearly if the eyes are sufficiently sensitive – as those of many nocturnal animals are.*

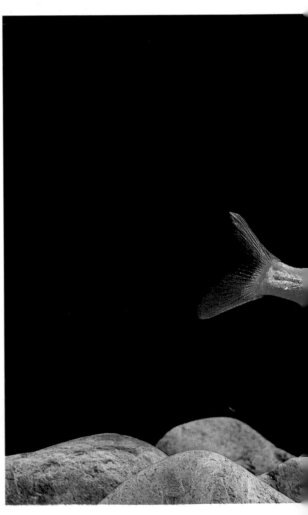

▼ *Blind characin fish from the underwater caves of Mexico. Many cave animals that live in permanent darkness lose their powers of sight. This is probably because the eye is a complex organ whose construction is an energy-expensive exercise. If it is no longer needed, natural selection favors its loss.*

▶ *The capercaillie's mating call has been described as a knocking sound, followed by a cork being pulled and a knife being ground. The human ear fails to appreciate the low-frequency sounds that harmonize with these odd noises. It is the infrasound component that carries over long distances.*

## Sensitivity

What determines the sharpness of the senses? At first sight, it may seem advantageous to be as sensitive as possible, but acute sensitivity would be an expensive luxury for many animals, and it could sometimes be a drawback. If human beings had an improved sensitivity to touch, for example, it might well make our skin crawl, while the background noise from our environment might intrude if we sharpened our sense of hearing. In these cases, further refinements are simply not advantageous.

Senses are often deliberately designed to respond only to a narrow spectrum of stimuli. Perhaps animals would be swamped with information if they were universally sensitive. The senses are rather like filters; they register inputs that are of particular interest, while rejecting others. For example, our eyes are only sensitive to a narrow segment of the electromagnetic spectrum – the part we call visible light. By contrast, many animals, such as certain birds and insects, see ultraviolet rays, and others can detect infrared radiation. Similar limitations attend our perception of sound. Some of our fellow creatures have different concerns; many small mammals for example, communicate via a range of very high-pitched whistles and pips – ultrasound – while pigeons may hear natural infrasounds, and use them in navigation (◗ page 222).

It may occasionally pay an animal to ignore certain types of information altogether. Octopuses, squid and their allies (the cephalopod mollusks) lack hearing organs, a rather puzzling defect in these otherwise advanced creatures. Some scientists believe that deafness may help them resist predators, such as toothed whales, which are thought to stun their victims with intensely loud sounds. No squid could escape the explosive power of a whale at close range, but deafness may protect them when these predators are a little way off, and give them the opportunity to escape.

## Measuring daylength

Many organisms must time reproduction or migration to coincide with certain times of the year, and in temperate regions they generally keep track of the changing seasons by monitoring daylength. In mammals, a part of the brain called the pineal gland plays a key role in the process. The gland secretes a hormone, melatonin, but only at night – it is controlled by information relayed from the eyes. The amount of hormone in the blood is therefore related to daylength, and provides a chemical signal to other tissues. Certain creatures sense daylength with an additional photoreceptor in the brain. Birds have such a device in, or near, a part of the brain called the hypothalamus. Remarkably, it responds to the light that filters through the feathers and skull.

Plants are also readily influenced by daylength, especially in reproduction. For some species, short days induce flowering, while for others long days are required. However, it is the length of the dark phase of the daily cycle that seems to be the critical factor, because short nocturnal interruptions with bright lights will disrupt the normal response. Although scientists have yet to work out all the steps in the process, the light-sensitive pigment known as phytochrome is initially involved in the response, which culminates in changes in levels of hormones and induction of flowering.

## A sense of time

An awareness of time is important to many animals and plants. It allows them to regulate their activities to coincide with the most favorable moment, whether in the daily cycle of 24 hours, the lunar cycle of 28 days, or the yearly cycle of 365 days.

Plants and animals can use daylength changes to monitor the yearly cycle, but for shorter cycles – such as the switch from day to night – responding to changes as they happen is not enough. Living organisms need to be ready in advance, physiologically, to make the most of the opportunities available. So "biological clocks" have evolved that can keep time, independently of external signals. Left to themselves they are not all that precise, however, and need regular cues from outside to keep accurate time. Kept in constant darkness, a mouse will maintain its normal cycle – activity during the night and rest during the day – but its times of rising and retiring will get a little later every day. This approximate nature of the clock (which is reflected in the term "circadian rhythm" – circa diem means "about a day") is not necessarily a bad thing. The need to reset its clock every day enables the animal to adjust to changing daylength at different seasons of the year. A perfectly precise clock would leave the animal out of step with the real world.

Although circadian rhythms are much the most common, other internal clocks are known in the animal kingdom. Circalunar rhythms exist, lasting a lunar month, and circannual rhythms, lasting a year. These circannual rhythms have been studied in birds, and apparently prepare them for the breeding season before daylength changes can take effect. The question of how any of these clocks actually work is still unresolved.

*In the deep sea, some fish produce their own light to see by*

## Adaptation to the environment

An animal's senses must, of course, be tailored to suit its particular way of life. Although this is true of all senses, the special adaptations found in the eyes of a range of animals illustrate the point with particular clarity.

The first important consideration in the design of an eye is the time of day at which its owner is active. Eyes can be adjusted to deal with limited changes in brightness, but nocturnal animals must resort to special techniques. Often their eyes are equipped with extra-large pupils, which help them form relatively bright images at night, but can close up to protect the eye by day. There may also be a shiny layer behind the retina, as in the domestic cat. This layer, known as the tapetum, reflects any stray light passing through the retina, so that it has a second chance to fall on the visual cells. Both ploys improve the eye's chances of detecting low levels of light. But other techniques can be equally important. The nocturnal tawny owl, for example, is a hundred times more sensitive to light than the diurnal pigeon, but its superiority depends on the way its retina combines the signals from several adjacent receptor cells. This gives enhanced sensitivity, (though at the expense of detailed resolution), because groups of cooperating cells act as much larger "effective receptors". This is a common feature of the retina in nocturnal animals.

Some insects have evolved a special version of the compound eye for night vision. The compound eye is composed of thousands of separate optical units called ommatidia, each of which has its own lens and its own private view of the world. In day-flying insects each ommatidium acts in isolation. But certain nocturnal moths and beetles have improved on the basic design. In their eyes, groups of ommatidia can join forces to produce a bright overall image by overlapping their separate images of the outside world. Movable "screens" of pigment between the ommatidia keep them in isolation during the day, but withdraw to allow cooperative vision at dusk.

The eyes of diurnal animals are more concerned with discerning fine detail in the visual scene – an ability referred to as visual resolution, or acuity. For an eye to perceive two neighboring points of light as distinct entities, its images of the points must fall on receptors that are separated by at least one unilluminated cell. So an eye designed for high acuity should have rather small, independent visual cells – in contrast to the eye of nocturnal creatures. The large eyes of the diurnal birds of prey are prime examples of eyes that are geared to high resolution.

Acuity and sensitivity seem incompatible, but eyes can obtain the best of both worlds by some ingenious compromises. For example, different parts of the eye can be specialized for different tasks. As in the human retina, a central fovea, where acuity is high, may be accompanied by a more light-sensitive periphery, with lower acuity.

An animal's visual pigments must also be adapted to the environment, and fish provide many examples of this. For instance, fish living in blue waters tend to lack red-sensitive visual pigments. For those that migrate from blue ocean water to redder rivers, such as the salmon and eels, this could create problems, but they overcome these by altering their visual pigments to coincide with their migrations. The skipjack tuna, which views its prey from beneath, has a visual pigment that is maximally sensitive to the general color of its marine environment. This arrangement intensifies the contrast between silhouetted prey and surrounding water.

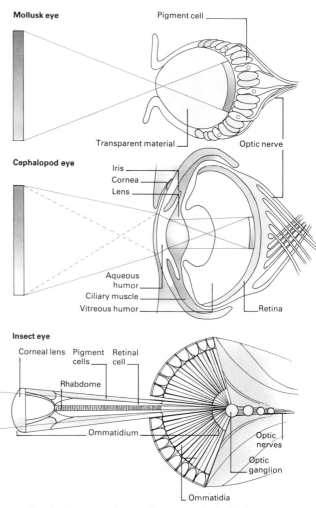

▲ *The simplest type of eye, as in most mollusks (1), has no lens. In cephalopod mollusks, this has evolved into a sophisticated structure (2) that is remarkably similar to the vertebrate eye. An insect's eye (3), though also highly developed, has a very different construction.*

▼ *An African hare, with light reflecting from its tapetum.*

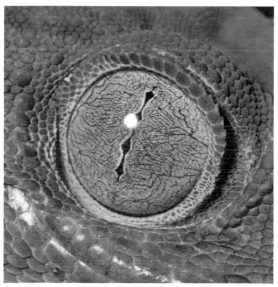

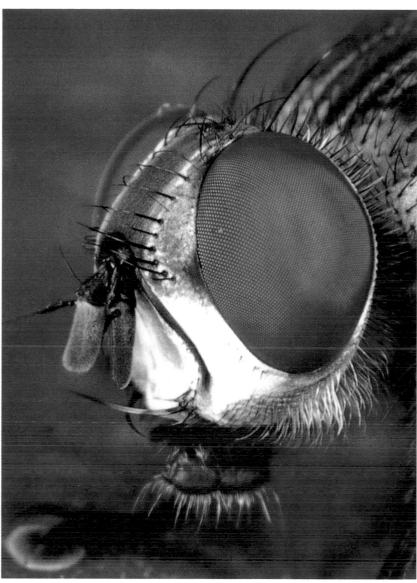

▲ Vertebrates can operate in a range of light intensities, by having a very sensitive retina and adjusting the amount of light admitted through a pupil. This reaches its height of development in the geckos (center), whose pupils close to leave just a few pinhole-like openings. In diurnal insects like flies (right) the ability to adjust to different light intensities is more limited, and is achieved by the movement of pigment within the ommatidia.

▶ Red light is entirely absent in the deep sea, and many small deep-sea animals are colored red for camouflage. This predatory deep-sea fish has light organs on its head that emit red light for the detection of such animals.

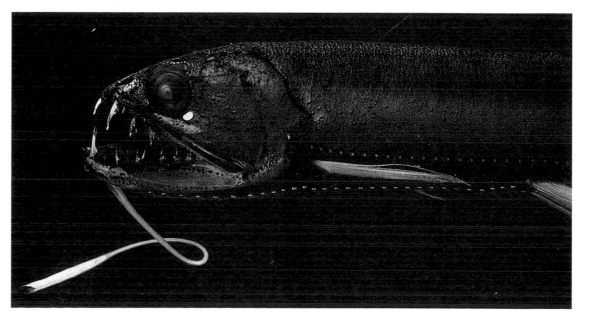

## Specific sensory tasks

The senses underpin many of the most impressive feats of animal behavior. Nowhere is this more dramatically illustrated than in the lives of predatory creatures. For example, certain snakes, such as pit vipers and pythons, detect warm-blooded prey by sensing emissions of infrared radiation or "heat". The rattlesnake is one exponent of the art. Its face bears a pair of special structures called pit organs, each of which has a thin membrane, only $15\mu$m thick, inside it. This flimsy sheet of tissue houses sensitive heat detectors, and since the pits have rather narrow openings, they act a little like pinhole cameras, forming dim, blurred images of infrared emmisions from the outside world. This system tells the snake the position of a warm-blooded bird or mammal, even in complete darkness.

Predators' senses are often extraordinarily sensitive. The barn owl, for example, is a nocturnal hunter that relies on a fine sense of hearing to locate its prey. It monitors small differences in the times that sounds arrive at its two ears, as well as differences in loudness. These subtle cues enable it to pinpoint sound sources with great accuracy. In addition, the opening of the left ear is set higher on the head than that of the right and this helps it determine whether sound comes from above or below.

Other hunters use sound in a rather different way. A range of creatures – including bats, a few birds, and many whales and dolphins – listen for the echoes of their own voices and use them to gather information about obstacles and potential prey. Bats estimate the distances of objects by monitoring the time it takes for echoes to return, or, in some cases, by the nature of the echoes themselves. Echolocation permits them to detect objects, even very small ones, and home in on them with no other clues at all as to their whereabouts.

Bats use sounds of extremely high pitch for echolocation purposes. Our hearing stretches to 20kHz (20,000 cycles per second), while their calls can reach to 200kHz. Because they have a short wavelength, these sounds can convey information about very small obstacles. The immensely skillful greater horseshoe bat, for example, is aware of threads as narrow as 0·05mm in diameter. Not surprisingly, the bat's sonar is an effective detector of potential meals, whether they be airborne insects or fish making ripples at the water's surface.

Chemoreception also plays a large part in the search for food. For animals that live on land, a distinction can usually be drawn between smells, which are borne on air currents and are detected at a distance from their source, and tastes, which are only perceived on contact. But the distinction breaks down in aquatic animals such as fish. Moreover, the taste buds of fish are distributed all over the body, so they must provide an unimaginably panoramic taste sensation.

◄ **This python has a row of heat-sensitive pit organs in pits along its upper jaw. They can detect a warm-blooded animal even in complete darkness.**

► **It was once thought that barn owls, too, could detect infrared radiation. But by using a cold "bait" in a lightproof room, it was shown that they hunted by sound. Only when the bait was moved (by pulling on a string) did the owl pounce.**

◄ *Most spiders have six or eight simple eyes (not compound eyes, as in insects and crustaceans). In jumping spiders (left) two of the pairs are enlarged to give good forward vision for hunting. The other two are much smaller and located on the animal's back.*

▶ *Lazzaro Spallanzani (1729–1799), the Italian naturalist who discovered that hearing is the crucial sense in bats.*

### Echolocating bats — a history

*The bat's remarkable nocturnal activities were once attributed to Satanic possession, but we now know that they merely rest on a devilishly complex feat of sensory physiology. Lazzaro Spallanzani (1729–1799) began the scientific study of their echolocation. He discovered that although bats could find their way around in complete darkness, they began to falter when he tied little hoods over their heads. Spallanzani first thought that this showed that some form of vision was at work, but later he discovered that a blind bat could fly, whereas one with its ears plugged could not. In 1920, the British physiologist Hamilton Hartridge proposed that a form of echolocation, based on the production of very high-pitched sounds, was involved, and his suggestions were proved correct by the American biologist Donald Griffin and his colleagues in 1938.*

# Navigation

### Navigation

Salmon, eels, turtles and many birds migrate vast distances, crossing oceans and continents to reach their breeding areas. Their powers of navigation depend, primarily, on the ability to set a compass course and stick to it – this, combined with an instinctive knowledge of how long to keep going before changing direction, or stopping, is the initial basis of navigation in the majority of birds. Day-flying birds use the Sun as their main compass, compensating automatically for its daily motion across the sky by reference to a biological clock (◊ page 217). This is known as time-compensated solar navigation. But not all birds migrate by day. Many that are normally diurnal choose to migrate at night and they mostly steer by the stars. Those in the northern hemisphere use the Pole Star as an indicator of north and fly away from it to go south.

Many animals are also equipped with a magnetic compass, which comes into its own when the sky is completely overcast. Dolphins, birds, mice, snails, moths, algae and even bacteria are among the creatures to display this "sixth sense". Moreover, experiments suggest that birds must first calibrate their solar compass against the magnetic one, before using the former. Scientists do not yet know how the magnetic sense operates, but they have found deposits of magnetic material in the pigeon's skull and in its neck muscles.

Setting a compass course is one thing, but finding the way home from a strange place is an ability of a different order. Birds, the supreme navigators, need to be able to do this because they run the risk of being blown off-course during their long journeys. And the same ability has provided amusement for generations of pigeon racers. But how is it done?

Birds such as petrels, displaced thousands of miles from their nests, are known to set off in the right direction and fly straight home. To do this, starting from an unfamiliar place, a bird must be able to work out where it is, and the direction from there to home. It was once believed that birds used the Sun for this, but to do so they would need to compare the Sun's movements across the sky with those remembered from home, and register minute differences between the two. Apart from extraordinary powers of computation, this would require a biological clock of phenomenal precision. The consensus of opinion now holds this to be impossible, and some other basis for homing has been sought. The main candidate is a map based on features of the Earth's magnetic field, but how this might work is not known.

Nearer home, and over more familiar terrain, however, maps based on remembered features might be of importance. The map need not necessarily be a visual one. For terrestrial creatures particularly, and for those few birds with a good sense of smell, a map based on patterns of scents could play a part. It has also been suggested that a map based on infrasound could be used. These exceedingly loud but low pitched sounds can be generated by air masses colliding with mountain ranges or stormy seas breaking on a shore. Infrasounds travel enormous distances so they could be particularly useful in navigation.

### Polarized light

Even nocturnal migrants can use the Sun to set a compass course, by observing the pattern of polarized light in the evening sky before setting out on their travels. Light consists of waves which usually vibrate in any plane. If vibrations are restricted to one plane only, the light is said to be polarized. When sunlight is reflected from a clear sky, it is polarized in a way that depends on the position of the Sun. So if animals can detect polarized light, they can get their bearings from the sun, even at dusk. Some day-flying animals, such as bees, also use polarized light for navigation.

▲ *Dolphins have been shown to follow submarine escarpments during migration. They may use their powers of echolocation to discern the shape of the seabed.*

▼ *Migrating geese fly in family parties, so the offspring benefit from their parents' experience, but for many other birds, the young make their first migration alone, guided only by instinct.*

▲ Spiny lobsters living in shallow coastal waters of the western Atlantic migrate to deeper water for the winter. The animals travel in single file, each one keeping contact with the one ahead, by placing its antennae on the other's abdomen. Exactly how they navigate is unknown, but they may be able to sense the direction of water currents. It has recently been shown that they also have a magnetic sense.

▶ Navigation is more easily studied in flightless birds because their exact course can be recorded. Some Adelie penguins were taken to a flat featureless area many miles from their nesting colony. On being released, the penguins looked around them and, if the Sun was out, set off in the right direction. But when it clouded over they wandered at random. This is true navigation using the Sun – something that is still not understood.

### By the light of the Moon

One potential source of compass information is the moon, but this has apparently not been exploited by birds or mammals, although some invertebrates do use it. Sandhoppers, for example, must be able to get back to the sea if they are blown inland, and experiments with an artificial light source, have demonstrated that they use the Moon to set their course. Some from the west coast of Italy were taken to the east coast, and released near the shore on a moonlit night. Instead of going toward the sea, however, they moved inland, showing that they were following a compass direction appropriate to home.

## Mapping the world

In advanced animals, certain senses can develop to the point where they provide a continually updated picture of external space. For humans, vision plays this role. Not all of the information it gathers is of immediate importance in survival, but a general awareness of the surroundings helps us predict likely events and react accordingly.

Visual information is processed by the visual cortex of the brain, where the cells are laid out in the form of a two dimensional "map" of the retina. Points close to one another in outside space are dealt with by neighboring cells in the visual cortex. However, parts of the map are drawn to different scales. The important area at the center of the visual field, the fovea, is given a far greater share of the map than its size alone warrants.

Sensory maps are widespread among other animals. For example, the brain of the barn owl holds a representation of outside space derived from its sense of hearing, while all mammals have maps for the sense of touch. Touch maps depict the body's surface and, as with the visual map, they are distorted to reflect the relative importance of various areas, such as the touch-sensitive whiskers of the muzzle.

The rattlesnake's brain also has a map for its infrared sense. This is organized along the same lines as its visual map – an arrangement that may enable the brain to compare inputs from both senses for any region of space. Biologists have found a variety of nerve cells that link the two. Some will respond to infrared stimuli or visual stimuli, while others will only react if both inputs are provided. The latter cells are stimulated most effectively by warm, mobile objects – hence their name of "mouse detectors".

## Keeping changes in focus

All animals are surrounded by a vast array of sensory information – far too much for them to take in and make sense of at once. Sense organs are therefore required to register important events in the environment, and they will be most useful if they react strongly to changes, while tending to ignore constancy. How is this accomplished? Just as bacteria become insensitive to a steady level of a chemical (◀ page 213), advanced sensory systems often adapt to constant stimuli: the number of nerve impulses generated by such a stimulus is initially high, but it decreases over time. This phenomenon has been studied in sea hares, where it seems to be brought about by a long-term modification of ion channels in the nerve cells, which alter the nerve's normal response (◀ page 204). Some receptors, such as touch receptors in the skin, adapt much more quickly than others – those signaling pain, for example, are very slow to adapt. Other types of receptor respond only to the onset or the cessation of a stimulus.

There is often a similar need to emphasize changes across space – for the discontinuities in a scene reveal the shapes and positions of objects. Eyes commonly use a technique called lateral inhibition to accentuate the edges of objects in a visual image. In the compound eye of the horseshoe crab (*Limulus*), for example, adjacent ommatidia interfere with one another's response to light. They reduce the electrical activity of their neighbors in proportion to their own degree of excitation. Ommatidia picking up the edge of a bright object will therefore give a stronger signal than those viewing its center – since some of their neighbors are in the dark and so inhibit them less. The upshot is that the animal sees a more pronounced view of the edge than would otherwise occur.

▲ *A parrot holding its head on one side to get a a better view of an object directly above it, by focusing it onto the fovea – a central spot on the retina which has maximum acuity.*

▼ *These black tandan catfish have both touch and chemical sensors on their chin barbels, so they can simultaneously taste and feel the riverbed when they forage by night.*

*Attack and defense – common to all life-forms...
Chemical weapons and physical barriers...Destroy or
damage strategies...The art of bluff and camouflage...
Unpalatable animals and their mimics...The costs of
defense – The biological "arms race"...PERSPECTIVE...
The chemical weapons of plants...Self-sacrifice of the
soldier termites...The immune system...Camouflage
for hunters*

A great many organisms live off other organisms, either by eating them, by sucking out their body fluids, or by invading them in search of food and other chemical supplies. This means that just about all living things are subject to attack, and must defend themselves if they are to have any chance of surviving long enough to reproduce.

Both attack and defense can be found at many different levels. Large creatures, such as mammals, are invaded by microscopic pathogens and parasites – viruses, bacteria, protozoa and fungi. They are also parasitized internally by invertebrates such as flatworms and nematodes, and externally by blood-sucking creatures such as mosquitoes and leeches. Furthermore, they must escape from, or fight off, the attacks of much larger predators. In general, the larger the organism the greater its range of enemies, but even the smallest creatures are subject to attack. For example, bacteria are infected by viruses (known as bacteriophages), eaten by protozoa and attacked chemically by the "antibiotics" which some organisms produce. Protozoa are attacked by bacteria and viruses and preyed on by other protozoa, plus a variety of small metazoan predators and larger filter-feeding organisms.

At all levels of size and complexity, the living world is a complex battleground with many creatures embroiled in both attack and defense on many fronts at the same time. Regardless of whether we classify them as parasites, pathogens or predators (◀ page 179), many organisms feed off other organisms as well as being someone else's prey.

### The immune system
*Of all defensive adaptations, one of the most complex is the battery of "immune defenses" set up by mammals such as ourselves against invading microorganisms. The first of these defenses are "non-specific", since they are active against a wide range of different microorganisms. They include the physical barriers of skin, the protective "mucus" covering soft tissues such as the throat and lungs, the wax within the ear and the acidity of the stomach.*

*The rest of the non-specific immune defenses are mainly mediated by various white blood cells which circulate throughout the body, not just in blood, but sometimes permeating in and around most of the other body tissues as well. Many white blood cells can engulf bacteria and viruses by "phagocytosis" (◀ page 170), and thus defeat many invasions by microorganisms at an early stage. Other white blood cells, known as "natural killer cells" can kill body cells that have become tumorous, or infected with viruses, for example. Many white blood cells also release various defensive proteins, such as "interferons", which stimulate the immune system in ways that are still poorly understood.*

*The immune system can also produce much more specific "antibodies" to eliminate particular infections. Antibodies are only one aspect of the "specific" immune defenses, which are mediated by two types of white blood cells known as T-cells and B-cells. These cells owe their specific effects to receptor proteins carried on their surface which can bind to foreign antigens such as the proteins found on the surface of an invading microorganism. Each T- or B-cell can bind only to a specific type of antigen, and a mammal contains cells able to bind to millions of different antigens overall. Whenever a T- or B-cell binds to a foreign antigen, it is activated to destroy or neutralize the microorganism to which the antigen belongs.*

*Activated T-cells generally eliminate microorganisms by destroying whole infected cells, and by helping to activate B-cells. It is the B-cells which release "antibodies" – large protein molecules able to bind to microorganisms carrying their particular antigens. Once attached, the antibody can make it easier for a phagocyte to engulf the microorganism, or just physically prevent the microorganisms from entering the body's cells.*

*When one bout of some particular infection stimulates the vertebrate immune response, it can leave the animal "immune" to further attacks. This is because the first infection generates the manufacture of large numbers of T- and B-cells able to bind to, and eliminate, the microorganism responsible. Once the first infection has been fought off, the number of these cells declines, but it never falls down to the small number present before the infection. Instead, a significant number remain in the body as "immune memory" cells, ready and waiting to fight off any fresh attack.*

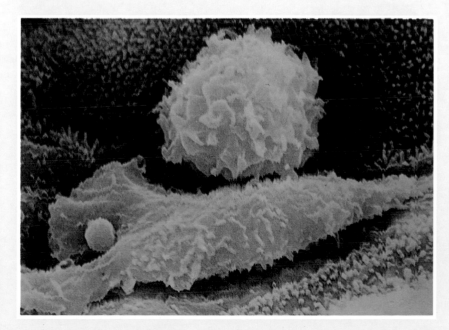

**◀ Two macrophages (phagocytic cells) in a human lung. The one at the bottom has elongated to engulf the small round particle at the left. Macrophages clear the lungs of dust, pollen, bacteria and other foreign matter.**

*Destroying or damaging the attacker is one form of defense*

Defensive adaptations include chemical weapons, such as toxins, cellular defensive systems, such as the immune system, physical barriers, such as thick skins and shells, behavioral adaptations, such as running away, and many more. Generally speaking, living things defend themselves by *destroying* or *damaging* their attackers, by *frightening* potential predators off, by somehow making themselves *unpalatable*, by *hiding or camouflaging* themselves, or by *physically resisting* attack in some way. These categories are not clear-cut, and one strategy may grade into another, but they provide a useful framework for considering defensive tactics in the living world.

One of the simplest examples of a "destroy or damage" strategy is hygiene – the removal of ectoparasites by cleaning, preening, bathing and so on. With larger attackers "destroy or damage" is more problematic, but they may sometimes be physically killed or fought off. Some small mammals, such as the ratel or honey badger of Africa and the Tasmanian devil, are geared to defensive strategies of this type and can deter predators much larger than themselves. The ratel, for example, has a formidable bite and is equipped with very loose skin on the back of its neck which allows it to twist round and bite a predator that seizes it from behind. These attributes, combined with great ferocity, protect the ratel from most predators. Many "destroy or damage" strategies are much more subtle than this, however. Plants and many invertebrates release toxic or irritating secretions, which kill or damage predators, or at least encourage them to look elsewhere. One of the most startling examples is the "bombardier beetle", which propels a jet of hot, toxic chemicals at any approaching threat. The jet is produced by the combination of two chemicals that the beetle synthesizes and stores in its body. When threatened, it allows the two to combine, and they react explosively, forcing the corrosive mixture out of the beetle's anus. The stings of bees, jellyfish or nettles are other, less dramatic examples of the same sort of strategy.

### The chemical weapons of plants

Plants have special difficulties in defending themselves against being eaten. They cannot run away or beat off an attack, so many plants have complex chemical defenses to repel invaders. Some of these defensive chemicals are present within or on the surface of the plants all of the time, while others are only produced in response to an attack.

Plant defensive chemicals can work in a variety of ways. Some are powerful poisons, such as cyanide, but others are produced simply as repellents, to make herbivores look elsewhere for food. Thistles, for example, produce repellent substances that keep various species of insect away.

Some of the other chemical strategies that have evolved in plants are much more subtle. Many plants manufacture chemicals that interfere with the growth and development of potential insect predators, often by mimicking the insects' own hormones (◀ page 197).

The wild potato plant manufactures an insect "alarm pheromone", released by aphids to alert one another to some danger. This protects the potato against aphids by warning them away from a danger which is not really there.

Another chemical warfare strategy adopted by plants is to make their tissues indigestible or nutritionally less useful to animals that might want to feed off them. The tannin produced by oak leaves combines with the plant proteins to make them indigestible to caterpillars and other herbivores. It is stored in membrane-bound "vacuoles" in the cells near the surface of leaves, and these vacuoles burst open and release their tannin as soon as a leaf is damaged. Most legumes (peas, beans etc) contain chemicals that make their proteins less digestible by inhibiting the enzymes various herbivores use to digest them.

Insects are some of the main targets of plant chemical defenses, and in some cases they have "fought back" in a spectacular manner. Some leguminous plants, for example, produce an unusual amino acid (canavanine) which is toxic to many animals because it is incorporated into proteins in place of arginine, making crucial enzymes and structural proteins non-functional. But one beetle is insensitive to this toxin, because it has evolved a more discriminating amino-acyl-tRNA synthetase enzyme (◀ page 140) that does not confuse canavanine with arginine.

Other insects have not only become resistant to the chemical weapons of certain plants, but have even developed ways of exploiting them for their own defense. Many butterflies do this, accumulating the toxins in their bodies to make themselves unpalatable. Certain grasshoppers have gone one better, storing a defensive poison obtained from milkweed plants in special glands, and then using it as a spray to repel predators.

◀ *A gerenuk feeding on an acacia tree, undeterred by its thorns. This small antelope has a narrow pointed muzzle and highly mobile lips. These enable it to pick out succulent leaves from between the sharp thorns. Such adaptations which overcome another organism's defenses are part of the continuing "biological arms race" – a process of coevolution that goes on between attackers and defenders.*

### Soldier termites — devoted to defense

Insects have developed a widely varying array of chemical and physical defenses, but the most dramatic examples are found in the termite caste of "soldiers" – individual organisms devoted solely to the defense of their colony, to the extent that they cannot even feed themselves or reproduce. A soldier termite is simply a walking weapon. The weaponry of soldier termites includes both physical and chemical components. As soon as a colony is attacked (usually by ants) the soldiers will rush forward in an utterly selfless defensive onslaught. In some species the heads of the soldiers are shaped like plugs which are used to physically seal off all the entrances to the colony. The soldiers of all species are equipped with powerful biting mouthparts which are used in a furious effort to bite off any intruders' legs and damage their bodies. But much of the most effective weaponry is chemical.

In some species the soldiers release toxins or anticoagulants (substances that prevent blood from clotting) from special glands as soon as their bodies become heated up by the exertion of battle. These secretions inevitably enter into the fresh wounds of the invaders, either killing them or preventing their wounds from healing. Other species, the "daubers", have an enlarged upper lip which acts like a paintbrush, daubing poisons all over the attackers. Others have a snout like tube extending from a modified forehead through which a thick "glue" is squirted. The attackers soon get tangled up in this glue, leaving them open to attacks from both soldier and worker termites.

In evolutionary terms, the death of soldier termites in battle is of little consequence to the colony as a whole, as they can soon be replaced. The loss of a single soldier has been likened to the loss of a dead skin cell from the human body. In some species, however, they are protected from their own poisons by special detoxification enzymes, and can live to fight another day.

▲ African porcupines in the Kalahari Desert. Their spines can do considerable damage to a predator – even a large animal such as a leopard or lion. By quickly running sideways or backward into its attacker, the porcupine can leave the easily-detached spines embedded in its aggressor's flesh. Though not poisonous, they are very painful and can produce septic wounds which later prove fatal.

◄ The fleshy outgrowths, known as cerata, on the back of this sea slug contain stinging cells, or nematocysts, obtained from hydroids. The sea slug feeds on these hydroids and can somehow prevent the nematocysts from discharging. Instead, they are coated with mucus, swallowed, and stored in the cerata. When attacked, the sea slug can release a few nematocysts into the water. If the predator swallows them they discharge their poison.

*Many animals try to bluff their way out of a dangerous situation*

Frightening an attacker off by pure bluff is a less reliable defense but one used to good effect by many species, including reptiles, amphibians and insects. Several butterflies, moths and other flying insects have realistic-looking "eyespots" on the wings that are usually covered when the insect is at rest, but can suddenly be displayed if it is approached or attacked. The apparent similarity of the eyespots to the eyes of owls, cats or stoats, suggests that these displays are defensive adaptations which frighten off small birds by simulating the presence of their own predators.

But are birds fooled that easily? To avoid the pitfalls of "storytelling" when describing something as an adaptation (◀ page 12) biologists must test such explanations, and this was done by the Dutch ethnologist Niko Tinbergen and his colleagues. They devised a box with a light inside which could display various patterns: crosses, circles, simple eyespots and more realistic eyespots. The latter had highlights and shading, as seen in many moths and butterflies, creating a striking three-dimensional effect. Birds were tempted down onto the box, and the light turned on as they approached – simulating the sudden display of eyespots by an insect. It became clear that realistic eyespots were most effective in scaring the birds off, suggesting that the eyespots are indeed effective deterrents, which help to protect the insects. Some caterpillars take this strategy further, and are elaborately patterned to resemble snakes, but whether this disguise really is effective, given the enormous size difference between a caterpillar and a snake, is open to question.

It is not just insects that try to bluff their way out of trouble. A growling dog, hissing cat, or tail-rattling rattlesnake are all trying the same trick. Toads react to danger by puffing themselves up to almost twice their normal girth and rocking from side to side, and many young birds, cornered in the nest by a potential predator, will fluff out their feathers and hiss loudly. These are last-ditch attempts to scare the attacker off – they may not work but they are worth trying.

▲ *Not all eyespots are for scaring off predators. Some, such as those of the meadow brown butterfly, serve to deflect attack from the butterfly's head, by providing a more noticeable target at the wing-tip. That this works is confirmed by the number of butterflies found with peck-marks in the eyespot regions.*

▲ *The elaborate eyespots of an emperor moth. Experiments have shown that birds are more frightened of such realistic eyes than of two concentric circles – confirming that natural selection for increasing realism in the pattern would be possible.*

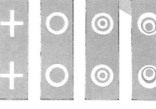

◀ *To test the hypothesis that eyespots deter predators, a box with a light inside was used to display various patterns (far left). Captive birds were lured down onto the box with tasty grubs. As each one approached the food, the light was turned on, and the bird's reactions recorded. Of the four patterns, crosses startled a few birds, circles were more effective, and two concentric circles more frightening still. The most effective deterrent was the realistic eyespot. The reactions of the birds to these patterns appeared to be instinctive.*

▲ The extraordinary ruff of skin on the neck of the frilled lizard seems to be used solely for scaring off predators – an example of defense by pure bluff.

◄ Several caterpillars of different species appear to mimic snakes. Despite the size difference, this disguise could work, because birds cannot judge distance – and therefore size – all that accurately.

► The chicks of a frogmouth (a nightjar-like bird) fluff out their feathers and hiss loudly in an attempt to appear larger and more threatening.

*Toxins or unpleasant tastes, combined with warning coloration, can keep predators off*

▲ *The bee beetle mimics a bumble bee, and so gains protection from predators such as birds which mostly avoid bees and wasps, because of their stings.*

▼ *The lionfish's spectacular fins warn that it is venomous. After one encounter, predators will associate its striking appearance with danger.*

Making themselves unpalatable to predators is an adaptation favored by many insects and plants. One of the best insect examples is the monarch butterfly, which accumulates toxic chemicals that are obtained from its foodplant, a milkweed. These will cause a small bird to vomit within minutes of eating a monarch. Of course, this does not help any butterfly that is eaten, but it soon teaches birds not to eat monarchs, and it is presumed to have evolved by kin selection (◀ page 15), whereby the death of an unpalatable individual would increase the survival prospects of relatives carrying the same genes – including those that promote the storage of the toxic chemicals. Like many other unpalatable animals, monarchs have "warning coloration" to advertize their distastefulness. Bold patterns of yellow, orange or red, combined with black, are the commonest form of warning, and it is thought that this general warning pattern is learned by predators, so that all animals carrying it have some sort of protection.

Some perfectly palatable butterflies have exploited the unpalatability of species such as the monarch by developing mimicry. That is,

their coloration is so similar to the distasteful species that birds and other predators avoid them as well. This form of defense – known as Batesian mimicry, after the Victorian naturalist H.W. Bates who first described it – only works if the mimic is less common than the model. If there are more palatable than unpalatable versions on the wing, birds are unlikely to learn to avoid them. Batesian mimicry is quite widespread, especially among tropical butterflies.

More general forms of mimicry, in which a whole group is mimicked, rather than a single species, are even more common. Bees, wasps and ants are the usual models, because of their powerful stings and bites. Thus a whole family of flies, known as hoverflies, mimic bees and wasps. Some clearwing moths mimic hornets, there are small beetles that mimic wasps, and even a beetle that looks like a bumblebee. Ant mimics include various spiders and the juvenile stages of some stick insect species. The ant-like spiders often complete their disguise by holding the first pair of legs off the ground to simulate antennae, leaving just six pairs for walking, as in insects.

◀ Warning colors often include red, orange or yellow, striped with black, as in these tree frogs from South America, whose skin produces a deadly toxin.

◀ Least palatable of all, to a predator, is a corpse – so many animals sham death to repel their attackers, as this European grass-snake is doing.

▲ The English naturalist, Henry Bates, after whom Batesian mimicry was named, being mobbed by curl-crested toucans in the Amazon rainforest.

▼ The African foam-locust's red-and-black coloration warns of the foul-tasting secretion that will froth out of its joints if the attacker comes any closer.

# Camouflage

### Defense by camouflage

Merging into the background is a superb method of defense that is employed by many invertebrate animals, some vertebrates, and even a few plants. In many cases, just adopting the color and general background pattern is sufficient camouflage, as in green tree snakes, and in bottom-dwelling fish like flounders, which are mottled to resemble a sandy seabed. Other animals take camouflage a step further, and resemble specific objects, such as twigs, leaves (dead or alive, half-eaten or intact), stems, flowers, chunks of dead wood, pieces of bark, lichens, thorns, bird droppings and even rabbit pellets. For aquatic animals, the buoyancy of water allows even more bizarre body shapes, and fish that live among waterweed are often elaborately disguised with frilly, plant-like outgrowths to their bodies. This sort of camouflage has much in common with mimicry (◀ page 231). After all, a moth, such as a lappet moth, that looks just like a dead beech leaf, is not all that differently adapted from the hornet clearwing moth, that precisely mimics a large wasp.

Many camouflaged insects have a second line of defense that comes into play if they are discovered. A brightly colored area of the body, or a pair of eyespots, that were previously hidden, are suddenly revealed in a dazzling and unexpected display. This serves to startle the predator and may deter it completely, or at least give the victim a chance to escape.

### Camouflage for hunters

Defense is just one use of camouflage – many predatory animals also rely on disguise to help them capture prey. Prettiest of these are the tropical flower-mantids (◀ page 12) which attract insects to them by mimicking flowers, then grab their prey in a lightning movement. In temperate climates, they are emulated by several species of white, pink or yellow crab-spiders, which lurk inside nectar-rich flowers. Among larger predators, one of the most remarkable is the alligator snapping turtle which is camouflaged to match the rotting vegetation on the river bed and sits motionless with its mouth open, virtually invisible but for a pink worm-like outgrowth in its mouth. Fish are attracted to this "bait", and promptly eaten.

▲ The frogmouths are nocturnal hunters. During the day, they rely on camouflage to protect them from danger. If disturbed, they point their beaks skywards to perfect their disguise as chunks of wood.

◀ The "living stones", Lithops, are remarkable plants whose camouflage helps them escape the attentions of herbivores. There are several species, each resembling a particular type of rock.

▶ ▲ A Sargassum fish among the weed from which it gets its name, and which it matches perfectly. A camouflaged predator, it has a lure on its snout for attracting invertebrate prey.

▶ Wild boar with their offspring. Young mammals and birds are often striped or speckled for camouflage.

▶ ▶ A leaf-mimicking katydid from Central America. Katydids are masters of disguise.

Defense based on physical protection has its most obvious manifestation in the shells of armadillos, tortoises, crabs and oysters, the spines of hedgehogs and porcupines, and the thorns of roses and cacti. But even our own rather thin skin presents a formidable defensive barrier to microorganisms, and in many plants and animals the outer surface is toughened and thickened to make invasion and damage more difficult. If these barriers are breached, other lines of defense may be employed. Once a plant has been damaged, for example, cells directly beneath the injured area produce a range of chemicals that quickly set up a barrier to invading microorganisms. This can localize the damage and improve a plant's chance of survival.

## The costs of defense

Living things only develop defensive adaptations at some cost to themselves, because all defenses use up materials and energy, both of which may be in short supply. In some cases these costs may be relatively small, while in others they may be dramatic. Snails, tortoises and other shelled creatures must obviously devote considerable amounts of materials and energy to the production of their thick shells, and carrying the shells around with them must consume yet more energy. Obviously the disadvantages of setting up defenses must be outweighed by the benefits the defensive adaptations confer, or they would not have been developed and retained.

The evolution of defensive systems can be thought of as a biological "arms race", in which no creature really wants to waste materials and energy in the development of defenses, but they are forced to by the attacks of other organisms. The defensive mechanisms and the attacking strategies of predators and parasites gradually evolve together, with any new advance in either attack or defense giving rise to further adaptations of other creatures to counter it. What looks like the status quo, in which attack and defense seem to be evenly balanced, is really a dynamic, ever-changing balance, rather than a static one. Over the long timescale of evolution some species eventually lose the battle and go extinct, while other species "win" and thrive – only to be challenged by the new adaptations of other species, to which new responses must be found if extinction is to be avoided.

**How a parasite evades the immune system**
*The protozoan parasite* Trypanosoma brucei *is one of the most damaging to humans and livestock. Spread by the tsetse fly, it infects the blood of humans and domestic cattle, causing a progressive disease that ends up as the fatal condition known, in humans, as "sleeping sickness". Much of the success of the trypanosome can be attributed to its ability to survive the attacks of the immune system by constantly "changing its coat". This presents the immune system with an ever-varying challenge.*

*Any parasitized individual becomes infected with a population of similar or identical trypanosomes, all covered with the same type of thick protein coat. The immune system of the infected organism recognizes these coat proteins as foreign antigens, and so sets up a powerful immune attack on them.*

*But from time to time the trypanosome suddenly changes its coat – switching off the gene responsible for making the existing coat, and switching on a gene for a new and different coat. This is composed of antigens that cannot be recognized by the antibodies directed against the first coat, so the trypanosomes can multiply to cause a new bout of disease.*

*The infected animal's immune system responds by initiating a new defensive assault against the antigens of the new coat. But by the time this new assault is becoming effective, some of the parasites will have changed coats once more, again allowing them to evade the immune system.*

*Each immune assault may kill up to 99 percent of the trypanosomes circulating throughout the body, but a small percentage always survives and multiplies by virtue of having changed coats. The infection is never defeated but spreads in repeated waves, eventually causing death of the host. Perhaps evolution will, in time, provide the host's immune system with new weapons to get round the trypanosomes' trickery, but at the moment the parasite is well ahead in the arms race of attack and defense.*

► *A trio of highly defended organisms struggle for survival in the arid landscape of Namibia. This young acacia plant is armed with thorns, and termites have begun their mound around it to prevent animals from trampling it underfoot. Ultimately, of course, the growth of the termite mound will kill the young acacia from which it now derives protection. To defend their colony the termites are guarded by a special soldier caste but still have their enemies, including the ant- and termite-eating pangolin. This extraordinary mammal is covered by bony plates that protect it from its insect prey – and ward off larger animals. If threatened it can roll up into a tight ball, or lash out with its armored tail.*

*Asexual reproduction...Sexual reproduction – in simple organisms and animals and plants...How genetic material comes together...Fertilization...Parental care...Bearing the young...PERSPECTIVE...Splitting of flatworms...Why sex?...Virgin birth...Male, female – or hermaphrodite?*

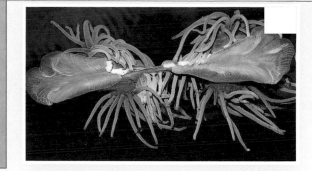

▲ *A snakelocks anemone splits into two daughter organisms. Sea anemones can easily undergo fission because they are of simple construction and radially symmetrical.*

▼ *A Hydra demonstrates another way in which cnidarians can reproduce asexually – budding. With an earlier offspring beside it, this Hydra is producing a new bud near its base.*

Reproduction is the means by which plants and animals ensure that their genes are passed on to the next generation (◀ page 9), and much of their biology and behavior has evolved to achieve reproductive success. In simple organisms, reproduction is just an extension of the growth process. Bacterial cells, for instance, split in half when they reach a certain size. This is called fission, and it produces daughter cells which are simply smaller copies of the parent. This is an effective way of reproducing, since it allows a rapid increase in numbers, but it is only feasible for unicellular organisms, such as bacteria, protozoa or yeasts, and a few higher organisms with a simple body plan, like the radially symmetrical sea anemones and sponges. In more complex organisms, reproduction is separated from growth, and becomes a specialized process with specific tissues.

Fission is just one kind of asexual reproduction, by which a single individual can produce genetically identical "daughters". The two commonest forms of asexual reproduction in higher plants and animals are spore production and budding. A spore is a group of unspecialized body cells packaged in a resistant coat, together with a simple source of nutrients. As well as being a means of reproduction, spores can provide a dispersal mechanism, or a way of overcoming adverse conditions that kill the parent, or both. If conditions are right, the spore produces a new individual that is genetically identical to the parent. Sponges produce enormous numbers of spore-like bodies called gemmules – nutrient-rich cells enclosed in a hard calcareous coat. The gemmules of freshwater sponges survive the death of the parent in the fall and only germinate in spring. The gemmules of marine species may even have a short free-swimming existence to give them a chance to disperse.

Budding, the second major method of asexual reproduction, generates a whole new individual from part of the parent. It is often described as *vegetative reproduction* although it also occurs among animals. Bulbous plants such as daffodils reproduce by budding off new bulbs, which serve as resistant storage organs, as well as reproductive bodies. Other plants, like the household "spider-plant" *Chlorophyta*, produce long aerial runners, extending some distance from their source. The daughter plant develops from a bud at the tip.

Among animals, freshwater *Hydra* reproduce by budding throughout the summer. Each bud starts as a simple swelling on the side of the parent, but then develops its own mouth and tentacles. When it does detach from its parent, it can immediately establish an independent existence. The marine worm *Syllis* can also bud off partly formed individuals. In some species these develop from the posterior segments, so parent and daughter run in tandem before separating. In others, new individuals can bud off from segments all along the body, so the parent looks like a miniature mobile Christmas tree.

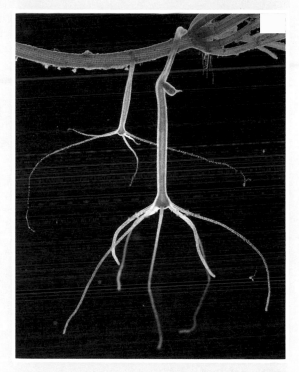

### Fission and senescence in flatworms

*Flatworms are some of the most complex animals to reproduce by fission. The tail holds onto the substrate, while the head moves forward, tearing the body along a predetermined plane. The head end can continue to feed, but the tail has to wait about two weeks for regeneration to occur. Theory suggests that the best strategy for rapid reproduction is to split halfway, but in fact the head gets about 75 percent of the body. This is probably because in streams where these animals live, a large tail without a head to guide it could easily be swept away. The most interesting aspect of this process is that lines derived from successive tail fragments are virtually immortal, but those lines derived from successive heads eventually die out. Because the brain is retained with the head it ultimately causes the aging process, whereas tails can reorganize and grow new brains.*

*Some animals are both sexes at once, and others can change sex.*

## Sexual reproduction

The option of reproducing sexually is found in almost all organisms, except for some bacteria and a few higher organisms that have secondarily lost the ability. Most plants and fungi, and some invertebrate animals, have also retained their asexual processes, whereas the majority of vertebrate animals and many invertebrates are limited to sexual reproduction.

The critical feature of sexual reproduction is the mixing of genetic material from two parents. In most life cycles this involves the fusion of two sex cells called gametes. The most notable exceptions to this are bacteria and some protozoa, where genetic material is donated directly from one cell to another during the process of "conjugation". Most fungi are also rather different, in that the fusion of specialized hyphae known as gametangia is the first step in sexual reproduction (◀ page 40). Except in bacteria, sexual fusion leads to the formation of a zygote with a double dose of chromosomes, so that meiosis (◀ page 24), the process by which the genetic material is halved, must occur before gametes are formed again. But this can take place at almost any stage in the life cycle. In animals it occurs just before gamete formation, but in bread molds, for example, it follows immediately on from zygote formation.

### Hermaphroditism

*Not all plants or animals have separate sexes. Many invertebrates, and all but a small proportion of flowering plants are hermaphrodite – both male and female simultaneously. This is advantageous if an individual can achieve greater reproductive efficiency than it would as a member of just one sex. In flowering plants, both males and females would have to produce costly floral displays in order to attract pollinators, so they economize by having both functions. If an organism is simultaneously male and female, it also has the potential, in an emergency, to fertilize its own eggs. Seaweeds that grow at the top of the shore where fertilization is difficult are frequently self-fertile.*

*Elsewhere this strategy is outweighed by the risks of inbreeding, and in many flowers, the pollen is released well before the female organ (the stigma) becomes receptive, so that the chances of self-fertilization are much reduced. However, some plants, such as the haricot bean, always fertilize themselves, and have closed flowers that prevent access by alien pollen. Why they should do this, and how they avoid the "inbreeding depression" seen in other species, is not fully understood.*

◄ Conjugation in bacteria, with one bacterium (right) donating genetic material to two others. The DNA is transferred through protein tubes. This process differs from sex in plants and animals in several ways. Only part of the genome is transferred and there is no reciprocation. The wholesale fusion of two separate genomes that characterizes sex in higher organisms is absent.

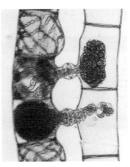

◄ Filaments of the alga, Spirogyra, engaged in sexual reproduction. Individual cells develop conjugation tubes with adjacent cells. Then the cell contents of one passes into the other and fusion occurs. A resistant zygospore develops from the zygote, and meiosis occurs within it, to restore the haploid condition. From the zygospore, a new filament develops.

▲ Slipper limpets are gastropod mollusks, but they feed by filtering the sea water with their gills, much as bivalves do, and therefore do not need to move about to feed. They live in stacks of up to nine, in which the two or three largest mollusks, at the bottom, are female and the top two or three – the smaller ones – are male. One or two mollusks in the middle are usually in the process of changing sex. Small slipper limpets joining the pile always develop into males, but if a young one settles on bare rock and founds a stack of its own it may develop straight into a female, and not go through a male stage.

◄ Roman snails mating. As hermaphrodites, they go through a complex courtship ritual which prepares each snail for the simultaneous insertion of its penis into the other's body – quite a tricky operation. During courtship they rear up and press their muscular foot against their partner's, stroke each other with their tentacles and secrete large amounts of mucus. After several hours of this, they inject sharp calcareous darts into each other, an apparently painful exercise but one which stimulates them to complete the mating act.

## Sex determination

In those organisms with different sexes, the process of sex determination may be genetic or environmental. In many animals there is a pair of chromosomes which differ in appearance, and these are responsible for sex determination (♦ page 27). Most fish and many reptiles do not have distinct sex chromosomes but sex-determining genes have nonetheless been shown to exist. For some insects and mites, sex is determined by the presence or absence of part of the chromosomal complement, while in bees, wasps and ants, males develop from unfertilized eggs and females from fertilized ones.

In other cases, sex depends on the environment. The nematodes which attack vegetable crops grow from eggs laid on their host's roots. Nematode larvae cause the plant to develop side nodules in which they will live and feed. Females are larger than males and need up to 35 times as much food. If parasite densities are high, then the roots become crowded and nutrition is poor, so the majority of adults turn into males. Under low density conditions, when food is abundant, most nematodes emerge as females. Evidently feeding conditions determine the sex which nematode larvae develop. Similarly, among maple trees, a higher proportion of females develop in good growing conditions.

A different environmental sex-determining system, dependent on temperature, has been found in alligators. When a female alligator lays her eggs in a warm dry place, the young which hatch are all males. If she puts her eggs out in the cooler, damper swamp, then daughters are produced. The same sort of system operates in turtles, and in both cases the adaptive significance is far from clear.

In some species, individual organisms may change sex during their lifetime. Often sex changes with size, because only large individuals have the resources to produce worthwhile batches of eggs.

Sperm, by contrast, are cheap to make, so small individuals can be male and grow at the same time. The slipper limpet can be found in stacks of up to nine animals. The small ones on top are male and the larger individuals on the bottom are female.

In sex-changing plants, a switch to maleness is often associated with stress, such as drought, while change to female follows a good growing season. Jack-in-the-pulpit Arisaema depends for its annual growth on energy stored in its corm. Only after a good year are there enough nutrients to ensure that the plant can be a productive female.

## Egg swapping in the black hamlet

Hermaphrodites with internal fertilization usually have a long courtship ritual which culminates in simultaneous fertilization of both partners' eggs. For species with external fertilization, this would not be a good idea, as their own eggs and sperm would mix and run a high risk of self-fertilization. The black hamlet is a hermaphrodite fish which fertilizes its eggs externally, and this has led to an unusual piece of behavior, known as an egg-trading ritual. Two fish get together for a series of spawning bouts, but only one functions as a female in each bout, and it does not release all its eggs, just a small package. In the second bout the partners swap roles and the fish that first acted as a male, reciprocates with eggs of its own. Fish that act as females first but get no reciprocation, terminate courtship immediately. But where the partner responds correctly, up to nine spawning sequences have been recorded. This trading of eggs has obvious advantages for the individual fish. It prevents cheating by mutant individuals which might try to fertilize a great many energy-expensive eggs provided by others, without always reciprocating with eggs of its own. It also accounts for the maintenance of hermaphroditism, since mutant male-only fish would quickly die out because they would have no eggs to trade.

▶ When reproducing by parthenogenesis, aphids bear live young. These develop from unfertilized eggs, are all female, and genetically identical to the mother aphid. They are produced in vast numbers during the summer, when food is plentiful.

◀ The evolution of different types of gametes – male and female – has had far-reaching consequences for sexual reproduction. The male gametes are generally smaller, so the males can produce them in huge quantities. As a result, one male can fertilize several females, and this fuels sexual selection (♦ page 13), a process which favors any characteristic that increases a male's mating success. The horns of stag beetles are products of sexual selection, and here two males use them in a fight.

In many simple organisms, such as the single-celled algae, the gametes are identical, a condition known as isogamy. But in all animals and terrestrial plants the gametes are of two distinctive types: very small mobile gametes (the sperm or pollen) which fuse with, and activate, a much larger gamete (the egg or ovum). This arrangement, known as anisogamy, probably evolved because bigger gametes make better zygotes, with food stores to nourish the developing young.

But large gametes (defined as female) are less mobile, and need small, mobile gametes (defined as male) to seek them out and fertilize them. Intermediate types are neither large enough nor sufficiently mobile, so they are outcompeted by the extremes which become increasingly different. Male gametes are small and cheap to produce but have to disperse widely to find the female gamete, so they are usually produced in vast quantities. Hazel bushes may produce 600 million pollen grains of which few ever achieve their goal of fertilization. Male animals similarly tend to produce sperm in large and renewable quantities. The reasons for this over-supply seem obvious in marine organisms with external fertilization, such as sea urchins or codfish, but large quantities are often produced in species with internal fertilization. A man produces twice as many sperm every second as a woman produces ova in her whole lifetime. This may have evolved as a result of competition between males. When females copulate with several mates, those with most sperm may increase their chances of fertilizing the eggs.

Anisogamy has the effect of limiting mating to male–female interactions only. But isogamous organisms cannot necessarily mate indiscriminately. Often there are two or more mating strains which must mate with a gamete of a different strain. This is the case for many fungi. In most such species, all the offspring from a cross will not necessarily be of the same mating type, so this does not *prevent* inbreeding, although it could help to reduce its incidence.

### Virgin birth

Some organisms with sexual ancestors have subsequently given up sex. The same tissues are used by females to produce eggs, but these develop into embryos without fertilization.

Virgin birth, or "parthenogenesis", is generally associated with unstable or colonizing conditions typified, among plants, by pioneer species such as the hawkweeds Hieracium and blackberries Rubus. Plants germinating in isolation on an uncolonized plot can establish a new colony rapidly by parthenogenesis: the lack of a sexual partner does not hold them back, as it would with other plants.

Parthenogenesis also occurs among a number of fish and reptiles. Some of these are complex genetic hybrids produced by the interbreeding of two or more distinct species, and this may make them unable to produce gametes. Like parthenogenetic plants, they usually occur in unstable or marginal habitats.

Among sexually reproducing species, parthenogenesis may be used as an alternative strategy. The bulk of the summer population of greenfly, or aphids, are females which have colonized fresh leaves and produced vast numbers of daughters by parthenogenesis while food supplies are plentiful. As fall approaches, the dwindling food supply for the dense population produces severe overcrowding. This, together with the shorter days, stimulates the greenfly to produce male offspring, and mating then occurs. The eggs that result from this are equipped with a resistant coat to endure the winter and because they are produced sexually, they ensure the production of a diverse stock to face the unpredictable conditions of the following year. This type of mixed strategy is called "facultative parthenogenesis".

### Parthenogenetic fish that still need males

The mollies, a group of freshwater fish, often form unisexual populations of females which can reproduce parthenogenetically from unfertilized eggs. Each unisexual species lives alongside a sexual species to which it is related. The two species compete very closely for all the available resources such as food and space. Since the parthenogenetic species can produce two females for every one produced by its sexual competitor, it seems surprising that the sexual species is not rapidly outnumbered.

The explanation for this apparent anomaly may be linked to the fact that the eggs of the parthenogenetic species cannot develop without being activated by sperm from a sexual male. In some species the sperm merely stimulate development. In others, the paternal chromosomes are temporarily incorporated into the zygote but are never passed on when eggs are produced. Asexual mollies still depend on other females' mates and are reproductively limited by their abundance.

▼ Male kangaroos fight to establish the right to mate with a female in estrus. Sexual selection can operate in three ways: through male–male fighting as here, through male competition for territory which then attracts females (as in many songbirds, for example), or through the female's choice of mate. It is by the latter route that elaborate male adornments, such as the peacock's tail, evolve.

*Breeding behavior must be synchronized and there are many ways of achieving this*

## Living together: sex loses its value

*Some organisms involved in mutualistic association (◀ page 179) live inside their partner, enjoying a buffered and predictable environment, regulated by their hosts. It has been discovered that sexual reproduction is much less common among such species, even when densities of individuals within the host are high enough to ensure that isolation is not preventing them from finding a mate. For example, species of unicellular algae living within mollusks, flatworms or corals rarely engage in sex. This suggests that the maintenance of sex is weaker in stable environments, and offers some support for the idea that sexual reproduction confers advantages in variable environments, allowing organisms to keep pace with external change.*

◀ *A sponge emitting a huge cloud of sperm. Chemical signals released into the water can stimulate other organisms to release their gametes, and thus obtain synchronization.*

▶ *In the mating dance of scorpions, the male drops a sperm packet and moves the female over it.*

▼ *A female southern right whale chased by 3 males.*

## Bringing gametes together

When organisms reproduce sexually, the problem of getting the gametes (or gametangia in the case of fungi) together at the same time in the same place has to be solved. In temperate latitudes most breeding cycles are tied to seasons. Inevitably some times are better for producing young than others. Woodland plants usually flower in the spring before the tree canopy develops, so that their bright petals will be most obvious to pollinating insects.

Many animals also breed early in the year. Large freshwater flatworms, for example, breed as soon as lake temperatures begin to rise in late winter so that their offspring will have the longest possible time to grow before the next winter. The population can be synchronized in its breeding activity because temperature changes in water are a highly predictable cue.

Terrestrial animals and plants are more likely to use cues such as daylength (◀ page 217) to tell them where they are in the breeding timetable. The gonads of male birds show a considerable change in size in response to daylength changes, and the related changes in hormone levels affect other activities, like territorial defense and song, which are part of breeding.

Some birds breed over a fairly extended season, but for others precise timing is more important. In the large, traditional nesting colonies of gulls and terns, for example, the birds breed simultaneously, which reduces the impact of predators by "flooding the market" with thousands of young birds at once. These birds are probably able to synchronize their breeding because the behavior of each bird produces an effect on others observing it. The sight of courtship behavior in one pair can stimulate the hormonal changes that bring neighboring birds into breeding condition.

Among marine animals, less subtle methods of synchronization are available. When marine urchins release their millions of gametes into the water for external fertilization, they are accompanied by a chemical cue which stimulates neighbors to spawn at the same time. This is advantageous for all concerned, since it maximizes the chances that eggs will be fertilized.

## Why sex?

*Detailed theoretical analysis, using mathematical modeling, reveals that sex is a very inefficient way of reproducing. The inefficiency lies in making male offspring. In the majority of sexual species only the female contributes energy and resources to the young. In contrast the males rarely contribute more than the minimum – a tiny sperm carrying genes, but devoid of other resources. If a female switches to parthenogenesis (◊ page 238) she redirects her investment into offspring that carry all her genes, instead of only half, effectively doubling her genetic output.*

*Given that sex is so inefficient, why is it so common? Four theories have so far been proposed, but unfortunately none of them has sufficient generality to be credited as a truly satisfying explanation of the origin and maintenance of sex.*

*The first explanation concentrates on advantageous mutations. In a sexual population, if these occur in different individuals, they can be brought together through mating. This is not the case in asexual species. Biologists have suggested that this could speed up the rate of evolution, but detailed calculations of the costs and benefits show that sex is not particularly advantageous in this respect, except when there is very frequent and violent change in the environment, or when populations are small.*

*The ratchet theory is similar to the above idea, but concentrates on bad mutations. These can accumulate in a population, whether sexual or asexual, and once established are difficult to lose, because reverse mutations are very rare – hence the analogy with a ratchet. But sex can partly overcome the ratchet. Through mating and recombination (◊ page 24) some offspring are produced with fewer bad mutations, while deleterious mutations are offloaded into other gametes. If these gametes, or the offspring they produce, have too many deleterious mutations they die, and the number of bad mutations in the population is thereby reduced. Alexey Kondrashov, a Russian mathematician, has estimated that the advantages of this outbalance the cost of sex, but few biologists agree with his analysis.*

*The two other theories both evoke short-term advantages rather than long-term ones. The first suggests that variability of offspring from sexual parents reduces competition between the offspring. But having just a few variable offspring is only better than having a larger number of similar offspring where there is really intense competitive selection, and this is rare in the natural world.*

*Finally, another advantage attaching to variable offspring has been put forward by William Hamilton. It is that variability is a defense against parasites and pathogens. These are continually under selection to adapt to the existing host population, so the best bet for the host is to be continually changing – and sex is a means of achieving this. Because sexual reproduction keeps producing novel ranges of genotypes it may help to hold disease in check by forcing them continually to adapt to their hosts. But again this is a fairly specific condition to favor sex, and there is as yet little supporting evidence.*

*Internal fertilization ensures that the gametes meet*

Timing apart, there is the problem of actually getting the gametes together, and this is much more tricky for plants and sedentary animals than it is for mobile ones. Things are not so bad for aquatic species, because in water, sperm can swim to the eggs, as they can in the damp terrestrial habitats where mosses and ferns breed (◀ page 50). But for higher plants, gamete transfer – pollination – depends on some external agent, such as wind or insects, and they have evolved elaborate mechanisms to improve their successful exploitation of these vectors (◀ page 62). Where the parents are mobile, they can meet up, and either release sperm and eggs in close proximity, as many fish and amphibians do, or undergo internal fertilization, where the male places sperm inside the female.

Males and females are brought together either by one sex, often the female, signaling its position to the other or, like toads and elephant

◀▼ **In both mammals and birds, the eggs are fertilized internally. In mammals, this is achieved by an intromittent organ, the penis. Most birds simply press their cloacas (combined reproductive and excretory openings) together. This requires absolute cooperation from the female bird, who must move her tail aside and keep quite still while the male is on top of her. A few birds, notably the ducks, do have an intromittent organ.**

▲ **Male golden toads gather at a breeding pool in the cloud forests of Costa Rica. Most frogs and toads breed communally, attracting others with their croaking. Some return to a traditional breeding site every year.**

▶ **A pair of yellowtail moths mating. The female has only just emerged from her cocoon, which can be seen on the left. As soon as she emerges she emits a pheromone to attract the male.**

seals, by the arrival of both sexes at traditional breeding grounds. Signaling can involve sound, sight, scent or even vibrations ( ◀ page 215). Female moths emit volatile substances, known as pheromones, that can attract males over enormous distances, while female fireflies and glowworms use biological light to lure their mates. By contrast, among midges it is the males which attract females by swarming in enormous clouds which form around prominent markers such as trees. In Africa these clouds may number many millions and can be seen for miles on warm, still evenings. Male birds also attract their mates, usually with complex songs delivered from prominent posts. The European sedge warbler is one example, whose song is used solely for this purpose. As soon as he has found a mate, the male bird stops singing. In other species, the song has other functions as well, notably the defense of territory.

*The male gamete is screened for vigor and suitability before fertilization occurs*

## Fertilization

The aim of all breeding behavior is fertilization, in which the gametes fuse, but in animals as well as plants, the female tissue sets a series of chemical tests which most male gametes fail to pass. This may constitute a weeding out of the ineffective gametes, or active female choice. For example, many female plants have chemical mechanisms for detecting the genetic makeup of the pollen and, if it is too similar to her own, she rejects it – a barrier to inbreeding. The animal sperm also has to penetrate the egg's protective coats. In sea urchins there is jelly and several cell layers before reaching the egg's outer membrane. In some amphibia, only part of the egg coat is receptive and in trout there are tiny channels which allow only a single sperm through to the egg. The final stage of fusion may take up to an hour, but it is significant in stimulating a chemical change which activates the new zygote's respiration, protein synthesis and development.

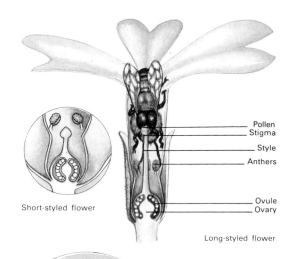

Short-styled flower

Pollen
Stigma
Style
Anthers
Ovule
Ovary

Long-styled flower

**Incompatible**
*The pollen grains from the same plant (or a closely related plant), will all carry the same S-alleles and none will be able to penetrate the stigma.*

**Semi-compatible**
*If the plant producing pollen has some of the same S-alleles, then some pollen grains will be able to penetrate the stigma but others will not.*

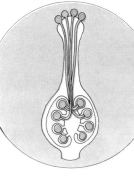

**Compatible**
*Pollen grains from a completely unrelated plant will share none of the S-alleles, so all its pollen grains will be able to develop.*

▲ *Cross-pollination is preferable to self-pollination for many plants, and for this reason several species have two types of flower, long-styled and short-styled. Pollen from the anthers of a short-styled flower is most likely to be deposited on the stigma of a long-styled flower, because they are at the same level in the flower, and vice versa. The value of this is to reduce pollination between flowers on the same plant, which will all be of one type. Such barriers to inbreeding are often backed up by genetic incompatibility systems.*

◄ *Like many flowers, those of the rosebay willowherb produce their pollen first, before the stigma is ready. This prevents self-fertilization within each flower. The bottom of the spike blooms first, and since bees usually work from the bottom to the top, self-fertilization within the spike is rare.*

▼ ▶ *Grunion lay their eggs in moist sand on the beaches of southern California, the female wriggling down into the sand, as the male twists around her, fertilizing the eggs (below). Their spawning coincides with the twice-monthly "spring" tides, when the high tide reaches the farthest up the beach, so that the eggs are as far as possible from the water and its predators. The young hatch 15 days later, taking advantage of the next spring tide to wash them into the sea. The spawning may be synchronized by the tide itself, by the Moon, or by an internal clock (◆ page 217).*

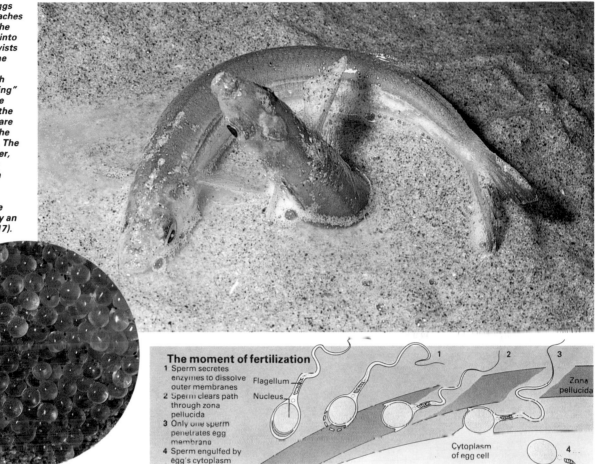

### The moment of fertilization

1 Sperm secretes enzymes to dissolve outer membranes
2 Sperm clears path through zona pellucida
3 Only one sperm penetrates egg membrane
4 Sperm engulfed by egg's cytoplasm

Flagellum
Nucleus
Zona pellucida
Cytoplasm of egg cell

▼ ▶ *Cross-section of a mammalian egg with approaching sperm cells (below). As the sperm reach the ovum the follicle cells disperse and the sperm cluster around the egg surface (right). Penetration of the egg by the sperm is shown in the diagram above right. The sperm release enzymes that dissolve the outer membrane and clear a path through the zona pellucida.*

### A mammalian egg

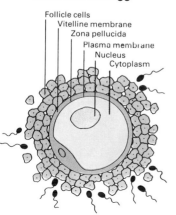

Follicle cells
Vitelline membrane
Zona pellucida
Plasma membrane
Nucleus
Cytoplasm

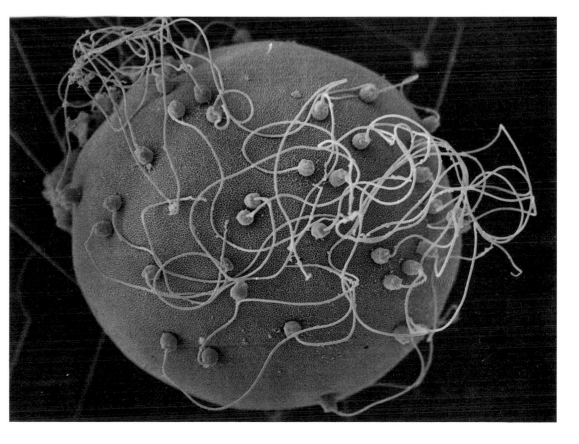

*It is usually the female that cares for the young, but not always*

▲ *A pair of coots with their chicks. The parents must feed them for the first four weeks, as well as keeping them warm at night and warding off predators.*

▼ *Several species of mangrove retain their seeds, which germinate on the parent tree. They grow a long, hard, pointed root that can implant itself in the mud below.*

## Parental care

Parental interest in reproduction often ends with the despatch of gametes, or at fertilization, so most animals and lower plants enter the world alone, as nothing more than fertilized eggs. The profligate cod releases gametes in vast numbers to fuse and form zygotes in the plankton, and makes no further investment in the developing offspring. Huge wastage occurs, and of the 6–7 million eggs released by a single female cod, only a few will become adult fish. An alternative way of ensuring reproductive success is to have extended parental care. This may take many forms, from simple protection of the developing young through added nutrition during development, to extended care for weeks, months or even years. The trend in many taxa has been to increase the investment made in each offspring and to decrease the number of offspring produced. The total investment made is a trade-off for the parent, between increasing the likelihood of its offspring surviving on the one hand, and risking its own survival, with its potential for breeding again in subsequent seasons, on the other. Among birds, it is interesting to note that smaller, shorter-lived species devote a higher relative proportion of energy to reproduction than do larger, long-lived species.

Among plants, an evolutionary trend towards increasing care of the young is noticeable. Ferns distribute their spores and leave the gametophytes to look after themselves, but gymnosperms and angiosperms retain the gametophyte on a spore-producing leaf ( page 51). The

◄ *A male seahorse carrying eggs. The female is more brightly colored, and takes the active role in courtship – something also seen in the few bird species where males alone rear the young.*

▲ *A green turtle lays its eggs in the sand of a tropical beach. It abandons the eggs, so the young turtles must dig themselves out of the nest and make their way to the sea alone.*

▼ *Leeches place their eggs in a nutrient-rich package, or cocoon. In most leeches this is deposited as soon as the eggs are laid, but in one group it is retained on the body until the eggs hatch.*

added investment is significant: the cones of primitive cycads which help to protect the gametophyte weigh up to 30kg. These higher plants also provide the developing sporophyte embryo with nutritive tissue, so that when it lands in a suitable habitat there is a store to support the seedling until its own leaves and roots can take over.

Among animals, parental care has evolved independently many times. Although it is most highly developed in mammals and birds, it also occurs in many invertebrates. Freshwater leeches *Glossiphonia* carry their young around after birth, and wolf spiders *Lycosa* carry both the eggs – seen as a white package trailing from the female's abdomen – and the newly hatched spiderlings. It is not necessarily the female who cares for the young, however. Among seahorses, the males have special pouches in which to brood the eggs and young, and in several other fish the eggs are guarded by the male. Among amphibians, too, male care is seen in several species (◀ page 102), while birds show every conceivable permutation from an equitable sharing of responsibility to exclusively male or exclusively female care.

It need not even be the parents who look after the young. Elder siblings often help, an act of apparent altruism that can be explained by kin selection for they share, on average, half their genes with a sibling (◀ page 15). Perhaps the most elaborate form of investment is seen in the social insects where particular non-reproductive castes do nothing but tend to the needs of eggs and larvae. They feed them, clean out bacteria, and ward off potential enemies.

## Bearing live young

A less common but quite widespread form of care involves retaining the eggs inside the mother's body and giving birth to live young, a strategy known as viviparity. The young that are eventually produced are fewer in number but further developed. Viviparity is common to all mammals, apart from the egg-laying echidnas and platypus, but it has evolved in several other animals as well, including some bivalve mollusks, polychaete worms, insects, fish and reptiles. In many, the eggs are merely retained within an incubation chamber, which serves primarily as a physical buffer. This is often referred to as ovoviviparity, to distinguish it from true viviparity, in which the link is more intimate, and the young are nourished by their mother.

The placenta of eutherian mammals sustains the developing embryo (◀ page 119) and it has parallels in the structures by which some fish and other viviparous species nourish their unborn young. Where such structures are absent, the young may actually feed inside the mother's body. Thus some species of caecilians (◀ page 101) rasp off special nutritive cells produced inside the mother, while some young sharks cannibalize their young siblings.

Where a placenta-like structure *is* present, considerable physiological adjustment is required on the part of the parent. In sexually reproducing species, there is the problem of the immunological difference between the mother and her offspring (which carries some of the father's genes) to be overcome. Somehow the automatic response of the immune system to attack foreign cells must be repressed, and in mammals this too is achieved by the placenta, which creates a barrier between the blood of the fetus and the mother.

Investment in parental care is not confined to sexually reproducing organisms. Asexually produced offspring may experience just as much care. When the strawberry extends a runner it does not simply dump its new daughter. The runner acts as a vital supply line to nourish and water the new plant until it has established its own roots and leaves. In aphids, the young, produced asexually by parthenogenesis, are born alive, and at quite a large size compared with the mother.

▼ *A white-tailed deer licks clean her newborn fawn. Because the embryo is linked to the mother, birth is a much more traumatic event than in ovoviviparous animals.*

▲ *A brittle star releasing her offspring. Many echinoderms abandon their eggs, but several species in harsh environments – the deep sea or very cold waters – are ovoviviparous.*

▲ *A female swordtail "gives birth". As well as brooding eggs in an ovarian cavity, swordtails are of interest for their ability to change sex. Females can become males, but not vice versa.*

# Credits

Key to abbreviations: ANT Australasian Nature Transparencies; BHPL BBC Hulton Picture Library; BCL Bruce Coleman Ltd.; GSF Geoscience Features; NHPA Natural History Photographic Agency; OSF Oxford Scientific Films; PEP Planet Earth Pictures; SPL Science Photo Library
b bottom; bl bottom left; br bottom right; c center; cl center left; cr center right; t top; tl top left; tr top right; l left; r right.

1 OSF/Peter Parks 2-3 BCL/Francisco Erize 4-5 BCL/C. & D. Frith 7 OSF/David Thompson 8 OSF/ Peter Parks 9l, 9r BHPL 11l PEP/A. Kerstich 11r Dr. L. M. Cook 12l Jacana 12r Premaphotos Wildlife/ K. G. Preston-Mafham 13 BCL/John Shaw 14t Mansell Collection 14c BHPL 14b Bildarchiv der Osterreichische Nationalbibliothek 15 BCL/D. & R. Sullivan 17 BCL/J. & D. Bartlett 18t Imitor 18cr Zefa 18br Sinclair Stammers 21t Ann Ronan 21b A-Z Botanical Collection 22l, 22tr, 22br Linda Gamlin 24-25 (all pictures) Professor Bernard John, Research School of Biological Sciences, Canberra 26t, Biofotos/ H. Angel 26b GSF 27tl Ian Wyllie 27r GSF 27bl BCL 28 OSF/J. Dermid 29 Stanley B. Prusiner 30 Topham Picture Library 31, 34 Ann Ronan 36-37 CNRI/SPL 36cr, 36br, 37cl, 37bl SPL/Dr. T. Brain & D. Parker 38cl BHPL 38cr Biozentrum/University of Basel/SPL 39t OSF/Michael Fogden 39b BCL 42t SPL/E. Gravé 42b SPL/Darwin Dale 43 SPL/Robert Knauft 44bl NHPA/John Shaw 44tr OSF/Barrie E. Watts 45t PEP/ Peter Scoones 45b OSF/Peter Parks 48bl Biofotos/ H. Angel 48-49 SPL/James Bell 49b BCL/Hans Reinhard 52t G. R. Roberts 52c Premaphotos Wildlife/ K. G. Preston-Mafham 52b Biofotos/H. Angel 53 Graham Bateman 54tl Premaphotos Wildlife/K. G. Preston-Mafham 54tr G. R. Roberts 54br BCL/Peter Ward 55 (main picture) Premaphotos Wildlife/K. G. Preston-Mafham 55 (inset) Biofotos/H. Angel 56tl NHPA/A. Bannister 56bl OSF/Michael Fogden 56-57 Biofotos/H. Angel 57b BCL/Hans Reinhard 58 Premaphotos Wildlife/K. G. Preston-Mafham 59 Linda Gamlin 60tl Biofotos/H. Angel 60br Graham Bateman 61l OSF/J. A. L. Cooke 61r BCL/Kim Taylor 62tr, 62cl, 62bl OSF/J. A. L. Cooke 63l OSF/David Thompson 63cr SPL 63br OSF/David Thompson 64 BHPL 65t BCL/Fritz Prenzel 65bl K. Wheeler 65br OSF/B. E. Watts 66tl OSF 66cl Linda Gamlin 66br Mansell Collection 67 PEP/Nancy Sefton 68r OSF/Kathie Atkinson 68c OSF/G. I. Bernard 69, 70 OSF/Peter Parks 71tr SPL/L. Stepanowicz 71cr SPL/John Walsh 71bl C. Howson 74, 74-75 OSF/ Kathie Atkinson 75l BCL/Inigo Everson 75r BCL 76t Biofotos/H. Angel 76b PEP/K. Lucas 77 SPL/Dr. T. E. Thompson 78t BCL 78b SPL 79 BCL 80t OSF/ G. I. Bernard 80b, 81 NHPA/Anthony Bannister 82t NHPA/S. Dalton 82b SPL/Dr. R. Shuster 83 BCL 84tl OSF/R. H. Kuiter 84bl Premaphotos Wildlife/

K. G. Preston-Mafham 84br BCL/C. & D. Frith 85l NHPA/G. I. Bernard 85r OSF 86bl NHPA/ A. Bannister 86tr Premaphotos Wildlife/K. G. Preston-Mafham 86br BCL/Jane Burton 87l Jacana 87r BCL/Jane Burton 89 BCL/Bill Wood 90tr PEP/ Richard Chesher 90cl BCL/F. Sauer 90bl NHPA/G. J. Cambridge 91 OSF/G. I. Bernard 92 PEP/C. Petron 93 OSF/Peter Parks 94 Professor E. N. F. Clarkson 95 BHPL 97 PEP/C. Roessler 98bl Popperfoto 98tr D. Allison 99 PEP/Rod Salm 101t Kenneth T. Nemuras 101b OSF/Michael Fogden 102t, 102c Michael Fogden 102b Biofotos/H. Angel 103 BCL/ J. & D. Bartlett 106-107 Agence Nature 106b E. & D. Hosking 107 NHPA/S. Robinson 110cl BCL 110bl, 110tr Michael Fogden 110br NHPA 111 BCL 112 BCL/J. & D. Bartlett 113 BCL/Kim Taylor 115t, 115b Jacana 116tl BCL/J. & D. Bartlett 116br BCL/ G. Zeisler 117bl Survival Anglia Ltd/Alan Root 117tr Survival Anglia Ltd/J. & D. Bartlett 118 Jacana 119 Biofotos/C. A. Henley 120t NHPA/J. Sauvanet 120c NHPA/A. Bannister 120b NHPA/Lacz Lemoine 121 Jacana/J. Prévost 122t Jacana/Arthus-Bertrand 122bl NHPA/A. Bannister 128bl Survival Anglia Ltd/ J. Foott 128tr NHPA/S. Dalton 130 Frank Lane Agency/H. Eisenbeiss 132 Rob Judges 133 NHPA/ Biophoto Associates 137 SPL/CNRI 141 Paul Brierley 142 A. C. Barrington-Brown/Weidenfeld & Nicholson Archives 143 Sio Photo 144-145 OSF/J. A. L. Cooke 147 Gerry Cranhams Colour Library 148 Crawford S. Dow, University of Warwick 149b Ann Ronan 150 Biofotos/H. Angel 151b SPL/Dr. T. Brain 151b BCL/ Patrick Baker 154bl PEP/Gregg Dietzmann 154tl PEP/Robert Hessler 155 Biophoto Associates 158-159t K. Wheeler 158-159b PEP/F. Jackson 160bl Drs. E. McBeath & K. Fujiwara 160cr A. V. Grimstone, University of Cambridge 161 Premaphotos Wildlife/ K. G. Preston-Mafham 162 OSF G. I. Bernard 165 (all pictures) OSF/Peter Parks 166 ANT 167 PEP/Roy Manstan 168 BCL/Jane Burton 169 BCL/Peter Davey 170, 171b SPL/Michael Abbey 171tl K. Wheeler 172-173 BCL 174t PEP/Bill Wood 174cl PEP/A. S. Edwards 174bl Biophoto Associates 175t PEP/Bill Wood 175b OSF/J. A. L. Cooke 176tl BCL/John Shaw 176bl SPL/Dr. J. Burgess 176br Survival Anglia/ M. & D. Plage 176-177 K. Wheeler 178l BCL/J. Shaw 178tr NHPA/S. Dalton 178br GSF 179t SPL/Sinclair Stammers 179b PEP/Peter David 180t BCL/Gunter Zeisler 180bl BCL/Kim Taylor 180br OSF/G. I. Bernard 181 SPL 182t BCL/Kim Taylor 182b NHPA/ S. Krasemann 183 OSF/Doug Allan 184 K. Wheeler 185 Michael Fogden 186-187 Anthony Bannister 186br BCL/David Hughes 187b ANT/R. & D. Keller 188t NHPA/Nigel Dennis 188-189 BCL/C. B. Frith 189t BCL/G. Doré 190-191 OSF/Doug Allan 190br BCL/ A. J. Deane 191br OSF/Carstan Olesen 192 OSF/Sean Morris 193 SPL 194BCL/N. G. Blake 195t BCL/Hans Reinhard 195b BCL 196 BCL/Jane Burton 196-197

BCL/Orion Press 197b Biological Photo Service 200bl Y. Uehara, J. Desaki & T. Fujiwara 200-201 Survival Anglia Ltd/J. Foott 201tr BCL/Kim Taylor 201br Michael Fogden 202tl Jacana/Viard 202br OSF/G. I. Bernard 204tr, 204cr, 206 Mary Evans Picture Library 208t, 208b NHPA/S. Dalton 209, 210 BCL/Kim Taylor 211t SPL/E. Gravé 211b SPL 213 BCL/Frieder Sauer 214-215t BCL/Hans Reinhard 214b Biophoto Associates 214-215b BCL/Jane Burton 215br Michael Fogden 216tl, 216cl OSF/S. Dalton 216tr Survival Anglia Ltd/J. & D. Bartlett 216-217b, 217t, 218, 219tl, 219cl BCL/Jane Burton 219tr ANT/Cyril Webster 219br PEP/Peter David 220bl NHPA/A. Bannister 220tr Frank Lane Agency/L. West 220-221b Kim Taylor & Jane Burton 221t Mary Evans Picture Library 222t BCL/M. P. Harris 222b BCL/Kim Taylor 223t BCL/Robert Schroeder 223b OSF/Doug Allan 224t BCL 224b ANT/A. G. E. Schmida 225 SPL/Dr. A. Brody 226 OSF/Edwin Sadd 227t NHPA/A. Bannister 227b BCL/R. M. Borland 228bl BCL/Adrian Davies 228tr NHPA/S. Dalton 229t Michael Fogden 229bl Anthony Bannister 229br ANT/Cyril Webster 230t Premaphotos Wildlife/R. A. Preston-Mafham 230b PEP/Alan Colclough 231cl Michael Fogden 231bl BCL/Jane Burton 231tr Anthony Bannister 232bl Premaphotos Wildlife/ K. G. Preston-Mafham 232tr Ardea/D. Hadden 233t OSF/David Shale 233bl BCL/Hans Reinhard 233br Michael Fogden 234 BCL/J. & D. Bartlett 235t OSF/ J. Cheverton 235b BCL/Kim Taylor 236, 237tl BCL/Jane Burton 237tr SPL/Professor L. Caro 237cr GSF/M. Hirons 238l BCL/Jane Burton 228-239t Premaphotos Wildlife/K. G. Preston-Mafham 239b ANT/Tony Howard 240t PEP/Peter Scoones 240-241b BCL/Francisco Erize 241t Anthony Bannister 242bl BCL/G. Zeisler 242br BCL/M. Freeman 242-243t Michael Fogden 243b BCL/Kim Taylor 244 Biophotos/Heather Angel 245tr, 245cl Survival Anglia/Jeff Foott 245br David M. Phillips, The Population Council 246t OSF/Barry Walker 246b NHPA/Ivan Polunin 247tl OSF/Rudie Kuiter 247tr Survival Anglia/C. Buxton & A. Price 247br NHPA/ G. I. Bernard 248bl BCL/Leonard Lee Rue 248tr Anthony Bannister 248br BCL/J. Burton

Specialist advisers Jane Burton, Robert Burton, Dr Terry Catchpool, Sarah Fox, Dr Ian Jackson, Dr Christine Janis, Priscilla Sharland, Kim Taylor, Dr Alwyne Wheeler, Dr Peter Williamson.
Artists Trevor Boyer, Robert and Rhoda Burns, Kai Choi, Nicholas Hall, Alan Hollingbery, Richard Lewington, Vanessa Luff, Kevin Maddison, Tony Maynard, Coral Mula, Colin Salmon, Mick Saunders, Milne & Stebbing Illustration.
Indexer Linda Gamlin.
Media conversion and typesetting Peter MacDonald and Ron Barrow.

# Further Reading

**General**
Alexander, R. M. *The Collins Encyclopedia of Animal Biology* (Collins)
Berry, R. J., Hallam, A. *The Collins Encyclopedia of Animal Evolution* (Collins)
Darwin, Charles *The Illustrated Origin of Species* (abridged and annotated, with an introduction) (Faber and Faber in UK/Hill and Wang in US)
Keeton, W. T. *Biological Science* (W. W. Norton)
Luria, S. E., Gould, S. J., Singer, S. *A View of Life* (Benjamin/Cummings Publishing Company Inc.)
Margulis, L. and Schwartz, K. V. *Five Kingdoms: An Illustrated Guide to the Phyla of Life in Earth* (W. H. Freeman and Co.)
Maynard-Smith, J. *Evolution Now: A Century after Darwin* (Macmillan)
Maynard-Smith, J. *The Problems of Biology* (Oxford

University Press)
Maynard-Smith, J. *The Theory of Evolution* (Penguin)
Villee, C. A., Solomon, E. P. and Davis, P. W. *Biology* (CBS College Publishing)
Watson, J. D. *Molecular Biology of the Gene* (W. A. Benjamin Inc.)

**Specific Topics**
Attenborough, D. *Life on Earth* (Cambridge University Press)
Banister, K. and Campbell, A. *The Encyclopedia of Aquatic Life* (Facts on File)
Banister, K. and Campbell, A. *The Encyclopedia of Underwater Life* (invertebrates and fish) (George Allen & Unwin)
Barrington, E. J. W. *Invertebrate Structure and Function* (Van Nostrand Reinhold Ltd.)

Halliday, T. and Adler, K. *The Encyclopedia of Reptiles and Amphibians* (George Allen & Unwin, Facts on File)
MacDonald, D. *The Encyclopedia of Mammals* (in 2 vols. George Allen & Unwin: UK; single volume Facts on File: US)
O'Toole, C. *The Encyclopedia of Insects* (George Allen & Unwin, Facts on File)
Perrins, C. M. and Middleton, A. L. A. *The Encyclopedia of Birds* (George Allen & Unwin, Facts on File)
Prime, C. T. *Plant Life* (Collins)
Salisbury, F. B. and Ross, C. W. *Plant Physiology* (Wadsworth Publishing Company Inc.)
Stanier, R. Y., Doudoroff, M. and Adelberg, E. A. *General Microbiology* (Macmillan in UK, Prentice-Hall in US)
Tweedie, M. *Insect Life* (Collins)

# Glossary

Several of the words used in biology have more than one meaning. Here, the definition or definitions applicable to this book are given first, with alternative definitions given afterwards, in brackets. Many words are explained in the text, and if they are not listed here, the definition can be found by use of the index.

**Acid**
A substance that ionizes to give hydrogen ions, or protons ($H^+$); a proton donor.

**Alkali**
See BASE

**Amino acids**
The building blocks of PROTEIN (◆ page 134)

**Amniotes**
Reptiles, birds and mammals: animals having an amniotic and allantoic membrane associated with the embryo (◆ page 103).

**Analogy**
A similarity between two organisms due to parallel or CONVERGENT EVOLUTION. See also HOMOLOGY.

**Autotroph**
An organism that makes its food for itself using carbon dioxide as a source of carbon, rather than requiring preformed ORGANIC molecules in its diet, as HETEROTROPHS do. Most autotrophs (the plants and cyanobacteria) use sunlight as their source of energy, and are therefore said to be photosynthetic. But a few bacteria obtain energy from chemical reactions involving inorganic molecules, and these are said to be chemosynthetic (◆ page 148).

**Bacteriophage**
A virus that attacks bacteria.

**Base**
A substance that can accept hydrogen ions and thus neutralize ACIDS; a proton acceptor. The word is also sometimes used for the purines and pyrimidines (◆ page 138).

**Carnivore**
A type of HETEROTROPH whose diet consists largely of other *living* animals or protozoa. Compare with HERBIVORE, OMNIVORE, SAPROTROPH. A carnivore may be a PREDATOR or a PARASITE. The term is sometimes also used to refer solely to members of the mammalian order Carnivora, a group that includes cats, dogs, bears, badgers, weasels etc.

**Catalyst**
A substance that increases the rate of a chemical reaction without becoming used up by that reaction.

**Cerci**
A pair of spike-like appendages that extend horizontally from the last segment of the abdomen on insects. They are often sensitive to vibrations.

**Chemosynthesis**
A means of obtaining energy to synthesize organic compounds by harnessing the chemical reactions of inorganic compounds (◆ page 148). See also AUTOTROPH.

**Chromosomes**
Strictly speaking, the structures that carry the genetic information in eukaryotic cells only (◆ page 23). They are made up of DNA and proteins and have a complex structure (◆ page 142). (The much simpler genetic material of prokaryotic cells, consisting of a loop of DNA or RNA with just a few associated proteins, is sometimes referred to as a bacterial chromosome.)

**Cilium**
A hair-like cell process (◆ page 211).

**Cloaca**
In vertebrates, a combined opening serving the digestive, urinary and reproductive systems.

**Coenocytic cell**
A cell having several nuclei.

**Convergent evolution**
A process whereby two or more groups (species, genera, families etc.) that are not closely related acquire similar adaptations independently of each other, through living in the same sort of environment, adopting the same diet, or defending themselves against similar predators. When the groups involved are fairly closely related, but still evolved their similar features *independently* of each other, the phenomenon is known as parallel evolution.

**Corolla**
Collective term for the petals of a flower.

**Cytoplasm**
The cell's contents but excluding in eukaryotic cells, the region inside the nucleus.

**Defecation (defaecation)**
The process of depositing FECES.

**Differentiate**
Of cells and tissues, to take on different forms during development or regeneration (◆ page 165).

**Digit**
In vertebrates, the extremities of the limbs (toes and fingers in humans).

**Diploid**
Having two sets of chromosomes. See also HAPLOID.

**Diurnal**
Active during the day.

**Ecology**
The study of the relationships and the interactions of living organisms, with each other and with the physical world.

**Enzyme**
A protein that acts as biological catalyst (◆ page 134).

**Epiphytes**
Plants that grow on other plants, but do not derive any nutrients or water from them.

**Excretion**
The elimination of waste products from within the cell of the organism (◆ page 181). (Sometimes used more narrowly, to mean the elimination of nitrogenous waste only.)

**Facultative**
Able to exchange to another mode of nutrition, another type of habitat etc. The opposite is OBLIGATE.

**Feces (faeces)**
Waste matter ejected from the digestive tract, consisting largely of indigestible food.

**Feral**
Descended from a domesticated animal that has escaped into the world.

**Flagellum**
A long whip-like cell process (◆ page 211).

**Gametes**
Cells produced for the purpose of sexual reproduction – ova (eggs) and sperm. Except in parthenogenetic species they must fuse with another gamete before development can take place.

**Gametophyte**
In plants, the generation that is HAPLOID and produces the gametes. See also SPOROPHYTE.

**Gene**
A unit of hereditary information (◆ page 22). Each gene produces a single polypeptide chain (◆ page 26).

**Genome**
The total genetic complement of an organism.

**Habitat**
In ecology, the type of environment that an organism inhabits.

**Haploid**
Having one set of chromosomes. See also DIPLOID.

**Herbivore**
A type of HETEROTROPH whose diet consists largely of plants, algae or fungi, or plant products, such as seeds and fruits. Compare with CARNIVORE, OMNIVORE, SAPROTROPH.

**Heterotroph**
An organism that needs preformed ORGANIC MOLECULES, produced by other living things, in its diet (◆ page 169).

**Homeostasis**
The maintenance of constant conditions in the internal environment of animals.

**Homology**
A similarity between two organisms due to descent – the inheritance of a feature or features from a common ancestor that had those feature(s). See also ANALOGY. The concepts of homology and analogy are important in taxonomy, where homologous structures point to true relationships between species, but analogous structures are "false guides" (◆ page 33). The adjective, homologous, pair of chromosomes have identical loci (◆ page 23) and pair up during meiosis and mitosis.

**Homozygous**
In genetics, having the same allele at both loci of a pair (◆ page 23).

**Internode**
In plants, the length of stem between two NODES.

**Leguminous**
Plants of the pea and bean family.

**Metabolic rate**
The general level of metabolism (◆ page 136) in an animal, in terms of the amount of energy expended (usually excluding that involved in movement etc). It is calculated by measuring the amount of oxygen consumed.

**Mucus**
A viscous fluid secreted by living organisms, often for defensive purposes.

**Mutualism**
See SYMBIOSIS.

**Neuron**
A nerve cell.

**Niche**
In ecology, the totality of interactions of a given organism. It includes the HABITAT it lives in, its food sources, parasites and predators, its special requirements for a burrow, nest or other living space, and all other factors affecting its survival. The niche of each species is assumed to be unique, because if two species had exactly the same niche, one would inevitably do better and the other become extinct.

**Node**
In plants, the point at which a leaf or leaves develop from the stem.

**Obligate**
Obliged to be – as in "obligate parasite". The opposite is FACULTATIVE.

**Omnivore**
A type of HETEROTROPH whose diet consists of a mixture of animal and plant material. Compare with CARNIVORE, HERBIVORE, SAPROTROPH.

**Organism**
Any living thing.

**Organic molecules**
Complex carbon-containing molecules (◆ page 130).

**Ovipositor**
A structure used for depositing eggs, in female insects. It is often elongated and may be able to pierce plant or animal tissues.

**Parallel evolution**
See CONVERGENT EVOLUTION.

**Parasite**
An organism that lives in or on another organism (the host) and is metabolically dependent on it. Two criteria are used to distinguish parasites from predators. First, predators generally have a lower rate of reproduction than their prey, whereas parasites have a higher rate. Second, predators kill their prey whereas parasites do not immediately kill their hosts. Despite these distinctions, there is no clear dividing line between parasites and predators, nor between parasitism and other forms of SYMBIOSIS (◆ page 179).

**Peptide**
A chain formed from two or more amino acids. When several amino acids are involved, the chain is known as a polypeptide. These names are applied to a partially synthesized PROTEIN, to the fragments obtained during the digestion of proteins, to short chains synthesized in the laboratory, or to single chains that form part of a larger protein molecule.

**pH**
A numerical measurement, from 0-14, of the acidity or alkalinity of liquids. A pH of 7.0 is neutral, less than 7.0 is acidic, more than 7.0 is alkaline.

**Phage**
See BACTERIOPHAGE.

**Photosynthesis**
A means of obtaining energy to sustain life by harnessing the energy of the Sun's radiation (◆ page 148). See also AUTOTROPH.

**Plankton**
The community of microscopic organisms that float at or near the surface of the sea or lakes.

**Polypeptide**
See PEPTIDE.

**Predator**

Commonly defined as "an organism that kills and eats other living things", but used in different ways by different biologists. One has even described the fungus that causes Dutch elm disease as a "predator". This points to two crucial problems. First, how can predators be differentiated from parasites? – for a consideration of this, see PARASITES. Second, should the word predator be applied to HERBIVORES as well as CARNIVORES? Although the common-sense concept of a predator is that of a carnivorous animal, in ecological terms a herbivorous animal that eats the whole plant, or at least kills it, or any fungus that kills its host plant is effectively acting as a predator and can usefully be compared with carnivorous predators. However, in this book, the word predator is used in the narrower sense, to mean a carnivorous, non-parasitic animal.

**Prostomium**

In annelids, the head region, in front of the first true segment.

**Protein**

A complex bio-molecule, made up of one or more chains of amino acids (◆ page 134). Where made of several chains, each of these is known as a POLYPEPTIDE chain.

**Protoplasm**

The contents of the cell. In eukaryotes it is divided into the nucleus and CYTOPLASM.

**Respiration**

Strictly speaking, the breakdown of food molecules in the presence of oxygen, a biochemical process which releases energy (◆ page 153). (May also be used to mean the process by which oxygen is obtained – in mammals, for example, the movement of air in and out of the lungs.)

**Saprobe**

A term sometimes used instead of SAPROTROPH.

**Saprophytes**

A term used to describe the nutritional characteristics of those fungi and bacteria that live on dead matter or excretory products. The word has now largely been replaced by SAPROTROPH or SAPROBE; the ending -phyte reflected the mistaken idea that fungi were plants.

**Saprotroph**

A type of HETEROTROPH that obtains its nutrients from the dead bodies or excretory products of other organisms. The term embraces animals such as dung beetles carrion beetles, as well as the fungi, once described as SAPROPHYTES.

**Sessile**

Of animals; fixed to the seabed, riverbed or other substrate, either permanently or for most of the time. (Also used in botany, to describe leaves with no stalk.)

**Social insects**

Insects that live in a colony of related individuals. The truly social (eusocial) insects have a set of distinct castes, some of which are non-reproductive, whereas the presocial insects show less developed forms of social life. All social insects belong to the Hymenoptera order (bees, wasps and ants) or to the termites.

**Spore**

A rather general term applied to a great variety of small reproductive or resting bodies. Unlike a GAMETE, a spore does not need to fuse with another cell prior to development (although some spores germinate to give gametes). In plants, algae, fungi and slime molds the spore is a simple reproductive body, usually consisting of a single cell with a protective coat. The coat may be very thick and allow the spore to survive a period of adverse conditions. Some protozoa also have reproductive bodies that are known as spores, but these tend to have a more complex, multicellular structure. The term spore is also applied to structures that have no reproductive role, such as bacterial spores, where one bacterial cell yields only one thick-coated spore. Its function is the survival of adverse conditions, rather than multiplication and dispersal.

**Sporophyte**

In plants, the generation that is DIPLOID and produces the SPORES. See also GAMETOPHYTE

**Stigma**

The tip of the STYLE, in the female reproductive organs of plants. It is the part which receives the pollen (◆ page 60).

**Style**

An extension of the carpel (◆ page 60) in flowering plants. It carries the STIGMA.

**Symbiosis**

A close relationship between organisms of different species (◆ page 179).

**Thallus**

A simple type of plant body, as found in the seaweeds (algae), mosses and liverworts. It is not sharply differentiated into stems, roots and leaves as the bodies of higher plants are, and tends to be either filamentous or flat, the latter having plate-like or ribbon-like growth form.

**Tracheids**

Water-conducting cells found in gymnosperms and other lower plants; they inter-connect by means of lateral pits (◆ page 64). They are replaced in flowering plants by VESSELS.

**Undulipodium**

The eukaryotic flagellum.

**Vascular system**

A system for transporting fluids around the body of an organism. The term is mainly used in connection with plants, but can also include the circulatory system of animals, or the water-vascular system of echinoderms (◆ page 87).

**Vessels**

Water-conducting cells of flowering plants (◆ page 64).

**Vestigial organ**

One which has lost its function in the course of evolution, and is usually much reduced in size.

**Xylem**

The woody, vascular tissue that conducts water and gives support to plants. It is found in flowering plants, gymnosperms and pteridophytes (ferns etc.) and may include TRACHEIDS or VESSELS.

**Zygote**

The cell that results from the fusion of two gametes; a fertilized egg. It is usually DIPLOID.

# Word Stems

Many biological terms are made up of frequently occurring word stems. With a knowledge of these, technical terms can be understood, but it is important to remember that some names (e.g. protozoa, saprophyte) were coined long ago, and are based on misconceptions about the nature of the organisms or structures in question.

**Alb-** white as in albumen
**Anther-** relating to pollen or sperm (as in antheridium)
**Anti-** against (as in antibiotic)
**Arche- (archae-)** ancient, primitive (as in Archaeopteryx)
**Arthr-** relating to joints (as in arthropods)
**Auto-** self (as in autotroph)
**Bio- (-biotic)** living (as in biochemistry)
**Brachi-** arm (as in brachiopods)
**Bryo-** moss (as in bryophytes)
**-cardi-** relating to the heart (as in pericardial cavity)
**-cele (-coel)** enlarged cavity (as in hemocoel, coelom)
**Cephalo-** relating to the head (as in cephalopods)
**Cerebro-** relating to the brain (as in cerebro-spinal fluid)
**Chrom-** colored (as in chromosomes)
**Crypt-** hidden (as in cryptogam)
**Cyto-** relating to cells (as in cytoplasm)
**-dactyl-** digits – toes, fingers (as in pterodactyl)
**-derm-** skin or outer covering (as in echinoderm)
**-dont-, dent-** relating to teeth (as in sphenodonts)

**Ecto-** outside (as in ectoderm)
**Endo-** inside (as in endoderm)
**Epi-** upon, immediately above, or on the outside of (as in epiphyte)
**Eu-** true (as in eumycota)
**-fer, -fera** bearing (as in conifer)
**Gam-** breeding, mating (as in gamete)
**Gastro-** relating to the stomach (as in gastropods)
**-gen** producing, growing (as in antigen)
**-germ-** relating to reproduction (as in germination)
**-gnath-** jaws (as in agnathans)
**-gramin-** seed (as in graminivores)
**Hemo- (haemo-)** (as in hemoglobin)
**Herbi-** of, or relating to, plants (as in herbivore)
**Hetero-** others (as in heterotroph)
**Homeo-** similar (as in homeostasis)
**Homo-** same (as in homosporous)
**Hyper-** excessive (as in hyperventilate)
**Hypo-** below, deficient (as in hypothalamus)
**-ichthy-** fish (as in ichthyosaur)
**-karyo-** cell (as in prokaryote)
**Lact-** relating to milk (as in lactation)
**Lepid-** scales (as in Lepidodendron)
**Mega-** large (as in megafauna)
**Meso-** middle (as in mesoderm)
**Micro-** small (as in microscope)
**Mono-** one (as in monocotyledons)
**-morph-** shape, or type (as in polymorphism)
**-myc-** of, or related to, fungi (as in myxomycota)

**Myxo-** slime (as in myxobacteria)
**Neo-** new (as in neo-Darwinism)
**Neuro-** nerve (as in neurotransmitter)
**Oligo-** few (as in oligochaete)
**Oo-** relating to egg or ovum (as in oomycete)
**-ornis-, -ornith-** bird (as in Ichthyornis)
**Paleo-, palaeo-** old, ancient (as in Paleocene)
**Pedo-, paedo-** juvenile (as in pedomorphosis)
**Peri-** around, outside (as in pericarp)
**-phage** eater or destroyer (as in bacteriophage)
**Phyto-, -phyte** of, or relating to, plants (as in phytochrome)
**-plasm** living matter (as in protoplasm)
**Platy-** flat, broad (as in platyhelminths)
**-pod-** leg (as in tetrapod)
**Poly-** many (as in polychaete)
**Pro-** before (as in prokaryote)
**Proto-** first (as in protozoa)
**Pseudo-** false (as in pseudoparenchyma)
**Pterido-** fern (as in pteridophytes)
**-ptero-, -pteryx** flying, wings (as in Lepidoptera)
**Sapro-** decaying (as in saprotroph)
**-saur-** reptile (as in pterosaur)
**-sperm-** relating to sperm, or to seeds (as in gymnosperm)
**Syn-, sym-** together, alike (as in symbiosis)
**-therm** temperature (as in endotherm)
**-troph** of feeding (as in autotroph)
**-vore** eater (as in carnivore)

# Index